MONEY LAUNDERING LAW

In the past twenty years action in respect of the profits of crime has moved rapidly up the criminal justice agenda. Not only may confiscation orders be made, but there are also now serious substantive criminal offences of laundering the proceeds of crime. Moreover, the consequences of the regulatory régimes put in place by the Money Laundering Regulations 1993 and the Financial Services Authority are very significant. This book examines critically the history, theory and practice of all these developments, culminating in the Proceeds of Crime Act 2002, which marks another step in the move towards greater concentration both on the financial aspects of crime and on the internationalisation of criminal law. The Act puts in place the Assets Recovery Agency, which will be central to the strategy of targeting criminal monies and will have power to bring forfeiture proceedings without a prior criminal conviction and to raise assessments to taxation. The author subjects the law of laundering, especially the novel aspects of the Proceeds of Crime Act itself, to thorough analysis and a human rights' audit.

Money Laundering Law

Forfeiture, Confiscation, Civil Recovery, Criminal Laundering and Taxation of the Proceeds of Crime

PETER ALLDRIDGE

·HART·
PUBLISHING

OXFORD – PORTLAND OREGON
2003

Hart Publishing
Oxford and Portland, Oregon

Published in North America (US and Canada) by
Hart Publishing c/o
International Specialized Book Services
5804 NE Hassalo Street
Portland, Oregon
97213-3644
USA

© Peter Alldridge 2003

The author has asserted his right under the Copyright, Designs and Patents
Act 1988, to be identified as the authors of this work

Hart Publishing is a specialist legal publisher based in Oxford, England.
To order further copies of this book or to request a list of other
publications please write to:

Hart Publishing, Salter's Boatyard, Folly Bridge,
Abingdon Road, Oxford OX1 4LB
Telephone: +44 (0)1865 245533 or Fax: +44 (0)1865 794882
e-mail: mail@hartpub.co.uk
WEBSITE: http//www.hartpub.co.uk

British Library Cataloguing in Publication Data
Data Available
ISBN 1-84113-264-0 (hardback)

Typeset by Hope Services (Abingdon) Ltd.
Printed and bound in Great Britain on acid-free paper by
Biddles Ltd, www.biddles.co.uk

Preface and Acknowledgements

This book deals with a range of legal mechanisms that are directed towards the proceeds of crime. They are confiscation, 'civil recovery' and taxation of those proceeds, together with the offences of criminal money laundering and, so far as relevant, the more ancient power of forfeiture. The law of England and Wales has come a long way since *Cuthbertson* in 1979. Twenty years ago, a person making profits through the commission of crime was liable to be punished, but not, without more, liable to disgorge the profits to the State. Taxation of the proceeds of crime was little more than a theoretical possibility. Such a person could walk into a bank, announce that s/he wished to open an account, fill in a form and deposit some cash. No identification was called for and if the client chose to hold the account and to supply specimen signatures in the name 'Donald Duck' that was perfectly acceptable. The bank's only concern was to ensure that the person who made withdrawals from the account was the same person as the person who opened it. To do that, there was no need for the bank to know the client's real identity. This book traces the development of the law on the first phenomenon, and its impact upon the second. It deals primarily with substantive and procedural criminal law, including the law of forfeiture and confiscation. Because of the link to financial institutions, however, it has been necessary to include some consideration of the civil law and of the regulatory framework. Confiscation and forfeiture provisions were criminal law at the margins. They are now at centre stage in the formulation of domestic criminal justice policy, in the moves for the internationalisation of criminal law and in the prosecution of a war.

The book is, in part then, a criminal law emergence study, but it also attempts two other tasks. The first is to examine the supposed rationales for the legal responses to proceeds of crime. This is particularly important at a time when money laundering has come to be blamed for many of the evils of the world. The law has developed piecemeal, and so justificatory accounts have to be constructed and tested. The book will suggest that the bases upon which forfeiture is permitted should, in principle, be much more limited than those currently embodied in English Law, that confiscation going beyond the profits acquired by a criminal from crime is unjustified, and that special attention needs to be given to the relationship between, on the one hand, taxation and, on the other the seizure of the assets of criminals. The second is to generate a human rights audit of the current state of the law of confiscation and forfeiture. Confiscation and forfeiture provide many important tests for the Human Rights Act 1998, and the judicial responses to confiscation and forfeiture cases brought under the Act are indicators of the wider response in the relationship between executive, legislature, courts and human rights. The refusal of the courts or Parliament to engage with strong arguments against forfeiture in many forms and or to provide principled limitations to confiscation, whether or not they are categorised as human rights arguments, is a continuing source of bemusement. I am not starry-eyed about the Human Rights Act, but it does have important attributes. First, notwithstanding that it has not been amended significantly to adapt to changes over 50 years, it does provide a relatively coherent standpoint from which to make a liberal critique of any criminal justice system. Secondly, although the interpretations that have been placed on it by courts have frequently disappointed the liberal, it does at least provide arguments to which the courts of England and Wales must respond. Thirdly, the same Government is responsible for the Proceeds of Crime Act 2002 as for the Human Rights Act 1998. It is not unreasonable to want to hold it to its own professed precepts. The citique is liberal in the uncomplicated sense that I believe in the rule of law, rights, democracy and the elimination of status-derived inequality.

Collection of material for the book ceased on 1 August 2002, but I have tried to state the law as at the date (as yet unknown) upon which the Proceeds of Crime Act 2002 will come into force. In fact, most provisions of the Act will only apply to offences committed after that date, and it will take a good deal of time for the old law fully to be worked out of the system.[1] The Drug Trafficking Offences Act 1986 was replaced by the Drug Trafficking Act 1994, but the courts were still dealing with cases to which it applied in 2001.[2] Consequently, and also because a good deal of the law is unchanged by the 2002 Act, the book contains a good deal of reference to the law before 2003. The Proceeds of Crime Act 2002 is a long and complex piece of legislation and the book does not purport to give a comprehensive account of it. For such an account there is a range of alternatives.

The book deals with the law of England and Wales. There are analogous provisions dealing with Scotland and Northern Ireland. Parts of the book have been published in the *Journal of Money Laundering Control*, *Buffalo Criminal Law Review*, *British Tax Review* and the *Modern Law Review*. I owe debts to many. Bob Sullivan and David Campbell read the first four chapters and made incisive comments. Kevin Dowd gave expert advice on chapter three. Michael Levi first interested me in the subject. He, Keith Smith and Ann Mumford all read the entire typescript and made many helpful comments both as to substance and style. No responsibility for what follows attaches to any of them. I am grateful to Richard Hart for his encouragement and April Boffin for her sharp editorial eye. The book is dedicated, with love, to Ann and Freddie.

---

[1] Even longer if the civil recovery procedure is held to be covered by Art 7 and consequently not able to be retroactive.

[2] Re Norris [2001] UKHL 34.

Contents

Table of Cases

Table of Legislation

United Kingdom

Statutory Instruments

1

Introduction

Clean money is worth more than dirty money. Clean money—money untainted by criminal association—can be invested in profitable activities, or spent on consumption, more or less conspicuous, without risk of incrimination. Dirty money can generally only be invested or spent less profitably, less visibly, and at the risk of punishment. It also carries the risk of being used as evidence of the initial crime. With the exceptions of small thefts of fungibles like cash, and the fantasy case of the criminal art collector who wishes to sit alone gloating over a painting so famous that it could not be resold, virtually all income from criminal activities must be disguised to be of use to the criminal. Money laundering[1] is that process of disguise. In many ways, notwithstanding the very low conviction rate and small amounts of monies recovered in the United Kingdom, money laundering was the 'crime of the 1990s'.[2] It will remain high on the law enforcement agenda during the years that follow. It has moved quickly from being marginal in the early 1980s, not even a ground for confiscation, let alone a crime, to a position at the centre of efforts at co-operation in the 'war on drugs', the 'struggle against organised crime' and the 'war on terrorism'. These efforts are international in scope and consequently require revision of the traditional view of the relationships between national systems of criminal justice.

Until 1986, drug dealers, when apprehended, were able to retain the profits of their crimes and, perhaps upon emerging from prison, to enjoy them. Now not only are they are not allowed to keep the proceeds, but attacks are being made upon all of the principal mechanisms by which they conceal their links to the money—banking secrecy laws, lawyer-client privilege and anonymous dealings in 'front' companies. Much police activity is now directed towards making criminal disposals of assets more difficult and to monitoring money movements. Furthermore, laundering itself now constitutes a series of independent crimes.

---

[1] For Jack Blum *et al*, Financial Havens, *Banking Secrecy and Money-Laundering*, UNDCP technical series issue 8 (New York City, NY, United Nations 1998) 6, the origin of the term is in the use of cash based retail service industries like laundries to disguise the origins of cash acquired through rackets in the United States. The object was to mix legally and illegally obtained cash to avoid the attention of corrupt police officers, competitors, and (from the time that prosecution for tax evasion came to be a potent weapon in the hands of authorities unable to bring successful prosecutions for specific substantive offences) the tax authorities.

[2] G Richard Strafer, 'Money laundering: the crime of the '90s'' (1989) 27 *American Criminal Law Review* 149.

These developments have not occurred in a vacuum. As late as 1980, the ability to set criminal law was still one of the most significant attributes of the Nation-State. This is no longer the case. The instantiation of the international response to money laundering has been one of the principal factors in this radical shift. Many international developments, including co-operation against drugs and organised crime within the European Union, have focussed around the area.[3] Late in 1999, the Tampere European Council meeting[4] placed enormous emphasis upon money laundering, calling, in particular, for an increase in consistency in the definition of predicate offences, the adoption of the Amending Directive[5] and the greater availability of relevant information for the purposes of international exchange, irrespective of arguments from banking secrecy. Within 24 hours of the attacks on the United States of 11 September 2001 the Prime Minister, Tony Blair, announced that the ability of terrorists to launder money was a significant contributory factor to the threat they present and that a great deal of heroin sold in the UK was of Afghan provenance, and that provided a justification for the military expedition.[6] Warfare had become a mechanism of crime control.

This book seeks to present a critical analysis of the responses to money laundering, from three perspectives. It considers accounts of the manner in which the law has developed, including the growing internationalisation of criminal law and the economics of laundering, within a socio-legal context. It reviews the justifications that are advanced within criminal law theory for regulation and criminalisation in this area, and then, and against that background, engages at a more detailed level with the statutes, cases and law reform proposals in the area, dealing both with substantive and procedural law. An important critical perspective is supplied by the jurisprudence of human rights, particularly those to private life and property, to fair trial and against double jeopardy. When these rights do not have the purchase they should have, a critique is supplied of the operation of the Human Rights Act.

HOW IS IT DONE?[7]

Money laundering, then, is the process of transforming the proceeds of illegal activities into legitimate capital. In principle, any financial transaction could be

---

[3] And the section below ch 5, The European Union.

[4] The conclusions of the Tampere Special European Council are at <www.europa.eu.int/council/off/conclu/oct99> See Julian Schutte, 'Tampere European Council Presidency Decisions' (1999) 70 *Revue Internationale de Droit Penal* 1023 at 1034–35.

[5] See the section below ch 5, The Amending Directive.

[6] See the section below, 11 September 2001.

[7] And see William C Gilmore, *Dirty money: the evolution of money laundering countermeasures*, 2nd edn (Strasbourg, Council of Europe Press, 1999) 27–48; Financial Services Authority, *The Money Laundering Theme: tackling our new responsibilities* (London, FSA, 2001) 8–10; Michael Levi, 'Following the Criminal and Terrorist Money Trails' in Petrus van Duyne and Klaus von Lampe (eds), *Criminal Finances and Organizing Crime in Europe* (forthcoming).

an act by which unlawfully acquired money is laundered. There are consequently an infinite number of mechanisms whereby money, commonly, is laundered.[8] The oldest international mechanisms for laundering are alternative remittance systems that operate outside established regulatory systems to move value from one place to another without physical movement of currency.[9] Typically they were developed as mechanisms by which immigrant workers sent money to their families, but they are now frequently used in respect of drug money. A far-sighted criminal might have a mixture of lawful and unlawful income. If the unlawful income can be used so as to pay those bills either that cannot be traced or that will not attract suspicion, then that will leave lawful income to discharge liabilities which are more closely scrutinised.

One of the perceived trends in laundering[10] is away from using the services of banks (foreign exchange transactions, cashier's cheques, wire transfers, bearer instruments, travellers' cheques and derivative transactions) toward the increasing use of non-banking financial institutions and non-financial businesses for money laundering. If laundering could be done though banks and trust companies, building societies, savings and loan companies and credit unions, then it could also occur via brokers or securities dealers, currency dealers, cheque cashers, issuers of travellers cheques and money orders and transmitters of funds. If these further areas are effectively regulated, (on the assumption that the launderers act rationally[11]) launderers will seek less regulated areas. A fuller account of markets through which laundering takes place would include (at least) precious metals dealers and brokers, commodities dealers, casinos and some non-financial markets, for example cars, art, spread bookmakers and real property and derivatives markets.[12] Any market—especially any international market—is a means by which laundering can take place, and so there will be increasing pressure to regulate more markets.

---

[8] Financial Action Task Force, *Report on Money Laundering Typologies* (Paris, OECD, 2000) 4; Jack Blum *et al*, *Financial Havens, Banking Secrecy and Money-Laundering, UNDCP technical series issue 8* (New York City, NY, United Nations, 1998) 8 *et seq.* And see Marie-Christine Dupuis, *Finance criminelle: comment le crime organisé blanchit l'argent sale*, (Paris, Presses Universitaires de France, 1998). See also United Nations Drug Control Program, *World Drugs Report* (Oxford, Oxford University Press, 1997), cited in Cabinet Office Performance and Innovation Unit, *Recovering the Proceeds of Crime* (London, Cabinet Office, 2000) (hereinafter 'PIU Report') 16.

[9] And see Financial Action Task Force, Report on Money Laundering Typologies (Paris, OECD, 2000) 4 *et seq.*: this is said to be a consequence of the imposition of effective regulation in the areas mentioned.

[10] FATF typologies report 1996–97.

[11] 'As successful criminal entrepreneurs, they are likely to take a more rational approach to the disincentives to crime.' *PIU Report*, para 3.12.

[12] See Sanjay Sharma, 'Dirty Money: How the UK Securities and Derivatives Markets are used to Launder Money' (2001) 4 *Journal of Money Laundering Control* 309.

HOW MUCH?[13]

There can be few areas of crime in which the 'dark figure' (the proportion which is unreported or unprosecuted, as opposed to that which does come before courts), is so difficult to quantify.[14] The usual techniques for identifying the 'dark figure' do not provide reliable data in this area. Victim reports are obviously inapplicable: self-reports are only of dubious value because the definition of the crime is sufficiently technical that even in the case of a willing self-reporter they will not know.

The reaction of governments to money laundering during the 1990s and 2000s is predicated upon the assumption that the incidence and dangers generated by the crime are both huge. Estimates vary enormously but do not go down below the Gargantuan. Robinson, for example, holds that in terms of the total sums involved laundering is the World's third largest industry.[15] The International Monetary Fund has stated that the aggregate of money laundering in the world 'could be somewhere between two and five *per cent* of the world's gross domestic product'.[16] Using 1996 statistics, these percentages would indicate that money laundering ranged between $590 billion and $1.5 trillion. The lower figure is equivalent to the total output of an economy the size of Spain.[17] A 'guesstimate' of $500 billion per year world-wide is said by the Financial Action Task Force (FATF) to be plausible.[18] For the UK between 7 and thirteen per cent of GDP has been proposed.[19]

At the outset, two definitional provisos are, first that the *quantum* of laundering will depend upon how widely it is defined. In the UK legislation, laundering is defined very widely—in particular, it seems,[20] to include activity directed towards the disposal of money which is the product of tax evasion,[21] in which case as much money will be laundered in any given economy as is equivalent to the entire black economy of the jurisdiction in question. The second

---

[13] J Walker, 'How Big is Global Money Laundering?' (2000) 3 *Journal of Money Laundering Control* 25; Sanjay Sharma, 'Dirty Money: How the UK Securities and Derivatives Markets are used to Launder Money' (2001) 4 *Journal of Money Laundering Control* 309 at 310–11.

[14] And a claim with such spurious specificity as $937 billion (Jonathan Fisher and Jane Bewsey. 'Laundering the Proceeds of Fiscal Crime' (2000) 15 *Journal of International Banking Law* 11, 11) needs to be treated with especial care.

[15] Jeffrey Robinson, *The Laundrymen* (London, Pocket Books, 1995).

[16] Quoted with approval by Bob Ainsworth MP, HC Standing Committee B, 17 January 2002, col 979.

[17] See FATF Policy Brief July 1999.

[18] Vito Tanzi, *Money Laundering and the International Financial System*, IMF Working Paper 96/55, (Washington DC, International Monetary Fund, 1996) 3.

[19] J Walker, 'How Big is Global Money Laundering?' (2000) 3 *Journal of Money Laundering Control* 25.

[20] And see the section below ch 9, Tax Evasion and the Predicate Offence to Criminal Laundering.

[21] The 1994 agreement between the US and Mexico refers specifically to tax evasion. On whether or not domestic and foreign evasion constitutes a predicate offence in England and Wales, see below, 156, 206.

definitional issue is whether the count is made *by transaction* or *by money and its product*. If $1m in cash is laundered via 10 bank accounts the amount of money laundered is $1m: the amount by laundering transactions is $10m. Attempts to quantify need to be clear as to the method of accounting.[22]

So far as concerns drug money, the FATF statistics reflect its assumption that 10 per cent of illegal drugs are seized. These huge figures are not reflected in activity in the courts in England and Wales. The rate at which launderers are convicted or at which money is seized from them, while increasing, remain low. The numbers of convictions either for the specific offences under the Criminal Justice Act 1988 and Drug Trafficking Act 1994 or under the Money Laundering Regulations 1993 has hitherto been relatively trivial,[23] but reports by professional advisers (lawyers, bankers and accountants) are increasing in number as greater emphasis is placed upon their being made by the National Criminal Intelligence Service (NCIS).[24]

Attempts at a more systematic quantification of the amounts laundered have proceeded along various lines. Early estimates of the quantum of laundering in a given jurisdiction, based upon its cash-to-GDP ratio, declined in significance as the growth of cash substitutes made cash a poor economic measure. Quirk[25] distinguishes between the following sources of information, none of which is particularly helpful: the literature on money laundering itself, which is largely anecdotal; the literature on the underground macroeconomy; the literature on the economics of crime; and statistics on cross-border flows of cash (which have become increasingly poor indicators as cash has been supplanted by other forms of money and as foreign exchange trading has increased exponentially with the introduction of derivatives trading). Van Duyne[26] assesses all the estimates, especially that of the FATF, critically. He argues that if the sums laundered had approached the highest estimates then the visible consequences should have been far greater than they have been:

> [L]et us face the simple fact that the proceeds of crime are not exported to the moon, but have to surface finally in the world to be transformed into production relations, assets or services which are the components of the legitimate economy.

His point is that if there were as much laundering as is claimed, the visible effects would be far more obvious. This is a useful corrective, both to claims about the quantum of money laundered and to claims about the harms involved.

[22] Vito Tanzi, *Money Laundering and the International Financial System*, IMF Working Paper 96/55, (Washington DC, International Monetary Fund, 1996) at 3.

[23] HC Debates 19 Feb 1998: Col 787 (Alun Michael MP), below, 187: *PIU Report*, n 8 above, para 4.18 *et seq*.

[24] And see Table 6 om the section below ch 12, The Mechanics of Reporting.

[25] Peter Quirk, *Macroeconomic Implications of Money Laundering*, IMF Working Paper 96/66 (Washington DC, International Monetary Fund, 1996) 6.

[26] Petrus van Duyne, 'Money-laundering: Pavlov's Dog and beyond' (1998) 37 *Howard Journal of Criminal Justice* 359, 360: see also Petrus van Duyne and Hervy de Miranda, 'The Emperor's Clothes of Disclosure: Hot Money and Suspect Disclosures' (1999) 31 *Crime, Law and Social Change* 245.

Recent Government pronouncements are more guarded,[27] but the sums claimed to be involved are still enormous. The Regulatory Impact Statement accompanying the Proceeds of Crime Bill states:

> The value of criminal proceeds available to be confiscated from those perpetrating acquisitive crime (not including the criminal justice costs of prosecuting such offenders) was estimated in May 1995 as being as much as £650 million per annum. While there is no methodology for gauging the accuracy of this figure or the extent of criminal proceeds, amounts of this order (and anecdotal evidence from the law enforcement agencies is that the amount has grown steadily since 1995) are both unacceptable in themselves and have potentially harmful economic effects. For example, if such money is not targeted in a systematic way, failures of legitimate businesses could occur due to criminally financed competition.[28]

The Minister made the following claim in Parliament:

> Organised crime is big business and the sums involved are huge. The value of drugs seized last year exceeded £735 million, and the value of illegal drugs transactions has been estimated at up to £1.5 billion annually. Cigarette smuggling annually costs the Exchequer almost £3 billion and loose tobacco smuggling about £900 million. The assets derived from organised crime represent about 2% of the United Kingdom's gross domestic product. Globally, the profits of some drug cartels are comparable to those of some of the world's major companies.[29]

Levi offers a more qualified view:

> . . . we lack more than a modest understanding of the incidence and prevalence of current techniques [of laundering] even from the systematic analysis of detected cases, let alone from those that are *undetected*. Instead of overly ambitious 'global' data and pattern estimates . . .—however organisationally and politically useful—it may be better to build up from the ground more modest analyses of what we can plausibly know about criminal money management.[30]

Nonetheless, whether or not they know how much money is laundered, enough influential people behave as though there is a significant problem for their statements to become self-authenticating, at least within the political process.

MONEY LAUNDERING AS A LAW EMERGENCE STUDY

The arguments for control of illegally obtained income (essentially that people should not be allowed to profit from crime) have always applied to the proceeds of corruption, pornography, contraband, prostitution and any other crimes creating profits: after the abolition of forfeiture there was, however, no signif-

---

[27] HC International Development Committee Fourth Report (March 2001) paras 129 *et seq.*

[28] <http://www.homeoffice.gov.uk/proceeds/ria.htm> section B

[29] HC Debates 30 October 2001 col 757 (John Denham MP, Minister for Police, Courts and Drugs).

[30] Michael Levi, 'Following the Criminal and Terrorist Money Trails' in Petrus van Duyne and Klaus von Lampe (eds), *Criminal Finances and Organizing Crime in Europe* (forthcoming).

icant general confiscation legislation anywhere in the world until 1986. The combination of the 'war on drugs'[31] moving into a struggle against 'organised crime', fraud and corruption with the movement generally called 'globalisation' has generated a strong political impetus to act. Greater integration of the world economy, the removal of barriers to the movement of capital, and the speed with which money can be moved have all increased opportunities both for lawful and unlawful commerce. Globalisation is characterised by increased deregulation, financial liberalisation[32] and privatisation. Cross-border capital flows have risen from five per cent to 13 per cent of world GDP over the last 20 years.[33] In response, criminal law is increasingly concerned with lawful and unlawful markets. This book describes and analyses a series of radical changes in the criminal law of England and Wales that have taken place over the last 20 years. They are sufficiently concerted and have taken place over a sufficiently long period of time that they cannot be ascribed to happenstance.[34] The question might be whether anything more general can be learned from these events for the study of criminal law. Why is it that something that attracted so little attention until relatively recently is now one of the major *foci* of one of central policing agencies worldwide? A full explanation of the development of money laundering will draw upon many of the sorts of accounts that have been given of criminal legislation.

Rational development of policy

One way in which legislation might be made is by following a rational deliberative model. The legislator will find out the extent of the 'problem', canvass a range of options according to the respective projected effects, attach weight to the factors to which regard may legitimately be had, and then decide upon a policy to pursue, according to the respective costs and benefits of the available alternatives. This method has been used surprisingly sparingly in the history of English criminal law, and it can hardly be suggested that the English law of money laundering was entirely a process of rational development of a policy towards a clear problematic.

> The dearth of empirical evaluation reflects the fact that money laundering law may be law without clear objectives and certainly law that was not the end product of a coherent analysis.[35]

---

[31] Steven Duke and Albert Gross, *America's Longest War* (New York City, NY, Putnam, 1993).

[32] Capital movements throughout the EU were fully liberalised as of 1 July 1990. Directive for the implementation of Art 67 of the Treaty. Council Directive 88/361, 1988 OJ (L 178) 5 (Capital Movements Directive).

[33] *PIU Report*, para 11.5.

[34] Compare, for example, the criminalisation of gross indecency, which seems to have been the outcome of unconsidered and unexpected behaviour: F Barry Smith, 'Labouchère's Amendment to the Criminal Law Amendment Bill' (1976) 17 *Historical Studies* 165.

[35] John Braithwaite, 'Following the Money Trail to what Destination? An Introduction to the Symposium' (1993) 44 *Alabama Law Review* 657 at 669.

The policing of money laundering provides a mechanism for the State to be better informed about the operation of markets and movements of money. Whilst criminal law was not amongst the first areas of law to attract the attention of economic analysis,[36] a good deal of attention is now being turned to it.[37] International bodies leading efforts to regulate and criminalise laundering frequently draw upon economic arguments to justify their concerns.[38]

Policy makers in the area have not, in the past, looked into alternatives to the criminal law, or even the 'inertia option' as a response to money laundering. They have not informed themselves of the costs of their money laundering policy, in terms of policing, the time of the professions involved in reporting, and also the less easily quantifiable costs of the intrusions upon the privacy of the relationships between bankers, lawyers and accountants and their clients. The conclusion has been advanced that the people involved in the making of policy are not so much problem solvers as problem owners.[39] It is they who benefit from the continuing discourse surrounding laundering, and their interests are better served by its perpetuation than by the provision of solutions.

In 2000 a Cabinet Office essay at 'joined-up government' finally made a commitment to this sort of consideration:

> There is a need for more detailed strategic economic analysis of the criminal markets and organisations operating within the UK. Asset deprivation is an economic intervention. To be used to best effect, it is important to establish a comprehensive picture of the market it is intended to damage. A better understanding of these markets will inform a more effective strategy against organised and financial crime generally.[40]

Years earlier, Braithwaite had formulated a further series of questions that should be addressed by legislators determining what to do about, and in particular whether to regulate, the laundering of drug money.[41]

Benefit Questions
1. What percentage increase in the price of drugs is likely to be accomplished by money laundering regulation?

---

[36] Criminal law was 'generally considered the domain *par excellence* of moral rather than economic thinking in law', Richard A Posner, 'An Economic Theory of the Criminal Law' (1985) 85 *Columbia Law Review* 1193 at 1230.

[37] And see Peter Alldridge, *Relocating Criminal Law* (Aldershot and Brookfield, VT, Dartmouth, 2000) 13–15 and materials there cited.

[38] See the section below ch 2, The International and Global Economic Consequences of Laundering.

[39] Petrus van Duyne, ESRC Seminar Series, Cardiff, April 2000.

[40] *PIU Report*, para 6.20: this document even cites Gary Becker, 'Crime and Punishment: An Economic Approach' (1968) 76 *Journal of Political Economy* 169, the *fons et origo* of economic consideration of criminal law.

[41] 'Following the Money Trail to what destination? An Introduction to the Symposium' (1993) 44 *Alabama Law Review* at 659–60. The article dealt with laundering on the assumption that it only applied to drug money: the questions are still valid so far as concerns that part of the laundering enterprise which deals with drug money, but little modification need be made for the more inclusive *régime* now in place.

2. Given what we know about the price inelasticity of demand for drugs, what percentage reduction in demand can we expect from such a price increase?
3. If it is a public benefit to exact retribution against evil people, how many such people get their just deserts as a result of money laundering regulation?

Cost questions

1. How much additional property crime is committed by addicts who choose to pay the increased price for drugs rather than curtail their demand?
2. What is the impact on the legitimate economy when drug users pays the higher price, thereby shifting their spending to the drug economy?
3. What is the efficiency cost to the banks of the new money laundering regulation? How much business does this shift to foreign banks not subject to regulation?
4. What are the costs to taxpayers of administering the new enforcement?
5. What are the costs of increasing monopolisation of drug markets by the most powerful groups as a result of enforcement that pushes less sophisticated groups out of the market?[42]
6. How many lives are lost as a result of enforcement operations?
7. How extensive is that loss of privacy which results from reporting and surveillance arrangements?

Analogous questions can be constructed in relations to other criminal markets. The fact that there has still been little attempt to address these questions indicates how far the development of money laundering law has hitherto been from an exercise in the rational development of policy.

'Progress'

There is a view, embodied in the Whig notion of history and frequently linked to the rationalist model of criminal law-making (though there is frequently little rational about it), that history is progress, that things are generally getting better, that this improvement is ineluctable, and that writing history involves describing progress. There have been some attempts to locate money laundering regulation within such an outlook. The continual deployment of the metaphor of 'fight' and 'struggle' is such an attempt, as is the use of the adjective of 'evolution' to describe the changing responses to laundering.[43] The images used in the following quotation are telling:

> Just as the 1991 Directive *moved ahead* of the original FATF 40 Recommendations in requiring obligatory suspicious transaction reporting, the European Union should continue to impose a high standard upon its member states, giving effect to or even going beyond the 1996 update of the FATF 40 Recommendations. In particular, the

---

[42] 'It is safe to assume that smaller criminal entrepreneurs will have more trouble getting around the law than powerful drug barons.' John Braithwaite, 'Following the Money Trail to what Destination?' (1993) 44 *Alabama Law Review* 657, 658.

[43] William C Gilmore, *Dirty money: the evolution of money laundering counter-measures*, 2nd edn (Strasbourg, Council of Europe Pres, 1999).

EU can *show the way* in seeking to involve certain professions more actively in the fight against money laundering alongside the financial sector.[44]

All this is correct if (but only if) it is 'the way'. Simply to present the argument in this way is to embrace the idea that the history of criminal law takes place outside human agency, and to present the actors as being swept along by a tide outside their control. This diverts attention both from the significance of human choices, and from the possibility of alternative strategies.

The General and the Particular in Criminal Lawmaking

Throughout the history of the legislation against laundering, two kinds of arguments resound, and their relationship has influenced the way in which the criminal law of England and Wales has developed in many areas. The first holds that there is a particular class of offences, be it drugs offences, or terrorism offences, or offences involving organised crime, which are graver by an order of magnitude than any other category of offence and which consequently require differential treatment, with more intrusive enforcement powers, rules of evidence less favourable to the defence, higher penalties, draconian confiscation powers and so on. The second holds that other offences are also very serious and that it is important that they be treated as equivalent to drugs offences, or terrorism offences, or offences involving organised crime (or whatever happened to be the current 'leading edge' category). The first set of arguments has typically been deployed to secure a derogation from a liberal position so far as concerns the selected offence, or enforcement power, and the second to bring all other offences to an equivalent position. The sequence has frequently been used to outflank the opposition that would have faced a direct assault on a liberal redoubt. This sequence—introducing acceptably specific legislation and then generalising from it on the basis of consistency—is seen throughout the relationship between the treatment of drugs offences and of other sources of laundered money. Repeatedly, harsh rules have been put in place for drugs offenders only later for an argument to be made from consistency that the same rules should apply elsewhere.[45] Rules that are introduced as exceptions are then extended because not to do so would preserve anomalies.[46]

---

[44] Preamble to draft amended EU Directive 2000: emphases added.

[45] Eg confiscation orders being made mandatory (not discretionary) for drugs offences, the criminalisation of failure to disclose knowledge or suspicion of drug money laundering, the assumptions in 'lifestyle provisions' being triggered by fewer convictions.

[46] *PIU Report*, para 8.12.

'Moral Panics'

Could the development of the legal responses to money laundering be placed within the general theory of 'moral panic'? This theory was originally used to account for the reactions that confronted 'Mods and Rockers' in the 1960s.[47] The idea is that a combination of press publicity and the actions of powerful individuals create an adverse public reaction towards a designated activity, and once the process of demonisation begins, it can be increased by continual publicity.[48] The investigation of money laundering necessitates, or is said to necessitate, more intrusive investigative powers than many other offences that are normally regarded as more serious. Gaining convictions for money laundering requires, or is said to require, that the prosecution be given the assistance of shifts in the burden of proof[49] and access to information that hitherto was regarded as privileged. These are the kinds of arguments that have been made throughout the ages in respect of whatever the current 'folk devil' happens to be.[50] The contrary argument is that it is precisely in the case of accusation of a crime considered at any given moment to be especially heinous that a defendant is in the clearest need of the parcel of protections associated with 'due process' rights.

It is clear that some elements of 'moral panic' and 'moral entrepreneurship'[51] can be seen in the development of the discourse surrounding money laundering. Take, for example, the language of the following quotation:

> Money laundering has devastating social consequences and is a threat to national security because money laundering provides the fuel for drug dealers, terrorists, arms dealers and other criminals to operate and expand their criminal enterprises. In doing so, criminals manipulate financial systems in the United States and abroad. Unchecked, money laundering can erode the integrity of a nation's financial institutions. Due to the high integration of capital markets, money laundering can also negatively affect national and global interest rates as launderers reinvest funds where their schemes are less likely to be detected rather than where rates of return are higher because of sound economic principles. Organized financial crime is assuming an increasingly significant role that threatens the safety and security of peoples, states and democratic institutions. Moreover, our ability to conduct foreign policy and to

---

[47] Stan Cohen, *Folk Devils and Moral Panics* (London, MacGibbon and Kee, 1972).

[48] Erich Goode and Nachman Ben-Yehuda, *Moral Panic: The Social Construction of Deviance* (Oxford, Blackwell, 1994); A Hunt, '"Moral panic" and moral language in the media' (1997) 48 *British Journal of Sociology* 629–48.

[49] And see the consideration of shifted burdens of proof in confiscation, below p 145, and in the criminal laundering provisions, below, p 195.

[50] They 'spreade their poison in secrete, making it nearly impossible to produce witnesses against them'. Archbishop Whitgift, letter to Lord Burghley, 15 July 1584, writing of blasphemy, quoted in Leonard Levy, *The Origins of the Fifth Amendment* (NYC, NY, Macmillan, 1968) at 139.

[51] The 'moral entrepreneur' thesis was advanced by Duster in respect of drug legislation: Troy Duster, *The Legislation of Morality* (NYC, NY, Free Press, 1971).

promote our economic security and prosperity is hindered by these threats to our democratic and free-market partners.[52]

Many of the sources do speak darkly of the consequential dangers of permitting laundering to take place, and the 'folk devil' required by the thesis is probably best thought of as a mixture between the late Pablo Escobar and a James Bond villain, complete with Persian cat and rare disability—that is, somebody who is very wealthy and who is prepared to use the power thereby acquired to cause damage on a world-wide scale.

Attempts have been made to portray Kenneth Noye in this light. As a result of his activities in disposing of the gold stolen in the Brink's Mat gold bullion robbery, Noye was convicted of handling stolen goods.[53] What had happened was that guards were terrorised into giving the codes by which access was achieved by robbers to large amounts of gold bullion. The subsequent dealings to convert the gold into saleable forms and to disguise the proceeds of sale never had any legal designation beyond handling of stolen goods.[54] At the time of his conviction in 2000 for the murder of someone who annoyed him on the M25,[55] the press portrayed him as an evil mastermind and described his participation in the bullion robbery—melting bars down and selling on the anonymised gold—as 'laundering'.[56] The Noye case draws attention to the question of nomenclature. Renaming is one of the techniques used in amplifying the perceived gravity of a given phenomenon. In the same way that street robbery attracted far greater sentences when repackaged as 'mugging'[57] and drug 'dealing' or 'pushing' when renamed 'trafficking', so 'handling' or 'fencing' takes on a more sinister aspect when recast as 'laundering'. So too, on a far larger scale, (and had it fallen within the jurisdiction of the English courts) was the 'laundering' of IMF money which had been granted to Russia.[58] Throughout the scandal[59] the expression 'money laundering' has been used to describe what might in another age have been described as theft and handling. Immediately upon the attacks on the United States of 11 September 2001, attention was directed against 'laundering' of money by terrorists, even though the financial resources of terrorists

---

[52] US Department of State, Bureau for International Narcotics and Law Enforcement Affairs *International Narcotics Control Strategy* (1997) at 2, cited by Jimmy Gurulé 'The 1988 UN Convention against illicit traffic in narcotic drugs and psychotropic substances—a ten year perspective: is international co-operation merely illusory?' (1988) 22 *Fordham International Law Journal* 74, 76–7.

[53] Andrew Hogg, *Bullion. Brink's Mat: the story of Britain's biggest gold robbery* (Harmondsworth, Penguin, 1988). And see *Brinks Ltd v Abu-Saleh and others (No 1)* [1995] 1 WLR 1478; [1995] 4 All ER 65.

[54] Whether on common law tracing principles or under Theft Act 1968, s 24.

[55] *The Observer*, 16 April 2000.

[56] *The Times*, 15 April 2000.

[57] Stuart Hall *et al*, *Policing the crisis: mugging, the state and law and order* (Basingstoke, Macmillan, 1977).

[58] The 'Bank of New York' scandal, as to which see Dolgor Solongo, *Russian Capitalism and Money Laundering* (NYC, NY, United Nations, 2001).

[59] *PIU Report*, Box 3.9.

might be lawful in provenance. The point of departure both from the Bond villain stereotype and from Noye, and the respect in which the stereotype fails, was that in neither of those cases, unlike the attacks on the United States, was there any particular desire to disrupt the way in which the Government functioned.[60]

So far as concerns money laundering, two things are missing from the 'moral panic' account. One is the element of public recognition. There are some representations of laundering in popular fiction and films, but there has been more governmental and less media action than is usually identified with moral panics. This is partly at least because the crime, almost alone among serious offences, lacks any element of overt harm which allows people unversed in law to recognise, be annoyed by and condemn. A person laundering money might well look like any other person going into a bank to make a deposit: unlike motor scooters, it is not even mildly annoying to watch and is difficult to get angry about it, and unlike a fraud, there is no readily perceptible victim with whom to empathise when the truth becomes known.

The second factor absent from a standard 'moral panic' account of money laundering is the international element. The accounts which have been developed within criminology, sociology and history to account for changes in criminal law and law enforcement have almost all been directed at activity within a given jurisdiction, and at least in some cases tell us more about the jurisdiction than the actual development. When dealing with legislation that is international in provenance (unless people who work for international organisations dealing with law enforcement constitute such a community) there is no identifiable community in whose interest (at some level) the legislation prohibition worked. The international organisations which are the driving forces underlying much of the legislation under discussion wear a cloak of anonymity behind which it is far less easy to identify the contribution of individual actors.

At one level, all that was necessary to explain the advent of the legislation is to say that the UK was obliged to sign and then to implement the UN Convention, the EU directive, the Conventions of the OECD and the Council of Europe, because that is the nature of the obligation undertaken by a State playing the role to which the UK aspires in those organisations. The difficult issue is how to know enough about the formation of policy and laws at the international level. The combination of international sources and multi-national agencies has generated a plethora of acronyms[61] that obfuscate the identification and motives of those formulate changes in law and policy. There are elements from the development of the regulatory structure surrounding money laundering which can be brought within most of the established means of accounting for developments in criminal law. Early work on the criminalisation

---

[60] And see Petrus van Duyne, 'Money-laundering: Pavlov's dog and beyond' (1998) 37 *Howard Journal of Criminal Justice* 359.

[61] BBA, FATF, JMLSG, NCIS, FINCEN, FAP, CCAB, FIUs, MLATs and so on. See generally Department of the Treasury. Financial Crimes Enforcement Network, *The Global Fight Against Money Laundering*, (Washington DC, no date given)

of laundering in the United States relates it less to public outcry about drugs than 'to a broader concern with financial crime, and to a cadre of experts pro-actively crafting and implementing a legal solution to a problem of which the public and Congress were little aware and which they understood poorly'.[62] The painstaking methodology of work like EP Thompson's classic account of the enactment and operation of the Black Act[63] is not easy to replicate in any area, but the international element presents especial difficulties. The decision-making processes are not transparent and it is difficult to identify either the *locus* of power or the means of its exercise. Levi's methodology is to conduct interviews with policy makers at the various international bodies most directly concerned in the regulation of laundering.[64]

The Rhetoric of the Debates

The forces of 'crime control' have frequently alighted upon groups who can find few or no defenders, and legislated, or put in place severe enforcement strate-gies, against them. People who profit from crime fall easily within that category. They are demons *par excellence*. No sophisticated set of accounts is required as to why somebody ought not to be permitted to benefit from crime. One of the reasons crime controls arguments have such rhetorical force[65] is that, whether the appeal is to a desired result in a specific case ('Should drug dealer *x* be allowed to emerge from prison to enjoy his ill-gotten fortune?) or the general principle ('What is the point of making things crimes if you still let people profit from them?) the answer 'stands to reason'.[66] Those arguing for a different posi-tion always enter the public debate (in the way in which it is conducted in Britain at least), disadvantaged by the absence of easily accessible, rhetorically power-ful, examples of criminals who should be allowed to retain the proceeds of their crimes. Arguments against regulation, or for less regulation or less draconian laws, follow from the general costs of having such laws, and seldom (except in third party cases) their application in particular instances.

---

[62] Jeanne Bickford, *Filthy Lucre: A Socio-Legal study of the Criminalization of Money Laundering* (PhD Thesis, University of California, Irvine, 1986).

[63] EP Thompson, *Whigs and Hunters* (Harmondsworth, Penguin, 1975).

[64] Michael Levi, 'Money laundering and its regulation' (2002) 582 *Annals of the American Academy of Political and Social Science* 181; Michael Levi and William Gilmore, 'Terrorist Finance and Money Laundering: A New Paradigm for Crime Control' (2002); Michael Levi, 'Following the Criminal and Terrorist Money Trails' in Petrus van Duyne and Klaus von Lampe (eds), *Criminal Finances and Organizing Crime in Europe* (forthcoming).

[65] Stuart Hall *et al*, *Policing the crisis: mugging, the state and law and order* (Basingstoke, Macmillan, 1977).

[66] And see Tony Blair, foreword to *PIU Report*: '. . . it simply is not right in Modern Britain that millions of law-abiding people work hard to earn a living, whilst a few live handsomely off the prof-its of crime. The undeserved trappings of success enjoyed by criminals are an affront to the hard-working majority.'

A proper account of the development of the law in this area should not be too determinist, but must admit the possibility that individuals' choices have impacted upon the development of law, and also that they have operated within the context of wider forces, particularly those arising out of globalisation. Borrowing from Thompson, one phenomenon that helps to gainsay a version based entirely upon a conspiracy of powerful interests, is judicial behaviour which asserts the liberal values of the rule of law. There have not been a great many examples, but the refusal of the Court of Appeal to be driven to accept the imposition of reduced burdens upon the prosecution[67] is one, and some assertions of human rights in this area another.[68] The movement towards more 'draconian' (a word which recurs very frequently in the debates[69] and judgments[70] dealing with this legislation) legal standards is consistent but not entirely concerted.[71]

Symbolic Legislation

Another volume in the library of accounts of the development of criminal legislation is that of 'symbolic legislation'. This expression describes legislation that achieves some objective simply by reason of having been on the statute book. Some legislation has been relatively successful in achieving a change of attitudes without having been enforced vigorously through the courts. Is the money laundering legislation 'symbolic' in this sense? This depends upon the target group identified. There is little doubt that the UK Government and its enforcement agencies, especially the National Criminal Intelligence Service (NCIS)[72] and the new Assets Recovery Agency,[73] has, and at all relevant moments has had, every

---

[67] The aftermath of *Dickens* [1990] 2 QB 102; [1990] 2 All ER 626.

[68] And see (extra-judicially) Lord Lloyd of Berwick. 'One sometimes forgets that the Convention is intended as a minimum, not a maximum, of what is required for the protection of what I still like to call the liberty of the subject. I do not care whether or not Part 5 will fall foul of the European Convention. It is sufficient for me that it falls foul of what I regard as acceptable in English law.' HL Debates 25 March 2002 vol 633 col 48.

[69] Tony Blair, then shadow Home Secretary, at the second reading debate on the Criminal Justice Act 1993: HC Debates 14 April 1993 Volume 222 Column 870, and countless times during the passage of the 2002 Act.

[70] Eg, *Attorney-General Of Hong Kong v Lee Kwong-Kut* [1993] AC 951, *per* Lord Woolf at 964; *R v Central Criminal Court, Ex Parte Francis & Francis* [1989] 1 AC 346; [1988] 3 All ER 775; *R v Southwark Crown Court, ex Parte Customs and Excise Commissioners* [1990] 1 QB 650 *per* Watkins LJ at 661; *R v Tivnan* [1999] 1 CAR(S) 92 *per* Rose LJ at 96–97. In *McIntosh v HM Advocate* 2001 JC 78; 2000 SLT 1280, Lord Prosser said: 'I am in no way suggesting that draconian penalties are inappropriate in combating drug trafficking. But Draco was concerned with the severity of penalties, not with imposing them without establishing or even suggesting facts which are prerequisites of liability to particular penalties. (Aristotle says that there was nothing noteworthy in Draco's laws except the severity of the punishments).'

[71] And, on the interpretation of the legislation, see the section below ch 4, A Note on the Interpretation of Money Laundering.

[72] See section below pp 17–18.

[73] See the section below ch 11, The Assets Recovery Agency.

intention of seizing as many assets from criminals as possible, has deployed significant resources in these efforts, and that the imposition of draconian penalties upon those charged under the criminal laundering provisions is sought by prosecutors. The crime control rhetoric directed against laundering has indeed been backed by law enforcement will. It has simply been unsuccessful.[74]

The area of money laundering legislation that has not been enforced with any great vigour is that which enlists the professions, especially banking and accountancy, to make reports upon their clients in the event of suspicious transactions being undertaken. There has been a great deal of publicity given in the media to inform those professions about the laundering laws, and requirements have been put in place and advice has been given by professional bodies and journals. The number of actual prosecutions of alleged launderers is negligible.[75] This might alter with the introduction of the new regulatory framework involving enhanced powers for the Financial Services Authority.[76] Enhanced police activity is also likely to follow the enlargement of the understanding of the scope of the legislation by the NCIS. After a low-key start to the policing of laundering provisions, concentrating upon drug money, the current enforcement programme seems committed to bringing all activity in the black or grey economies under the classification of money laundering. This would place the laundering laws, so far as they deal with the professions, in the category of legislation whose effective implementation depends more upon changing the attitudes of the people directly concerned than upon making effective threats. The new legislation is accompanied by a Government target of doubling the receipts from seizures by 2004, by deploying additional resources, expertise and greater international co-operation.[77] Whatever may have been the position in the past, the 'symbolic legislation' account is now difficult to sustain.

A Functionalist Account of Confiscation, Criminalisation and Internationalisation

The rhetoric of 'war' in the 'war on drugs' or the 'war on terrorism' implies that if there were no longer any money laundering, or even if there were to be a substantial diminution in the incidence of money laundering, then that would be the satisfaction of an important objective. Once it becomes clear that there is little

---

[74] The failure of the legislation is starkly admitted in *PIU Report*, para 8.6: 'The intention of the UK's confiscation law is clear: that offenders should be deprived of their criminal benefit. But this is not happening.'

[75] *PIU Report*, figure 9.1 shows the numbers of prosecutions in England and Wales to be 80, 50 and 115 for 1997, 1998 and 1999 respectively, with convictions hovering around 40. The provisional figures for 2000 show 16 convictions from 73 prosecutions for drug money laundering and 23 convictions from 45 prosecutions for other crimes. HL Debates 25 June 2002 Col 1320 (Lord Falconer).

[76] See the section below ch 12, The Financial Services Authority and its Powers.

[77] HC Debates 30 October 2001 col 758 (John Denham MP, Minister for Police, Courts and Drugs).

or no serious probability of the 'war' being won, and that all policy-makers who are reasonably well informed must know that, then the search for different accounts begins. On this basis, the money laundering crusade could be presented as an exercise in futility—lawmaking and law enforcement along the lines of Prohibition, which multiplies expenditure upon enforcement whilst generating crime (criminogenesis) and recovering little from criminals. But there is another way of looking both at Prohibition and at the manner in which the law of confiscation, criminalisation and internationalisation now operates. It is to adopt the functionalist strategy of asking who benefits from the fact that the laws and enforcement procedures have been put in place. Viewed along these lines, the developments in the law make some sense by identifying the people who benefit, analogous to the Yankee in Gusfield's study in whose (at some level) interest Prohibition worked.[78] These are described by van Duyne as the 'Threat Assessment Industry':

> [T]his consists of public agencies, private firms or persons, who are primarily interested in conveying an image of organised crime that suits their purposes. Frequently this image is an apocalyptic one; a huge threat of the sinister forces of darkness. The threat assessment reports are composed accordingly and sold for not too modest prices.[79]

The crusade against money laundering has put in place incentives for different career trajectories within the police forces and international organisations. It is having an impact upon the financing of police activity. In the United States the police forces concerned in the operation of these laws actually have access to the funds that are seized.[80] In the reorganisation of policing within the United Kingdom, one of the driving forces is the crusade against money laundering. The National Criminal Intelligence Service has an Economic Crimes Unit, the agency to which reports should be addressed, which receives reports of money laundering. The Europol National Unit is within the NCIS and the Economic Crimes Unit of the NCIS is part of the UK delegation to the Financial Action Task Force (FATF) and is the Financial Intelligence Unit (FIU) for England and Wales. Its continued significance depends upon the importance ascribed to money laundering.

From 1992, the NCIS had existed without a specific statutory basis under the *aegis* of the Home Office, and it was placed upon a statutory footing in 1997.[81] Its functions include liaison with financial institutions, trade associations and

---

[78] Joseph Gusfield, *Symbolic Crusade* (Urbana, IL, University of Illinois Press, 1963).

[79] Petrus van Duyne, 'Money Laundering: Pavlov's Dog and Beyond' (1998) 37 *Howard Journal* 359. For a less cynical view see Michael Levi, 'Evaluating the 'New Policing': Attacking the Money Trail of Organised Crime', (1997) *Australia and New Zealand Journal of Criminology* 3.

[80] As erstwhile Attorney-General Richard Thornburgh put it, '[I]t's satisfying to think that it's now possible for a drug dealer to serve time in a forfeiture-financed prison after being arrested by agents driving a forfeiture-provided automobile while working in a forfeiture-funded sting operation.' (Seized Drug Funds to Pay for Prisons, *Washington Times*, 28 Sept 1989).

[81] Police Act 1997 Part 1.

regulatory bodies regarding the education and training of money laundering reporting officers, and the exchange of financial intelligence and participation in training with foreign FIUs. It provides assistance to other countries seeking to establish them. It is the primary enforcement body involved in the enforcement of the money laundering provisions. The objectives established for it by law are:

(a)   to provide high quality and relevant criminal intelligence[82] leading to—
    (i)   the dismantling or disruption of criminal enterprises engaged in serious and organised crime, and
    (ii)   the arrest and prosecution of criminals, whose activities take place in or impact on the United Kingdom;
(b)   to provide high quality and relevant criminal intelligence and information to law enforcement agencies, having regard to the Command Paper entitled 'Tackling Drugs to Build a Better Britain—the Government's Ten-Year Strategy for Tackling Drugs Misuse'[83] and in order to suppress the availability of controlled drugs in the United Kingdom.[84]

Particularly striking in this document is the aim to *disrupt* organised crime. This fits within a move from reactive to proactive policing and away from the use of the traditional tools of crime prevention. It also coincides with greater interest in the policing of criminal markets and in treating 'organised crime' as *organisations* whose functioning can be detrimentally affected.

It is not just the careers of police and prosecuting and defending lawyers that have prospered in the upsurge of concern about money laundering. The political career trajectory most closely linked to legislation and international action on the profits of crime is that of Tony Blair. From the 'tough on crime and tough on the causes of crime' speech,[85] his speeches as shadow Home Secretary during the passage of the Criminal Justice Act 1993, through to the decision to prioritise the reform that became the Proceeds of Crime Act 2002,[86] and the speedy identification of money laundering as one of the issues which needed to be confronted after the events of 11 September 2001, Mr Blair has been central to the development of the law over the past years. The Labour Party has traditionally been regarded as electorally vulnerable on 'law and order', and it was clearly part of the 'New Labour' project to make the issue, at the very least, a neutral one. Optimally this had to be done without jeopardising core support, and so the selection of 'rich' stereotypes against whom to act was convenient. It also

---

[82] 'Criminal intelligence' is an expression used as a response to the argument of those who argued that the functions of the NCIS should be limited to information for 'the prevention of crime' and those who wished it to be more proactive.

[83] Cm 3945.

[84] The NCIS (Secretary of State's Objectives) Order 1999 (SI 822).

[85] Labour Party Conference 30 September 1993.

[86] In this sequence of events the reference to the Cabinet Office Performance and Innovation Unit, which produced the *PIU Report* was crucial.

struck chords with the many Labour backbenchers.[87] It is, however, important not to ignore the personal appeal for Tony Blair of morality. He does engage in moral crusades that others would avoid. He does not attack people benefiting from crime just to secure political capital. He believes it to be a wrong-in-itself, from which consequential wrongs also follow, for people to profit from crime. That view underpins his commitment to the developments outlined in this book.

From Drugs and Banks to Markets and Organised Crime to International Terrorism

When originally put in place, confiscation powers were focussed on the profits of drug dealing (and, to a largely symbolic extent, terrorist property) and the *locus* of regulation was banks. The last 10 years, both at the national and international levels, have seen increased concern with other specific areas of crime and with the fact that the crime is 'organised', and that it takes place within criminal markets. 'Organised crime' is associated with continuing profits, from a trade in illegal goods and services. The activities extend beyond drugs to arms, prostitution and illegal immigration. The incorporation of 'international organised crime' as one of the principal *foci* of law enforcement has led to the increased deployment of the police in covert, proactive roles, together with the instantiation of systems of information gathering and exchange, and to a far greater emphasis on the financial aspects of crime. This has in turn cast the regulatory focus wider so as to seek to cover other categories of the (potentially infinite) range of mechanisms by which value can be translated from one form to another. The burden upon, and the powers of, the organisations charged with monitoring transactions have concomitantly increased.

The international drive against laundering has led to pressure for homogenisation of substantive criminal laws and enforcement mechanisms as between countries. In so doing it has helped recast the relationships that existed between Nation-States. From the point of view of individual States, it has provided the strongest challenge to the traditional idea of criminal law as being one matter in respect of which the sovereign Nation-State is still the predominant political unit. English criminal law is now unashamedly the handmaiden of international markets.

---

[87] During the passage of the Proceeds of Crime Bill many liberalising amendments from the Conservatives, particularly in respect of the duties of the regulated sector, were met by claims that they were attempting to protect their rich friends. See, eg, 'Would my right hon. Friend also consider amending the current balance between penalties and rewards for those engaged in money laundering? The profits are enormous and the penalties, especially for lawyers, accountants and bankers in the City of London and elsewhere, who assist terrorists to hide their money, are slight. Does he agree that publicly hanging a couple of lawyers would greatly assist with concentrating the mind?' Ian Davidson, HC Debates vol 372 col 952 15 October 2001.

A City free of regulatory abuse but open to fraud, corruption and money laundering is not one that will survive and grow in the current international climate.[88]

The contrast between the amounts of money that have been mentioned by enforcement authorities as representing the quantum of money laundered in the jurisdiction, and, on the other, the sums actually seized has generated a typical conflict between two sets of responses. One is to say that the estimates were too high, and that the 'problem' is not nearly so serious as had been imagined, and that no further legislative action is appropriate. Would-be enforcers claim, on the other hand, that the reason the level of seizures remains comparatively low is that that the requisite powers have still not been granted.[89]

Internationalisation and Small Jurisdictions

The process of internationalisation is not simply one in which the most (economically) significant jurisdictions enter into agreements one with another in the knowledge that all others will follow suit out of self-interest. The developing law of laundering has led to far greater attention being paid to jurisdictions in which, by virtue of the respect granted in those legal systems to corporate secrecy, banking secrecy and professional privilege, money laundering is enabled. The common stereotype is that havens like the Turks and Caicos Islands, Cayman Island and British Virgin Islands, for all of whose foreign policy the UK is responsible, attract huge amounts of money and that their banking and corporate secrecy laws allow the money to be protected from prying eyes. For such jurisdictions, there are significant advantages in laundering. 'The thing about the TCI is that you don't mention the money laundering. It's bad form. You talk about asset-management structures and tax-beneficial operations.'[90] The effect of globalisation is that so long as there is one jurisdiction that offers greater opacity to the 'money trail' than all the others, it will attract the most 'dirty' money and its existence will be enough to frustrate law enforcers. The process of homogenisation of laws through various international groups has involved the bringing to bear of pressure on such jurisdictions to conform to the wishes of 'the international community'. Absolute banking secrecy has now been abolished, for example in Switzerland. It is here that the traditional emphasis upon the self-expression of the Nation-State through criminal law breaks down entirely.

---

[88] Helen Liddell MP, HM Treasury News Release 119/97. 'Multilateral action is, however, much to be preferred, so as to have maximum impact and to avoid the costs on legitimate transactions with the UK being higher than with our international competitors.'

[89] This is seen most clearly in the argument for 'civil forfeiture' powers. See the section below ch 11, Forfeiture and Confiscation by Other Means.

[90] *The Observer*, 2 April 2000. And see *PIU Report*, paras 11.40 *et seq.*

Despots' Deposits

Until relatively recently, one of the perks of being a dictator was that if he survived his eventual overthrow he could look forward to a comfortable retirement in some agreeable exile living off funds which had been looted from his country during his period of office and stashed in a secure secret overseas bank account. Since 1989, with the end of the Cold War, the position has been different. Former tyrants are pursued.[91] The advent of mechanisms of accountability, elsewhere than in the country governed, for acts done while in government has generated demands for controls over the use of such assets. The matter became an embarrassing one for the United Kingdom Government when the former Nigerian dictator, Sani Abacha, was found to have deposited some £1.3bn in London banks,[92] 15 of which were found to have had significant control weaknesses,[93] and for Switzerland, when some at least of the money allegedly looted by former President Marcos of the Philippines was frozen in Swiss accounts. The nature of these cases is that the character of the activity generating the wealth will not be known at the time of the deposit, but will come to be known after the end of the dictatorship. At that time what will be most important for the new *régime* is to freeze the funds in whatever account they can be traced to so as to take action to secure them. Only relatively recently have effective mechanisms for doing this become available.

11 September 2001

On 11 September 2001, hijackers crashed two planes into the World Trade Centre in New York City, one into the Pentagon, and a fourth crashed in Western Pennsylvania after passengers had fought with hijackers. Slightly over 3,000 people were killed. A good deal of the immediate response to the attacks was upon the ways in which terrorism was financed, and upon the national and international legislative responses which were required to reduce the probability of a recurrence. The acts of terror challenged the established boundaries of criminal justice and international relations. If the actions fell within the criminal justice paradigm, then international pressure, extradition, trial and punishment were the outcomes. If they were acts of war, then sanctions by the United

---

[91] Consider, for example, the application to extradite Augusto Pinochet to Spain: *R v Bartle and the Commissioner of Police for the Metropolis, ex parte Pinochet (No 1)* [2000] 1 AC 61; [1998] 4 All E.R. 897: *R v Bartle and the Commissioner of Police for the Metropolis, ex parte Pinochet (No 2)* [2000] 1 AC 119; [1999] 1 All ER 577.

[92] The Select Committee on International Development heard evidence (25 January 2001) from HE Prince Bola A Ajibola on the looting conducted by Abacha in Nigeria (Select Committee on International Development Fourth Report Evidence, March 2001, Questions 658–79). See Standing Committee B, 17 January 2002 cols 1014–16, (Ian Davidson MP).

[93] 'Plundered $1bn to be returned to Nigeria' *The Times* 18 April 2002.

Nations or military action followed. The responses actually blurred the established boundaries. Crime was presented as warfare, and military reprisal as crime control.[94]

On 23 September 2001 the US President, George W Bush, issued an Order targeting terrorists and blocking the accounts of a number of organisations and individuals.[95] Congress enacted the Financial Anti-Terrorism Act of 2001.[96] The Security Council of the United Nations resolved that all States should have in place a legislative framework to deal with the financing of terrorism,[97] and in particular that States should criminalise the provision of funds to carry out terrorist acts,[98] and that assets be frozen which are in the hands of persons who 'commit or attempt to commit terrorist acts or participate in or facilitate the commission of terrorists acts' or bodies controlled directly or indirectly by them.[99] The United Nations resolved that member nations ensure that their financial institutions report transactions thought to be related to terrorism and put in place measures to criminalise the financing of terrorist acts, and freeze the assets of suspected individual and organisations.[100] Meeting in Washington DC the G7 finance ministers extended the remit of the FATF,[101] to include the financing of terrorism.[102] At the initiative of the G7 Finance Ministers and Central Bank governors, an extraordinary plenary meeting of the FATF was held in Washington DC on 29–30 October 2001 to address new initiatives to combat money laundering and terrorist financing. The FATF agreed to establish a set of Special Recommendations on Terrorist Financing committing members to detect, prevent and suppress the financing of terrorism and terrorist acts. The EU's leaders backed a new package of EU measures to counter terrorism, including an EU-wide arrest warrant,[103] fast-track extradition procedure, and close co-operation between EU intelligence services and those in the US.[104] In particular there was strong pressure to resolve the log-jam that surrounded the Amending European Union Directive.[105] The principled claims of those who resisted encroachments into lawyer/client secrecy were no weaker or stronger as a result of the attack, and no one claimed that if only there had been a fuller or

[94] And see Michael Levi, 'Following the Criminal and Terrorist Money trails' in Petrus van Duyne and Klaus von Lampe (eds), *Criminal finances and organizing crime in Europe* (forthcoming).

[95] Executive Order Blocking Property and Prohibiting Transactions with Persons who commit, threaten to commit, or support Terrorism (Executive Order 13224 23 September 2001 66 *Federal Register* 49079).

[96] HR 3004, <http://www.gop.gov/committeecentral/docs/bills/107/1/bill.asp?bill=hr3004>.

[97] UN Security Council Resolution 1373 (28 September 2001).

[98] *Ibid*, Art 1(b).

[99] *Ibid*, Art 1(c).

[100] UN Security Council Resolution 1373 (28 September 2001).

[101] See the section below ch 5, Financial Action Task Force.

[102] *The Independent*, 6 October 2001.

[103] *Report of the European Union Committee on The European Arrest Warrant* (16th Report HL Paper 89).

[104] *The Independent*, 22 September 2001.

[105] See the section below ch 5, The Amending Directive.

more rigorous reporting requirement placed upon lawyers the attacks would have been averted. Nonetheless, something 'had to be done'.

In the United Kingdom, the Financial Services Authority investigated the possibility of profits having been made from the attacks.[106] The Chancellor of the Exchequer, Gordon Brown, announced the freezing of $88m of assets linked to the Taleban régime[107] and around the world measures were put in place. A new terrorist finance unit has been set up within NCIS. Emergency anti-terrorism legislation was introduced, inter alia, to 'build on the provisions of the Proceeds of Crime Bill[108] to deal specifically with terrorist finance through monitoring and freezing the accounts of suspected terrorists.'[109] The police were given new powers to disrupt terrorist finances, and it was made a criminal offence for financial institutions not to report transactions that raised suspicions.

The events of 11 September 2001 provided the impetus for a further shift in the focus of money laundering control to consider the means by which terrorism is financed. The expression 'laundering' was continually applied to the means by which terrorist organisations were financed. The use of the pejorative expression was doubtless deliberate. The analytical truth is that funding for terrorism is either itself the profits of crime, in which case it is covered already, or it is not, in which case the seizure of money intended for terrorist use, when no action has been taken towards its deployment, smacks of 'thought-crime' and does not fall within traditionally accepted notions of laundering, because the money is clean in the first place. This was obscured in the rhetoric and the association of Afghanistan with heroin sales.[110]

Similarly, the introduction of closer monitoring of suspected bank accounts by financial information orders had already been put in place, so far as concerns the accounts of persons suspected of involvement in terrorism.[111] Somehow, however, the more widespread deployment of these orders was presented as being a necessary response to the attacks.[112] In this case the legislation probably would have occurred anyway, and the attacks simply provided a convenient issue by reference to which to overcome any opposition on civil liberties grounds.

---

[106] FSA/PN/122/2001 <http://www.fsa.gov.uk/pubs/press/2001/122.html>

[107] Labour Party Conference, 1 October 2001.

[108] The Proceeds of Crime Bill was introduced shortly afterwards.

[109] HC Debates 15 Oct 2001 Col 923 (David Blunkett MP, Home Secretary), introducing what became the Anti-Terrorism, Crime and Security Act 2001.

[110] After the attacks on the US, Tony Blair stated repeatedly that 90% of heroin sold in Britain was of Afghan origin. (Labour Party conference 2 October 2001; 'Air Strikes on Afghanistan: Prime Minister's Speech' *The Independent*, 8 October 2001; HC Debates 8 October 2001 cols 814 & 821). The conceptual differences were, however, made clear by the Chancellor of the Exchequer, Gordon Brown, HC Debates 15 Oct 2001, col 943.

[111] See the section below ch 10, Financial Information Orders (Bank Circulars).

[112] 'G7 approves plan to choke terror funds', *The Guardian*, 26 September 2001.

THE FUTURE?

Will the 'crime of the 1990s' fade from view or will it continue to have a dominant role? There is much to be said for Williams' view:

> . . . in spite of this emphasis on following the money trail as a way of countering and disrupting transnational criminal organisations, the advantages remain with the criminals. The global financial system provides many more opportunities than law enforcement can ever hope to forestall or block. Consequently, law enforcement is playing a game of catch-up that it is almost certainly destined to lose.
>
> Moreover, for a variety of reasons the advantages accruing to the criminals are likely to increase rather than decrease in the next decade. Developments such as smart cards and cyber-money will facilitate money laundering activities and provide new opportunities for money transfers that are difficult if not impossible for government authorities to monitor and detect. Although anti-money laundering efforts remain an essential part of holistic or comprehensive strategies against drug smugglers and other transnational criminal organizations, therefore, expectations about their overall effectiveness should be modest. There will be some spectacular successes and substantial inroads will be made against some criminal organizations—but the overall impact will remain limited as criminal groups find ways to circumvent new restrictions and display the kind of ingenuity that is difficult to counter.[113]

MONEY LAUNDERING AS A CASE STUDY IN CRIMINAL LAW THEORY

One approach, then, to money laundering is to understand it as a piece of law-making to be described and analysed in socio-legal terms. Another approach is to seek justifications for the law in criminal law theory. The three sets of powers under examination in this book—forfeiture, confiscation and criminalisation as responses to dealings with the proceeds of crime, have different histories and follow from differing governing rationales.

Forfeiture laws, which give the State property in the thing by, with or in which the offence is committed, are not a product of sophisticated moral thinking, and they attract very widespread condemnation amongst academics. The strongest defence of them is in terms of the symbolic importance of the particular item that is the subject of forfeiture,[114] but it is hardly compelling. In the case of *confiscation* laws, by contrast, where the State exacts an amount equivalent to that by which a criminal benefited from crime, it is not difficult to find substantial support for the principle that criminals ought not to be allowed to benefit from their crimes. Difficulties arise when it becomes apparent that a system that attempted to deprive every criminal of the profits of his/her crime would

[113] Phil Williams, 'Money Laundering' (1997) 5 *South African Journal of International Affairs* 71.
[114] Paul Schiff Berman, 'An Anthropological Approach to Modern Forfeiture Law: The Symbolic Function of Legal Actions Against Objects' (1999) 11 *Yale Journal Law & Humanities* 1.

neither be practical nor desirable, and that there is a need to distinguish those crimes in respect of which the criminal is and those where s/he is not to be deprived of the proceeds of crime. Amid the rhetoric of denunciation, little attention has been devoted to this important distinction. Moreover, even where there is support in principle for depriving the criminal of his/her profits, there are two important constraints. The first is the expense of enforcement. There is a balance to be struck between, on the one hand, the costs of the investigations and the proceedings to recover the assets, and, on the other, the value of the assets recovered. The second is the rights, including the human rights, of the owner of property against whom the proceedings are brought. The relationship between the two is crucial. The greater the attenuation of the rights of the owner of property, whether by reversal of the burden of proof, or confiscation without a criminal conviction, obligatory disclosure, compelled reports from the owner's professional contacts (banker, lawyer, accountant), or any of the other evidential and procedural devices to be considered, the less costly the proceedings and the more lucrative they are likely to be to the State.

Criminalisation of laundering is problematic. In the context of the legislation to be considered in this book, the argument that criminals ought not to be allowed to profit from their crimes is a reason for 'reparative' confiscation, but not for criminalisation. In liberal theory, every imposition of criminal liability requires a sufficient justification. The central concepts by reference to which criminal law theory seeks such justifications are harm and fault. On this account, criminal liability is morally justified (at least) when a sufficiently serious harm is brought about with a sufficiently culpable mental state. The criminalisation of money laundering occurred in response to international initiatives and so its rationale has seldom been made explicit. Without such a statement it is difficult to differentiate bad from not-so-bad cases in sentencing and other decisions within the penal process. Differing consequences follow according as to whether the harm is described in economic terms or by reference to the harm involved in the predicate offence. The extent to which it is caused by a single act of laundering is unclear, and the mental state that is required is (quite exceptionally among serious offences) quite unrelated to the supposed harm.

One of the recent developments in this area is that the complexity of money laundering systems and resulting difficulties in pursuing criminal sanctions against perpetrators to attempts at civil actions against financial advisers and others through whose hands money has passed. In those cases the most significant development is the introduction of an Assets Recovery Agency separate from the police with power to bring proceedings for the confiscation or forfeiture of the property of suspected criminals *without convictions in respect of the activities generating the property.*[115]

The legal régime governing money laundering puts in issue at many stages in the criminal justice process the assumptions that are central to the definition,

---

[115] See the section below ch 11, Forfeiture and Confiscation by Other Means.

investigation and prosecution of more traditional crimes. Enforcement powers are available to determine whether somebody has benefited from a crime that are analogous to the powers to investigate whether a crime has been committed. Relationships between bankers and clients or accountants and clients, which were hitherto either completely secret or at least privileged absent a court order, are now conducted on the basis that the 'professional' is under a duty to inform the authorities in the event of certain suspicions arising.

At the Labour Party conference in September 2000, Tony Blair proclaimed, 'You cannot beat drugs gangs according to the Queensberry rules'.[116] The meaning of the metaphor is clear. Human rights may be trumped by public interest considerations. The use, by politicians and others with a commitment to increased criminal justice expenditure and the rhetoric of crime control, of the money launderer as a 'soft target' has many benefits for the advocates of forms of proactive policing and the diminution of the rights of accused persons.[117] Once it had been held that confiscation and forfeiture fell outside the scope of Article 6(2) of the European Convention, they became attractive mechanisms for a Government that seems increasingly prepared to go to some lengths to promulgate rhetoric about human rights but to avoid their being granted meaningful effect. It is therefore no surprise that, especially with the advent of a direct human rights jurisdiction in the United Kingdom,[118] it should be the human rights of alleged money launderers that are in issue. The issues arising include implied and express reversal of the onus of proof in respect of criminal liability,[119] liability to confiscation[120] and forfeiture,[121] double jeopardy,[122] retroactivity of legislation[123] and the general legitimacy of confiscation[124] and forfeiture rules,[125] financial secrecy and privacy, lawyer/client confidentiality,[126] the right to pay a lawyer of choice an appropriate fee,[127] and the questions in

---

[116] *The Guardian*, 27 September 2000.

[117] This is the argument for 'civil forfeiture' powers. See the section below ch 11, Forfeiture and Confiscation by Other Means.

[118] The Human Rights Act 1998 came into force on 2 October 2000.

[119] *R v Colle* (1992) 95 CAR 67: *R v Gibson* [2000] Crim LR 479. See discussion in the section below ch 9, Defences and the Burden of Proof.

[120] *HM Advocate v McIntosh (Sentencing)* [2001] UKPC D1; [2001] 3 WLR 107; *Phillips v United Kingdom* (2001) 11 BHRC 280; *R v Rezvi* [2002] UKHL 1; *R v Benjafield* [2002] UKHL 2 .

[121] *Goldsmith v Customs and Excise* [2001] 1 WLR 1673.

[122] *R v Smith (David Cadman)* [2001] UKHL 68; [2002] 1 All ER 366.

[123] *Welch v United Kingdom* (1995) 20 EHRR 247, *Wadsted v Barretto* [1994] QB 392; [1994] 1 All ER 447, *US v Montgomery (sub nom Re M (Restraint Order: External Confiscation Order))* [1999] 1 All ER 84; [1998] 2 FLR 1035. And compare *United States v Monaco* (1999) 194 F 3d 381 (statute applies to proceeds generated before enactment of the statute).

[124] *R v Benjafield* [2001] UKHL 2.

[125] *Air Canada v United Kingdom* (1995) 20 EHRR 150 and see n 43 below.

[126] See the section below ch 12, Lawyer/Client Confidentiality.

[127] *Barham (Edward John Frederick), Re* (unreported) *Sub nom: In the Matter of the Drug Trafficking Offences Act 1986, Re* (1995). And see the section below ch 12, Lawyer/Client Confidentiality.

policing and evidence which arise from the forms of international activity deployed against money laundering.[128] These concerns were considered during the passage of the legislation[129] and will be addressed at various points throughout the book. Many important questions for the courts will be generated by the Proceeds of Crime Act 2002.

THE HARM IN LAUNDERING

One approach to money laundering, derived from the theories of labelling and social construction, is to adopt the position of saying that nothing 'real' has changed, or at least that there is no clear evidence that anything relevant has changed over the last 20 years, and that the legal responses have changed for reasons independent of the phenomena. On this analysis the focus is the way in which the discourse surrounding laundering constructs and amplifies the perceived harm. On the other hand we might accept that so much attention is being given, and so many resources are being spent, by people who are not all cynical careerists, that there might actually be identifiable phenomena involved. There is a problem in the 'real world' and it requires analysis. The arguments adduced by the proponents of money laundering regulation require, at the least, to be considered on their own terms. The claim that runs through much of the literature on laundering, not always fully explicitly, is that laundering does economic damage, generally, and most significantly, that it detrimentally affects the efficient operation of markets. This set of arguments is sufficiently important to require full separate consideration.[130]

CONCLUSIONS

The legal developments to be described in this book are bewildering. In the face of enforcement results that, on the terms set for the enforcers have made the laws failures,[131] money laundering law has vaulted to the top of the criminal justice agenda. The debates surrounding laundering show powerful rhetoric overwhelming any attempt at rational assessment of the policy questions in point.

The study of money laundering shows not merely that the way in which we think about the substance of criminal law has been changed, and with it the relationship between civil and criminal law, and between accomplice and

---

[128] In *R v Radak, Adjei, Butler-Rees & Meghjee* [1999] 1 CAR 187; [1999] *Criminal Law Review* 223, the defendant's right to equality of arms enshrined in the European Convention on Human Rights 1950 Art 6(3)(d) was said to be compromised by this activity. See RE Bell, 'Undercover Sting Operations in Money Laundering Cases' (2001) 4 *Journal of Money Laundering Control* 333.

[129] Joint Parliamentary Committee on Human Rights, *Third* and *Eleventh Reports* (2001 and 2002 respectively).

[130] Ch 2, below.

[131] For levels of confiscation, see the section below ch 7, Levels of Confiscation.

bystander. The crusade against money laundering also impacts upon the way in which we think about the international role in the creation and enforcement of criminal law, and the diminution in the significance of the sovereign Nation-State. It represents an admission that the traditional approach to punishment, especially prison, does not 'work' (in the sense of changing conduct by means of law) and that proceedings against assets will take on a new emphasis. It demands attention.

2

The Economics of Money Laundering

T HIS CHAPTER WILL address the claim that money laundering regulation should be put in place so as to prevent the economic damage which would otherwise flow from laundering. The argument is to be found most explicitly in publications of international bodies in favour of controls. The validity of their contentions is critical to the justifiablity of the regulatory structure as a rational enterprise.

THE ECONOMIC CONSEQUENCES OF LAUNDERING IN INDIVIDUAL JURISDICTIONS

For any given government, there are clear advantages to having money laundered into its own economy rather than into another. A single anecdote serves to make this point forcefully. In the wake of the collapse of the USSR, criminal codes were put in place in a number of former Soviet Socialist republics that mirrored more closely the legal framework and values of the West. Consultants were employed in their drafting. In a meeting between one of these consultants and a very senior government minister in one such republic, the minister, reviewing a provision outlawing money laundering, said (loosely translated); 'Let me get this straight: money laundering is where people make money unlawfully elsewhere and bring it to this country and invest it—correct?' The consultant's answer was in the affirmative. 'Why should I be against that?' came the response from the minister.[1] The benefits to the host country are related to the benefits of inward investment: they include job creation enhanced tax revenue. The *realpolitik* of the minister reflects the 'dominant strategy' which game theory produces for any given jurisdiction, of *permitting* money laundering.[2] If there are two countries, A and B, deciding on the basis of economic self-interest whether or not to criminalise money laundering, one of the considerations will be what the other country does. If country B chooses to criminalise laundering, then country A's self-interest will be to permit money laundering, because then

---

[1] And see Vito Tanzi, *Money Laundering and the International Financial System*, IMF Working Paper 96/55 (Washington DC, International Monetary Fund, 1996) at 5: 'Recently some small countries have almost advertised their willingness to accept laundered money'.

[2] And see Brent Fisse and David Fraser, 'Some antipodean skepticisms about forfeiture, confiscation of proceeds of crime, and money laundering offenses' (1993) 44 *Alabama Law Review* 737; R Norton, 'In defense of money laundering' (1999) 140 *Fortune* 37. For the game theory approach see Matthew B Comstock, 'GATT and GATS: A Public Morals Attack on Money Laundering' (1994) 15 *Journal of International Law and Business* 139 at 161 *et seq.*

A will receive all the profits (as between A and B) of laundering, and B will shoulder the burdens of law enforcement. On the other hand, if B chooses to permit laundering, the optimal choice for A is also to permit (for the same reasons). However, if both countries permit laundering, then the outcome is said[3] to be Pareto inefficient[4] (because both sets of financial institutions benefit less) and also to provide a policy basis for controlling the underlying criminal activity, which damages the licit economy.

If money laundering were to be considered simply to be the problem of individual jurisdictions, then an economic approach to the questions whether and how to regulate would also include consideration of the costs of regulation, which include bureaucracies, courts, prisons and tax revenue foregone when criminal organisations are prevented from laundering money into legitimate businesses that pay tax and create honest jobs. It would also include less tangible costs such as loss of privacy. For any given jurisdiction, whether or not to regulate would turn upon a range of considerations. If single jurisdictions are considered, the arguments for controls are not so strong. Action against money laundering can therefore be argued to require a facilitative international framework.

THE INTERNATIONAL AND GLOBAL ECONOMIC CONSEQUENCES OF LAUNDERING

International agreements dictated by economic self-interest are possible, because, unlike the case of the prisoner's dilemma,[5] the parties are able to communicate one with another. Comstock argues that the Vienna Convention[6] creates incentives for some nations to cheat. An unscrupulous nation knows with near certainty that many states will act against laundering, so the dilemma does not arise. It can attract laundered money without fear of competition.[7] Comstock's view rests upon the absence of a system of sanctions for refusal to criminalise, and argues for a system of penalties through the international trade régime (in particular, the World Trade Organisation) for failure to criminalise.

---

[3] Matthew B Comstock, 'GATT and GATS: A Public Morals Attack on Money Laundering', 15 *Journal of International Law and Business* 139 at 162, quoting Barbara Webster and Michael S. McCampbell, *International Money Laundering; Research and Investigation Join Forces* (Washington DC, National Institute of Justice, 1992) at 6.

[4] Pareto optimality is an efficiency condition devised by the economist and political scientist Vilfredo Pareto (1848–1923). An allocation or distribution of goods and services in an economy is said to be Pareto optimal if no alternative allocation could make at least one individual better off, without making anyone worse off.

[5] The dilemma, frequently referred to in game theory, is the case of two suspects in custody, isolated from one another, both of whom know that his own position will be best in the case that they both refuse deals with the police, but that they will be worse off in the cases where he does not deal with the police but his confederate does.

[6] United Nations Convention against Illicit Traffic in Narcotic Drugs and Psychotropic Substances 1988: see the section below ch 5, The Vienna Convention.

[7] Above, n 3 at 162.

These systems permit sanctions on public morals grounds, for whose invocation he argues.

Whether or not his account is correct in its entirety,[8] Comstock does highlight the point that laundering is behaviour whose dangers only exist to a larger community than the Nation-State, and in the sense that it provides a common enemy, this can serve to provide a focus for those attempting to enhance international solidarity and co-operation over a range of issues. Money laundering is the first serious crime whose existence can be directly related to global economic concerns, rather than those of individual jurisdictions. That, more than any other reason, is why its emergence has coincided with the advent of globalisation. It therefore makes sense to assess the accounts which are to be found of the *international* economic ramifications of laundering—its effect upon global markets and the global economy. It is in this area that the economists working for major international organisations, particularly the International Monetary Fund, have been very active.[9] This chapter will review their work.

Money Laundering has the Capacity to Undermine Financial Markets

The major economic contention resounding through the literature is that laundering has a detrimental effect on the operation of markets.[10] Some argue that the protection of the financial sector against corruption is the major motive underpinning global anti-laundering measures.[11] An IMF economist, Tanzi, argues that the resources that go into illegal activity might otherwise be directed legally.[12] Money laundering allocates dirty money around the world not so much on the basis of expected rates of return but on the basis of the ease of avoiding controls, and this is inefficient.[13] As a consequence, the world allocation of resources is distorted, first by the criminal activities themselves, and then

---

[8] The major problem is that he fails to distinguish criminalisation as a matter of law from active pursuit as a matter of criminal justice policy. The underlying assumption of his analysis is that levels of enforcement do not vary significantly as between nations that criminalise. A nation attempting to secure the benefits of being part of the 'International Community' and some of having money in its economy rather than another country's might well allow a disjunction between the rhetoric and the reality of its approach.

[9] It should also be noted at the outset that the economic arguments are generally expressed to show some detrimental outcome from laundering. What the writers have done, however, is to concentrate upon the overall effect of laundering. This does not necessarily argue for any particular legal response. In particular, in order to provide a coherent basis upon which to criminalise it is necessary to supply more about the role of the individual participant. To move from that outcome to the claim that criminalisation is an appropriate response requires further argument to be supplied.

[10] *PIU Report* 20: *Second Commission Report to the European Parliament and the Council on the Implementation of the Money Laundering Directive* COM (1998) 401 final 18–19.

[11] Mark Pieth, 'The Prevention of Money Laundering: a Comparative Analysis' (1998) *European Journal of Crime, Criminal Law and Criminal Justice* 161.

[12] Vito Tanzi, *Money Laundering and the International Financial System*, IMF Working Paper 96/55 (Washington DC, International Monetary Fund, 1996).

[13] Cabinet Office Performance and Innovation Unit, *Recovering the Proceeds of Crime* (London, Cabinet Office, 2000) (hereinafter '*PIU Report*') para 11.34.

by the way the dirty money is allocated.[14] Now it may be the case that economic statistics are skewed by laundering. Without more, however, this is hardly a reason to put in place criminal offences commanding serious sanctions and other very significant enforcement mechanisms. It is simply a reason to find more reliable means of generating economic statistics.

The argument from efficiency and the allocation of dirty money, if it can be substantiated, is far the more serious of the two, and requires fuller consideration. The total assets controlled by criminal organisations may, so it is said, be so large that to transfer them from one jurisdiction to another may have important economic consequences. At the national level, the argument runs, this will affect exchange and interest rates. Now it is true that a large stock of capital might bring instability to the world market, but there is no reason to suppose that the fact that it is laundered would bring greater instability than any other stock of capital. The sums of money crossing national borders are already huge, and do not seem to present much of a concern.

Masciandaro[15] argues further that laundering has a pollutant effect—that once it takes place then more and more property will become tainted.[16] This is true—and particularly true if tax evasion is to be treated like other forms of 'criminal conduct' for the purposes of money laundering, but the very rate at which the pollution spreads might be regarded more as a function of the high degree of criminogenesis attributable to attempts to regulate laundering, and actually a reason not to regulate.

Walter roots his analysis of the economics of money laundering in the economics of financial secrecy. Secrecy has value.[17] People will pay for secrecy because it costs less than disclosure. To the person in possession of money deriving from illegal sources the dangers of disclosure relate to the possibility of prosecution and imprisonment. The process of money laundering holds out the prospect of gaining lasting concealment of the information dealing with the provenance of the money. On the demand side, a person holding assets acquired from illegal sources should be willing to expose him/herself to a reduced rate of return or a higher rate of risk or both. Rational launderers may prefer conservative portfolios. One conservative choice is to expatriate the money. On the supply side, if the channels of conventional interbank fund transfers were to be closed due to exchange controls, or to appear unattractive

---

[14] Tanzi, above n 12 at iii.

[15] Donato Masciandaro, 'Money laundering: the economics of regulation' (1999) 7 *European Journal of Law and Economics* 225. And see Donato Masciandaro, 'The economics of money laundering' [L'economia del riciclaggio e della politica antiriciclaggio] (1995) LIV *Giornale degli economisti e annali di economia* 211.

[16] And see G Goisis, 'Economic impact of rules against money laundering' [Profili economici della legislazione antiriciclaggio] (1996) XLIII *Rivista internazionale di scienze economiche e commerciali* 303.

[17] Ingo Walter, *The Economics of International Money Laundering* (NYC, NY, Institute of Latin American and Iberian Studies, Columbia University, 1993) section headed 'Confidentiality versus Risk and Expected Returns'.

due to the risk of disclosure, then alternatives would be sought. This might involve cash or counter cheques or bearer bonds (all of which carry a risk of loss or theft) and other securities. There are also increased incentives for launderers to move into precious metal, antiques, *objets d'art*, real estate, spread betting (buying both sides) and so on. Walter traces these consequences into the investment behaviour of launderers.

> One would be tempted to argue that, in terms of their investment behaviour, money launderers and those associated with them should be a conservative lot. Since they are already substantially exposed to risk in terms of the origins of their need for secrecy, they ought to have relatively little tolerance for risk in their asset portfolios. One would conclude that they therefore want a high degree of secrecy and a high degree of safety. Given the trade-offs provided by the market, they would thus be willing to pay a high price, in terms of earnings foregone, for the dual attributes. This may not be quite so true if taxation is taken into account. Since money launderers may well operate entirely or largely free of tax in the financial markets they use, the after-tax returns comparison may not look quite as bad in comparison with those of (taxed) investors not concerned with secrecy. Moreover, the absence of tax on income as well as on assets, estates and capital gains may increase the secrecy seeker's interest in somewhat more risky assets, since the expected returns are effectively higher. In the real world, it appears, a significant proportion of money launderers are not particularly risk-averse.[18]

The accumulated balances of laundering are said to be economically dangerous because they might be used to corner markets or even smaller economies, and there is a further possibility that control of economic activity can be compounded by insider trading using the balances. These claims are substantially overstated. There are three issues: the size of the balance, the danger of cornering markets and insider trading. Only the size of the balance is directly linked to laundering. If there are monopolies or insider dealing, then appropriate legislation should deal with it, whatever the source of the money. The IMF position has not gone unchallenged,[19] but it dominates modern responses to laundering. One obvious limitation to regulation which should follow is that if the harm of laundering is to do with international movement of money, then only laundering involving international movement of money need be regulated.[20] A further response might be that if there are harmful economic consequences of laundering, they do not follow directly from laundering itself but from not allowing banking and corporate secrecy. That is to say, the regulatory effort might not be worth its costs.

---

[18] *Ibid*, section headed 'Value of laundered Financial Assets'.

[19] 'Any macroeconomic effect of money laundering is only marginal in a major industrialised economy.' Second Report on the implementation of the European Directive, 20, quoting an unnamed national delegation whose opinion was not controverted, but was ignored.

[20] Yet the FSA explicitly concentrates on laundering without an international element. Financial Services Authority, *The Money Laundering Theme: Tackling our new Responsibilities* (2001) para 1.8.

The Microeconomic Effects of Laundering

The microeconomic effects of laundering are more tangible and may well be more significant. The effects of laundering upon an identified business which is driven under, and whose owner loses her job and house, because the business of the competitor was subsidised by drug money, is much more direct and telling.[21] There are two sorts of responses available. One is to challenge the stereotypes of how the money is deployed. This can only be done by attention to the microdata. Van Duyne[22] suggests that the incidence of this sort of competition is far less than is suggested by the law enforcement agencies. Secondly even if he is wrong and the microeconomic consequences of laundering are indeed widespread, in these sorts of cases the remedy might best be found in competition law. What causes the damage is the cross-subsidy, not the fact of its illegal source. The harm accrues whether the money comes from drug dealing or a legacy to the company. If the cross-subsidy is *ipso facto* illegal, then the provenance of the money does not matter. If the cross-subsidy is not illegal, then the fact that damage is done by it might be thought a reason for dealing with it within the context of competition law, rather than for the deployment of measures of confiscation or criminalisation. If it cannot be dealt with within competition law, because many cross-subsidies are not illegal, that is a reason for altering competition law.

There are also microeconomic effects militating against regulation, or at least regulation in the present form. Since the confiscation régime began, confiscation orders have taken priority over secured and unsecured creditors. The system of recovery orders creates rights *in rem* in the Assets Recovery Agency, and so they too will confer priority to the representatives of the State over other creditors. This will have the effect that upon insolvency, unpaid creditors will lose. This is a clear negative effect of regulation. Its extent is proportional to the amount of enforcement.

Corruption of Professionals

A further argument upon which little reliance can be placed is that allowing money laundering invites corruption of the professions, particularly lawyers, bankers and accountants.[24] Quirk, for example, suggests that one of the ways in

---

[21] *PIU Report*, above n 13 para 6.5.

[22] Petrus van Duyne, 'Money-laundering: Pavlov's Dog and beyond' (1998) 37 *Howard Journal of Criminal Justice* 359, 361 *et seq*: Petrus van Duyne and Hervy de Miranda, 'The Emperor's Clothes of Disclosure: hot Money and suspect Disclosures', (1999) 31 *Crime, Law and Social Change* 245.

[24] For example, in a statement commenting upon statistics for numbers of reports and urging the European Commission to go even further than the draft amended directive, Economic Secretary to the Treasury Melanie Johnson highlighted money laundering's 'capacity to undermine financial markets and to corrupt professional advisers'. 'Treasury Urges EC to do more to fight Money Laundering', *Accountancy Age*, 14 October 1999.

which laundering affects the banking sector is by corrupting bank officials.[25] He claims:

> Money laundering activities can corrupt parts of the financial system and undermine governance of banks. Once bank managers have become corrupted by the sizeable sums of money involved in money laundering, non-market behaviour can be introduced into operating areas other than those directly related to the money laundering, which creates risks for the safety and soundness of the bank. Bank supervisors also can be corrupted or intimidated, which would reduce the effectiveness of supervision.[26]

Even if there were empirical evidence to bear this contention out, it still need not amount to a compelling argument for confiscation provisions or for criminalisation. It may just argue for different systems of banking regulation. However, there are jurisdictions in which there are long traditions of banking without asking questions about the provenance of the money, which nonetheless command enormous confidence. Switzerland, until the banking secrecy laws were revoked,[27] and Lichtenstein (still) have such reputations. The phenomenon Quirk contemplates does not seem to present too much difficulty in those jurisdictions. That is to say, Quirk's argument has force only if the bank officials can be corrupted. In a jurisdiction where (for whatever reason, whether it be moral rectitude or the efficacy of their supervision) there is little danger of bank officials being corrupted the argument has no force. On the other hand, in a jurisdiction where bank officials can be bought in significant numbers, then that is itself likely to be a serious problem and there are very probably greater concerns than money laundering. It may very well be that the same kind of response can be made to the more general 'corruption of the professions' argument. In any event, better evidence of the propensity towards corruption is necessary before the argument is taken seriously.

A Specific Consequential Claim—Harm to the Banking System

Amongst the wider consequential claims, the effect of laundering upon the banking system is frequently a particular concern. Smith writes:

[25] Peter Quirk, *Macroeconomic Implications of Money Laundering* IMF Working Paper 96/66, (Washington DC, International Monetary Fund, 1996) 24.

[26] In a footnote he adds: 'Traditionally, anti-money laundering efforts are closer to the responsibilities of government bodies such as ministries of justice. Anti-money laundering efforts tend to be more politically sensitive than the traditional areas of central banking and an assumption of such responsibilities could possibly lead to less autonomy for the central bank, with spill-over effects into the monetary policy area.' (at 25).

[27] Shelby R Du Pasquier, 'The Swiss Anti-Money Laundering Legislation' (1998) 13 *Journal of International Banking Law* 160; Guy Stessens, *Money Laundering: A New International Law Enforcement Model* (Cambridge, Cambridge University Press, 2000) 100 *et seq*.

[T]he fear of financial regulators is that when credit and financial institutions are used to launder proceeds from criminal activities . . . the soundness and stability of the [particular] institution concerned and confidence in the financial system as a whole could be seriously jeopardised.[28]

Likewise Cranston asserts that '[Money laundering] affects public confidence in, and the stability of, the banking system.'[29] This is clearly a commonly held view, but why exactly is it that the fact that a bank launders money adversely affects confidence either in that bank or in banking generally? One of the dangers is said to be in banking liquidity. The argument goes like this: if a bank deals with investors the provenance of whose money is illegal, then the kinds of demands which those investors will make are less predictable than those coming from more conventional investors. The proportion of its assets which a bank will need to keep liquid to meet such eventualities without collapsing entirely are affected by the sorts of clients with whom they choose to do business. It is, however, by no means clear that these kinds of effects have arisen in banks that launder money. If it is to provide a basis for the laundering régime, the banking liquidity arguments require strong empirical evidence.

If a particular bank is taking investments from money launderers, how does that constitute any threat either to that bank, or to the system as a whole? There are clear reasons why banks might regard launderers as desirable customers. They will not care whether or not the highest rates of interest are available, but will be happy to receive a lower or even negative rate. The bank need not make any risky investments with their money, and it can conform easily to any liquidity requirements.[30] The Cabinet Office claims that the collapse of BCCI made it more difficult for small banks to attract deposits because of a 'flight to quality'.[31] One answer may be, however, that it is a good thing that investors look harder to identify high quality investments.

Those who make the argument that money laundering endangers banks frequently do so by reference to the most famous example of the collapse of a bank that did a great deal of business laundering money, the Bank of Credit and Commerce International (BCCI).[32] The rise and fall of the BCCI was 'the greatest scandal in the history of banking.'[33] The bank was incorporated in Luxembourg in September 1972 and received a banking licence from the

---

[28] Geoffrey Smith, 'Competition in the European Financial Services Industry: the Free Movement of Capital versus the Regulation of Money Laundering' (1992) 13 *University of Pennsylvania Journal of International Business Law* 101 at 111.

[29] Ross Cranston, *Principles of Banking Law* (Oxford, Oxford University Press, 1997) 75.

[30] Compare Banking Act 1987 s 60, appearing to think special provision necessary.

[31] *PIU Report*, above n 13 Box 3.10.

[32] See John Kerry and Hank Brown, *The BCCI Affair: a report to the Committee on Foreign Relations United States Senate*, (Washington DC, US Govt Printing Office, 1992) (102d Congress 2d Session Senate Print 102–140).

[33] Per Lightman J in *Bank of Credit and Commerce International SA (in liq) v Ali and others (No 2)* [1999] 4 All ER 83.

Luxembourgeois authorities.[34] BCCI Holdings (Luxembourg) SA (Holdings) was incorporated in Luxembourg in December 1974 as a non-bank holding company. From September 1976, the bank was a wholly-owned subsidiary of Holdings. Bank of Credit and Commerce International (Overseas) Ltd (Overseas) was incorporated in November 1975 in the Cayman Islands and was at all times a wholly owned subsidiary of Holdings, itself owned primarily in the Middle East. The Bank and Overseas were the two principal operating subsidiaries of Holdings. By the end of 1982, the group had 280 branches or offices in 57 countries. Between 1982 and 1988 the group added a further 137 branches and offices in 16 countries so that it had 417 branches in 73 countries and employed 14,000 persons world-wide. As at 5 July 1991, the group operated in some 69 countries and employed some 12,000 persons in its operations world-wide. Of these the bank had 47 branches in 13 countries; Overseas had 63 branches in 28 countries; and other subsidiaries and affiliates had 260 entities in 30 countries.

In October 1988 the US Federal Government charged that BCCI and nine of its officers were involved in laundering more than $32M in drug money. Federal prosecutors alleged that bank officers of US branches of BCCI took funds which they knew to be from US cocaine sales, invested them in certificates of deposit issued by BCCI banks in France, the UK, Luxembourg, the Bahamas, Panama and South America, and made loans to drug dealers. The loan proceeds were eventually wired to the Florida branch of BCCI.[35] They were then transferred back without further ado to members of the Medellin cartel. The subsequent indictment in Tampa precipitated closer regulatory scrutiny of all of the groups' activities. 'Before the Tampa arrests BCCI (in common with many other financial institutions in the UK) had made no disclosures to the National Drugs Intelligence Unit (NDIU).[36] Thereafter, following steps to overhaul and tighten compliance with international guidelines on the prevention of money laundering, many disclosures were made. The opinion of the NDIU is that after a late start BCCI made a positive move in the direction of due compliance.'[37] The

---

[34] The following account is derived from the judgment of Lightman J in *Bank of Credit and Commerce International SA (in liq) v Ali and others (No 2)* [1999] 4 All ER 83. For a fuller account of the history, concentrating on the activity of British regulators, see Sir Thomas Bingham, *Inquiry into the supervision of the Bank of Credit and Commerce International*, HC 190 (London, HMSO, 1992) para 2.4–2.112. The Parliamentary response is Treasury And Civil Service Committee, *Banking supervision and BCCI: the implications of the Bingham Report* (London, HMSO, 1993). See also Nikos Passas, 'Structural sources of international crime: policy lessons from the BCCI affair.' (1993) 20 *Crime, Law and Social Change* 293–309; James Ring Adams, and Douglas Frantz, *A full service bank: how BCCI stole billions around the world* (London, Simon & Schuster, 1992); Peter Truell, and Larry Gurwin, *BCCI: the inside story of the world's most corrupt financial empire*, (London, Bloomsbury, 1992); Mark Potts, Nicholas Kochan, and Robert Whittington, *Dirty money: BCCI, the inside story of the world's sleaziest bank* (Washington DC, National Press Books, 1992).

[35] They would not have been subject to the $10,000 Cash Transaction Reporting rule. See the section below ch 12, Cash Transaction Reporting.

[36] Which preceded NCIS as the agency to whom reports had to be directed.

[37] Sir Thomas Bingham, *Inquiry into the supervision of the Bank of Credit and Commerce International*, HC 190 (London, HMSO, 1992) para 2.554.

bank's UK operation was closed by regulators on 19 July 1991. When it collapsed, BCCI was insolvent to the tune of $3.2 billion world-wide.[38]

Was there a causal connection between the collapse of the bank and the laundering to which it was a party, or did it just happen that a bank which committed huge frauds also permitted large amounts of laundering, and that, if the frauds had not taken place but the laundering had, the bank, upon being closed by the regulators for poor money laundering compliance, would have been found to be solvent and the creditors would have been paid? Although BCCI is inextricably connected in the public imagination with money laundering,[39] it is by no means clear that the laundering which undoubtedly took place was a causal contributor to the fact that when the Bank ceased to trade it was insolvent. The factor that most distinguished the bank was not the laundering but the frauds that took place. 'The systematic frauds now thought to have been practised in BCCI were on a scale which had never been known before.'[40] That is, the Bank closed because of the laundering, but when it was closed it was insolvent *because the money had been stolen, not because the bank laundered it.* The BCCI episode is not evidence that banks' solvency is endangered by laundering.

The BCCI crisis drew attention to two points. First, it became obvious, even if it had not been before, that the regulation of banking and the control of money laundering could be dealt with—if dealt with at all—only at an international level. Second, it corroborated existing doubts as to the competence of the banking regulatory framework, both in the UK and elsewhere, which had apparently allowed the BCCI house of cards to flourish. In response to this and other 'events' such as the collapse of Barings,[41] the banking regulatory framework in the UK has been adjusted so as to place responsibility outside the Bank of England, in the Financial Services Authority.[42] But it is a mistake to conclude that laundering is a cause of banking instability.

A final response that may be made to the claim that money laundering endangers the banking system is that it is of the (limited) nature of the claim that it can only provide a reason to intervene in money laundering which employs the banking system. Much of the current discourse surrounding laundering, including that dealing with the Amending EU directive,[43] is directed towards the

---

[38] Sir Thomas Bingham, *Inquiry into the supervision of the Bank of Credit and Commerce International*, HC 190 (London, HMSO, 1992) para 2.193.

[39] LEXIS searches in the news file for documents containing the two expressions 'Money Laundering' and 'BCCI' are interrupted because it probably will retrieve more than 1,000 documents.

[40] Thomas Bingham, *Inquiry into the supervision of the Bank of Credit and Commerce International* HC 198 (London, HMSO, 1992) para 2.3. And see, for example, *Bank of Credit and Commerce International (Overseas) Ltd (in liquidation) and another v Akindele* [2000] 4 All ER 221.

[41] EAJ George (chair) *Report of the Board of Banking Supervision into the Circumstances of the Collapse of Barings*, HC 673 (London, HMSO, 1995); Stephen Fay, *The Collapse of Barings* (London, R Cohen Books, 1996).

[42] Bank of England Act 1998 Part III, and, for the approach of the FSA see the section below ch 12, The Financial Services Authority and its Powers.

[43] See the section below ch 5, The Amending Directive.

expansion of the range of activities subject to the regulatory framework. Where laundering is conducted by other means than the banking system, for example by the use of *bureaux de change* or informal methods of transfer, the banking system is not endangered and there is no independent reason for State intervention supplied by the 'banking collapse' argument. There is no suggestion that *bureaux de change* or antiques markets will collapse as a result of failure to regulate against laundering. The case for banking to be treated differently in this regard should be viewed with scepticism.

Further Macroeconomic Effects of Laundering

Quirk attributes the following further series of macroeconomic harms to money laundering:[44]

(1) Policy mistakes due to measurement errors in macroeconomic statistics arising from money laundering;

(2) Changes in demand for money that seem unrelated to measured changes in fundamentals;

(3) Volatility in exchange rates and interest rates due to unanticipated cross border transfers of funds;

(4) Other country-specific distributional effects or asset price bubbles due to disposition of 'black money';

(5) Development of an unstable liability base and unsound asset structures of individual financial institutions (or groups) creating risks of systemic crises and hence monetary instability;

(6) Effects on tax collection and public expenditure allocation due to non- and under-reporting of income;

(7) Misallocation of resources due to distortions in relative asset and commodity prices arising from laundering activities;

(8) Contamination effects on legal transactions due to the perceived possibility of being associated with crime. Some lawful transactions with Russian entities, for example, have become less desirable because of their association with laundering.

Taking these claims in turn, argument (1) is that money laundering generates policy mistakes due to measurement errors in macroeconomic statistics. As a result of these unexpected capital movements,[45] policy-making is detrimentally affected. For example, the policy-makers of a country that, in the face of high inflation, overvalued exchange rate and a large fiscal deficit experienced capital

---

[44] Peter Quirk, *Macroeconomic Implications of Money Laundering*, IMF Working Paper 96/66 (Washington DC, International Monetary Fund, 1996) at 27–8.

[45] 'Seeming to defy the laws of economics'—Vito Tanzi, *Money Laundering and the International Financial System*, IMF Working Paper 96/55 (Washington DC, International Monetary Fund, 1996) at 7.

inflow might be less inclined to change its interest rate policies.[46] It was dismissed above.[47] (2) is little more than a function of (1). Changes in demand for money that appear unrelated to measured changes in fundamentals may be a consequence of laundering but it hardly provides a reason for criminalisation and huge expenditure on a regulatory structure. The simple response would be to get better economic data upon the basis of which to formulate policy. Furthermore, since data on international flows of cash have been discredited as indicia even of the amount of money that is laundered,[48] it is difficult to see why they should be taken so seriously for the purposes of generating economic policy. (3) and (4), volatility in exchange rates and other price 'bubbles' are the sorts of things that economists regard as being 'harms', but whether they are sufficiently clearly established as being caused by laundering, or sufficiently important in terms of avoidable damage done, is far less clear. Exchange rates are notoriously unpredictable. It is entirely lawful for someone with enough money to behave in such a way as to impact upon the exchange rate. That was the way in which, for example, speculators drove the pound out of the European exchange rate mechanism in 1993. (5) is best viewed in the context of the effects of money laundering upon banking. The more alarmist claims as to laundering and banking solvency are difficult to substantiate.[49] (6) is, if anything, an argument for better tax collection methods. The relationship between tax evasion and money laundering is central to the modern international campaign in respect of laundering, but the argument in this case seems overstated. Money that is laundered for reasons other than tax evasion also represents income that is an evasion of taxes, thus compounding the economic distortions. However, in general, taxpayers will not declare unlawful income, whether or not there is a regulatory régime in place in respect of laundering. If the argument is really that regulating laundering will reduce the incidence of initial crime, then better evidence is necessary. (7) simply restates (1), and should be met with the same response. (8) is the sort of anecdotal evidence that ought to be treated sceptically.

Alternative Units of Exchange

The other area of economics that has the potential to impact strongly upon the development of money laundering regulation is to the technology of money transfer. The advent of e-cash—alternative systems of payment that do not depend upon a system of exchange backed by a central bank—will create

---

[46] Tanzi, above n 12 at 7.
[47] See the section above ch 2, Money-laundering Has the Capacity to Undermine Financial Markets.
[48] See the section above ch 1, How Much?
[49] And, of course, this argument would not apply in jurisdictions or systems in which exchange rates are fixed.

greater challenges to any attempt to regulate.[50] If the objective of the commerciant is to transfer value between jurisdictions, then there have long existed ways of doing it so that the movement is difficult to detect. Jewels secreted about a person have been commonly used. There are already relatively well-developed systems for granting a credit ticket in one jurisdiction that can be redeemed in another jurisdiction for a different currency (in effect, travellers' cheques without the bank). The prospect of e-money, bypassing banks altogether, may diminish the role of banks further.[51]

Without a gold standard, convertability into other currencies is the only real 'guarantee' of the value of a currency. The 'value' of a system of exchange depends upon the confidence reposed in it. There is no necessary connection between this confidence and central bank control. This is where e-cash[52] and other alternative methods of exchange may become important. E-cash promises to allow value to be placed electronically upon smart cards or stored value cards), which can be used as an untraceable means of payment across jurisdiction. These systems offer all the benefits of the anonymity of currency together with the additional benefits of speed and cheapness. The effect of emoney on the traditional scheme of reporting of cash (US) to suspicious or unusual (Europe) transactions is potentially devastating. No government yet accepts e-money as legal tender, so e-money apparently operates outside the regulatory frameworks that deal with money. There is debate as to whether or not attempts to regulate would be either desirable or feasible. Unless e-money can be regulated then money laundering regulation, to the extent that it depends upon the reporting of transactions which will simply be unknown, and can take place without the involvement of an institution will be overtaken by technology which allows transfers without the involvement of a financial intermediary.[53]

---

[50] Laurie Law, Susan Sabett and Jerry Solinas, 'The Electronic Future of Cash: How to Make a Mint' (1997) 46 *American University Law Review* 1131.

[51] Timothy Ehrlich, 'Note: to regulate or not? Managing the risks of e-money and its potential application in money laundering schemes' (1998) 11 *Harvard Journal of Law & Technology* 833; Bruce Zagaris & Scott MacDonald, 'Money laundering, financial fraud, and technology: the perils of an instantaneous economy' (1992) 26 *George Washington Journal of International Law and Economics* 61–107; Julia Alpert Gladstone 'Technology, the law, and a changing world in the twenty-first century' (1999) 22 *Fordham International Law Journal* 1907; E Rederer, 'Money laundering using cybermoney—Or how traditional crime-fighting strategies are becoming worthless' (2000) 45 *Kriminalistik* 261.

[52] Timothy Ehrlich, 'To Regulate or Not? Managing the Risks of e-money and its potential application in Money Laundering schemes' (1998) 11 *Harvard Journal of Law and Technology* 833.

[53] Catherine Lee Wilson 'Banking on the Net: Extending Bank regulation to Electronic Money and Beyond' (1997) 30 *Creighton Law Review* 671.

THE COST OF REGULATION

The greatest costs of regulation fall upon the financial services industry.[54] The Home Office published a Regulatory Impact Statement setting out the costs of regulation.[55] The costs that are set out do not include the costs of enlisting the financial sector in the monitoring and reporting transactions, of training staff and the incidental costs of the régime. The most significant costs to the financial industry were for Customer Information Orders,[56] with estimated costs of £50m per annum for 1000 circulars served on 200 institutions. The Statement claims potential benefits to the fish of about £650 million per annum, but concedes that 'there is no methodology for gauging the accuracy of this figure'.

The Impact Statement does not regard the costs to small businesses as being significant. Nonetheless, costs will accrue as a consequence of the priority granted to confiscation and forfeiture proceedings over other creditors.[57] The Proceeds of Crime Act relies for its efficacy upon the use of receivers. The receivers will be remunerated out of the assets seized. At a time when the priority *in insolvency* of the Revenue is under review, it is in some respects odd that the State is asserting priority here.

CONCLUSIONS

This chapter has examined the arguments presented by economists for the proposition that money laundering is a harmful phenomenon. It is clear that this case can only be made out if the economic interests of various States are aggregated. It has been suggested that many of the minor arguments for the existence of harms are incorrect or inconsequential. It has also been suggested that the claim that laundering damages the banks through which it takes place, or the institution of banking itself, is unfounded. It is a precondition of the validity of the economic case for any form of regulation that money laundering does have a harmful effect upon the efficient operation of global markets. At the least this requires better evidence, and the cost of regulating (rather than allowing banking secrecy) needs to be assessed. There is much to Naylor's claim that reorientation of the criminal justice system towards seizing the profits of crime has 'its roots in a mixture of superstition, myth and misunderstanding about the nature and operation of the criminal marketplace'.[58]

[54] Duncan E Alford, 'Anti-money laundering regulations: a burden on financial institutions' (1994) 19 *North Carolina Journal of International Law and Commercial Regulation* 437.
[55] Home Office, *Proceeds of Crime Bill: Full Regulatory Impact Assessment* (2001) <http://www.homeoffice.gov.uk/proceeds/ria.htm>
[56] See the section below ch 8, Customer Information Orders.
[57] See the section below ch 7, Priority of Confiscation Orders Relative to Other Debts.
[58] RT Naylor, 'Wash-out: Follow-the Money Methods in Crime Control Policy' (1999) 32 *Crime, Law and Social Change* 1.

The economic arguments need not take the regulatory régime as given. There are two obvious alternatives, both of which can be quickly stated but with each having vast ramifications. One is to reduce the quantity of 'dirty' money in the world by legalisation of the conduct generating it. The markets in drugs are the clearest potential target. The other might be the concession that the regulatory framework has too many costs for any benefit that might accrue from it. This would argue for the restoration of banking secrecy in any jurisdiction that wished it. Then the principal economic argument for regulation of laundering— that investment does not go to the most economically beneficial arena—would disappear. The playing field can be levelled either by allowing no secrecy— which is very difficult—or secrecy in every jurisdiction that chooses it.

3

Theory: Justifications for Forfeiture, Confiscation and Criminalisation

THE PROCESS OF demonisation of the money launderer has directed attention away from any close consideration of the rationale for powers of confiscation and forfeiture of the proceeds of crime and for the criminalisation of laundering. This chapter will attempt to construct and criticise the sorts of justifying accounts that are or might be advanced within liberal theories of State powers. The arguments will vary according to which enforcement power is in point, and must be considered independently of one another. The fact that a case can be constructed for one of the three measures does not imply that it applies equally for the existence of a different power. Each power, if it should remain, requires an independent and sufficient justification.

CONFISCATION

Confiscation is said to be justified by a principle, deeply ingrained into the law, that people should not profit from unlawful activity in general and from crime in particular.[1] This principle follows from the requirement that if law is to impact upon people's behaviour, it should deliver coherent messages. It is not coherent, on the one hand, to try to prevent a particular form of behaviour, but, on the other, to permit someone who does it to benefit. Expressed in utilitarian terms, the message delivered by the establishment of disincentives to particular forms of behaviour should not be qualified by allowing the law to be used in order to secure profits from that behaviour. The principle is stated in the judgment of Lawton LJ in *R v Waterfield*:[2]

> The first thing the law should do is to ensure that those who break it . . . should not make any money out of their wrongdoing. . . . This court is firmly of the opinion that if those who take part in this kind of trade know that on conviction they are likely to be stripped of every penny of profit they make and a good deal more, then the desire to enter it will be diminished.

[1] Goff and Jones, *The Law of Restitution*, 5th edn (London, Sweet & Maxwell 1999) ch 37 'Benefits accruing to a Criminal from his crime'. And see the discussion by Ronald Dworkin, *Taking Rights Seriously* (London, Duckworth, 1977) 23 *et seq.* of *Riggs v Palmer* (1889) 12 American St Rep 819.

[2] *R v Waterfield* (17 February 1975, unreported).

There is no common law power for the State to seize the proceeds of crime, but the principle is evident in cases where the offender received a benefit as a result of committing a crime and the question is whether a victim has a right to recover, or where the offender claims or receives a benefit as a result of having committed a crime.

The principle is, however, not without exception—most notably the acquisition of land by adverse possession and the rules relating to the duties of occupiers of land to trespassers.

The principle is frequently referred to as providing a reason beyond which no further justification is required. It is, we are to believe, self-evident in a system that is directed against particular forms of behaviour, that those things cannot be allowed to generate profits. Hence, for example, the judgment of Fry LJ in *Cleaver v Mutual Reserve Fund Life Association:*[3]

> It appears to me that no system of jurisprudence can with reason include amongst the rights which it enforces rights directly resulting to the person asserting them from the crime of that person.

To like effect, famously, in *the Estate of Crippen, decd*[4] Sir Samuel Evans P stated the basis of the rule in these dramatic terms:

> The human mind revolts at the very idea that any other doctrine could be possible in our system of jurisprudence.

The doctrine that a criminal should not benefit from his/her crime is seen most vividly in the homicide cases. In *Cleaver*, Florence Maybrick had poisoned her husband. She was held to be unable to benefit from a life insurance policy on his life.[5] Crippen made a will in favour of his mistress, Ethel le Neve, before being executed for the murder of his wife. His wife had died intestate and had the normal rules for the devolution of property upon intestacy applied, her property would have passed to him, and thence, under his will, to le Neve. The court held that Crippen was removed from the category of people who could inherit.[6]

Whilst the devolution of property consequent upon a murder has operated satisfactorily by excluding the murderer, rigid applications of the same doctrine in cases of non-intentional killings were thought to give rise to unfairness. There has consequently been a relaxation of the harshness of the rule, mostly arising from cases of killing by persons suffering some mental abnormality, or unintentional but illegal killings of family members in road traffic accidents. Under the Forfeiture Act 1982, a discretion is conferred upon the court to modify the effect

---

[3] *Cleaver v Mutual Reserve Fund Life Association* [1892] 1 QB 147 at 156.
[4] *In the Estate of Crippen, decd* [1911] P 108, 112.
[5] And see Bernard Ryan (with Lord Havers), *The Poisoned Life of Mrs Maybrick* (Harmondsworth, Penguin, 1989).
[6] *In bonis Crippen* [1911] P 108.

of the forfeiture rule[7] so as to allow a person still to benefit under the will or intestacy of someone for whose death s/he is criminally responsible if

> it is satisfied that, having regard to the conduct of the offender and of the deceased and to such other circumstances as appear to the court to be material, the justice of the case requires the effect of the rule to be so modified in that case.[8]

The principles to be applied in the case of non-intentional killings have been worked through in a series of cases.[9] The most significant recent one is *Dunbar v Plant*,[10] in which the survivor of a suicide pact claimed to succeed to the estate of the deceased. The plaintiff, the father of the deceased, successfully applied to the court for an order that the proceeds of an insurance policy taken out by his son for the benefit of P should be forfeited to him as the administrator of the estate. On appeal it was held that where two people attempted to commit suicide together 'public policy' would not require forfeiture or prosecution of the surviving party. Although P had committed a criminal offence (of aiding and abetting her *fiancé's* suicide[11]), such as to warrant the imposition of the forfeiture rule, section 1(2) of the Forfeiture Act 1982 allowed the court to take a more sympathetic approach. The Court of Appeal held that the court should have exercised the power conferred upon it by the Act having regard to all the circumstances of the case, and, accordingly, that P should be granted full relief from forfeiture.

From this mix of cases it is clear that even in the strongest cases—those of deliberate killings—unless there is a conviction for murder, there is considerable flexibility as to whether the principle prohibiting the criminal from benefiting applies. The absolutist implications of the rhetoric in *Cleaver* and *Crippen* have been tempered by (seldom articulated) considerations to do with fairness and desert. The criminal, whether under the Forfeiture Act or otherwise, is allowed to benefit when justice requires. If justice may require that the criminal may ever be permitted to benefit from homicide, *a fortiori* any other crime. It is clear that the principle against allowing profit from crime is not absolute. Where a person intended to profit when committing the crime s/he has not been allowed to recover, but many others have.

Beyond homicide, significant consideration of the principle against allowing a criminal to benefit from his/her crime has been given to the economic

---

[7] The rule of public policy preventing a person benefiting under the will or intestacy of one for whose death they are criminally responsible: Forfeiture Act 1982 s 1.

[8] Forfeiture Act 1982 s 2.

[9] *Re S (Deceased) (Forfeiture Rule)* [1996] 1 WLR 235; [1996] 1 FLR 910; *Jones (John Keith) v Roberts (John Ronald)* [1995] 2 FLR 422; [1995] *Fam Law* 673; *Re Jones (Deceased); Jones v Midland Bank Trust Co Ltd And Others* [1998] 1 FLR 246; [1997] 3 FCR 697; *Manslaughter: Forfeiture of Widow's Pension, Re* [1999] Pens LR 1.

[10] *Dunbar v Plant* [1998] Ch 412; [1997] 4 All ER 289.

[11] Contrary to the Suicide Act 1961 s 2. The court did not advert to the possibility that he might also have been liable for intentional homicide in pursuit of a suicide pact which is, by virtue of Homicide Act 1957 s 4, a form of voluntary manslaughter.

consequences of bigamy. In *Whiston v Whiston* [12] the Court of Appeal invoked
public policy to rule that a deliberate bigamist was precluded from relief under
the Matrimonial Causes Act 1973. The Court held that bigamy was still a serious crime (even though female bigamists, if prosecuted at all, tend to attract
lenient sentences) and that to allow the respondent to claim financial relief
would be to permit her to benefit from her crime: both *Beresford* and *Crippen*
were cited with approval. In *J v S-T (formerly J)*,[13] however, a person born
female but pretending to be male went through a ceremony of marriage with
another (unsuspecting) female, this 'marriage' involving the commission of a
perjury offence. A differently constituted Court of Appeal (although Ward LJ
was a member of both) held that section 25 of the Matrimonial Causes Act
1973 conferred a wide discretion on the court when awarding relief and that
the Court should judge the applicant's crime in the context of the circumstances of the case. The discretion, on the facts, was exercised against the
applicant.

Effect of the 'Profit Principle'

The principle against permitting a person to profit from his/her crime has two
major uses. Passively, it can act as a bar to recovery by the criminal: actively, it
can supply a reason to compel the criminal to disgorge the profit of crime. At
common law, only the first was regularly invoked, because there was no power
at common law for the State to seize the profits of crime. Such actions as there
were to recover profits from criminals succeeded only where they fell within an
independent cause of action. These two will be taken in turn. The principle
against criminal profit, in its application to statutory interpretation, can apply
in both fields.

The Criminal Asserts Rights—Common Law

The effect of the principle against criminal profit is, in the first instance, that the
courts will not allow a criminal as plaintiff to benefit from his/her crime. This is
frequently done by reference to the maxim *ex turpi causa non oritur actio*.[14]
There is a distinction to be made between (on the one hand) a narrow reading
of the maxim, to mean that the courts will not be used as the means by which
profits are able to be acquired from wrongful action (which is its literal meaning), and (on the other) a much wider reading, holding the principle to authorise
seizure of those profits. That is, is the maxim about the courts or about the

---

[12]   *Whiston v Whiston* [1995] Fam 198; [1998] 1 All ER 423.

[13]   *J v S-T (formerly J)* [1998] 1 All ER 431; [1997] 3 WLR 1287.

[14]   In *R v Secretary of State for the Home Department, Ex parte Puttick* [1981] QB 767, 775,
Donaldson LJ observed that: 'it was well established that public policy required the courts to refuse
to assist a criminal to benefit from his crime *at least in serious cases* . . .'. (Italics added).

profit? Is it saying—'we [the courts] do not mind you having the profits of crime so long as you are punished for the crime, but do not expect us to sully our hands by helping you get the profits', or is it saying 'it is our duty, so far as we have power, to make you disgorge the profits'? The history of *ex turpi causa* suggests the narrower reading.[15] In *Smith v Jenkins*,[16] Windeyer J in the High Court of Australia analysed all the then authorities in Australia, the UK and other common law or Roman-Dutch law jurisdictions and concluded that the maxim itself, strictly speaking, applied only to the law of contract, with *turpi causa* meaning something like 'illegal consideration'. Confining the doctrine to the cases where the criminal attempts to benefit *by using the civil courts* is a useful limitation on the doctrine. *Ex turpi causa* would not be a defence, for example, to a private prosecution brought by a confederate, that if successful could yield a confiscation order, nor is it necessarily a defence to an occupiers' liability action by a burglar.[17]

The boundaries of *ex turpi causa* were considered in relation to the seizure of money acquired by drug dealing in the *Webb v Chief Constable of Merseyside*,[18] where the police seized property in the course of an investigation, and then, without bringing charges, held on to the property, arguing (and proving on the balance of probabilities) that the money was the product of drug dealing. The fact that the property had been acquired illegally did not prevent a good title passing, and, subject to exceptions that did not apply, the plaintiff did not need to assert the illegality in order to claim the property. The 'public policy' argument advanced by the police was rejected.[19]

Construing Statutes

The principle against allowing a criminal to benefit from his crime has significance for statutory interpretation whether it is the criminal or the victim who asserts rights. There are various general considerations to which all statutes are subject. For example, there is rarely provision in statutes creating offences that duress provides a defence, but all statutes are read as including such a defence.

---

[15] 'No court will lend its aid to a man who founds his cause of action upon an immoral or an illegal act.' Lord Mansfield CJ in *Holman v Johnson* (1775) 1 Cowp 342, 343; 98 ER 1120, 1121 (KB). The Plaintiff sued to recover the purchase price of tea pursuant to a sale made in Scotland. The court held that because the contract was perfectly legal in Scotland, the defendant could not raise as a defence the fact that the seller may have known that defendant buyer intended to smuggle the tea into England.

[16] *Smith v Jenkins* (1970) 44 AJLR 78 at 80–89.

[17] The view that *ex turpi* is a procedural rather than substantive bar to recovery prevailed in *Tinsley v Milligan* [1994] 1 AC 340.

[18] *Webb v Chief Constable of Merseyside* [2000] 1 QB 427; [2000] 1 All ER 209.

[19] Approved in *Attorney-General v Blake* [2001] 1 AC 268; [2000] 4 All ER 385 and followed in *Costello v Chief Constable of Derbyshire* [2001] EWCA Civ 381; [2001] 3 All ER 150. See Graham Battersby, 'Acquiring title by theft' (2002) 65 *Modern Law Review* 603. For full consideration of *Webb* and for the suggestion that the case contributes towards the argument for a statutory 'civil confiscation' strategy, see below, 226–8.

A similar effect has been read into statutes so far as concerns the principle against allowing people to benefit. In *R v Registrar General, ex parte Smith*, Staughton LJ expressed the interpretative dimension of the principle in these terms:

> In the case of statutory duties the rule is, in my opinion, based upon interpretation of the meaning intended by Parliament. It is not a rule imposed *ab extra* as in the case of contracts. To hold otherwise would come perilously close to infringing constitutional doctrine of major importance. . . . [T]he rule is that we must interpret Acts of Parliament as not requiring performance of duties, even when they are in terms absolute, if to do so would enable someone to benefit from his own serious crime.[20]

This statement should, perhaps, be read to include the qualification that such interpretations can only be adopted where the statute is unclear. If, as in the case of the Forfeiture Act 1982, there is a clear Parliamentary intention that the criminal *should* benefit, then the courts must accept that.

The Victim as Claimant—Restitutionary and other Remedies

The common law position was that matters between victim and perpetrator of crime were rigorously separated from questions about criminal liability. Powers to compel compensation to be made to a victim by an offender, without recourse to the civil law, were first put in place under the Powers of Criminal Courts Act 1973.[21]

Restitutionary remedies are the other major area of civil law in which the principle against allowing criminals to benefit from crime is critical. Wherever there is an identifiable 'victim' of the crime, s/he will generally have a right to recover against the criminal, for example for conversion, breach of fiduciary duty, one of the economic torts, vindication of property rights or the fact that the crime is a form of wrongdoing recognised as triggering restitutionary remedies.[22] Failing that, the prevailing view at civil law is that there is no general right of victims to recover, because the duty imposed by criminal law is owed to the state not to the victim, and because the introduction of such a general right is not properly a matter for the courts, the question of confiscation from offenders having been frequently and fully addressed by Parliament during the 1990s[23] without the explicit provision of a statutory right for victims (or the State) to sue.[24]

---

[20] *R v Registrar General, ex parte Smith* [1991] 2 QB 393 at 402.

[21] Powers of Criminal Courts Act 1973 s 35: now Powers of Criminal Courts (Sentencing) Act 2000 s 130 *et seq*.

[22] Graham Virgo, 'The Law of Restitution and the Proceeds of Crime—a survey' (1998) 6 *Restitution Law Review* 34 at 35.

[23] By the legislation to be examined below, see the section below ch 7, Confiscation Orders.

[24] *Halifax Building Society v Thomas* [1996] Ch 217; [1995] 4 All ER 673 per Glidewell LJ at 229–30 and Peter Gibson LJ at 230. The same argument is used in *Attorney-General v Blake* [2001] 1 AC 268 at 278; [2000] 4 All ER 385 at 402, *per* Lord Nicholls.

More extensive provision in respect of the victims of financial crimes is high on the current political agenda. The power under the Financial Services and Markets Act 2000 to make restitution orders is a very significant move in this area.[25] The court is given power to impose the order when a person has contravened, or has been knowingly concerned in the contravention of a relevant requirement,[26] and either s/he has profited, or others have lost. There is a wide discretion in the allocation of the money elicited.

As to the measure of damages, where s/he suffers damage equivalent to the profit made by the criminal, there is little problem (where the funds are actually available) in saying that the *quantum* should be identical. What of the case where the defendant's gain exceeds the plaintiff's loss?[27] If it can be said that the property is the subject matter of a trust,[28] or obtained in breach of a fiduciary duty, then the entire profit can be recovered. [29] A clear example of such recovery is the decision of the House of Lords in *Foskett v McKeown*,[30] where property held on an express trust for the plaintiffs had improperly been used to pay some of the premiums of a life assurance policy. The thief subsequently died. The question was whether the claimants were entitled to be compensated, if at all, to the extent of their loss, plus interest, or whether they were entitled to a share in the benefits of the policy proportional to the contribution stolen from them. The Court of Appeal held that the victims of the theft were not entitled to a proportion of the proceeds.[31] The House of Lords reversed the decision, awarding the victims a share in the benefits of the policy.

---

[25] Financial Services and Markets Act 2000 s 382.

[26] A duty imposed by the Financial Services and Markets Act or any other Act whose contravention falls within the prosecuting power of the Financial Services Authority or the Secretary of State: Financial Services and Markets Act 2000 s 382(9).

[27] Helen Norman, 'Tracing the Proceeds of Crime: An inequitable Solution?' in Peter Birks (ed), *Laundering and Tracing* (Oxford, Oxford University Press, 1995) 95.

[28] In *Westdeutsche Landesbank Girozentrale v Islington London Borough Council* [1996] AC 669, Lord Browne-Wilkinson said, 'The court by way of remedy might impose a constructive trust on a defendant who knowingly retains property of which the plaintiff has been unjustly deprived. Since the remedy can be tailored to the circumstances of the particular case, innocent third parties would not be prejudiced and restitutionary defences, such as change of position, are capable of being given effect. However, whether English law should follow the United States and Canada by adopting the remedial constructive trust will have to be decided in some future case when the point is directly in issue.' (at 716).

[29] See also *Halifax Building Society v Thomas* [1996] Ch 217 at 229–230; [1995] 4 All ER 673 at 682–683, where the defendant was convicted of conspiring to obtain a mortgage advance by deception. On the facts the plaintiff was held to have elected to affirm the mortgage despite the fraud. If the mortgage had not been affirmed and the defendant could have been shown to have benefited the claim would have succeeded.

[30] *Foskett v McKeown* (HL) [2001] 1 AC 102; [2000] 3 All ER 97.

[31] *Foskett v McKeown* (CA) [1998] Ch 265.

Civil Law Duty to the State

Where there is no other identifiable victim, the only possible civil claimant will be the State. Then, at civil law, the issue is whether there is a duty to the State to disgorge the proceeds, or whether the criminal can retain them. Prior to the advent of the confiscation legislation, various attempts were made to establish a common law basis for the State to acquire the proceeds of crime. Statutes of Queen Anne gave informants the right to sue for multiples of the size of an unlawful (or unlawfully large) wager[32] or for usury.[33] Nonetheless, the mere fact that property was acquired through the illegal conduct of a trade did not of itself generate a right to confiscate. In *Gordon v Chief Commander of the Metropolitan Police*,[34] for example, income from illegal betting was held to belong to the bookmaker.

Limited claims were made during the twentieth century to argue that all profits of crime were held on constructive trust for the Crown, or that there was a duty to account for them. This approach prevailed in the House of Lords in *Reading v Attorney General*,[35] in which the appellant, a sergeant in the army stationed in Cairo, on several occasions, while in uniform, boarded a private lorry and escorted it through Cairo, thus enabling it to pass the civilian police check-points without being inspected. The lorry was loaded with cases, the contents of which were unknown. On each occasion the sergeant received from a civilian a large sum of money of which the military authorities later took possession. The House of Lords held that any position which enabled an employee to earn money by its use gave the employer a right to receive the money so earned even though it was earned by a criminal act; this right being derived from an implied term in the contract of employment that he would account to his employer for any moneys he might receive by reason of his employment. The grounds for the decision remain unclear but there is some support for the view that it is the breach of fiduciary duty in this case which makes the difference.[36]

The same kind of argument from breach of fiduciary duty continues to be made in bribery cases, but it does not extend to a general principle that the proceeds and profits of crime are held on trust for the Crown. One specific area in which the 'principle' has been invoked is as to the 'literary proceeds of crime'. Typically the cases will involve the publication of a book describing the com-

---

[32] 9 Anne, c 14, enacting penalties against gambling, and giving half the penalty to the poor of the parish in which the offences is committed and imposing in certain circumstances (s 5) a forfeit five times the value of the sum of money or other thing won.

[33] 12 Anne c 16. And see Leon Radzinowicz, *A History of English Criminal Law and its Administration: Vol 2: The Enforcement of the Law* (London, Stevens, 1956) 287 *et seq.*

[34] *Gordon v Chief Commander of the Metropolitan Police* [1910] 2 KB 1080.

[35] *Reading v Attorney-General* [1951] AC 507.

[36] Graham Virgo, 'The Law of Restitution and the Proceeds of Crime—a survey' (1998) 6 *Restitution Law Review* 34.

mission of a crime.[37] There have been many such books.[38] In *Attorney General v Blake (Jonathan Cape Ltd, third party)*, the defendant published a book giving an account of the treason for which he was convicted in 1961.[39] He had subsequently escaped from prison and lived in Moscow. After the collapse of communism, legal relations between Moscow and London were restored and Blake attempted to have the profits from the book sent to him in Moscow. Blake's position was never likely to have much appeal for the courts,[40] but there were significant divergences as to why it was that he should be denied access to the money. There were two distinct grounds upon which the case was argued— the private law claim stemming from the confidentiality clause in Blake's contract of employment with the security services and a public law claim by the Attorney-General in his capacity as guardian of the public interest. It was the latter that succeeded in the courts below,[41] and the former in the House of Lords. The obstacle to deciding the case on contractual grounds was that a successful contractual claim did not necessarily convey with it the right to Blake's profit, but only, according to traditional contract doctrine, a right to damages. There was significant authority, binding on courts below the House of Lords that there was not a head of 'restitutionary damages' in contract. The House of Lords decided that Blake's was an exceptional case, and fell within a category where an account of profits was available as a remedy for breach of contract.[42]

Had there been no such clause, would the court still have been able to prevent his profiting? The other basis upon which the Attorney-General sued was as the guardian of the public interest for an interlocutory injunction. The order was expressed in interlocutory terms ('until further order'). But the substance of the order was permanent, because there was no event in contemplation whose occurrence could have altered the position so as for the rights of the parties in respect of the money conclusively to be determined. That is, the interlocutory order was to be used as a means of confiscation. But it is not the purpose of interlocutory

---

[37] And see Aric Freiberg, 'Confiscating the literary Proceeds of Crime' [1992] *Criminal Law Review* 96.

[38] Eg Jonathan Aitken, *Pride and Perjury* (London, HarperCollins, 2000) (although arguably there was no victim since the perjury was unsuccessful).

[39] *R v Blake* [1962] 2 QB 377; [1961] 3 All ER 125.

[40] 'For the respondent to receive the balance of the royalties would amount to the law being flouted. . . . The ordinary member of the public would be shocked if the position was that the courts were powerless to prevent the respondent profiting from his criminal conduct', *per* Lord Woolf MR [1998] Ch 439 at 464: this is exactly the same argument as that in *Cuthbertson*, below, 92, which, had it succeeded, would have generated a common law power to seize the profits.

[41] *Attorney General v Blake* (QBD) [1997] Ch. 84; [1996] 3 All ER 903: *Attorney General v Blake* (CA) [1998] Ch 439, [1998] 1 All ER 833.

[42] *Attorney General v Blake* (HL) [2001] 1 AC 268; [2000] 4 All ER 385. The leading speech was delivered by Lord Nicholls, with whom Lord Goff and Lord Browne-Wilkinson agreed. Lord Steyn delivered a concurring judgment. Lord Hobhouse dissented, holding that the creation of a category of 'restitutionary damages' in the law of contracts was not justified. See Steve Hedley, ' "Very much the wrong people": the House of Lords and publication of spy memoirs' (2000) 4 *Web Journal of Current Legal Issues* and David Campbell, 'The treatment of *Teacher v Calder* in *AG v Blake*' (2002) 65 *Modern Law Review* 256.

orders to alter the legal rights of the parties, simply to preserve the position pending a final determination. A permanent injunction would have involved a determination as to the ownership of the money and if it were to be determined that the money belonged to the Crown, then that would have involved creating a common law power to confiscate. But the House held that such a power has never formed part of the common law,[43] and that since Parliament had spent so much time engaging with profits of crime during the 1990s there was no scope for further judicial creativity, even had it been desirable.[44] It follows from this decision that in the absence of a contractual, fiduciary or other duty[45] there is no power to deprive a person of the 'literary proceeds' of crime. A number of the United States have enacted specific laws preventing such profits, but in their absence and the absence of any other special reason, it appears that there is no general right for the victims of crime to seek redress against the proceeds of the sales of books describing the offences, and no right in the State to seize them.

It is in this area that the advent of the Assets Recovery Agency (ARA) will constitute a radical departure. The Proceeds of Crime Act 2002 grants the Director of the Agency a proprietary interest in proceeds of crime in the hands of criminals or their transferees, and power to bring proceedings for its enforcement. This power will be discussed fully later.[46]

QUALIFYING AND LIMITING THE PRINCIPLE AGAINST ALLOWING CRIMINALS
TO KEEP THE PROFITS OF CRIME

The entire area of law to do with the penalisation of laundering and the confiscation of proceeds would have a different shape were it based upon one single simple precept—that of depriving criminals of the profits of their crimes. A fuller account can be sought by attempting to distinguish the cases in which a person is and those where they are not permitted to retain the benefit.

What the principle really propounds is a doctrine of pragmatic consistency. It is rooted in a notion of *what law is for*.[47] If criminal law is seen as an attempt to

---

[43] [2001] 1 AC at 289, citing *Attorney-General v De Keyser's Royal Hotel* [1920] AC 508 and *Burmah Oil v Lord Advocate* [1965] AC 75: simply to cite these cases signals the constitutional significance the judges attach to the case.

[44] The case therefore provides an interesting contrast between areas in which judges regard themselves as free to legislate ('common law' areas like contractual remedies) and those where they do not (confiscation, where there are statutes aplenty). The underlying premise is that Parliament gives a 'keep off the grass' warning to the courts by legislating a 'statutory code' in a given area. Doubt was cast upon a number of cases (*Chief Constable of Kent v V* [1983] QB 34, *West Mercia Constabulary v Wagener* [1982] 1 WLR 127, *Chief Constable of Leicestershire v M* [1989] 1 WLR 20) cited in *Webb*, see the section below ch 11, Forfeiture and Confiscation by Other Means) in which Chief Constables had been granted interlocutory injunctions freezing the proceeds of crime in circumstances where there had not yet been a conviction for a criminal offence.

[45] Blake was not—at the time the book was written—a fiduciary.

[46] See the section below ch 11, The Assets Recovery Agency.

[47] Lon Fuller, *The Morality of Law* (New Haven, CT, Yale UP, revised edn, 1969).

discourage some forms of behaviour, then that objective can best be achieved when conflicting messages are not delivered. The designation 'crime' should not hold out any potential gains that can be defended within the system. The trouble is that a large number of crimes generate, directly or indirectly a wide range of profits, and only relatively few of them are challenged.

The Hodgson Committee asked:

> What about environmental crimes, where there are very large profits to be made from disobedience to law. What of the developer who pulls down a listed building, the polluter or the enterprise which enhances its own profits by operating in breach of health and safety laws?[48]

The 'principle' does not account for the homicide cases in which the killer *is* allowed to inherit, or the bigamy cases in which the discretion is exercised for the bigamist. Nor does it account for the environmental and other offences where little or no attempt is made to assess and confiscate the profits of criminal actions. At the least, it would be necessary to supply some further distinction between the killings which 'count' and those which do not, perhaps by resurrecting and refining some kind of distinction between *mala in se* and *mala prohibita*,[49] so as to be able to explain the offences in respect of which the principle is applied vigorously and those where it is not.

The simple position that '[t]he key to ensuring that crime does not pay is for confiscation to be applied as a matter of routine in all cases where criminals have profited, and where there are assets available for recovery',[50] is thus incomplete. It is simply not true that, ' . . . the recovery of the proceeds of crime can never be unjust.'[51] There seem to be four major arguments against an attempt to locate and seize whatever profit is made out of crime in *every case where there is a conviction*. One is based upon resources, the second upon fairness, the third upon the existence of remedies elsewhere which generate appropriate consequences, and the last upon the limitations in the rights of owners of property that would be required by effective legislation to seize the profits of crime.

As to *resources*, it may well be that there should also be a *de minimis* category of cases where, even in an ideal world, the criminal should not be deprived of the proceeds of crime. Assume, for example, that it can be established clearly

---

[48] Derek Hodgson, *Profits of Crime and their Recovery* (London, Heinemann, 1984) (hereinafter *Hodgson Report*) 7.

[49] 'Blackstone's presentation of [*mala in se*] is the first occasion of our hearing of the acute distinction between *mala in se*, and *mala prohibita*: which being so shrewd, and sounding so pretty, and being in Latin, has no sort of occasion to have any meaning to it: accordingly it has none.' Jeremy Bentham, 'A Comment on the Commentaries' (1776) (JH Burns and HLA Hart eds, London, Athlone Press, 1977). On the distinction see Patrick Devlin, 'Real Crimes and Quasi-Crimes' in *The Enforcement of Morals* (Oxford, Oxford University Press, 1965) 26; Patrick Fitzgerald, 'Real Crimes and Quasi Crimes', (1965) 10 *Natural Law Forum* 21.

[50] Cabinet Office Performance and Innovation Unit, *Recovering the Proceeds of Crime* (London, Cabinet Office, 2000) (hereinafter '*PIU Report*) para 8.19.

[51] HL Debates 22 April 2002 col 46 (Lord Rooker). The statement is clearly inconsistent with the policy of the Forfeiture Act. See above, text accompanying n 7 *et seq.*

that someone broke the speed limit on the way to pick up a bargain in a sale, and they arrive just before the sale ends, in time to save ten pounds. Clearly the saving is a profit made by committing a crime. Is this a matter that ought to concern the law? The pragmatic utilitarian argument is that there might come a point at which attempts to deprive criminals of the profits of their crimes would not, on balance, be worth it. Put bluntly, if a serious attempt were made to recoup *all* the profits of *all* known crimes the result might very well be circumstances, as with the Prohibition amendment and its subsequent repeal, where the evils created by the enforcement effort outweighed those against which the law was intended to militate.

As to *fairness*, positive enforcement of a principle against allowing benefits from crime must necessarily involve some degree of selectivity. So few such offenders will successfully be made the object of confiscation that there are dangers of capricious and/or discriminatory enforcement. This would introduce further elements of chance into the criminal law. *Alternative remedies* are available in the case of many crimes with victims. Legislation to provide for a civil law right of recovery in the case where a person's economic interests are damaged by corruption[52] will deal with cases not already governed by the economic torts. The instantiation of restitution orders under the Financial Services and Markets Act 2000 is a further move along these lines. When a victim of crime chooses to avail him/herself of civil law remedies, then s/he should be considered to have priority over the State in claiming the money.[53] In the case of offences with identifiable victims one approach taken hitherto is to regard the victim as the primary enforcer and the primary beneficiary, whether by restitution and/or compensation orders.[54]

Lastly, attenuation of the privacy (to which value attaches) of relationships between lawyers, accountants, bankers and so on (on the one hand) and their clients (on the other) is not without cost. The professions have to expend resources on operating a reporting system, and training people to comply with the system. Confiscation legislation can operate only by using these means. Appropriate legislation should afford some value to individual privacy and that may prevent the seizure of some profits. Any legislation that invades privacy in such a way requires a strong justification.

The 'principle' that criminals should not be permitted to profit from crime is not absolute, but since it is by reference to this principle that the argument is made for confiscation, there are two simple implications in the cases in which it does apply which have of the utmost importance. They can be briefly stated, but the failure of legal systems to respect them has generated much draconian and unjustifiable legislation. First, the principle against allowing people to profit

---

[52] Implementing the Civil Law Corruption Convention of the Council of Europe (ETS 174, 1999).
[53] Eg Proceeds of Crime Act 2002 (hereinafter PCA 2002) s 6(6).
[54] These are orders available under the Powers of Criminal Courts (Sentencing) Act 2000, ss 130 and 148, respectively compelling compensation for injury and the restitution in respect of stolen goods.

from crime is only ever a reason for preventing people from profiting from crime: it can never justify the seizure of sums exceeding the profits. As a matter of principle, the Hodgson Report was correct to say that if the objective of the confiscation order is to place the criminal in the economic position which he occupied prior to the offence, then it can be regarded as 'reparative', but that if the order goes beyond that by any amount, then the orders take on the characteristics of a punishment for crime and the extraction of the proceeds becomes a punishment.[55] Secondly, the principle against allowing people to benefit from their crimes is a reason for confiscation or restitution or refusal to grant a civil law remedy, but it is not necessarily a reason for making it a crime to benefit from crime. The moves towards confiscation of proceeds rather than profits[56] and towards criminalisation of laundering[57] both require justifications, independent of the appeals which are made to the internal coherence of the message delivered by the legal system.

The Nature of the Claim of the State to the Profits or the Proceeds of Crime

The major change in attitude introduced by the Proceeds of Crime Act 2002 is to assert a far stronger claim by the State to the proceeds of crime. The nature of the claim is seldom made explicit, and is the subject of much rhetoric. There are at least four major bases upon which the State could claim the profits of crime: it can assert the right to take the property from the criminal:

(1) to prevent the criminal having or (the 'prophylactic rationale'); or
(2) because the criminal had no proper title to it (the 'propriety rationale'); or
(3) because the crime confers upon the State a better claim to the property than the criminal has (the 'priority rationale'); or
(4) because the fact that the property was obtained by crime the State acquires a proprietary interest in them (the 'proprietary rationale').

It can be seen that the shape which the law is to take depends upon which claim the State makes against the property alleged to be the proceeds of crime. The first rationale does not assert any right in the State to deploy the profits in any particular way, simply to deprive the criminal of them. The limited objective of depriving the criminal would be satisfied if the profits were turned into cash and buried at sea. The common law, up to and including *Attorney-General v Blake*, did not develop a doctrine that the State necessarily has a proprietary interest in the proceeds (or even the profits) of crime. The important thing was to deprive

---

[55] See the speech of Lord Ackner, HL Debates vol 540 cols 744, 749 (22 Nov 1992) and compare *PIU Report* para 4.11 (claiming that the UK régime is reparative, in spite of *Welch v United Kingdom* (1995) 20 EHRR 247). For further procedural consequences—in particular as to the availability of the privilege against self-incrimination, see below, 183.

[56] See the section below ch 7, Proceeds Not Just Profits.

[57] See ch 9 below.

the criminal. The restitution cases are much more concerned with the position of the victim than of the State.

It is traditional in common law to think about personal property in terms of priorities and not in terms of an absolute right like the Roman law *dominium*.[58] Cases such as *Webb* are argued in terms of the assertion of competing rights. The fact that the property was acquired through crime does not *ipso facto* stand in the way of a proprietary claim. The 'priority rationale', and a challenging application of it, was invoked by Lord Falconer in the debates on the Proceeds of Crime Act 2002 concerning the position of third party creditors of a person against whom a confiscation order was made. In the House of Lords Report stage Lord Falconer said: 'Society's claim to the proceeds of crime is better than that of an unsecured creditor.'[59] Now, before the legislation, the State did not have a prior interest as against the criminal (though that has been altered by the wider availability of cash forfeitures).[60] A *fortiori* it did not have priority as against the unsecured creditor. Lord Falconer's statement, whilst having initial rhetorical appeal, does not bear very much analysis. The problem is that the interests of society might be thought to include the protection of honest traders from bad debts.

At another point in the same debate, however, Lord Falconer said:

> . . . the person in possession of the proceeds of unlawful conduct should not be able to retain such wealth, on the basis that it never properly belonged to him. If it did not properly belong to him, he had no right to promise it to other people.[61]

The notion of 'properly belonging' is, in English law, a novel one. The civil recovery procedure,[62] under which the State asserts a proprietary right in the profits of crime, goes down a road which cases like *Reading* and *Blake* avoided taking. At another point Lord Falconer said, 'The proceeds of crime belong to the victim, where one is identifiable, and to society, where one cannot be identified.'[63] The full consequences of the adoption of the view that property acquired by crime is either owned by or owed to the State requires fuller analysis than it was given during the passage of the Proceeds of Crime Act 2002. In particular, this view would be a complete departure from the limits developed in the history of the principle against allowing the criminal to benefit, and, if the State asserts beneficial (moral) ownership of the benefits of crime on no other grounds than that they are the benefits of crime, there is no basis upon which the profits may legitimately be taxed.[64]

---

[58] *Armory v Delamirie* (1722) 1 Strange 505; 93 ER 664.

[59] HL Debates 25 June 2002 col 1234 (Lord Falconer).

[60] See the section below ch 6, Broadening Customs Seizure, Detention and Forfeitures of Cash.

[61] HL Debates 25 June 2002 col 1236 (Lord Falconer).

[62] See the section below ch 11, The 'Civil Recovery' Power.

[63] HL Debates 22 Jul 2002 col 49.

[64] For the increased emphasis upon taxation of the proceeds of crime, see the section below ch 11, Taxation, Money Laundering and Criminal Justice. For the changes in priorities in bankruptcy made by the Enterprise Act 2002, see below, ch priority of confiscation orders relative to other debts.

Justifying Forfeiture[65]

Forfeiture provisions allow the seizure of the *impedimenta*, or 'instrumentalities', of crime. These are the things with which, or in which, or by possession of which, crime is committed. The principle against allowing people to profit from crime cannot itself supply a reason for forfeiture. The ancient fiction, 'about as irrational and unjust a proposition as a sober mind can concoct',[66] is that there is something criminal about the thing.[67] Because the thing is guilty, the State can seize it and arguments from double jeopardy can be side-stepped. Forfeiture, in addition to criminal sanctions is not, on this account, double punishment.[68] By Blackstone's time, forfeiture provisions were regarded as having a 'superstitious purpose' derived from the 'blind days of popery'.[69] Forfeiture as a doctrine seems to survive on no better ground than that was it was always done. Pollock and Maitland attribute proceeding against inanimate objects to 'that unreasoning instinct that impels the civilised man to kick, or to consign to eternal perdition, the chair over which he has stumbled.'[70]

The underlying fiction was that the thing is guilty of the offence,[71] but the fiction is only a fiction.[72] If the fiction of the guilt of the chattel is put aside, what justification could be advanced for forfeiture? What kind of claim does the State have to the item with which a crime is committed? A number of possible justifications can be advanced for forfeiture. They are independent of one another. Each justification has limitations. If forfeiture is to be justified it is critical to be aware of the supposed justification. Forfeiture of instrumentalities attracts the clearest criticism.

---

[65] For excellent general critiques of forfeiture see David J Fried, 'Rationalizing Criminal Forfeiture' (1988) 79 *Journal of Criminal Law & Criminology* 328 and Leonard Levy, *A License to Steal: The Forfeiture of Property* (Chapel Hill, NC, University of North Carolina Press, 1996).

[66] Jacob Finkelstein, 'The Goring Ox: Some Historical Perspectives on Deodands, Forfeitures, Wrongful Death and the Western Notion of Sovereignty' (1973) 46 *Temple Law Quarterly* 169 at 257.

[67] Paul Schiff Berman, 'An Anthropological Approach to Modern Forfeiture Law: The Symbolic Function of Legal Actions Against Objects' (1999) 11 *Yale Journal Law & Humanities* 1.

[68] *United States v Ursery* (1996) 518 US 267; 116 S Ct 2135.

[69] Leonard Levy, *A License to Steal: The Forfeiture of Property* (Chapel Hill, NC, University of North Carolina Press, 1996) 15 quoting 1 Blackstone, *Commentaries* 300.

[70] 2 Frederick Pollock and Frederic Maitland, *History of English Law*, 2nd edn (Cambridge, Cambridge University Press, reissued 1968) 474.

[71] Michael Schecter, 'Note, Fear and Loathing and the Forfeiture Laws' (1990) 74 *Cornell Law Review* 1151 at 1154.

[72] 'Goods, as goods, cannot offend, forfeit, unlade, pay duties, or the like, but men whose goods they are.' *Sheppard v Gosnold* (1671) Vaugh 159 at 172; 124 ER 1018 at 1024 *per* Vaughan CJ, approved in *Mitchell v Torup* (1766) Parker 227 at 236; 145 ER 764 at 767 *per* Parker CB.

Forfeiture as Fine in specie

Forfeiture may be justified as a fine *in specie*—that is, an enforcement mechanism for a fine or a confiscation order having a separate and sufficient justification. In this case, which is not forfeiture properly so called (it is not seizure solely because the item was employed in the commission of crime), there is a justification supplied by the purpose. Seizing the asset is simply one way for the State to recover a debt that is due. If the penalty is justified, then the use of forfeiture is simply a serendipitous enforcement mechanism, and there can be no objection to it. There are three clear limitations to the availability of forfeiture as a fine *in specie*. First, there must be a conviction. Secondly, the item must have a market value. If possession of the object forfeited is unlawful—as in the case of drugs or firearms—it can have no legitimate market value and so cannot satisfy a fine. Thirdly, forfeiture that is justified upon this ground must be set off against any other punishment that is imposed. This is the justification for forfeiture in English Law now advanced as a matter of course. Really, however, it is more of an excuse for forfeiture than a justification. If all that forfeiture achieves is the imposition of a fine, then this is most efficiently and transparently accomplished by treating it as part of sentencing, rather than as being the outcome of a further set of proceedings.

Objects of Crime

English law does not recognise a distinction between the object of crime (the gun in the offence of unlawful possession of firearms) and the instruments of crime (the knife in a murder, the getaway car in a robbery), though it might be helpful to do so, because the possible rationales for the forfeiture differ.[73] Instances of forfeiture of the *objects* of crime can be justified on the ground that the forfeitures prevent further crime.[74] Some things may not be lawfully possessed, or in the case where they can lawfully be possessed, may not lawfully be alienated.[75] Among these contraband items are drugs, firearms, explosives and offensive weapons. If a person is found to be in possession of such an item, there will be a concomitant power to seize the item.[76]

---

[73] *Guy Stessens, Money Laundering: A New International Law Enforcement Model* (Cambridge Cambridge University Press, 2000) 43–47.

[74] If this is the basis, then there is no need to insist upon a conviction before imposing forfeiture.

[75] *R v Blake* [1997] 1 All ER 963; [1997] 1 WLR 1167.

[76] Possession is generally a preliminary step towards the commission of some more serious offence.

Instrumentalities of Crime

Prevention of crime does not, however, justify the seizure of an item that was lawfully acquired, was used once in the commission of crime, is unlikely to be used in the same way again and has a range of lawful uses. There is a significant difference between, on the one hand, the car used to commit an offence, and, on the other, a pistol or an incorrectly calibrated weighing machine possessed unlawfully. The pistol and the scales may not be lawfully used. The car may. In the case where no further crime is prevented, the behaviour of the State in taking away an item used to commit a crime is rather like that of a parent taking away a toy with which a child does something wrong, and saying, 'If you can't play with it properly, you can't have it at all'.[77] The difference is that the child can easily be thought of as having the toy on a revocable loan from the parent, whereas the claim that people hold property at the indulgence of the State opens the difficult underlying issues as exactly to what is meant by the right of property. Within political theory the more absolutist accounts of proprietary rights, deriving from Locke, would hold that, except in certain very special cases, the State does not have any analogous role of oversight of the use by competent adult of his/her own property. The countervailing considerations are, first, that other accounts of property, in particular more socialist or communitarian accounts would not embrace the absolutist position but would regard property rights as being subject to claims of common good,[78] and second, that there is a tradition of legal pragmatism that asserts a power to forfeit property on the grounds of 'common sense' without reference to political theory.

Prevention of Crime

Prevention of crime can also justify taking away from somebody something they intended to use to commit the crime, at least until such time as they are not likely to use it to commit crime. Even where there is no such express statutory power, this sort of *forfeiture* power would be justified on the ground that its exercise prevents crime.

Customs Forfeitures

Customs forfeitures are a special case which might fall both within objects and instrumentalities of crime. Forfeiture, typically without conviction, of contraband

---

[77] 'Confiscation of the instrumentalities of crime rests on the assumption that the convicted [person has shown himself *unworthy* to use property by using it for criminal purposes'—Guy Stessens, *Money Laundering: A New International Law Enforcement Model* (Cambridge, Cambridge University Press, 2000) 43 (emphasis added). The more absolute notion of property would hold that a person who owns property does not need to demonstrate any further worthiness. Compare above, 57–59.

[78] Renounced by the English courts in *Bradford Corporation v Pickles* [1895] AC 587.

substances whose possession is not *per se* punishable but on which duty is payable[79] is of long standing.[80] It may be argued that a person choosing to travel between jurisdictions subjects him/herself and his/her chattels to greater enquiry in the customs hall than elsewhere.[81] Even if it is acceptable for customs powers to work in this way, extensions of the customs powers of seizure and forfeiture beyond ports should be closely scrutinised. Likewise, extension of the forfeiture power beyond the means and the object of a crime requires close examination, and the same is true for forfeiture on account of the intention with which the property was held.

Chattel as Symbol

After *Bennis v Michigan*,[82] a further justification that might cover some cases of forfeiture is that there may be cases where the chattel will be to hand and there is difficulty in finding the owner to determine whether or not s/he was at fault. The symbolic force that attaches to the forfeiture of that particular chattel—a car that was one of the items causing nuisance to the inhabitants of the road in question—is said to justify the forfeiture provision. While this is the strongest justification for forfeiture it is not clear how it could overcome those against.

Objections to Forfeiture

There are several objections that can be made to forfeiture consequent upon conviction. First, forfeiture is arbitrary since it does not link the value of the goods seized to the value of the property the crime was committed to acquire. The extent of the forfeiture will depend upon whether an expensive car or a bicycle was used to commit the theft. So the operation of forfeiture provisions can give rise to the 'hanged for a sheep' counsel of despair. If a dealer will face forfeiture of a car for using it to transport drugs, irrespective of whether the drugs in question are marijuana or heroin, the incentive is to put it to the most profitable use. Risks of violence are increased.[83] Secondly, there is the question of the relationship between forfeiture provisions and third party rights.[84] The fiction underpinning forfeiture—

---

[79] The general forfeiture provision dealing with property on which duty is payable is Customs and Excise Management Act 1979 s 49 but there are many other specific customs forfeiture provisions.

[80] Leonard Levy, *A License to Steal: The Forfeiture of Property* (Chapel Hill, NC, University of North Carolina Press, 1996) 21 *et seq.*

[81] In *R v HM Customs and Excise Commissioners, ex parte Hoverspeed et al.* [2002] EWHC 1630 (Admin) the Court held that HM Customs and Excise were not empowered to use greater powers at national borders than they used elsewhere in the collection of excise duty, as this would impede free movement of goods contrary to EU Law. This consideration only applies (i) where the goods are such that it is lawful to possess them but they carry Excise or some other liability to duty; and (ii) within the EU.

[82] *Bennis v Michigan* (1996) 517 US 1163; 116 S Ct 984, see the section below ch 6, A Comparator—United States' Jurisprudence.

[83] Donald J Boudreaux and AC Pritchard, 'Civil Forfeiture and the War on Drugs: Lessons from Economics and History' (1996) 33 *San Diego Law Review* 79, 92.

[84] And see Sandra Guerra, 'Family Values? The Family as an Innocent Victim of Civil Drug Asset Forfeiture' (1996) 81 *Cornell Law Review* 343.

that the thing is guilty—implies that forfeiture provisions should prevail over third party rights in the item forfeit.[85] This is the consequence arrived at in *Bennis*.[86] Indeed, if the 'symbolism' argument for forfeiture[87] is adopted, it ought not to matter whether the item is stolen or not. Most statutory forfeiture provisions do now include some kind of provision protecting third party rights. Thirdly, leaving aside the exceptional cases where possession of the item is itself criminal or the item can only have a criminal use, the State has no right to seize property simply because it is *used* in the commission of crime. This is an objection of principle speaking to questions of human rights, and in particular the right to quiet enjoyment of property.[88] Fourthly, a most obvious objection both to forfeiture and to confiscation is that they can generate double punishments for the same offence. Even if the general acceptability of forfeiture is granted, some response must be provided to the double jeopardy argument which states that a person should not be punished twice for the same offence.[89]

On all of the grounds above it is suggested that forfeiture of the instrumentalities of crime simply because they are instrumentalities of crime is unjustified. Whilst not involving double punishment, the principal objection to forfeiture provisions operating in the absence of a criminal conviction is that 'it can too easily be used as a way of penalising conduct without the safeguards of the ordinary criminal process'.[90] These are straightforward but enormously important considerations. If they are correct, then the forfeiture provisions in English law are unjustifiable, whether or not they are consistent with the European Convention on Human Rights. This is crucial because the recent extensions of the scope of money laundering law in the areas of terrorism and cash forfeiture depend upon its legitimacy.

JUSTIFYING CRIMINALISATION

Much of the legislation and practice of the attempts to bring legal regulation to bear upon the proceeds of crime have involved mechanisms beyond the traditional criminal law resources of forbidding designated types of behaviour

[85] Leonard Levy, *A License to Steal: The Forfeiture of Property* (Chapel Hill, NC, University of North Carolina Press, 1996) 161 *et seq*.

[86] Above, n 85.

[87] Paul Schiff Berman, 'An Anthropological Approach to Modern Forfeiture Law: The Symbolic Function of Legal Actions Against Objects' (1999) 11 *Yale Journal Law & Humanities* 1.

[88] And see the section below ch 6, First Protocol—the Right to Property.

[89] And see generally Martin L Friedland, *Double Jeopardy* (Oxford, Clarendon Press, 1969); George C Thomas, III, *Double Jeopardy: The History, The Law* (NYC, NY, NY University Press, 1998). The recent review of double jeopardy by the Law Commission—Law Commission, *Consultation paper No 156, Double Jeopardy* (London, The Stationery Office, 1999) in the wake of the MacPherson enquiry into the investigation of Stephen Lawrence's killing limited itself to considerations of double *exposure* to condemnation. There seems to be no clearly established independent principle in English Law prohibiting double *punishment*. See the section below ch 6, Forfeiture Proceedings and Double Jeopardy.

[90] D Hodgson, *Profits of Crime and their Recovery* (London, Heinemann, 1984) (hereinafter *Hodgson Report*).

and trying and punishing people who perform it. The deployment of policing activity to disrupt criminal activity, together with activity directed against property under the control of the suspect, marks a distinctive move away from that tradition. The enforcement of criminal laundering provisions is not central to the international effort against laundering. It is, nonetheless, a clear requirement of many of the international actions against laundering that there be prohibitory provisions in place, because they trigger reporting requirements and they in turn generate important analytical questions within criminal law theory.

The assertion of a general principle that a person should not be permitted to benefit from crime—even the application of that principle far more rigorously than is currently done in English Law—would not necessarily justify the criminalisation of dealing with the proceeds. Indeed, if the confiscation provisions were to operate ideally, and no profits actually were made from the predicate offences to which the laundering provisions applied, then the independent argument for criminalisation would be considerably weakened. The various arguments for criminalisation require some disentangling, but, broadly speaking, it is possible to distinguish between, on the one hand, the sorts of moral arguments which are the usual means by which the limits of the most serious criminal offences are set—identifying a harm against which it is appropriate for the law to militate, identifying a guilty mental state and then, perhaps, sets of aggravating and mitigating characteristics, and, on the other, the set of economic arguments why laundering should be considered an issue sufficiently serious as to justify invoking the criminal law.[91]

The shape of the offence to be put in place depends upon the choice of rationale, which ought also to govern sentencing policy. Sentencers need to know what it is wrong with the behaviour that they have to punish so that they can know how the offence in question differs from the 'standard' form of that offence, what matters might amount to aggravating and what mitigating factors, and so on. The difficulty that they faced in some of the early laundering cases was a lack of clarity about the reason laundering was a crime. Is it like theft or fraud, or counterfeiting, or drug dealing, or smuggling, or handling stolen goods, or what?[92] If laundering is to remain a crime then it is necessary to have a clearer idea of precisely what is wrong with it.

Arguments for Criminalisation

When a phenomenon is the subject of such great interest, and such large quantities of resources are being directed against it by governments and law enforcement agencies, it is easy to forget that if we are to have a morally defensible

---

[91] This distinction is by no means a hard and fast one. Deliberately to cause economic damage is immoral. Perhaps a more accurate way to state the distinction in the text might be between arguments those which deal with long range economic harms and those which do not.

[92] And see below, pp 207–14.

criminal law then the proscriptions that it lays down must be subject to moral, as well as to political, justification. This section will restate and consider the group of moral arguments for the criminalisation of money laundering.

Punishing Laundering Removes the Incentive to Commit Predicate Offences[93]

This argument is a very simple one, akin to the assertion of the principle against allowing profit from crime. There are two major sets of objections. First, it is frequently taken for granted that if laundering were to be more difficult, there would be substantially fewer predicate offences. This is by no means self-evident. Even if there were to be perfect enforcement of laundering offences, the profits to be made from drugs are such that there would still be ample incentive for the dealer simply to hold the money in cash until they are ready to use it. Criminalisation of money laundering does not prevent the use of safe deposit boxes for cash to be spent later.

Second, but more importantly, the argument depends for its validity upon an implausible and unproven empirical claim. If the predicate offence is already a crime and there exists power to confiscate the profits of the offence, what additional force do provisions have which make it a crime to dispose of the money? If somebody contemplating a course of conduct involving the unlawful acquisition of money followed by its laundering is not put off by the existence of the predicate offence nor by the existence of the power to confiscate, it is hardly likely that the existence of the laundering offence will make much difference. The deterrent argument would be slightly stronger if the chance of being detected for the predicate offence is significantly lower than for laundering (which will seldom be the case), or where the penalties for the laundering offence are so much higher than for the predicate offence as to make a difference to a rational, calculating criminal. It would, however, be difficult to justify such a sentencing régime.

Laundering is a Form of Complicity in Predicate Offences

At common law there was a branch of the law of complicity dealing with 'accessories after the fact'[94] into which persons now categorised as launderers might have fallen. This mode of participation really had more to do with shielding the offender from justice than assisting in the crime itself. The closest the offence came to modern notions of laundering was where a defendant was convicted as accessory after the fact through removing evidence against the perpetrator,[95] but it is the interference with justice that is critical, not the fact of the disposal. The modern equivalent is the offence under section 4 of the Criminal Law Act 1967: the launderer is not without more, liable under that section.

---

[93] The expression 'predicate offence', borrowed from the Vienna Convention and many subsequent international instruments, describes the offence by which the profits were acquired.

[94] Glanville Williams, *Criminal Law: The General Part*, 2nd edn (London, Stevens, 1961) 409.

[95] *Levy* [1912] 1 KB 158.

The argument for regarding laundering as a form of complicity is slightly different. It is that laundering is a form of participation in another offence, for example either drug consumption or drug dealing, however described. It is clear that inchoate liability in English Law has extended significantly beyond the traditional trio, rooted in common law, of attempt, conspiracy and incitement. There is now a large group of statutory inchoate offences, including threats offences, going equipped for stealing, possession of firearms, explosives or scales which give false measures. They have extended significantly the scope of the conduct covered by attempt, conspiracy and incitement. In consequence of these statutes, criminal law now enjoins conduct that is significantly earlier in time and further removed causally than an attempt.

Money laundering could have been defined so as to establish it as a form of complicity, but, in English Law, it was not. The two main objections to treating money laundering as a form of complicity in the predicate offence are: first, that it is by no means clear from which predicate offence the objectionable part of laundering is derived; and secondly, that as a matter of labelling, complicity does not properly encapsulate the significance of the harm. Identification of the predicate offence is important because the usual account of complicity at common law holds that the degree of culpability of the accomplice is limited to that of the principal.[96] If the launderer is regarded as an accomplice to possession, then that differs from, and usually is treated far less seriously than, being an accomplice to dealing. At the least, if this is the argument then it needs to be explicated far more fully. The sentences that are set in English Law for money laundering do not express any particular concern for the nature of the offence by which the money was acquired.[97] If, on the other hand, the 'harm' in laundering is some more remote economic harm done by the launderer, then it is not relevant what the source of the money is.

Punishing Laundering Attacks the 'Real' Criminals

Discourse about 'organised crime' in general and drug dealing in particular is peppered with references to the idea that 'the criminal fraternity', when organised, typically operates along the same sort of hierarchical lines as the Mafia in any of a number of films such as *The Godfather*. That is, at the top of all criminal organisations there is someone who keeps most of the profits, lives a very comfortable life in an exclusive quarter, and rules the subordinates with a rod of iron. If this stereotype has any basis in reality,[98] it is easy to believe that people in the upper levels of such an organisation can distance themselves,

---

[96] Sandford Kadish, 'Complicity, Cause and Blame: a Study in the Interpretation of Doctrine' (1985) 73 *California Law Review* 323.

[97] And see below, pp 207–14.

[98] The extent to which there are significant numbers of criminals conforming to the stereotype is unclear: Petrus van Duyne, 'The emperor's clothes of disclosure: hot money and suspect disclosures' (1999) 31 *Crime, Law and Social Change* 245–271, suggests that there are very few.

morally, psychologically and geographically, from the ugly ground level criminal activities. The argument then made for criminalising laundering is that these people cannot distance themselves from the profit, because that is why they are in the enterprise.[99] The really significant criminals can be identified and punished if the money can be traced to them.

If this is indeed the justification, it has a far more wide-reaching impact. It embodies a curious ambivalence towards the effect of legislation. If the 'real' criminal fulfils this stereotype, then s/he will be guilty of serious offences. In cases where there is evidence that the money is linked to the crime, s/he probably will be an accomplice, and failing that, conspiracy charges could be brought. Where there is no evidence that the money is linked to the crime, there will be no independent case for a crime of laundering. Where proof that the money is linked to the crime will depend upon shifting the burden of proof, criminalisation—whether as accessory to or conspirator in the predicate offence or for a distinct offence of laundering—will depend upon the legitimacy of shifting the burden.[100] But whether or not shifted burdens are acceptable, there is no independent case for criminalisation. What the rhetorical deployment of this stereotype really argues for is a category of complicity based upon instigation, which would be a significant (if long overdue) reform of the law of complicity towards which the Law Commission groped.[101]

There is another way of stating the 'real criminal' argument, which relates to the effect of overt disobedience to law on the regard in which law is held. If people without jobs, who do not claim benefit, are able to buy expensive cars and houses and appear to emerge unscathed by the law, then this is an example to others that ought not to be given as to how to make money. Members of the police claim that public satisfaction follows the apprehension of such people, and this view has been endorsed at the highest level.[102]

The responses that can be made are: first, that this is an argument for confiscation, not necessarily for criminalisation; and secondly, that the person who lives well without apparent means of support should be regarded in the first instance as an appropriate target for the tax authorities. They can be investigated for tax evasion. Whether or not they are appropriate subjects for *prosecution* in respect of whatever the criminal conduct is which generated the money is another question.

The Neglected Steps in the Economic Argument

The arguments outlined in chapter two suggest that at least some money laundering has serious detrimental *economic* effects. That is enough, perhaps, to support greater efforts to improve the rate at which the profits of crime are

---

[99] See *PIU Report* para 1.3.

[100] And see the section below ch 9, Defences and the Burden of Proof.

[101] Law Commission Consultation Paper No 131: *Assisting and encouraging crime* (London, HMSO, 1993).

[102] Tony Blair, foreword to *PIU Report*, quoted in ch 1 n 66 above.

confiscated. But it is not enough, without more, to argue for criminalisation. Within a liberal account of the proper limits of the criminal law, further arguments would need to be made out. First, there is the question of the place of criminal law in the legislative armoury. Feinberg provided[103] the most searching analysis of the sorts of harms against which, in a liberal society, it was legitimate to invoke the criminal law, and the cases where it might be legitimate to invoke the criminal law notwithstanding the absence of harm. Many other liberal theorists[104] argue that criminalisation should be regarded, not as a knee-jerk response, but as a last resort, only to be invoked when all other methods of legal regulation of the phenomenon in question have been canvassed and found wanting. There is a range of alternative means of regulation that could be tried. In particular, if confiscation works successfully to deprive criminals of the overwhelming preponderance of their profits, then there is little independent case for criminalisation: alternatively, if confiscation is ineffective, then strong evidence would be required to show that criminalisation is likely to be efficacious.

The second neglected step is the leap from identification of a harmful phenomenon to its attribution to a single perpetrator. Even if the most serious claims for the harms of money laundering *as a phenomenon*[105] are correct, the causal contribution of any given individual launderer to any of these macroeconomic effects will almost always be negligible. So the launderer makes a very slight contribution to the risk that power will be grasped by a bad person, and, perhaps, that markets will operate below optimal efficiency. Even if it is assumed[106] that these threats are very grave, can they be linked to one of the justifications that are usually advanced for the invocation of the criminal law?

The claimed economic consequences of laundering do not, without more, provide a ground for criminalisation. Even if the empirical claims that the phenomenon of laundering causes great economic harm are granted, what must still be supplied is a justification for legislation punishing each individual launderer. The two analytical problems which immediately arise are, first, remoteness and causation; second, ascription and *mens rea*. If a launderer is to be blamed, not so much for dealing with the profits of crime, but for increasing the probability of some economic and political catastrophe occurring, then the extent of the contribution of the launderer needs to be able to be quantified. This is the point at which the claims about the extent of money laundering in the jurisdiction become counter-productive. Assume (as will be the case in the overwhelming proportion of cases) that D is charged with laundering, and that the amount of

---

[103] Joel Feinberg, *The Moral Limits of the Criminal Law* 4 vols (NYC, NY, Oxford University Press, 1984–7).

[104] Eg, Nils Jareborg, 'What kind of Criminal Law do we want?' (1995) 14 *Scandinavian Studies in Criminology* 17.

[105] Ie, see the section above ch 1, 'Moral Panics'.

[106] The clearest proponents of such a mechanical model were CMV Clarkson and HM Keating in early editions of their *Criminal Law: Texts and Material* (London, Sweet & Maxwell, 1st edn, 1984).

money involved is an insignificant proportion of the total which is said to have been laundered in that jurisdiction. Now, there is, of course, no doctrine of *de minimis* in English criminal law. Nonetheless, if the harm which is being ascribed to the defendant for the purposes of the imposition of serious punishment is that of creating or increasing a *risk* of the occurrence of the consequences set out in the direst prediction of the effect of laundering, then without proof that the defendant actually did materially increase that danger, there is no harm and no basis for punishment.

The second major difficulty with holding that laundering is a grave offence because it materially increases the danger of some catastrophe occurring is with ascription. Unless the launderer has detailed economic knowledge s/he will not know of the economic consequences of laundering, and so cannot be fixed with having intended them or been reckless as to their occurrence. It is, in the classical theory of ascription, inappropriate to fix him/her with responsibility for having created that risk. The point is simply made, but the structures put in place under the criminalisation régime depend, for their legitimacy, upon the development of a justifying account for this link.

The criminalisation of laundering is consequently very difficult to justify as an act of criminalisation, but reporting requirements are essential to the crusade against laundering. If there are to be reporting requirements, they must be triggered by suspicion of *something*. If that something is not itself a criminal offence, then (i) it is difficult to see why people should be expected to work unpaid to report it; and (ii) failure to comply with the reporting requirement is unlikely itself to be viewed seriously. It could have been a satisfactory way forward to use the offences simply as triggers for the reporting requirements, with few or no prosecutions. Amid the panic of recent years, however, prosecutions have been brought, and criminalisation of laundering is taking on increasing importance and requires analysis.

4

History of Forfeiture and Confiscation Provisions

An ANALYSIS OF the history of English Law in this area is necessary in order to understand the background against which the modern legislation has been put in place. Until the late twentieth century, civil courts were concerned with compensation among subjects. Criminal courts were concerned with punishment. Forfeiture for felony and various other devices, together with the powers of the Customs and Excise, provided supplements to the powers of the criminal courts, but the absence of any generalised confiscation power left a *lacuna* whose exposure, in a high-profile case was always likely to provoke a legislative response. The critical moment arrived with the decision of the House of Lords in *Cuthbertson*.[1] Legislation followed after six years. The legislation dealt originally only with drug trafficking offences, but the subsequent trend has been to apply the same set of rules more widely. In this chapter the trend away from the broadly liberal approach of the Hodgson Committee towards a far more repressive legislative response in the Proceeds of Crime Act will be traced.

FORFEITURE FOR FELONY

There is no common law power for the State to confiscate property.[2] At common law there was, however, no problem about the ownership of the proceeds of crime or any other property belonging to someone who was convicted of a felony. The doctrine of forfeiture held that the personal property of a convicted felon was forfeit to the Crown. The Crown was also entitled to one year and a day's waste of real property, before feudal escheat operated.[3] It was as simple as that. Forfeiture was unfair to the family of the defendant, but also to the victim of the felony, who could not sue before the criminal trial had generated a conviction,[4] yet could not

---

[1] *R v Cuthbertson* [1981] AC 470; [1980] 2 All ER 401. See the section below, The Origins of Confiscation Law.

[2] *Attorney-General v De Keyser's Royal Hotel* [1920] AC 508: *Burmah Oil v Lord Advocate* [1965] AC 75.

[3] *Hodgson Report*, 12–16. Escheat was the doctrine whereby the land reverted to the feudal lord. Leonard Levy, *A License to Steal: The Forfeiture of Property* (Chapel Hill, NC, University of North Carolina Press, 1996) 28 *et seq.*

[4] Holdsworth, *History of English Law* (London, Methuen, vol 10, 1932) 331–3; *Smith v Selwyn* [1914] 3 KB 98.

sue after a conviction because there was no property for which to sue. The doctrine was abolished in 1870.[5]

Deodands[6]

The ancient *deodand* was only available in the case where death was caused, and had, in all probability, a compensatory role and some of the elements of a tax.[7] The coroner's jury decided precisely what property was forfeit. The local community was responsible for paying uncollected *deodands*. They retained their legal existence till 1846. They were abolished when a right for relatives to sue for loss of a breadwinner was provided by Lord Campbell's Act.[8] It is probable that what led to the passing of the latter Act was that the London and Birmingham Railway Company had a year or two earlier been amerced in the sum of £2,000, representing the value of a railway engine that had run over and killed a man, thus becoming a *deodand*.[9]

Dealing with Profits from Crime

The first significant attempts to deal with profit-making from crime, going beyond *deodand* and forfeiture for felony, were made in the late seventeenth and early eighteenth centuries to deal with the handling of stolen goods.[10] The courts adopted a narrow view of the crime of larceny and refused to hold that a person who handled stolen goods was guilty as an accessory to larceny unless the principal had been convicted.[11] It was during the dominance of Jonathan Wild that the activities of receivers came to be perceived as a threat of a different sort to those posed by individual thieves. Wild's Act[12] was enacted after a series of decisions restricting the liability of the handler of stolen goods (as accessory to theft) to the cases where the thief was convicted.

[5] Forfeiture Act 1870.

[6] And see Leonard Levy, *A License to Steal: The Forfeiture of Property* (Chapel Hill, NC, University of North Carolina Press, 1996) 1–20.

[7] Jacob Finkelstein, 'The Goring Ox: Some Historical Perspectives on Deodands, Forfeitures, Wrongful Death and the Western Notion of Sovereignty' (1973) 46 *Temple Law Quarterly* 169.

[8] 9 and 10 Vict c 62.

[9] See Harry Smith, 'From *Deodand* to Dependency' (1967) 11 *American Journal of History* 389, cited in *Hodgson Report*, 15.

[10] Jerome Hall, *Theft, Law and Society*, 2nd edn (Bloomington, IN, Bobbs Merrill, 1952) 34–58; Leon Radzinowicz, *A History of English Criminal Law and its Administration Vol 2 The Enforcement of the Law* (London, Stevens, 1956) 21 *et seq*.

[11] 1 Anne c 9 (1702) (receivers guilty of misdemeanour absent conviction of perpetrator); 5 Anne c 31 (if felony proved as against perpetrator, handler guilty of felony).

[12] 'Jonathan Wild's Act', 4 Geo 1 c 11 (1717); see generally Gerald Howson, *It takes a Thief: the Rise and Fall of Jonathan Wild* (London, Cresset Library, 1987); Leon Radzinowicz, *A History of English Criminal Law and its Administration Vol 1: The Movement for Reform* (London, Stevens, 1948) 682–84. See also 25 Geo 2, ch 36 (1752) (threatened a £50 fine against either the advertiser or the printer of a 'no questions-asked' reward offer).

The idea that some other goods might represent the goods that were the subject matter of a theft arises early[13] but takes on great significance during the twentieth century. The civil law doctrine of tracing[14] has the effect that proprietary claims may be asserted by the original owner in respect of property that has taken the place of the property originally stolen. Consequently the property 'belongs to another'[15] and is capable of being stolen. There is also a statutory extension of the notion of 'stolen goods' for the purposes of the handling offence.[16]

Statutory Forfeiture

Beginning in the seventeenth century, certain statutes—especially customs and revenue statutes and under the Navigation Acts (which protected the British maritime industry) allowed *in rem* forfeiture without a criminal conviction.[17] So far as concerns forfeiture upon conviction, it was only with the abolition of forfeiture for felony that specific forfeiture provisions take on any great significance. Forfeiture is a blunt instrument, and has consequently given rise to questions as to exactly what property is to be forfeit.[18] In modern times, forfeiture has been used to seize the equipment of a radio pirate[19] and an aircraft on which drugs were smuggled,[20] and forfeiture is one of the weapons the Government is attempting to use to combat illegal immigration,[21] and is central to recent attempts to prevent smuggling of tobacco and alcohol.[22]

---

[13] *Taylor v Plumer* (1815) 3 M & S 562; 105 ER 721.
[14] And see the section below ch 11, Recoverable and Associated Property.
[15] For the purposes of Theft Act 1968 s 4.
[16] Under Theft Act 1968 s 24:

> (2) For purposes of those provisions references to stolen goods shall include, in addition to the goods originally stolen and parts of them (whether in their original state or not),—
>> (a) any other goods which directly or indirectly represent or have at any time represented the stolen goods in the hands of the thief as being the proceeds of any disposal or realisation of the whole or part of the goods stolen or of goods so representing the stolen goods; and
>> (b) any other goods which directly or indirectly represent or have at any time represented the stolen goods in the hands of a handler of the stolen goods or any part of them as being the proceeds of any disposal or realisation of the whole or part of the stolen goods handled by him or of goods so representing them.

[17] Leonard Levy, *A License to Steal: The Forfeiture of Property* (Chapel Hill, NC, University of North Carolina Press, 1996) 40 *et seq*.
[18] A question of the severability of property arose in *R v Attarde* [1975] *Criminal Law Review* 729. The court forfeited a car which had had an extra petrol pump fitted, to siphon fuel from other cars. The car, not just the additional fuel pump, was forfeit.
[19] *R v Blake* [1997] 1 All ER 963; [1997] 1 WLR 1167 (acting under Wireless Telegraphy Act 1949 s 14(3)).
[20] *Air Canada v United Kingdom* (1995) 20 EHRR 150, see the section below ch 6, First Protocol—the Right to Property.
[21] Under the Immigration and Asylum Act 1999. See *International Transport Roth GmbH and another v Secretary of State for the Home Department* [2002] EWCA Civ 158; [2002] UKHRR 479.
[22] *Lindsay v HM Customs and Excise Commissioners* [2002] EWCA Civ 267; [2002] 3 All ER 118: *R v HM Customs and Excise Commissioners, ex parte Hoverspeed and others* [2002] EWHC 1630 (Admin).

Section 27 of the Misuse of Drugs Act 1971 states:

> Subject to subsection (2) below, the court by or before which a person is convicted of an offence under this Act may order anything shown to the satisfaction of the court to relate to the offence, to be forfeited and either destroyed or dealt with in such other manner as the court may order.

In *Cuthbertson*[23] (the 'Operation Julie' case[24]) the section was scrutinised by the House of Lords. An attempt had been made to use the section as a confiscation provision. At the conclusion of a trial an order had been made for the forfeiture of property valued at £750,000, which included British and foreign currency, the contents of safe deposit boxes abroad and monies in foreign bank accounts. It is rare indeed for a judgment to begin, as Lord Diplock's did: 'My Lords, it is with considerable regret that I find myself compelled to allow these consolidated appeals.'[25] The House of Lords held that there was no jurisdiction to make such orders because the conspiracies to which the defendants had pleaded guilty were not 'offences under the Act' within section 27(1), but conspiracies either at common law or under the Criminal Law Act 1977. However, their Lordships thereafter refused to make an order for the return to the appellants of the property in this country that had been seized from them.

The supposed deficiencies in the law to which the decision drew attention could have been remedied simply as a matter of the drafting of section 27. But a more fundamental objection was the distinction that was made between the means by which the offence is committed, and the profits flowing from that offence. The House held that Parliament had never intended section 27 to be the means by which traffickers were to be relieved of the total profits of their unlawful enterprises.

> . . . To ascribe to the section any more extended ambit would involve putting a strained construction on the actual language that is used, and so far from there being any grounds for doing so, it seems to me that if it were attempted to extend the subject-matter of orders of forfeiture to choses in action or other intangibles, this would lead to difficulties and uncertainties in application which it can hardly be supposed that Parliament intended to create.[26]

So one limitation on the subject matter of an order for forfeiture is that it must be something tangible. There is also another: that what is forfeited must be shown to relate to an offence under the Act of which a person has been convicted by or before the court making the order. For the purposes of section 27 one is therefore looking for

[23] *R v Cuthbertson* [1981] AC 470; [1980] 2 All ER 401.
[24] Dick Lee & Colin Pratt, *Operation Julie—how the undercover police team smashed the world's greatest drugs ring* (London, WH Allen, 1978).
[25] [1981] AC at 479; [1980] 2 All ER at 402.
[26] And note *R v Khan; R v Crawley* [1982] 1 WLR 1405, holding that choses in action cannot be the subject of forfeiture (footnote added).

an offence which is not only an offence under the Act but also is an offence which in its legal nature is of a kind to which something tangible and thus susceptible to forfeiture can be said to 'relate.' This cannot, in my view, be properly said of the offence of conspiracy, which in its legal nature does not involve any dealing by the offender with anything tangible at all, but consists entirely of an unperformed agreement to do so.[27]

Section 27 was thus confined to being a forfeiture provision, and not a confiscation provision. In *Beard*,[28] Caulfield J held that a house was not included in the word 'anything' in section 27, and further restrictive applications followed.[29] The absence of a general common law power to confiscate, together with the narrowness of the forfeiture provisions left what was perceived to be an important gap. Out of these expressions of judicial regret came the body of legislation dealing with confiscation.

The historical reasons for the absence from English law of an active confiscation principle, revealed by *Cuthbertson*, are difficult to identify. One (unlikely) answer might be that income from unlawful activity was subject to taxation, and that the Inland Revenue's powers of investigation, fines and confiscation were thought sufficient. Until relatively recently these powers could be exercised in a largely administrative manner without regard to the procedural rights available to 'normal' criminal defendants. Another might be that the recognition that large amounts of money could be made from illegal trade was not generally made until the second half of the twentieth century. A third might be the antipathy of the common law for executive powers of seizure. Finally, the argument for a confiscation power only arose after the abolition of forfeiture for felony.

The Hodgson Committee

Whatever the reasons for the omission, *Cuthbertson* was a turning point. The modern law of confiscation derives directly from concerns engendered by it. The Hodgson Committee was formed by, but independent of, the Howard League, and with some assistance from the Home Office.[30] Following upon a consultation process, its report forms the basis for all subsequent discussion. At the time it was written there were already some provisions dealing with powers of compensation, restitution and forfeiture. The issue with which the committee was most occupied was that of confiscation law, the defects that had been exposed by *Cuthbertson*. The committee distinguished three areas in which confiscation might be relevant.

---

[27] [1981] AC at 483; [1980] 2 All ER at 405.

[28] *R v Beard* [1974] 1 WLR 1549 (and see *R v Pearce* [1996] 2 CAR(S) 316)).

[29] The power to order forfeiture under Misuse of Drugs Act 1971 s 27 applies only to property shown to be connected with the offence of which the offender is convicted, and not to property (such as working capital) intended to be used to facilitate the commission of other offences: *R v Llewellyn* 7 CAR(S) 225, [1985] *Criminal Law Review* 750.

[30] The composition of the committee can be found in D Hodgson, *Profits of Crime and their Recovery* (London, Heinemann, 1984) (hereinafter 'Hodgson Report') vi.

... 'victim-crimes', the paradigms of which are fraud and theft; 'non-victim' crimes, for example, the drug and pornography rackets, unlawful gaming, the transportation of illegal immigrants and corruption of officials; and there are those regulatory offences that involve less obvious criminality; for example the property developer who enormously increases the value of his land by demolishing a listed building or cutting down protected trees, the haulier who overloads his lorries, the manufacturer who pollutes a river with his industrial effluent, or the trader who systematically contravenes the rules of fair trading. The profits made out of this last method of transgressing the law can be enormous and the fines imposed are frequently derisory in comparison; the fine which is imposed is often a cheap price to pay for the profit made.[31]

This classification of offences is by no means the only way in which the matter could have been approached, and the third category appears particularly dated in the light of greater knowledge of the relative significance of white-collar and other crime, and of means of regulation other than the criminal law.

The only significant exception which the committee identified to a general failure to address the harm done and the profit made by crime is the power of Inland Revenue and Customs and Excise to impose penalties.[32] It provides, in effect, for the confiscation of the gains of perpetrators of criminal offences falling within their respective areas of operation. Even then, the committee noted that:

[b]y the payment of penalties the fraudulent evader of taxes escapes the obloquy of a criminal conviction,[33] a privilege denied to the shoplifter or to the embezzler. If society is content that as tax fraudster should escape conviction by the payment of a penalty, why not also the porn merchant, the corrupter of officials and the transporter of illegal immigrants ... ?[34]

So far as concerns the objective that the proposed confiscation legislation was to have, the committee was clear.

We think it should be to restore the *status quo* before the offence.[35] This would require confiscation of only the net proceeds of offending. If drug traffickers have paid their suppliers, confiscation of the gross proceeds would go further than would be necessary to put them in the same position as if they had not offended.[36]

This limited position was not to survive long.

The Committee's central recommendation was that there be put in place a power, upon conviction, to order confiscation.[37] The Committee's view was that

---

[31] *Hodgson Report*, 9.

[32] The powers of the Customs and Excise are now to be found in Customs and Excise Management Act 1979 s 139 and those of the Inland Revenue in Taxes Management Act 1970 Part X.

[33] Without, it might now be added, losing the protection of Art 6(2) of the Convention.

[34] *Hodgson Report*, 9–10.

[35] Author's note: the restoration of the *status quo* would not require the operation of forfeiture in addition to confiscation provisions.

[36] *Hodgson Report*, 11.

[37] *Hodgson Report*, 74 and 151.

the burden of proving the amount of the gross receipts should be on the Crown, but that it was legitimate to have regard to evidence of the street value of the commodity (usually drugs).[38] The Committee considered[39] a possibility of forfeiture without conviction in cases where there was danger to the public—for example the power to forfeit counterfeit coins and forged banknotes and plates for their production.[40] They were absolutely clear, however, that the right to trial of someone faced with forfeiture should be retained.[41] The prospect of drawing adverse inferences about someone's financial affairs from their silence did not, in those days arise. Contemporary reaction to the report was positive, if qualified.[42] With the years that have passed since the report, the liberal principles[43] that informed it have come to be in danger of being forgotten.

There was a slight delay caused by the legislative programme of the Home Office arising out of the Royal Commission on Criminal Procedure,[44] but it was not long before the Hodgson Report was to form the basis for legislative action. Two major parallel legislative threads followed. The first, dealing with drugs offences, is to be found in the Drug Trafficking Act 1994 as amended by the Proceeds of Crime Act 1995, consolidating the Drug Trafficking Offences Act 1986 and certain provisions of the Criminal Justice (International Co-operation) Act 1990 relating to drug trafficking. The second, dealing with other (relatively) serious crimes is to be found in part VI of the Criminal Justice Act 1988, as amended by the Criminal Justice Act 1993 and the Proceeds of Crime Act 1995.[45]

The Drug Trafficking Offences Act 1986

The original legislation putting in place power to confiscate was the Drug Trafficking Offences Act 1986. The Act owes much to the Hodgson Report. It is the Act to which are to be traced confiscation orders, restraint and charging orders, realisation and orders to make materials available. The Act also contained the offence of assisting another to retain the benefits of drug dealing,[46] which is the first criminal laundering provision.

---

[38] *Hodgson Report*, 75 and 151, para 11.

[39] *Hodgson Report*, 95.

[40] Under Forgery and Counterfeiting Act 1981 s 24(3).

[41] *Hodgson Report*, 97.

[42] Martin Wasik, 'The Hodgson Committee Report on the Profits of Crime and their Recovery', [1984] *Criminal Law Review* 708 at 724–25 suggested that the committee might have overstated a crusading case.

[43] See, for example, the remarks on the use of imprisonment, *Hodgson Report*, 6, and the presumption of innocence and the burden of proof, *Hodgson Report*, 82 *et seq*.

[44] The Royal Commission on Criminal Procedure (Phillips) gave rise to the Police and Criminal Evidence Act 1984 (a Police and Criminal Evidence Bill in 1983 fell at the 1983 election) and the Prosecution of Offences Act 1985.

[45] Since the advent of legislation dealing with terrorism there has always been additional provision dealing with money connected to terrorism. See the section below ch 10, Terrorist Fund-Raising.

[46] Drug Trafficking Offences Act 1986 s 42.

Criminal Justice Act 1988

The 1988 Act was a very substantial piece of legislation dealing with a range of matters, including torture, extradition, criminal injuries' compensation and the probation service. So far as concerns the proceeds of crime, Part VI extended the application of the rules on confiscation to a category of criminal conduct much more widely defined than under the drugs legislation. Its provisions were still significantly less harsh than those for drugs offences. In particular, the court was given discretion to impose a confiscation order, (not an obligation so to do) when the offence was not a drug trafficking offence.

Criminal Justice (International Co-operation) Act 1990

The crimes in question are amongst the most international. The money that is generated from unlawful trade can only be recovered in jurisdictions in which there are mechanisms in place that permit enforcement between jurisdictions. One common means of laundering is by means of foreign exchange trans-actions: another is by expatriating the money. The impetus behind the Criminal Justice (International Co-operation) Act 1990 was the Vienna Convention.[47] The 1990 Act received the Royal assent days before a World Ministerial Summit dealing with the drug trade in general, and cocaine in particular, in London in April 1990. The Act enabled the UK Government to ratify the 1957 European Convention on Mutual Legal assistance (Part 1) and the 1988 Vienna Convention. It extended the law relating to the manufacture of drugs to embrace the case of manufacture of a substance to be used in the production of a controlled substance.[48]

The alteration which the 1990 Act made to the law of money laundering was to make it an offence to conceal, disguise, convert or transfer the proceeds of drug trafficking for the purpose of avoiding prosecution for a drug trafficking offence, or the making or enforcing of a confiscation order,[49] or to conceal, disguise, convert or transfer another's proceeds, knowing or having reasonable grounds to suspect that they are such proceeds. For both offences the maximum was 14 years imprisonment. Again, the 'special' nature of the drugs trade was behind the differentiation between drug and other crime. The Act also provided power[50] to enforce overseas court orders for the forfeiture of property used in the commission of serious offences, including offences corresponding to or similar to offences of trafficking and laundering. It also contained provisions dealing with the seizure if cash.[51]

---

[47] See the section below ch 5, The Vienna Convention.
[48] Criminal Justice (International Co-operation) Act 1990 s 12.
[49] Criminal Justice (International Co-operation) Act 1990 s 14.
[50] Criminal Justice (International Co-operation) Act 1990 s 9.
[51] Ss 25 *et seq.*

Criminal Justice Act 1993

The 1990 Act had put in place criminal laundering provisions that dealt with the proceeds of drug trafficking. The 1993 Act put in place criminal provisions dealing with money laundering, in compliance with Article 3 of the Vienna Convention. It inserted criminal money laundering provisions into the 1988 Act, applying otherwise than to drug trafficking offences, and supplying the concomitant enforcement provisions.[52] Article 7 of the Vienna Convention had adopted the civil standard of proof for showing that property was the proceeds of crime. In the 1993 Act, Parliament intervened to reverse the decision of the Court of Appeal in *R v Dickens*[53] that the prosecutor had to show beyond reasonable doubt that proceeds were of criminal provenance in order for a confiscation order to be made, and expressly made the civil standard the applicable one.[54]

In his speech in the second reading debate, the then shadow Home Secretary, Tony Blair, said:

> Those powers in the 1986 Act have been described as draconian. Clearly they are draconian; they were meant to be. Draconian powers are fully justified because of the appalling evil that they are designed to counter. It is clear that confiscation orders have been of considerable use. Secondly, it obliges the court, rather than simply permitting it, to make statutory assumptions about the defendant's assets. Whatever assets a defendant has, the assumption is that they are the proceeds of drug trafficking. [. . .]
>
> However, the accumulation of a lower standard of proof plus the assumptions that go a long way towards establishing proof and their mandatory nature somewhat restrict the ability of the court to take into account all the factors that it wishes to take into account.
>
> . . . [W]e should understand that there will have to be great changes in the ways in which those financial institutions operate. If there are not, quite lowly officials within the banking system may find themselves responsible in circumstances in which the real failure is the failure of higher management to give them proper training, to instruct them on the right things to look for and to ensure that they are able properly to keep track of the money with which they are dealing.[55]

The 1993 Act forms the beginning of the movement from concentration upon drugs to a much wider attack upon laundering, including controls of the financial services' industry.

Drug Trafficking Act 1994

The 1994 Act consolidated the 1986 Act and the provisions of the Criminal Justice (International Co-operation) Act 1990 that deal with drug trafficking.

---

[52] Criminal Justice Act 1988 s 93A (hereinafter CJA 1988) *et seq.*
[53] *R v Dickens* [1990] 2 QB 102, [1990] 2 All ER 626; See also *R v Enwezor* (1991) 93 CAR 233.
[54] CJA 1988 s 71(7A); Drug Trafficking Act 1994 (hereinafter DTA 1994) s 27.
[55] HC Debates 14 April 1993 vol 222 col 870.

Consequently decisions made under the preceding sections of those Acts are authoritative in the application of the Act.

Proceeds of Crime Act 1995

The 1995 Act was introduced as a private member's Bill by Sir John Hanham, with Government support. It was brought forward in the wake of the first Report of the Home Office Working Group on Confiscation.[56] It was the first Parliamentary sign of dissatisfaction with the operation of the régime put in place to remedy the defects revealed by *Cuthbertson*. Infrequent use had been made of confiscation orders, especially those under the 1988 Act.[57] The Act replaced the courts' discretion to confiscate with a duty where written notice was given by the prosecutor.[58] In line with the arrangements for drug trafficking, if the prosecutor did not tender a notice, the court was still able to make an order of its own volition. The Act also abolished the lower limit for confiscation orders[59] and cast the net for confiscation orders much more widely. The two related issues which were identified as important deficiencies were the question of repetitions of small offences, only a few of which were taken into consideration in sentencing (consequently lowering the sums available for confiscation) and 'criminal lifestyle' (persons living beyond their lawfully acquired means). Sir John said:

> The best example of that is the difficulty illustrated by pornographic videos. A criminal may copy and distribute thousands of videos a month, but the production of each video will constitute a separate offence. For the entire proceeds of that criminal enterprise to be confiscated under the 1988 Act, every offence would have to charged and convicted separately or taken into consideration by the court.
>
> . . . Unfortunately, the courts may take offences into consideration only with the defendant's consent and lifestyle criminals are well aware of the possibility of their ill-gotten gains being confiscated if they allow the court to take too many offences into consideration and will obviously not allow it. The new provisions[60] empower the courts to assume that all property passed through the defendant's hands in the past six years has come from crime. If the defendant cannot show that assumption to be wrong, in whole or in part, the court will be able to order the defendant to pay an amount equivalent to that assumed benefit. The Drug Trafficking Offences Act 1986 has always allowed similar assumptions to be made on the strength of one drug trafficking conviction.[61]

Courts were given the power to order the defendant to provide any information that it considers relevant to the making of a confiscation order, bringing the Criminal Justice Act 1988 into line in this respect with the Drug Trafficking Act

---

[56] Home Office Working Group on Confiscation, 1992, Report on Part VI of the Criminal Justice Act 1988 (London, Home Office, 1992).

[57] HC Debates 3 February 1995 col 1322 (Sir John Hanham).

[58] Proceeds of Crime Act 1995 s 1.

[59] It had been £10,000.

[60] Which became CJA 1988 s 72AA.

[61] HC Debates 3 February 1995, cols 1323–1324.

1994. The Act gave the courts the power to make the statutory assumptions[62] where the defendants were convicted of a wide range of serious or lucrative non-drug crimes, but the drug trafficking legislation was not 'updated'[63] to deal with the same lifestyle issues. It also provided greater powers of investigation. Powers to investigate whether or not whether any person has benefited from any criminal conduct were inserted in Part VI of the Criminal Justice Act 1988.[64]

Criminal Justice (International Co-operation) (Amendment) Act 1998

This short, *ad hoc* piece of legislation was introduced to provide a defence to a charge of manufacture and supply of scheduled substances under the 1990 Act that the manufacture or supply was done with the consent of a constable. The legislation was introduced simply to deal with the possibility that somebody might be authorised to continue their (lesser) role in order to catch a more serious collaborator. There was some discussion during its passage as to whether or not it was likely to generate greater use of *agents provocateurs* or sting operations,[65] but the legislation was almost wholly uncontroversial.

Terrorism Act 2000

There had been provisions dealing with the financing of terrorism stemming from the Prevention of Terrorism (Temporary Provisions) Acts 1974–1989. This Act put in place systematic provisions echoing those for confiscation under the Criminal Justice 1988 and the Drug Trafficking Act 1994, with the important difference that they were forfeiture not confiscation provisions.[66]

Anti-Terrorism, Crime and Security Act 2001

The Act, passed in the wake of the 11 September outrages, included a range of provisions, some but not all of which were directed against the sort of events that gave it rise. The provisions of the Terrorism Act 2000 dealing with cash seizures were extended, and the offence of failure to report dealing in terrorist cash was reinstated.

Proceeds of Crime Act 2002

After some preliminary urgings from the Home Office,[67] the principal moving force behind the 2002 Act was the Cabinet Office Performance and Innovation

---

[62] The progenitors of the 'lifestyle provisions'. See the section below ch 7, The Standard and Burden of Proof in Confiscation Proceedings—Applying the Lifestyle Provisions.

[63] Home Office Working Part on Confiscation 3rd Report *Criminal Assets* (1998) para 3.14. On this notion of progress see the section above ch 1, 'Progress'.

[64] Proceeds of Crime Act 1995 s 11, inserting CJA 1988 s 93H.

[65] HL Debates 16 Mar 1998 col 549 (Lord Williams of Mostyn).

[66] See the section below ch 10, Forfeiting Terrorist Property Upon Conviction.

[67] Home Office Working Party on Confiscation 3rd Report, *Criminal Assets* (1998).

Unit. It set out the administrative difficulties: '[A]n annual average of 15,000 such disclosures has led to only a handful of money laundering convictions. There are significant delays in processing suspicious transaction reports. In order for the reports to be acted upon effectively it is important that the turn-around time be fast.' The Cabinet Office review set targets of 24 hours in 75 per cent of most urgent cases, as against a 1999 average of seven to eight weeks. In view of the speed with which money can be moved, this sort of delay renders much of the reporting useless.[68] The Economic Crime Unit of NCIS has been said in the past to have been be understaffed.[69]

A single session of Parliament was to last from June 2001 till November 2001. The Queen's speech in November 2000 promised the publication of a draft Bill. This was done in March 2001.[70] The Bill was finally introduced in October 2001,[71] complemented by the publication of the Home Office's Assets Recovery Strategy[72] and received the Royal Assent on 24 July 2002. The defects in the existing law it was intended to remedy were clearly set out by the Minister of State in the Commons' Second Reading debate:

> Frankly, the legislation has failed to keep pace with the increasingly sophisticated measures used for hiding and laundering criminal assets.
>
> For a start, the separate treatment of drug trafficking and other criminal activity makes the legislation ineffective against today's versatile criminal entrepreneurs. When dealing with criminal groups, it is often in practice impossible to distinguish between the proceeds of their drug trafficking and those of other activities. The courts have called for the abolition of this distinction in the criminal law on money laundering.
>
> Secondly, to prosecute money laundering and confiscate criminal proceeds, it is necessary to find them. The law at present does not give the police and customs enough help; a search warrant on its own is of little use if they do not know where to search. With modern technology, money can be transferred from one bank account to another at the touch of a button. We need new investigative powers to facilitate the tracing of assets.
>
> Thirdly, even if investigators find the assets, they have no powers to freeze them. Restraint orders, which prohibit defendants and their associates from disposing of assets, are not available until the defendant is about to be charged. That is far too late. By that time, the defendant will often have realised that he or she is under investigation and will have placed their assets beyond reach. Moreover, the restraint procedures themselves are costly and inaccessible, which is why last year fewer than 300 such orders were made.
>
> The complexity of the confiscation system deters the courts and the practitioners.

---

[68] *PIU Report* para 9.1.

[69] FATF assessment of the United Kingdom, 1996: 'Representatives of the financial sector, who have been required by the various anti-money laundering initiatives to invest in resources in this area, have a legitimate expectation to see their efforts matched by greater law enforcement resources and priorities for money laundering.'

[70] *Proceeds of Crime Bill: Publication of Draft Clauses* CM 5066 (2001).

[71] Second Reading HC Debates 30 October 2001 col 757 *et seq.*—a debate of little quality.

[72] <http://www.homeoffice.gov.uk/proceeds/asset_recovery/asset_recovery.htm>

The system produces only about 1,200 confiscation orders each year, compared with over 65,000 defendants found guilty of offences in the Crown court, most of which are for acquisitive crime.[73]

The Bill emerged relatively unscathed from its Commons' stages, but in the Lords the drafting and structure of the Bill provoked some criticism.[74] It drew heavy fire from a Law Lord.[75] Meanwhile, the Joint Parliamentary Committee on Human Rights reported twice,[76] again drawing attention to respects in which the Bill might be deficient.

A Note on the Interpretation of Laundering Legislation

Before moving on to deal with specific provisions, it is necessary to address one general question that recurs throughout the consideration of the legislation. This is the matter of interpretation.[77] The legislation confers significant powers of search, seizure, detention, forfeiture and confiscation of property, and puts in place a series of serious criminal offences. How are the courts to approach it?

What Sort of Statutes?

The framework for the confiscation of laundered money and criminalisation of laundering is a statutory one, and, as such requires that principles of statutory interpretation be deployed. The confiscation provisions are also provisions as to the appropriation of property by the State from the individual, and in consequence they have much in common, both in length and complexity, with taxing statutes. Even if they have significant impact elsewhere, the law in this area is too technical to be subject to injunctions to keep the criminal law simple.[78] In theory at least, tax statutes and criminal law statutes are both subject to a special need for strict construction.[79]

---

[73] HC Debates 30 October 2001 col 759 (John Denham).

[74] Eg by Lord Goodhart HL Debates 25 March 2002 vol 633 col 28.

[75] Lord Lloyd of Berwick HL Debates 25 March 2002 vol 633 cols 44 *et seq.* See also HL Debates 13 May 2002 col 66; HL Debates 25 June 2002 col 1256 *et seq.* HL Debates 11 July 2002 cols 842–856, inflicting a defeat on the Government.

[76] Joint Parliamentary Committee on Human Rights, *Third* and *Eleventh Reports* (2001 and 2002 respectively).

[77] And see Guy Stessens, *Money Laundering: A New International Law Enforcement Model* (Cambridge, Cambridge University Press, 2000) 126 *et seq.*

[78] The Theft Act 1968 was introduced among murmurings of a brave new world of criminal statutes readily accessible to the general reader. The absurdity of this position became clear in *Treacy v DPP* [1971] AC 537; [1971] 1 All ER 110, where the House of Lords uttered platitudes about ordinary language and general accessibility and then divided 3–2 as to what 'demand' meant.

[79] John Bell and Sir George Engle, *Cross on Statutory Interpretation*, 2nd edn (London, Butterworths, 1987) 173 and 182.

The legislation on money laundering has frequently been said to be 'draconian'.[80] In other judicial periods it might have been construed *contra proferentem*. Lord Goff's statement that:

> ... it is a principle of English Law to give reasonably precise guidance as what kinds of conduct are criminal. This is the so-called principle of legality, which has a respectable theoretical foundation but can, perhaps, be a little unrealistic in practice.[81]

evinces a dissatisfaction with the principle of legality in criminal cases, and decisions on anti-avoidance provisions in taxation have shifted their emphasis more towards the Revenue. In *R v Smith (David Cadman)* Lord Rodger went further. He said:

> [The confiscation] scheme has the merit of simplicity. If in some circumstances it can operate in a penal or even a draconian manner, then that may not be out of place in a scheme for stripping criminals of the benefits of their crimes. That is a matter for the judgment of the legislature, which has adopted a similar approach in enacting legislation for the confiscation of the proceeds of drug trafficking.[82]

This involves a departure from the traditional canons—honoured more, admittedly, in the breach than the observance—of statutory interpretation. The *contra proferentem* rule states that the fact that one part of a provision (a penal law, or a taxing provision, or an exemption clause) generates harsh adverse consequences for a party is a reason why the courts should construe ambiguities in the provision against the powerful party responsible for its being in place. Lord Rodger turns this on its head. His argument is that because other parts of the confiscation provisions operate severely against the defendant, that is a reason why the particular provision in point should also be construed that way—that penal provisions should be construed *pro proferentem*.

In general, the courts, in the construction of the legislation on money laundering, in both its confiscation and forfeiture provisions and those creating criminal offences, have not been astute to adopt constructions against the State. Typical of the modern approach is the following:

> We bear in mind that, as a penal statute, the 1994 Act must, in the case of ambiguity, be construed favourably to the defendant. But we see no ambiguity. The plain words of the statute, in our judgment, provide for the making of an application for a further certificate and for an increase in the amount to be recovered under the confiscation order at any time after the original confiscation order was made. By this means drug dealers can be deprived of their assets until they have disgorged an amount equivalent to all the benefit which has accrued to them from drug dealing.[83]

As with the case law on the Theft Acts, where very few defendants have had convictions quashed on 'technicalities' having been found by a jury to be dis-

---

[80]   See the section below ch 1, The Rhetoric of the Debates.
[81]   *R v Preddy* [1996] AC 815 per Lord Goff at 831.
[82]   *R v Smith (David Cadman)* [2001] UKHL 68 Para 23.
[83]   *R v Tivnan* [1999] 1 CAR(S) 92 at 97 per Rose LJ.

honest,[84] so, so far as concerns confiscation orders, the defendants have started with the enormous disadvantage of having been convicted of a serious offence. Occasionally judges have adopted a more liberal position. The clearest example of this is *R v Dickens*[85] where the Court of Appeal held, under the 1986 Act that the onus was on the prosecution to prove to a *criminal* standard (ie beyond reasonable doubt) that the appellant had benefited from drug trafficking and the amount of such benefit. Lord Lane CJ (no liberal) said:

> In our judgment the context of the Act and the nature of the penalties which are likely to be imposed, make it clear that the standard of proof required is the *criminal* standard, namely proof so that the judge feels sure or proof beyond reasonable doubt.

The existence of the 'statutory code' for confiscation has led the higher courts to lean against anything that would operate as a common law supplement. *Blake*[86] and *Webb*[87] are both cases in which the courts have counteracted a movement that appeared to be taking root in the lower courts for the extension of existing remedies, especially interlocutory injunctions, to remedy what were perceived to be defects in the statutory scheme. *Blake* is particularly significant. The realisation that the confiscation statutes confer powers of enormous constitutional significance has eventually lead to their interpretations being argued within the context of the liberal, anti-executive tradition in the courts, dating back to the eighteenth century, rather than the more submissive posture associated with some period of the twentieth. This change is due, at least in part, to the changes that have taken place in the political complexion of the higher judiciary, but also to the altered atmosphere generated by the human rights jurisdiction. Even 10 years ago, a statement such as Lord Steyn's, 'Giving a member of the executive unnecessary powers is never a good idea',[88] would not have been written in a proceeds of crime case.

Nonetheless the harsh approach has been evident in the cases on the adjectival law of laundering. In *ex parte Francis & Francis* the majority of the House of Lords adopted a 'purposive' interpretation of an exception to the availability to legal professional privilege, allowing the police access to documents in the hands of innocent people.[89] In *HM Customs & Excise Commissioners v Duffy*[90] the Court interpreted a forfeiture provision which was silent as to whether or not it covered 'smurfing' (dividing up a larger qualifying transaction into several smaller non-qualifying transactions) so as to cover it.

---

[84] *R v Preddy* [1996] AC 815; [1996] 3 All ER 481 being the exception.

[85] *R v Dickens* [1990] 2 QB 102, [1990] 2 All ER 626.

[86] *Blake v Attorney-General* [2001] 1 AC 268; [2000] 4 All ER 385: see the section above ch 3, Civil Law Duty to the State.

[87] *Webb v Chief Constable of Merseyside* [2000] 1 QB 427; [2000] 1 All ER 209: Below Forfeiture and Confiscation by other means (226–8).

[88] *Blake v Attorney-General* [2001] 1 AC 268; [2000] 4 All ER 385: see the section above ch 3, Civil Law Duty to the State.

[89] ALE Newbold, 'The Crime/Fraud Exception to Legal Professional Privilege' (1990) 53 *Modern Law Review* 472.

[90] *HM Customs & Excise Commissioners v Duffy* [2002] EWHC 425.

Human Rights and Statutory Interpretation

The Human Rights jurisdiction has changed much. Section 3(1) of the Human Rights Act 1998 imposes a strong interpretative obligation on the courts. It provides: 'So far as it is possible to do so, primary legislation and subordinate legislation must be read and given effect in a way which is compatible with the Convention rights.' Emmerson and Ashworth's declaration that, '[t]he process of statutory interpretation is no longer dominated by a search for the intention of Parliament'[91] may be slightly premature but the approach to be adopted by the courts to the Proceeds of Crime Act will be a significant determinant of its approach to the Human Rights Act, and *vice versa.*

One of the surprising factors about the early years of the Human Rights' jurisdiction has been the amount of litigation in which the legislation in question was enacted post-1998. There are two procedural safeguards written into the Human Rights Act which were designed to ensure, if not that all post-1998 legislation was compliant, then at least that in any litigation the legislation would start with certain assumptions in its favour. These were the certification procedure[92] and the establishment of the Joint Parliamentary Committee on Human Rights. The ability of ministers to cite 'legal advice' without naming the adviser or publishing the advice[93] has brought the certification procedure into some disrepute.[94] The Joint Committee can only make its views known,[95] and if it is ignored, they are wasted ink.[96]

Nonetheless, many commentators have been disappointed by the levels of judicial activity under the Act, and the laundering legislation has been in point as much as any body of law. Challenges to the rules providing for the 'statutory assumptions' were at the heart of early trials,[97] and the courts were keen to emphasise the respective functions, under the Human Rights Act, of the courts and a 'democratically elected' legislature.[98] Even before the Human Rights Act there were indications that the Convention was not to provide quite the resource some had imagined for those against whom forfeiture or confiscation proceed-

---

[91] Ben Emmerson and Andrew Ashworth, *Human Rights and Criminal Justice* (London, Sweet and Maxwell, 2001) 132.

[92] Human Rights Act 1998 s 19.

[93] As was done by Lord Goldsmith in the debates on the Proceeds of Crime Bill HL Debates 13 May 2002 col 72.

[94] Andrew Ashworth, *Serious Crime, Human Rights and Criminal Procedure* (London, Sweet & Maxwell, 2002).

[95] As it did in Joint Parliamentary Committee on Human Rights, *Third* and *Eleventh Reports* (2001 and 2002 respectively).

[96] They could not be referred to by later courts: *Pepper v Hart* [1993] AC 593; [1993] 1 All ER 42 limits the availability of reference to Hansard generally to cases where the Parliamentary speaker is the relevant minister, who would not sit on the Human Rights' Committee.

[97] *HM Advocate v McIntosh (Sentencing)* [2001] UKPC D1; [2001] 3 WLR 107, *R v Rezvi* [2002] UKHL 1, *R v Benjafield* [2002] UKHL 2.

[98] *HM Advocate v McIntosh (Sentencing)* [2001] UKPC D1; [2001] 3 WLR 107 at para 36 *per* Lord Bingham. References to democracy generally preface judicial restraint.

ings were brought.[99] The dangers pointed out by the sceptics, in particular that the Convention would be taken to provide a standard of what is tolerable not an irreducible minimum, have been borne out in the early applications of the Act.

The most significant rights for the purposes of the money laundering jurisdiction will be those to private life, to property and to a fair trial, and, should the United Kingdom accede, the right not to suffer double punishment. Will the advent of the human rights jurisdiction make a difference to the interpretation of laundering law? Even in the aftermath of the events of 11 September 2001, Lord Woolf warned that any emergency legislation would still be subject to the Human Rights Act,[100] but the judges have been remarkably supine in the face of the moral panic surrounding laundering.

The decision of the (Scottish) Court of Criminal Appeal in *McIntosh v HM Advocate*[101] might have marked a move towards recognition of human rights' arguments. In this case the result was achieved not by interpretation of ambiguous legislation (the legislation putting in place the statutory assumptions is not, in the sense ambiguous), but by use of the power the Scottish courts have actually to strike down legislation.[102] On appeal, the Judicial Committee of the Privy Council[103] took the view that since proceedings for the determination of the extent of a confiscation order followed a conviction, Article 6 did not apply and so no derogation from the presumption of innocence was involved. This was followed by the European Court of Human Rights[104] and the House of Lords.[105]

The effects of the decision in *Lambert*[106] may be more significant. In that case the House of Lords held that although the natural meaning of the statute would have favoured the imposition of a probative burden on the defendant, that obligation would not have been justified as a proportionate departure from the obligation under Article 6(2), and consequently that the interpretative obligation[107] meant that the court could hold that a meaning which was not the natural meaning, but was not offensive to the language used (that the burden upon the defendant should be an evidential one only), be adopted.[108]

---

[99] *AGOSI v United Kingdom* (1987) 9 EHRR 1, *Air Canada v United Kingdom* (1995) 20 EHRR 150, *Raimondo v Italy* (1994) 18 EHRR 237.

[100] 'On the brink of war: Lord Chief Justice in human rights warning' *The Guardian*, 28 September 2001.

[101] *HM Advocate v McIntosh (Sentencing)* 2001 JC 78; 2000 SLT 1280.

[102] The alternative under the constitutional arrangements in England and Wales would be a 'declaration of incompatibility'. Human Rights Act 1998 s 4.

[103] *HM Advocate v McIntosh (Sentencing)* [2001] UKPC D1; [2001] 3 WLR 107.

[104] *Phillips v United Kingdom* (2001) 11 BHRC 280; [2001] Crim LR 817.

[105] *R v Rezvi* [2002] UKHL 1; *R v Benjafield* [2002] UKHL 2.

[106] *R v Lambert* [2001] UKHL 37; [2001] 3 All ER 577.

[107] Human Rights Act 1998 s 3(1) provides: 'So far as it is possible to do so, primary legislation and subordinate legislation must be read and given effect in a way which is compatible with the Convention rights.'

[108] And see *R v A* [2001] UKHL 25 for another significant application of s 3.

If Article 6 arguments have had limited success, there has been a recent victory for arguments from the First Protocol (that the powers to confiscate or impose forfeiture interfere with protected property rights). The battle under Article 8 in respect of the right to private life and access to financial information has yet fully to be joined.[109] It seems that a breach of the right to private life in the context of criminal proceedings does not necessarily imply a breach of the right to a fair trial.[110] Should the United Kingdom Government accede to the double jeopardy protocol[111] this will raise further challenges.

To the 2002 Act

Before the 2002 Act, there were two major parallel legislative threads. From the point of view of neatness, it would have been better if these provisions had a single legislative track. If there are two places to find confiscation provisions, then it is remarkable that it did not prove possible even to have consistency in the technique by which amendment is made. One way to update a particular area of legislation is to pass new Acts from and then, from time to time, to consolidate. The other is to update by textual amendment of the original Act. The Drug Trafficking Act 1994 was a consolidating measure. The Criminal Justice Act 1988 was the subject of much textual amendment.[112] This cannot have been the most efficient way to manage the statute book, and their consolidation in the Proceeds of Crime Act 2002 is, in this respect, a clear advance.

It was against the long-term background of the perceived failure of the incremental steps embodied in the previous legislation, and the short-term anxiety generated by the attack on the United States, that the 2002 Act was brought forward. The further element, of growing importance, had been the growing internationalisation of criminal law and procedure. This requires separate treatment.

---

[109] And see the section below ch 9, Privacy.

[110] *Khan v United Kingdom* (2001) 31 EHRR 45; [2000] 8 BHRC 310, *R v McLeod* [2002] EWCA Crim 989.

[111] ECHR Protocol 7, Article 4.

[112] And see DA Thomas' note to *R v Martin* [2002] *Criminal Law Review* 228, 230: 'If ever an illustration were needed of the absurdity of English sentencing legislation, and that applying to confiscation in particular, this case surely provides one. The Court of Appeal is forced to quash a confiscation order . . . exceeding £10 million . . . because of procedural errors which can be directly attributed to the difficulty of applying legislation which has been chopped and changed in a piecemeal fashion over a period of years.'

5

The International Dimension

A person might fall under the authority of different political units. S/he might be subject to laws made by a local council, a regional authority, a nation and by supranational organisations. So far as concerns criminal law, with the exception of relatively minor offences created by delegated legislation, the power to make criminal law, like the power to tax and to make treaties, has long been one of the identifying properties of the sovereign Nation-State. Formulating the criminal law, on the traditional account, is one of the principal ways in which a Nation-State creates and protects its identity. It is fundamental to that identity that the Nation-State should be able to determine, for example, its own age of consent to sexual intercourse, its own rule as to whether a person may kill in defence of property, its own policy as to whether or not polygamy and polyandry should be permitted, and so on.

The specifically modern countervailing force to the Nation-State has been the assertion of a power, not so much in other individual countries, but in the 'international community', to take an interest in matters which previously had been regarded as matters of internal sovereign governance. Criminal law is one of the last areas of law to be the subject of the movement for internationalisation. Its internationalisation will have very significant consequences for the substance of the law, for accused persons, for policing and for relations between States. The usual formal mechanism for harmonisation is international treaties or conventions, requiring signatory jurisdictions to put in place specified criminal prohibitions, reciprocal extensions of jurisdiction, reciprocal policing assistance evidence gathering and other legal assistance. There have been many of these. There are also organisations, of which the FATF is the most significant, disseminating non-obligatory advice, but where non-compliance still has great practical significance. Behind them, there is much inter-governmental contact, and contact between governments and international organisations, at varying levels of elevation and formality.

As history proceeds beyond the Nation-State,[1] embracing federalism and the introduction of a range of intranational constitutional structures, and with

---

[1] John Dunn (ed), *Contemporary Crisis of the Nation-State* (Oxford, Blackwell, 1995); Jurgen Habermas, 'The European Nation-State. Its achievements and its Limitations' (1996) 9 *Ratio Juris* 125.

sovereignty concomitantly less or differently prized,[2] two major developments in criminal law are taking place. The first (political) is a coalescence of Nation-States into larger political units that undertake reciprocal enforcement of obligations, render assistance one to the other in enforcement of criminal law and agree to criminalise the same things. The other development (economic) is the vast increase in the mobility of people and goods, tangible and intangible, across frontiers. The consequences are that the physical boundaries of the criminal law are being broken down, crossed and blurred. A system of criminal justice is now so closely bound into its political unit's system of international relations that the only States that can afford to conduct criminal law and criminal justice on a basis of isolationism are those that choose isolation more generally. In general, one country would not wish to be regarded as the harbour of the fugitives from another with which it wished to maintain reasonable relations. Conversely, if one country wished to maintain reasonable relations with another country that held sympathies for the fugitive, it would not wish to extradite to that country's enemy. There are prudential reasons why one country should have regard to the criminal law of others in fixing its criminal law. Even a country with a political commitment, for example, to the legalisation of heroin might still not legalise on its own for fear of the social consequences of attracting large numbers of addicts. A country that wished to maintain reasonable relations with countries that do not countenance drugs would come under pressure not to decriminalise. Internationalisation of criminal law means internationalisation of enforcement mechanisms, of the means of obtaining and using evidence and even of punishment. It also implies homogenisation of substantive laws and the creation of enforcement structures involving far greater interdependence between countries.

Beyond these practical considerations there is a clear expressive function in internationalisation, which is that the international dimension of criminal law allows a 'we' to be created across international frontiers[3] of legislators and other powerful groups, and for it to be juxtaposed against 'them'—the international (that is, most dangerous) criminal. 'Terrorism, fraud, drugs, paedophilia and organised crime bad: law and order good', is chanted like some kind of *mantra* in the struggle to extend jurisdiction and to gain greater enforcement powers. The movement to internationalise has been implemented by the mutual undertaking of treaty obligations followed (in countries like the United Kingdom where there is such a constitutional necessity) by legislating treaty obligations into domestic law.

---

[2] Neil MacCormick, *Questioning Sovereignty: Law, State, and Nation in the European Commonwealth* (Oxford, Oxford University Press, 1999).

[3] Interestingly described by Paul Mitchell as 'English-speaking justice'. See Paul Mitchell, 'English-Speaking Justice: evolving Responses to Transnational forcible Abduction after *Alvarez-Machain*' (1996) 29 *Cornell International Law Journal* 383.

One of the prime instruments of the New World Economic Order is the radical concept of mutual evaluation, which involves inspecting not just the enactment of legislation to ensure formal compliance but its implementation.[4]

While measures to combat domestic money laundering can, if necessary, be put in place at the national level, by each country acting with determination and appropriate policies, it is claimed that an effective solution to the international money laundering problem can be found only at the international level.[5] In a departure from the fairly insular history of jurisdiction in English criminal law, the Home Office review of jurisdiction[6] recommended that the instantiation of extra-territorial jurisdiction be considered where one of the following factors was present;

(i)   the offence is serious;
(ii) where, by virtue of the nature of the offence, the witnesses and evidence necessary for the prosecution are likely to be available in the United Kingdom;
(iii) where there is international consensus that certain conduct is reprehensible and that concerted action is needed, involving the taking of extra-territorial jurisdiction;
(iv) where the vulnerability of the victim makes it particularly important to tackle instances of the offence;
(v)   where it appears to be in the interests of the standing and reputation of the United Kingdom in the international community;
(vi) where there is a danger that the offences would not otherwise be justiciable.

Of these, a case can be made that (i) (ii) (iii) (v) and (vi) may be satisfied in the case of money laundering. It is central to the development of an internationalised criminal law.

GLOBALISATION

The globalisation of the world economy, and in particular of world capital markets, has been at the heart of the development of the international régime in respect of money laundering. To all intents and purposes, within the developed world, money can be moved anywhere instantly. Globalisation has many consequences that neo-classical economics holds to be desirable, but there are, it is conceded,[7] costs. One of the costs of globalisation is the danger of sudden, large

---

[4] Michael Levi, 'Terrorist Financing and Money Laundering: a new paradigm for Crime control?' (forthcoming).

[5] Vito Tanzi, *Money Laundering and the International Financial System*, IMF Working Paper 96/55 (Washington DC, International Monetary Fund, 1996) at 11. And see above, 48.

[6] Home Office Review of Jurisdiction (1996) cited at Home Office, *Raising Standards and Upholding Integrity The Prevention of Corruption* (London, Stationery Office, 2000) para 2.21.

[7] Eg Vito Tanzi, *Money Laundering and the International Financial System*, IMF Working Paper 96/55 (Washington DC, International Monetary Fund, 1996) at 1.

capital movements prompted by speculators, or investors with 'herd instincts'. Another is the easier access which countries with structural (rather than cyclical) deficits have to foreign borrowing, which gives easier access to capital markets for laundering. Here lies a paradox. With the advent of globalisation, currency controls are lifted. Yet concern with laundering gives a new set of reasons for the regulation of currency transactions. The European Council resolves it thus:

> [F]ar from being restrictive in nature and or an obstacle to liberalisation, a successful effort against money laundering is in fact an essential pre-condition for enhancing international trade and commerce, financial market liberalisation and the free movement of capital under optimal conditions.[8]

MOVING MONEY

Money laundering would never have become an issue for international legal co-operation unless it had been possible to move money between jurisdictions. There are innumerable ways in which this is done, both physically and electronically. The liberalised global financial system has taken on characteristics that are as conducive to money laundering as to any other form of money movement.[9] The Internet, too, has radically affected many areas of commerce. It allows the maintenance of a bank account in jurisdiction A by a person in jurisdiction B so asto buy goods in jurisdiction C with the currency of jurisdiction D for delivery anywhere in the world. Telephone and Internet banking places a strain on 'know-your-customer' requirements[10] because the amount of face-to-face contact between customer and bank is reduced.[11] Access can be from anywhere in the world, and the bank will only rarely be able to tell the location from which it is gained (because access will generally be indirect, via an Internet service provider). Transactions can take place without any bank employee/customer interaction at all. The nature of the Internet is such that a particular country may find it difficult to stop its citizens from setting up accounts elsewhere. A set of specific recommendations for control has been made by the FATF.[12]

Identification of the customer at the beginning of the business relationship, which is at the core of the FATF and EU systems of regulation, is not enough in the case where the customer subsequently begins to engage in laundering activ-

[8] Proposal for a European Parliament and Council Directive amending Council Directive 91/308/EEC of 10 June 1991 (Document 599PC0352).

[9] Jack Blum *et al*, *Financial Havens, Banking Secrecy and Money-Laundering*, UNDCP technical series issue 8 (New York City, NY, United Nations, 1998) 21.

[10] See the section below ch 12, 'Know Your Customer'.

[11] Hence the FSA's response to the recommendation in the Cruikshank report (*Report on competition in UK banking: assessment* (Norwich, Stationery Office, 2000): Financial Services Authority, *The Money Laundering Theme: tackling our new responsibilities* (2001) Annex B.

[12] Financial Action Task Force, *Report on Money Laundering Typologies* (Paris, OECD, 2000) 4.

ity. Money laundering might develop in these facilities, conducted by customers who are known to their banks. Even had currency controls not been abolished the Internet would have made their maintenance, except in areas totally insulated from the effects of globalisation, impossible. Such attempts as have been made to impose some degree of regulation in the area, however draconian, are unlikely to have much practical significance.

THE UNITED NATIONS

Global economics is one side of the internationalisation coin. The other is to be found in international law and politics. Although many of the developments, relating to money laundering, both Europe and the Americas, are regional, the starting point should be treaties of global effect. Efforts to put in place an international framework to deal with drug trafficking predate the United Nations.[13] The first duty to confiscate was imposed by the Convention for the Suppression of the Illicit Traffic in Dangerous Drugs.[14] The first serious venture of the United Nations in this area was the Single Convention on Narcotic Drugs,[15] Article 4 of which provides:

> The parties shall take such legislative and administrative measures as may be necessary: (a) to give effect to and carry out the provisions of this Convention within their own territories; (b) to co-operate with other States in the execution of the provisions of this Convention; . . .

Article 35 provides:

> Having due regard to their constitutional, legal and administrative systems, the parties shall: (a) make arrangements at the national level for the co-ordination of preventive and repressive action against the illicit traffic; . . . [of narcotic drugs]; (b) assist each other in the campaign against the illicit traffic in narcotic drugs; (c) co-operate closely with each other . . . with a view to maintaining a co-ordinated campaign against the illicit traffic; (d) ensure that international co-operation between the appropriate agencies be conducted in an expeditious manner; and (e) ensure that where legal papers are transmitted internationally for the purposes of a prosecution, the transmittal be effected in an expeditious manner to the bodies designated by the Parties; . . .

Article 37 provides for drugs substances and equipment to be liable to seizure and confiscation. The protocol to the Convention[16] was executed in 1972.[17]

---

[13] International Opium Convention, The Hague (1912); Convention Limiting the Manufacture and Regulating the Distribution of Narcotic Drugs (1931). See M Cherif Bassouni, 'Critical Reflections on International and National Control of Drugs', (1990) *Denver Journal of International Law and Policy* 388.

[14] Convention for the Suppression of the Illicit Traffic in Dangerous Drugs (1939) Article 10.

[15] Single Convention on Narcotic Drugs (520 UNTS 204, 1961).

[16] Protocol to the Single Convention on Narcotic Drugs (1972) (Cmnd 7466).

[17] Synthetic drugs were treated by the Convention on Psychotropic Substances (1971) 1019 UNTS 175.

The Vienna Convention

The pivotal development in the global crusade against laundering was the United Nations Convention against Illicit Traffic in Narcotic Drugs and Psychotropic Substances, made at Vienna in 1988.[18] Early drugs agreements regulated production and regulated dissemination. By the mid 1980s, the perception was that these initiatives did not deal effectively with the complexity of drug dealing, or provide adequate mechanisms for dealing with them. In December 1984 the UN General Assembly adopted a resolution expressing the conviction that 'the wide scope of the illicit trade in narcotic drugs and its consequences make it necessary to prepare a convention which considers the various aspects of the problem as a whole.'[19] A lengthy period of negotiation ended with the Vienna Convention.[20] Article 3 obliges signatory nations to criminalise a list of activities to do with drug trafficking and obliges them to criminalise intentional money laundering in relation to various offences of drug trafficking, and to take steps to ensure that bank secrecy does not impede enforcement, in particular cross-border enforcement. The other provisions were designed to ensure that drug-related crimes were treated seriously in all the jurisdictions concerned. Article 5 requires party States to enact domestic laws providing for the confiscation of all forms of property, proceeds or instrumentalities used in or derived from covered offences. It also provides[21] that each party signatory shall empower its courts or other competent authorities to order that bank, financial or commercial records be made available in such a way as to override its local banking secrecy laws. Article 6 provides for the extradition of launderers. Article 7 prohibits a State signatory from invoking banking secrecy as a reason not to proffer mutual legal assistance. The Convention entered into force on 19 November 1990, and by September 1994 had attracted 148 States and the European Community. In addition, the UK, which ratified in 1991, has acted to extend its application to jurisdictions for whose foreign affairs it is responsible, including Bermuda, the Cayman Islands and the British Virgin Islands.[22] Many producer nations accept its obligations. Failure to enact domestic legislation criminalising efforts at concealing or disguising the illicit source of drugs and money laundering proceeds constitutes non-compliance under the Convention.

---

[18] And see David P Stewart, 'Internationalising the War on Drugs: the UN Convention Against Illicit Traffic in Narcotic Drugs and Psychotropic Substances' (1990) 18 *Denver Journal of International Law and Policy* 387.

[19] William C Gilmore, *Dirty money: the evolution of money laundering counter-measures*, 2nd edn (Strasbourg, Council of Europe Press, 1999) at 50, citing General Assembly resolution on International Campaign Against Traffic in Narcotic Drugs, UN Doc A/RES/39/141 at 7.

[20] Convention against Illicit Traffic in Narcotic Drugs and Psychotropic Substances, Vienna, 1988.

[21] Art 5(3).

[22] William C Gilmore, *Dirty money: the evolution of money laundering counter-measures*, 2nd edn (Strasbourg, Council of Europe Press, 1999) at 50.

There is still some question as to the lasting effect that the Convention has had.[23]

Whilst the Convention marked the last legislative action of the United Nations in respect of drug money laundering, it by no means marked the end of the interest of the organisation. In 1993, the UN Model law on Money Laundering, Confiscation and International Co-operation in relation to Drugs[24] was promulgated, as an aid to civil law countries. The Global Programme against Money Laundering (1997–99), implemented by the Office for Drug Control and Crime Prevention, was a means of putting in place technical co-operation, including the transfer of expertise for the establishment of FIUs, and the use of preventative strategies against drug-related laundering, including the international money laundering information network (IMoLIN).[25] Immediately following the attacks on the United States in September 2001, the Security Council of the United Nations passed a resolution condemning it,[26] and shortly thereafter a resolution setting out obligations in respect of the financing of terrorism.[27]

THE COUNCIL OF EUROPE

The Council of Europe was established in 1949 with a human rights focus. It was originally conceived as the organisation ensuring and evangelising the values underpinning the European Convention on Human Rights. Nowadays its Conventions deal not so much with rights against the State, but with agreements by States to criminalise. For some years it filled the gap left by the diffidence of the EU to broach matters of criminal law. Now it struggles to maintain independent significance by looking eastwards. The Council of Europe does not have the power, as does the EU, to bind the UK. It does, however, have express power to deal in the area of criminal law (which had been omitted from the Treaty of Rome), by proposing criminal laws and giving recognition to the idea that a common policy must be pursued in order for anything to be achieved. The enormous significance of the requirements of the Council of Europe is that its membership extends to many of the areas, in particular Central and Eastern Europe, in or from which 'dirty' money is suspected to originate. Especially if

[23] Jimmy Gurulé, 'The 1988 UN Convention against illicit traffic in narcotic drugs and psychotropic substances—a ten year perspective: is international cooperation merely illusory?' (1998) 22 *Fordham International Law Journal* 74.

[24] United Nations, International Drug Control Programme, *Model law on Money Laundering, Confiscation and International Co-operation in relation to Drugs* (Vienna, United Nations, November 1995).

[25] And for other global law enforcement co-operation see William C Gilmore, *Dirty money: the evolution of money laundering counter-measures*, 2nd edn (Strasbourg, Council of Europe Press, 1999) 69 *et seq*.

[26] SRES 1368 (2001).

[27] Implemented in the United Kingdom by Terrorism (United Nations Measures) Order (SI 2001 No 3365).

the EU puts in place the proposed charter of rights, the focus of the future work of the Council of Europe will move east into Asia.

In the late 1970s, concern over a growing number of criminal acts like kidnapping prompted the Council of Europe to examine the problems that had arisen in European countries as a result of money laundering.[28] A select committee reported, and there followed a period of analysis and deliberation that culminated in 1980 with the adoption of a formal recommendation.[29] This recommendation focuses on prevention, particularly by means of the central banks, and on banks having identity checks. It was neither widely accepted nor implemented.[30] The historical significance of the recommendation is that it was the first time that any body that could be identified with the 'international community' had stated the position that the support of the financial sector was necessary to combat money laundering. This is, for example, the origin of the 'know-your-customer' requirement that requires financial institutions to identify customers through supporting evidence.[31]

In the late 1980s, the Council was responsible for the work underpinning the 1990 Convention. In 1986, the European Ministers of Justice, in consideration of the UN's work up to the 1988 Convention, asked the Council on Crime Problems to develop 'international norms and standards to guarantee effective international co-operation between judicial (and, where necessary police) authorities as regards the detection, freezing and forfeiture of the proceeds of illicit drug trafficking.' A select committee was established, whose work became the principal influence upon the 1990 Convention.[32] The Convention required the extension of the criminalisation of intentional money laundering beyond its association with drug trafficking.[33] Not only can laundered money be the product of *any* predicate offence, but the offence need not have occurred within the jurisdiction.[34] Subsequent Council of Europe instruments dealing with specific offences contain provisions relating to the laundering of their proceeds.[35] The Convention requires co-operation in the investigation and confiscation of proceeds. Since the Convention, the Council has been instrumental in the provision of conferences and seminar to countries of Central and Eastern Europe and promulgating a series of papers setting out best practice for the conduct of operations against fraud, drugs and organised crime. The political impact of

---

[28] This section relies upon William C Gilmore, *Dirty money: the evolution of money laundering counter-measures,* 2nd edn (Strasbourg, Council of Europe Press, 1999) 121–54.

[29] Measures Against the Transfer and Safekeeping of Funds of Criminal Origin: Recommendation and Explanatory Memorandum Council of Europe Rec No R (80) 10.

[30] Hans Nilsson, 'The Council of Europe Laundering Convention: A Recent Example of a Developing International Criminal Law' (1991) 2 *Criminal Law Forum* 419 at 423.

[31] And see the section below ch 12, 'Know Your Customer'.

[32] Council of Europe Convention on Laundering, Search, Seizure and Confiscation of the Proceeds of Crime (ETS 141, 1990).

[33] Art 6.

[34] Art 6(2)(a).

[35] Eg Council of Europe, Criminal Law Convention on Corruption (ETS no 173) Art 13.

such statements is significant. In particular, the statements of best practice can contribute towards the development of shared expertise.

The jurisdiction of the EU over laundering stems from its jurisdiction over markets. If the dangers of money laundering are really dangers to markets, then laundering is something to which the Union should have regard. There is a clear tension between this concern and the fact that the European Union still has no formal power to put in place criminal laws. Since the Treaty of Maastricht (1993), the original hesitance concerning bringing the law of the Union to bear upon criminal law has been much attenuated.[37]

The Money Laundering Directive

As against the United Nations and the Council of Europe, the EU has a special constitutional significance. Other treaties are exhortatory. Directives from the EU raise obligations. The first reference to laundering in the EU literature was in a resolution of the European Parliament in October 16 1986.[38] The Directive on Money Laundering[39] simply provides that member States shall ensure that laundering is prohibited, but without specifying the mechanism by which the prohibition is to be achieved.[40] The key features of the Money Laundering Directive are that: member States must ensure that laundering the proceeds of serious crimes is itself prohibited;[41] that credit and financial institutions[42] must require identification of their customers by means of supporting evidence when entering into business relations; that credit and financial institutions must maintain adequate records of transactions and identification for at least five years; that credit and financial institutions must co-operate with national law enforcement authorities and must inform them of any fact which might be an indication of money laundering; that credit and financial institutions must carry out adequate staff training to ensure that their staff are aware of the law and are trained to spot potentially suspicious transactions; and that member States must

---

[36] And see Konstantinos D Magliveras, n 36 above.

[37] Estella Baker, 'Taking European Criminal Law Seriously' [1998] *Crim LR* 361.

[38] And see Konstantinos D Magliveras, 'The European Community's Combat Against Money Laundering: Analysis And Evaluation' (1998) 5 *ILSA Journal of International & Comparative Law* 93.

[39] Council Directive 91/308: on the legislative history see Konstantin D Magliveras, 1994, 'Money Laundering and the European Communities', in J Norton (ed), *Banks: Fraud and Crime* (London, Lloyds of London Press, 1994) 171, 174–5.

[40] And see Ross Cranston, *Principles of Banking Law* (Oxford, Oxford University Press, 1997) 76.

[41] Art 2.

[42] This goes beyond simply banking. Credit Institutions are defined in accordance with the first banking directive, Council Directive 77/780 as amended (89/646) and financial institutions as defined in Art 1(6) of Council Directive 89/646/EEC.

extend the provisions of the Directive to any businesses that engage in activities which are 'particularly likely to be used for money-laundering purposes'.[43] It does not matter whether the predicate offence took place in a member or third party State.[44] The Directive requires customers and beneficial owners to be identified when entering into business relations, for example, when opening an account or setting up a deposit box facility. Records are to be kept and special attention is to be given to transactions that appear particularly likely, by their nature, to be connected to money laundering. The Directive is the source of the obligation upon banks to co-operate with the authorities.[45] It is in consequence of the Directive that the banking secrecy laws in the EU were broken down.[46] The Directive has been implemented outside the EU by various mechanisms.[47]

Magliveras[48] criticised the breadth of the definition of what is to amount to predicate offences for the purposes of the Directive. The definition includes 'the cultivation, production, manufacture, transportation and sale of narcotic drugs and the management or financing of any of these activities', and 'any other criminal activity designated as such for the purposes of this directive by each Member State.' Member States were consequently not *compelled* by the Directive to extend their national provisions beyond drugs. Any disparity will impact in areas where, like extradition and mutual legal assistance, there is a double criminality provision.

Implementation and Review of the Directive

Following the 1991 Directive, two reports were presented to the Council of Ministers and to the European Parliament assessing the success of its implementation. The first Commission report called for a more co-ordinated approach, including central reporting units.[49] The European Parliament considered this report and responded with a 21-point resolution calling for the extension of the Directive beyond drugs to the proceeds of all organised crime, and for the extension of the range of occupations governed by the Directive.[50]

---

[43] This synopsis is taken from Select Committee on European Scrutiny, *Twenty-Eighth Report*, para 17.2 (1999).

[44] Art 1.

[45] Arts 6, 8–10.

[46] And see Ayman Rizkalla, 'Money Laundering: The European Approach' (1998) 13 *Tulane European and Civil Law Forum* 111.

[47] Second Commission Report to the European Parliament and the Council on the Implementation of the Money Laundering Directive COM (1998) 401 final, 5–7.

[48] And see Konstantinos D Magliveras, 'The European Community's Combat Against Money Laundering: Analysis And Evaluation' (1998) 5 *ILSA Journal of International and Comparative Law* 93 at 99.

[49] First Commission report on Money Laundering Directive COM(95)54 final Brussels 3 March 1995.

[50] OJ No C 198, 8 July 1996; Appendix 2 to Second Commission Report to the European Parliament and the Council on the Implementation of the Money Laundering Directive COM (1998) 401 final.

The second report[51] recommended extension of the rules to cover the legal profession, and expressed concern as to markets not hitherto covered, for example in antiques. An appendix dealt with the increasingly important issue of the application of 'know your customer' rules in the case where, due to access taking place over the Internet or some other means, there is no face-to-face transaction.

Financial Intelligence Units[52]

Article 6 of the Money Laundering Directive placed credit and financial institutions under the duty to report to the competent authorities, on their own initiative, any fact which might be an indication of money laundering. The text left the implementation of the obligation to the individual States. The designation 'Financial Intelligence Unit' came later. The variety of responses has been characterised[53] as falling within three models—judicial, police, and independent. The problems that arise from the absence of congruity of model between countries amplify the normal difficulties which would arise from the storage and reciprocal transfer of information.

Jurisdictions entered into memoranda of understanding to iron out the creases in this provision. Mitselagis has identified the following problems in the operation of these memoranda. First, it is difficult for a unit that is constituted as independent of the State, or as an administrative body, to exchange information with one founded within the police. It is at the heart of the idea of constituting a judicial unit that sensitive information is not to be communicated to law enforcement authorities. Conversely, it is unconstitutional for many police units, as *State* units, to exchange information with independent 'non-state' bodies.[54] Secondly, there are differences in the definition of the predicate offence adopted in various jurisdictions.[55] Although the tendency is towards expansion of the notion of predicate offence, at least to 'all serious crime'[56] the definitions still vary from jurisdiction to jurisdiction. Tax evasion is a crime in respect of which there remains inconsistency among countries.[57]

---

[51] Second Commission Report to the European Parliament and the Council on the Implementation of the Money Laundering Directive COM (1998) 401 final.

[52] For fuller consideration see Guy Stessens, *Money Laundering: A New International Law Enforcement Model* (Cambridge, Cambridge University Press, 2000) 143–82.

[53] By Valsamis Mitsilegas, 'New Forms of Transnational Policing: The Emergence of Financial Intelligence Units in the European Union and the Challenges for Human Rights' (1998) 3 *Journal of Money Laundering Control* 147, 147.

[54] Mitsilegas, *ibid*, at 155.

[55] Mitsilegas, *ibid*, at 155.

[56] Second Commission Report to the European Parliament and the Council on the Implementation of the Money Laundering Directive COM (1998) 401 final.

[57] Guy Stessens, *Money Laundering: A New International Law Enforcement Model* (Cambridge, Cambridge University Press, 2000) 49–50.

An informal grouping (the Egmont Group) was formed in 1995 to try to improve the functioning of FIUs at their respective national levels, and to enhance co-operation at the international level. It adopted a common definition of FIU in 1996 with a certification procedure. Recognition in this way confers some benefits,[58] the most significant of which is access to the Egmont secure intranet and email system for information exchange.[59]

The Amending Directive

The generation of an amended or second directive was early agreed upon as an objective.[60] The Commission accepted that, although implementation was generally satisfactory, a new money laundering Directive was necessary to up-date and extend the coverage of the 1991 measure.[61] The Commission's Action Plan for Financial Services[62] made such an Amending Directive a priority.[63] Over a numbers of years, various proposals were the subject of scrutiny.

The Amending Directive had been foundering on the question of the extent of the encroachment of lawyer/client confidentiality, but the events of 11 September 2001, and the promulgation very soon thereafter of the idea that controls upon international terrorism required more effective control of money laundering, gave it fresh impetus.[64] After much wrangling between Member States, the text of the Amending Directive was finally agreed in a conciliation procedure between the European Parliament and the European Council on 19 November 2001.

The Amending Directive obliges Member States to extend their anti-money laundering régimes to combat the proceeds of all serious crime. The categories of criminal offences covered by the Amending Directive are now to be defined to include any of the drug trafficking offences defined in Article 3(1)(a) of the Vienna Convention; the activities of criminal organisations;[65] serious fraud;[66]

---

[58]   Mitsilegas, n 53 above, at 156.

[59]   And see Appendix 7 to Second Commission Report to the European Parliament and the Council on the Implementation of the Money Laundering Directive COM (1998) 401 final.

[60]   599PC0352 Proposal for a European Parliament and Council Directive amending Council Directive 91/308/EEC of 10 June 1991 on prevention of the use of the financial system for the purpose of money laundering (Feb 2001).

[61]   Second Commission Report to the European Parliament and the Council on the Implementation of the Money Laundering Directive, 4.

[62]   Financial Services—Implementing the Framework for Financial Markets: Action Plan. Commission Communication of 11.05.1999 COM(1999)232.

[63]   Select Committee on European Scrutiny, *Twenty-Eighth Report*, Para 13.1 Exchange of information by financial information units on Money Laundering Draft Decision on arrangements for co-operation between Financial Intelligence Units of the Member States in respect of exchanging information received under the provisions of the Council Directive on prevention of the use of the financial system for money laundering. (20342) 9961/99 CRIMORG 101.

[64]   Tony Blair, HC Debates 14 September 2001, cols 606 and 609: Jack Straw *ibid*, col 619.

[65]   As defined in Art 1 of Joint Action 98/733/JHA.

[66]   As defined in Art 1(1) and Art 2 of the Convention on the protection of the European Communities' financial interests.

corruption; and any offence which may generate substantial proceeds and which is punishable by a severe sentence of imprisonment in accordance with the penal law of the Member State. Legal professional privilege was restricted.

Beyond the Directives

There are other EU measures which impact upon money laundering. The Third Pillar of Maastricht generated a series of measures that impact in the area of money laundering. The Convention on the use of information technology for customs purposes[67] provides for direct access to data on the EU Customs information system for national customs authorities and other competent authorities, so as to achieve the aims of 'preventing, investigating and prosecuting serious contraventions of national laws.'[68]

The Second Protocol to the Convention for the Protection of the Communities' Financial Interests[69] contains provisions concerning laundering of the proceeds of fraud and corruption to the detriment of the Community budget, the responsibility of legal persons and the confiscation of the proceeds of such conduct, and co-operation between the commission and national prosecuting authorities. This provision has been used as a legal basis for the exchange of information between Financial Intelligence Units at EU level.

The idea that the major enemy is 'organised crime' is to be found in the Action Plan[70] on making it a criminal offence to participate in a criminal organisation, which was adopted by the Council on 28 April 1997. Chapter VI deals with organised crime and money laundering. It aspires towards high levels of co-operation and two-way information exchange between financial and fiscal institutions and law enforcement and judicial authorities.[71] The plan calls for the establishment of a system of information exchange, consistently with data protection provisions, at EU level to combat money laundering,. One of its recommendations was that money laundering provisions should extend beyond the 'classical financial sector' to other institutions. The European Parliament in March 1999 adopted a resolution calling upon the Commission to include estate agents, art dealers, auctioneers, casinos, *bureaux de change*, transporters of funds, notaries, accountants, advocates, tax advisers and auditors. The Commission agreed to these proposals, save for the inclusion of art and antique dealers and auctioneers. It considered that there would be serious problems in defining exactly the coverage provided by the rules, and could see nothing in principle to distinguish art dealers from car dealers, jewellery shops or stamp

---

[67] Convention on the use of information technology for customs purposes 27 Nov 1995 OJ C 316.
[68] Art 2(2).
[69] 1995 OJ C 89 15 March 1995.
[70] Joint action 98/733/JHA of 21 December 1998 on making it a criminal offence to participate in a criminal organisation in the Member States of the European Union 1998 OJ L 351; 1999 OJ L 57.
[71] Point 6g.

and coin dealers. Of course, there is nothing in principle to distinguish any one form of trade from any other. In the terms of the style of reasoning which has informed the development of criminal law, the logical step must be to extend the definition as widely as possible. The effect of any exclusion upon the rational launderer could only be that a greater proportion of money is laundered through the excluded categories. However had the legislation been introduced on the basis that all forms of commerce, or all transactions over a prescribed limit, were to be governed by prescriptions requiring the reporting of suspicious transactions, then there would have been great opposition.[72]

Article K.3 of the Treaty on European Union empowers the Council of Ministers to adopt joint actions in all matters of common interest in the fields of justice and home affairs, where the objectives can better be met collectively than individually. The areas of common interest include fraud, immigration and asylum. On 3 December 1998, the Council adopted a Joint Action on money laundering, the identification, tracing, freezing and seizing of the instrumentalities and the proceeds of crime.[73] Under the Joint Action, no reservations are to be made under Article 6 of the Strasbourg Convention,[74] in respect of any serious offence (defined by reference to a maximum term of imprisonment of 12 months). Article 6 deals with laundering offences, so the effect is that Member States have agreed to criminalise laundering the proceeds of all serious offences.

As a consequence of the 1998 Joint Action the Commission considered whether the reporting obligation should be extended to all 'serious offences' so defined, and adopted a more placatory position in respect of the people who would be doing the reporting than has the UK Government. The financial sector has expressed considerable reticence concerning any reporting requirement that would extend to an excessively wide range of offences,[75] even including relatively minor ones.[76]

The Commission concluded that for the purposes of the Directive, and its extension to certain non-financial activities, a reporting obligation based on serious offences might be too broad. The Commission proposed that the reporting obligation apply only to activities linked to organised crime[77] or damage to the financial interests of the European Communities. It was thought that a clearer sense of the objectives might give better guidance to the financial sector

---

[72] And see the section above ch 1, The General and Particular in Criminal Lawmaking.
[73] OJ L 333 9 December 1998.
[74] That is, the Council of Europe Convention.
[75] No criteria are given to determine what might be excess.
[76] Explanatory memorandum to proposal to amend 1991 Money Laundering Directive (Document 599PC 0532).
[77] Art 1 of the Joint Action defines 'organised crime': 'Within the meaning of this joint action, a criminal organisation shall mean a structured association, established over a period of time, of more than two persons, acting in concert with a view to committing offences which are punishable by deprivation of liberty or a detention order of a maximum of at least four years or a more serious penalty, whether such offences are an end in themselves or a means of obtaining material benefits and, where appropriate, of improperly influencing the operation of public authorities.'

than a reporting requirement based only upon specific penalties, which might not be known.[78]

Article 30 of the Justice and Home Affairs pillar provides for common action in the field of police co-operation, including the 'collection, storage, processing, analysis and exchange of relevant information, including information held by law enforcement services on reports of suspicious financial transactions, in particular through Europol, subject to appropriate provision in the protection of personal data.[79] Europol, established by the Council of Ministers in 1995, has a wide *aegis*.[80] It covers the laundering of the proceeds of the forms of serious crime.[81] It was granted operational powers in the Amsterdam Treaty.[82] Data are to be included in the Europol system not only relating to persons suspected of committing or being an accomplice to an offence within the Europol terms of reference, but also to persons in respect of whom 'there are serious grounds for believing they will commit criminal offences'. Systems for the dissemination of data of this nature are only as reliable as the information. The danger is to individual liberties as a consequence of unreliable tittle-tattle being presented as reliable information upon the basis of which the police should act.

OLAF & Eurojust

Community powers are restricted to co-ordination, co-operation and investigation. But the institutions are pushing the previous limits. Under the Maastricht version of Article 209 A EC, a Commission unit, UCLAF (*Unité de coordination de la lutte anti-fraude*) was set up and is given the task of leading the 'fight against fraud'. Although it was ultimately dependent on the Member States as far as the prosecution of cases is concerned, it was given powers of investigation of its own (of on-the-spot-checks and inspections) in the sphere of fraud and irregularities under Community law.[83] This regulation makes no provision to deal with the fact that such checks can be an interference with citizens' rights, especially national privacy rights and those under Article 8 of the European Convention on Human Rights[84] and has set a precedent for criminal law related competence of the EC. After scandals in 1998 a more wide-ranging office (OLAF) was created.

---

[78] Proposal for a European Parliament and Council Directive amending Council Directive 91/308/EEC of 10 June 1991 on prevention of the use of the financial system for the purpose of money laundering: COM/99/0352 final—COD 99/0152.

[79] Art 30(1)(b).

[80] The Europol Convention OJ C 316 1 (1995).

[81] Art 2(1) includes a non-exhaustive list concluding 'unlawful drug trafficking and other serious forms of international crime when there is an organised or transnational crime element in the case'.

[82] New Art 30.

[83] Regulation 2815/96, OJ 1996, L 292 p 2 was based on Art 235 (now 308) EC. And see Leonard Besselink, 'Sovereignty, Criminal Law and the New European Context' in Peter Alldridge and Chrisje Brants (eds), *Personal Autonomy, the Private Sphere and the Criminal Law—A Comparative Study* (Oxford, Hart, 2000) 93.

[84] Under Art 5 'economic operators' are required to grant access to 'premises, land, means of transport or other areas, used for business purposes'.

Member States are obliged under the terms of the Maastricht Treaty[85] to establish close liaison between their competent departments with the assistance of OLAF in order to protect the financial interests of the Community. The Advisory Committee on the Fight against Fraud (a committee of senior officials, especially those involved in customs) meets regularly. In 2002 Eurojust was instigated. It is a permanent unit of investigating judges with cross-border powers of investigation. The plan is that it will evolve into a judicial equivalent of Europol, to fight international crime and harmonise European law-enforcement procedures.

THE INTERNATIONAL MONETARY FUND AND THE WORLD BANK

The other non-regional[86] international organisations that have a significant impact upon money laundering are the IMF and the OECD. The establishment of the International Monetary Fund and the World Bank by the Bretton Woods Agreement in 1944 was part of a system that contemplated fixed exchange rates and exchange controls. The primary goals of the organisation are to promote exchange rate stability and to help members achieve balance of payments equilibrium. The move away from both has left the IMF, which is not without its critics,[87] pursuing other roles in international affairs. When the IMF monitors a country, one of the matters to which regard is had is the to treatment of 'dirty money', and when the World Bank lends money it lends on conditions, including conditions as to the local money laundering régime. The Fund also publishes highly influential works in economics.[88]

FINANCIAL ACTION TASK FORCE[89]

The major international body now involved in the attempts to deal with money laundering is the FATF established by at the G7 summit in Paris in 1989 in fulfilment of a pledge given at the Toronto summit of 1988. It is the only international body dedicated solely to the fight against money laundering.[90] It is an *ad hoc* grouping of governments with a single central concern. The FATF

---

[85] Art 209a(2).

[86] This book will not deal with regional organisations in the Caribbean or the Americas. On these see William C Gilmore, *Dirty money: the evolution of money laundering counter-measures*, 2nd edn (Strasbourg, Council of Europe Press, 1999) 27–48.

[87] Kevin Danaher(ed), *Fifty Years is Enough: the Case Against the World Bank and the International Monetary Fund* (Boston, MA, South End Press, 1994).

[88] As to money laundering see Peter Quirk, *Macroeconomic Implications of Money Laundering*, IMF Working Paper WP/96/66; Vito Tanzi, *Money Laundering and the International Financial System*, IMF Working Paper WP/96/55, discussed above, see ch 2 n 1.

[89] And see Alexander Kern, 'The international anti-money-laundering regime: the role of the Financial Action Task Force' (2001) 4 *Journal of Money Laundering Control* 231–48.

[90] William C Gilmore, *Dirty money: the evolution of money laundering counter-measures*, 2nd edn (Strasbourg, Council of Europe Press, 1999) 79–120.

includes representatives of 26 governments representing the world's financial centres.[91] With its support, a Caribbean FATF and the Asia-Pacific Group on Money Laundering have been established, and also newer groups in Africa. The objective is a world-wide network. It acts by the promulgation of a set of 40 recommendations as to how States should regulate financial services. The recommendations[92] place great emphasis upon financial institutions, laying down a series of concrete steps that banks should take. The 40 recommendations introduced duties of customer identification, record keeping and suspicious transaction reporting.[93] In 1991, the FATF issued a statement indicating that its members had agreed to a process of mutual assessment to ensure that the 40 recommendations were being put into practice.[94] The 40 recommendations were revised in 1996. The UK was evaluated in 1996 by the FATF and found to have an anti-money laundering system 'which meets, and in many areas goes beyond, the forty recommendations.'[95] It was the FATF that required, in 1996, the extension of 'predicate offences' beyond drugs offences to cover serious crimes. The rationale was that having a wider range of predicate offences should improve suspicious transaction reporting. It was the FATF also, in 1999, which issued guidance in the interpretation of the 40 recommendations requiring tax evasion to be recognised as a predicate offence.[96]

The FATF recommendations have no binding effect. There is a formalised procedure for the imposition of sanctions upon members who fail to comply. The most serious sanction short of expulsion is invocation of recommendation 21, which authorises FATF to urge financial institutions world-wide to scrutinise business relations with and in a designated country. Such a notice was issued against Turkey in 1996, in view of its failure to put in place money laundering laws. The defect was soon remedied.[97]

---

[91] The membership is listed at www.oecd.org/fatf. The European Commission is a full member.

[92] <http://www.oecd.org/fatf/recommendations.htm>. 'The Crown Jewel of soft law'—Guy Stessens, *Money Laundering: A New International Law Enforcement Model* (Cambridge, Cambridge University Press, 2000) 17. They are reproduced, with the 1996 revisions, in William C Gilmore, *Dirty money: the evolution of money laundering counter-measures*, 2nd edn (Strasbourg, Council of Europe Press, 1999) at 245–68.

[93] Recommendations 12, 13, 14, 15, 16.

[94] Ronald K Noble and Court E Golumbic, 'A new anti-crime framework for the world: merging the objective and subjective models for fighting money laundering', 30 *New York University Journal of International Law and Politics* 79 at 123.

[95] Cabinet Office Performance and Innovation Unit, *Recovering the Proceeds of Crime* (London, Cabinet Office, 2000) (hereinafter '*PIU Report*') Box 9.3.

[96] See the section below ch 7, Pecuniary Advantage—the Benefit.

[97] Further information may be found at http://www.oecd.org/fatf/. 'As the very final step we may also decide to prohibit financial transactions in the identified non-cooperative jurisdictions.' (Patrick Moulette, Executive Secretary of FATF, quoted in *PIU Report* Box 11.4). And see Financial Action Task Force, *Review To Identify Non-Cooperative Countries Or Territories: Increasing The Worldwide Effectiveness Of Anti-Money Laundering Measures* (Paris, FATF, 2000).

The first attempt to 'name and shame' by the publication of a blacklist of 'non-co-operative countries' took place in June 2000. Various respects were identified in which the countries in question had failed to comply with the 40 recommendations. The blacklisting process appears to have been relatively effective.[98] In the wake of the events of 11 September 2001, the FATF moved firmly into terrorist financing. It issued 8 'special recommendations'[99] and a plan of action.[100]

THE BASLE COMMITTEE

The major international agency dealing with banking supervision is the Basle Committee on Banking Regulations and Supervisory Practices. In December 1988 it adopted a statement of principles to counter money laundering. The first and most important safeguard was said to be the integrity of banks' own managements and their vigilant determination to prevent their institutions becoming associated with criminals or being used as a channel for money laundering. According to the Bingham report:

> The Basle Committee's statement of principles and the European Community Directive represented a step forward[101] in international thinking and practice. In most countries, banking supervisors had not had a role in detecting money laundering. It was during the 1980s, and against a background of growing concern about drug-trafficking, that it became accepted that bank supervisors should contribute to its prevention, although the supervisors primary concern remained to maintain the financial stability and soundness of banks.[102]

As the focus of regulatory activity dealing with money laundering has moved outwards from the banking sector, the significance of the Basle committee has waned,[103] but in 1996 the Committee produced 29 recommendations as to the effectiveness of the supervision of banks operating (as had BCCI) outside their national boundaries.[104] Subsequent activity has refined accounts of customer due diligence.[105]

---

[98] Jackie Johnson, 'Blacklisting: initial reactions, responses and repercussions' (2001) 4 *Journal of Money Laundering Control* 211.

[99] <www.oecd.org/fatf>

[100] For an excellent account and critique, see Michael Levi, 'Terrorist Financing and Money Laundering: A new Paradigm for Crime Control' (forthcoming).

[101] And compare 'Progress' in the section above ch 1.

[102] Thomas Bingham, *Inquiry into the supervision of the Bank of Credit and Commerce International* HC 198 (London, HMSO, 1992) para 1.72.

[103] And see Guy Stessens, *Money Laundering: A New International Law Enforcement Model* (Cambridge, Cambridge University Press, 2000) 134.

[104] <www.bis.org>.

[105] Basle Committee Publications, *Customer Due Diligence for Banks* (Consultative Document January 2001).

CONCLUSION

Money laundering law is a creature and has become the motor of international co-operation in financial surveillance. The development of money laundering law has been driven by international organisations, and it has blurred or removed many distinctions that previously were thought sacred. Banking secrecy has been broken down and far greater international co-operation put in place. The US has been one of the driving forces behind many of the initiatives in the internationalisation of criminal law.[106] The denial of certification invloves foreign assistance sanctions and a mandatory US vote against multilateral development bank loans.[107] The US holds greater sway at the OECD, the World Bank and the IMF than at the United Nations: developments in international efforts against laundering which come from the former are more likely to bear a US *imprimatur* than those from the latter. The principal moving forces have been the IMF, the World Bank, and, in particular, the FATF. Because of its jurisdiction over markets, the European Union has been central. Money Laundering Law is a microcosm within which the reconfiguration of national sovereignty and criminal justice is taking place.

[106] For example, corruption, as to which see Alldridge, 'Reforming the Criminal Law of Corruption' (2001) 11 *Criminal Law Forum* 287.

[107] Jimmy Gurulé 'The 1988 UN Convention against illicit traffic in narcotic drugs and psychotropic substances—a ten year perspective: is international cooperation merely illusory?' (1988) 22 *Fordham International Law Journal* 74 at 87.

6

Forfeiture Provisions

POWERS OF FORFEITURE of the objects and *impedimenta* of crime are now frequently found.[1] There is, for example, provision for the seizure and confiscation of scales and other measures made or modified for the purpose of giving short measure,[2] unlawful firearms[3] and knives.[4] Counterfeit coins and tools for making forgeries or false instruments are able to be forfeit by magistrates without a conviction.[5] Legislation governing street betting, poaching, pornography and fish conservation all contained similar provisions.[6] The Immigration and Asylum Act 1999 deals with restraint and forfeiture of transport involved in illegal immigration.[7] There are other specific powers linked to particular offences, most of which require a conviction.[8] Some, for example the power to forfeit obscene publications and counterfeit currency,[9] and powers of forfeiture by customs, do not. There were specific powers to seize and forfeit cash involved in drugs[10] and terrorism.[11] This power has been extended by the Proceeds of Crime Act 2002.

The other source of powers to forfeit was in order to enforce fiscal policies. The customs authorities have for many years had power to forfeit contraband that is being smuggled,[12] and there is apparently no question of this power being, in general, inconsistent with the European Convention.[13] It was suggested earlier that the rationale for customs forfeiture is different from that for other forfeitures, so there is a danger of a customs power spreading to areas in which it has no clear rationale.[14]

---

[1] D Hodgson, *Profits of Crime and their Recovery* (London, Heinemann, 1984) (hereinafter 'Hodgson Report') 94.

[2] Weights and Measures Act 1985 s 17.

[3] Firearms Act 1968 s 52.

[4] Knives Act 1997 s 6.

[5] Forgery and Counterfeiting Act 1981 s 7, s 24.

[6] *Hodgson Report*, 17.

[7] Immigration and Asylum Act 1999 s 25(6)

[8] *Hodgson Report*, 94.

[9] Forgery and Counterfeiting Act 1981 ss 7 & 24

[10] Drug Trafficking Act 1994 (hereinafter DTA 1994) s 42.

[11] Terrorism Act 2000 ss 28–30. In the wake of 11 September 2001 this power was extended beyond ports. Anti-Terrorism, Crime and Security Act 2001 Part 1 and Sch 1.

[12] Eg, Alcoholic Liquor Duties Act 1979 s 26(4) (and see *Hodgson Report*, 17).

[13] *AGOSI v United Kingdom* (1987) 9 EHRR 1 (*on appeal from Allgemeine Gold und Silberscheideanstalt v Customs and Excise Commissioners* [1980] QB 390; [1980] 2 All ER 138). See the section below in this ch, First Protocol—the Right to Property.

[14] See the section above ch 3, Customs Forfeitures.

FORFEITURE UPON CONVICTION

This general provision dealing with the means of commission or facilitation of crimes is section 143 of the Powers of Criminal Courts (Sentencing) Act 2000,[15] which, in the case where a conviction has been returned for an offence carrying a penalty of more than two year' imprisonment, enables the court to forfeit any interest which the defendant has in property that was used or intended to be used for committing or facilitating the commission of *any* offence. Property may only be forfeited under section 143 if it was in the possession or control of the defendant at the time of his/her arrest.[16] The other major forfeiture powers upon conviction are those in respect of the proceeds of terrorism, which are dealt with elsewhere in this book.[17]

FORFEITURE AS CRIME PREVENTION

When there is a conviction, section 143 allows forfeiture of property that has been used or was *intended* to be used for committing or facilitating the commission of a criminal offence. It follows that property may be forfeit without actually having been used in the commission of an offence. When operating in this way, the power of forfeiture is a mechanism of prophylaxis. It has been held that, where money found in the possession of a person convicted of supplying drugs is shown to be his working capital for the purchase of future supplies of drugs, it may be liable to forfeiture.[18] The objective of crime prevention could be achieved simply by seizing the property and holding it for as long as there is a danger that it will be used to commit a crime. However, the use of this power is rarely confined to crime prevention only, and frequently has a punitive element. Such use of a power of forfeiture requires further justification.

FORFEITURE AS AN ADDITIONAL PENALTY

Can forfeiture legitimately be used as an additional penalty? The Hodgson Committee was clear on this issue.

> We agree that [forfeiture] may be an appropriate type of penalty, but we think it would be wrong always to add forfeiture as an additional penalty because of some mystical connection to the wrong-doing (as with *deodand*). This type of forfeiture is in effect a fine *in specie*.[19]

---

[15] Replacing Powers of Criminal Courts Act 1973 s 43. There are also numerous specific forfeiture provisions that operate for serious offences.

[16] *R v Hinde* (1977) 64 CAR 213: compare, in this respect, the rules relating to the confiscation of after-acquired property. See the section above ch 3, Customs Forfeitures.

[17] See the section below ch 10, Involvement with Terrorist Money.

[18] *R v O'Farrell* [1988] 10 CAR(S) 74.

[19] *Hodgson Report*, 99.

The Committee consequently argued that a court should only be able to make a forfeiture order if the value of the property does not exceed the maximum fine for the offence, and where the defendant is also fined, the *total* of the financial penalties should not exceed the maximum fine. The interests of third parties are unaffected if they can show[20] that they did not consent to the defendant's possession of the item, or, if they did, that they did not know and had no reason to suspect the defendant's use of or plans for their property.[21]

In deciding whether or not to order forfeiture the court must have regard to the value of the property and to the likely financial and other effects on the offender.[22] This provision fell for consideration in *R v Buddo*,[23] where the appellant was sentenced to imprisonment for the offence in connection with which the motor caravan had been used. A forfeiture order was made depriving the appellant of his rights in the motor caravan. It was held that this was a substantial and unnecessary increase in the punishment. The court has a power, not an obligation, to apply a forfeiture order. Similarly, in *R v Joyce*[24] the court held that an order under (then) section 43, depriving an offender of his rights in property used to facilitate the commission of an offence, should be considered as part of the overall penalty for the offence and the other sentence should be adjusted accordingly. Only by adhering to this principle is the objection avoided that punishment varies according to whether or not the defendant uses his/her own property in order to offend.

In *R v Highbury Corner Stipendiary Magistrates' Court, ex parte Di Matteo*[25] the Divisional Court[26] held that a court sentencing a defendant for a criminal offence coming within what is now section 143 of the Powers of Criminal Courts (Sentencing) Act 2000, must ask itself whether, in respect of a particular offence, forfeiture of property, in conjunction with the other sentences or orders that the court proposes to make, inflicts too great a burden on the defendant and if that defendant has to be sentenced for more than one offence, the court must look at the total effect of the penalties imposed and measure that against the totality of his offending.

Under section 143, only the *defendant's* interest in the property is forfeit. The English rule does not, therefore, operate to generate objectionable consequences like those in *Bennis v Michigan*.[27] In doing this, the rule departs from its own historical rationale, which is that the *thing* is at fault. As a harbinger of other

---

[20] The burden being upon the third party: Powers of Criminal Courts (Sentencing) Act 2000 s 144(1)(b).

[21] Powers of Criminal Courts (Sentencing) Act 2000 s 144(1)(b).

[22] Powers of Criminal Courts (Sentencing) Act 2000 s 143(5).

[23] *R v Buddo* (1982) 4 CAR(S) 268.

[24] *R v Joyce* (1989) 11 CAR(S) 253.

[25] *R v Highbury Corner Stipendiary Magistrates' Court, ex parte Di Matteo* (1990) 12 CAR(S) 594; [1992] 1 All ER 102.

[26] Following a *dictum* of Russell J in *Scully* (1985) 7 CAR(S) 119, 120.

[27] Below, ch 6 A Comparator—United States' Jurisprudence (121–2).

rules incentivising policing,[28] forfeited property may be awarded by the courts directly to the police force that recovered the assets.[29]

CONFISCATION, FORFEITURE AND DOUBLE COUNTING

The harshness of forfeiture would be much reduced if it were used only as a form of confiscation *in rem* to satisfy an order for the confiscation of proceeds or a financial penalty. But if the underlying rationale is different, and if forfeiture is *neither* regarded as a punishment of a criminal nor as a means of preventing the criminal from making a profit from a crime, then there is no reason why the same object should not be the subject of a confiscation order and of forfeiture. This *reductio ad absurdum*[30] was seen in *R v Smith (David Cadman)*[31] where the House of Lords held that a person who smuggles cigarettes into the country is liable, in addition to whatever punishment is imposed upon conviction, to the forfeiture of the cigarettes and then also to a confiscation order to the value of the unpaid duty.[32]

HUMAN RIGHTS CHALLENGES TO FORFEITURE PROCEEDINGS

Forfeiture provisions are open to serious criticism in principle:[33] do they offend any human rights' precepts? There are three major options for a challenge.

First Protocol—The Right to Property

If the apparent absurdity of the *deodand* of a railway locomotive could generate change in the law to remove an archaic system in the middle nineteenth century, then it might have been imagined that the forfeiture of an aircraft would provide the challenge that would lead to the abolition of the forfeiture rules. Not so, it seems. The First Protocol to the European Convention on Human Rights states:

> Every natural or legal person is entitled to the peaceful enjoyment of his possessions except in the public interest and subject to the conditions provided for by law and by

---

[28] See below ch 11, Confiscation Without Conviction—'Civil Recovery'.

[29] Powers of Criminal Courts (Sentencing) Act 2000 s 145(1); Misuse of Drugs Act 1971 s 27(1).

[30] See also *R v Dore (Anthony)* [1997] 2 CAR(S) 152; [1997] Crim LR 299. The Court held that the statutory forfeiture procedure required that forfeiture was *subordinate* to confiscation, so that already confiscated drugs could not later be forfeited. This line was followed in *R v Berry (Paul Douglas)* [2000] 1 CAR(S) 352; [1999] Crim LR 855.

[31] [2001] UKHL 68.

[32] And the duty was apparently still payable. For critique, see the section below ch 7, Pecuniary Advantage—the Benefits.

[33] See the section above ch 3, Objections to Forfeiture.

the general principles of International Law. The preceding conditions shall not, however, in any way impair the right of a state to enforce such laws as it deems necessary to control the use of property in accordance with the general interest or to secure payment of taxes or other contributions or penalties.

The validity of *all* forfeiture legislation, with or without conviction, will turn upon its consistency with this provision. The question will be whether in imposing forfeiture a State is acting to 'control the use of property in accordance with the general interest'.[34] Do forfeiture provisions amount to a control by the State upon the use of property in accordance with the general interest such as to satisfy the proportionality test?

In *Sunday Times v UK*[35] the European Court of Human Rights explained two of the requirements that flow from the presence of the expression "prescribed by law" in ECHR Article 10(2). It said:

> The law must be adequately accessible: the citizen must be able to have an indication that is adequate in the circumstances of the legal rules applicable to a given case; (ii) A norm cannot be regarded as a 'law' unless it is formulated with sufficient precision to enable the citizen to regulate his conduct: he must be able—if need be with appropriate advice—to foresee, to a degree that is reasonable in the circumstances, the consequences which a given action may entail.[36]

In *Hentrich v France*[37] the Strasbourg court applied these principles in a case where the applicant complained of a breach of Article 1 of the First Protocol.

The European Court of Human Rights has held that although it involves a deprivation of possessions, forfeiture of property does not necessarily come within the scope of the second sentence of the first paragraph of Article 1 of Protocol.[38] In the *AGOSI*[39] case the applicants were a German company who had sold a quantity of Krugerrands subject to a retention of title clause, pursuant to which the ownership of the coins remained with them after the dishonour of the cheque tendered as payment. The Krugerrands, which were at that time prohibited goods, were seized on arrival in this country, and the purchasers were charged with an offence.[40] The court held that the forfeiture of the coins did, of course, involve a deprivation of property, but in the circumstances the

---

[34] Note that the (Strasbourg) Convention on Laundering, Search, Seizure and Confiscation of the Proceeds from Crime (emanating from the Council of Europe) does not authorise forfeiture of the instrumentalities of crime otherwise than as a means of seizing the proceeds of crime. Art 2 states: '1. Each Party shall adopt such legislative and other measures as may be necessary to enable it to confiscate instrumentalities and proceeds or property *the value of which corresponds to such proceeds*.' (emphasis added).

[35] *Sunday Times v United Kingdom* (1979–80) 2 EHRR 245.

[36] Para 49.

[37] *Hentrich v France* (1994) 18 EHRR 40.

[38] *Handyside v United Kingdom* (1979–80) 1 EHRR 737 para. 63; *AGOSI v the United Kingdom* (1987) 9 EHRR 1 para 51.

[39] *AGOSI v United Kingdom* (1987) 9 EHRR 1 (*on appeal from Allgemeine Gold und Silberscheideanstalt v Customs and Excise Commissioners* [1980] QB 390; [1980] 2 All ER 138).

[40] Under the statutory predecessor of Customs and Excise Management Act 1979 s 170.

deprivation formed a constituent element of the procedure for the control of the use in the United Kingdom of gold coins such as Krugerrands. However, the court seemed amenable to the argument that forfeiture without any kind of fault on the part of the owner should be held inconsistent with the protocol because,

> as a practical matter, where a person is free of any fault which could relate in any way to the purpose of the legislation, it is likely that the forfeiture of that property could not on any sensible construction of the legislation further the object thereof.[41]

In *Raimondo v Italy*[42] there is an indication that upon the expression in the protocol 'use of property otherwise than in accordance with the general interest' means 'in the commission of crime'. A retrenchment from that position has followed. There is no clear guidance yet on the consistency of non-prophylactic forfeiture provisions within the Convention. This is a crucial matter. In general the State does not punish a person on the basis of nothing more than an intention to commit crime. If the State is to have power to appropriate property for no other reason than that it was used to commit crime then an explanation—and little short of a theory of private property will do—must be offered.

A more fundamental human rights challenge to operation of the forfeiture rules could have come in *Air Canada v United Kingdom*.[43] The airline complained that by seizing an aircraft which had arrived at Heathrow carrying prohibited drugs, pursuant to the powers of forfeiture under the Customs and Excise Management Act 1979,[44] Customs and Excise Commissioners had violated Air Canada's rights to the quiet enjoyment of property and rights to a fair trial. Air Canada had appealed unsuccessfully against the seizure through the UK courts.[45] The European Court of Human Rights held that the exercise of the powers of seizure of the Commissioners of Customs and Excise did not involve the determination of any criminal charge under Article 6 of the Convention regarding a fair trial[46] and did involve a dispute about Air Canada's property rights. Because Air Canada had failed to apply for judicial review (and consequently had not exhausted their domestic remedies) it was not necessary to rule on whether the remedies available for the deprived property owner were adequate. The court intimated, however, that to seize an aircraft found carrying

---

[41] *AGOSI v United Kingdom* (1987) 9 EHRR 1 para 53.

[42] *Raimondo v Italy* (1994) 18 EHRR 237.

[43] *Air Canada v United Kingdom* (1995) 20 EHRR 150.

[44] Customs and Excise Management Act 1979 s 139 contains very wide provisions as to the detention, seizure and condemnation of goods.

[45] HM *Customs and Excise Commissioners v Air Canada* (CA) [1991] 2 QB 446; [1991] 1 All ER 570; reversing [1989] QB 234; [1989] 2 All ER 22.

[46] This is not beyond question: see Guy Stessens, *Money Laundering: A New International Law Enforcement Model* (Cambridge, Cambridge University Press, 2000) 63 *et seq.*, arguing that as confiscation and forfeiture are both punitive they should necessarily be taken to raise Article 6 questions. It is, however, the view to which the United Kingdom courts now appear committed. *Goldsmith v Commissioners of Customs & Excise* [2001] 1 WLR 1673 (customs forfeiture); *Butt v HM Customs and Excise* [2001] EWHC Admin 1066, (cash forfeiture); *R v Rezvi* [2002] UKHL 1 (confiscation).

prohibited drugs and then release it only in return for payment did not contravene the First Protocol. The court held that Member States were entitled to control the use of property insofar as to do so was proportionate to enforce policy in the general public interest. The seizure of the plane was not disproportionate to the aim of encouraging Air Canada to improve its security, bearing in mind the way security had lapsed, the value of the drugs found and a history of security lapses by the airline. The decision has been the subject of criticism[47] The main concerns expressed in the dissents by Judge Walsh, and by Judge Martens (joined by Judge Russo), were that a law which made no distinction at all between the innocent and the guilty could not be upheld as being in the general interest within the meaning of the second paragraph of Article 1 of the First Protocol.[48] Judge Pekkanen, for his part, said that the Act:

. . . gives practically unfettered discretion to the Commissioners with regard to both the seizure and the measures to be taken following it. Is this type of legal provision sufficiently precise to satisfy the criterion of 'foreseeability' required by the Convention according to the Court's case law?[49]

On the majority view it seems that the First Protocol gives individual States a wide discretionary power to interfere with property.[50] If the rules for forfeiture in respect of the use of aeroplanes or gold coins could form part of a legal régime dealing with the control of the use of those items, then it may be suggested that a provision permitting forfeiture of money could form part of a régime for the control of the use of money. Nonetheless the power to interfere with property is not an unlimited one. There are two limiting criteria. The first is *proportionality*. In cases concerning Article 1 of the First Protocol, the ECHR looks for a 'reasonable relationship of proportionality between the means employed and the legitimate objectives pursued'.

This . . . requirement was expressed in other terms in the *Sporrong & Lonnroth* judgment by the notion of the fair balance that must be struck between the demands of the general interest of the community and the requirements of the protection of the individual's fundamental rights. The requisite balance will not be found if the person concerned has had to bear an individual and excessive burden.[50a]

---

[47] By Simon Brown LJ in *International Transport Roth GmbH and another v Secretary of State for the Home Department* [2002] EWCA Civ 158, noting (at para 41) that the minority judgments were better argued and that Strasbourg jurisprudence has moved on since then. In *Hoverspeed* [2002] EWHC 1630 (Admin) Brooke LJ, at paras 157–8, held that the majority of the Strasbourg court was clearly influenced by the fact that the Commissioners did not exercise their strikingly wide powers of forfeiture until after a long series of alleged security lapses in relation to drugs importation had been drawn to Air Canada's attention, culminating in an express written warning to them that when they carried prohibited goods, the Commissioners would consider exercising their powers under CEMA, including the seizure and forfeiture of aircraft.
[48] See Judge Walsh at para 2 *et seq*, and Judge Martens at para 3 *et seq*.
[49] Para 1.
[50] Ewan Bell, 'The ECHR and the Proceeds of Crime Legislation' [2000] *Criminal Law Review* 783 at 785.
[50a] *James v United Kingdom* (1986) 8 EHRR 123, 144–5, para 50.

Although the Court was speaking in that judgment in the context of the general rule of peaceful enjoyment of property enunciated in the first sentence of the first paragraph, it pointed out that the search for this balance is reflected in the structure of Article 1 as a whole.[51]

In *De Freitas v Ministry of Agriculture*,[52] in giving the opinion of the Judicial Committee of the Privy Council Board on analogous provisions, Lord Slynn adopted a three-fold analysis from Zimbabwe. The questions arose:

Whether:
(i)   a legislative objective is sufficiently important to justify limiting the fundamental right;
(ii) the measures designed to meet the legislative objective are rationally connected to it; and
(iii) the means used to impair the right or freedom is no more than is necessary to accomplish the objective.[53]

There is clearly some scope for a proportionality challenge at least to some forfeiture provisions. The First protocol argument against *confiscation* was addressed in the Court of Appeal in *Benjafield*.

It is very much a matter of personal judgment as to whether a proper balance has been struck between the conflicting interests. Into the balance there must be placed the interests of the defendant as against the interests of the public, that those who have offended should not profit from their offending and should not use their criminal conduct to fund further offending. However, in our judgment, if the discretions which are given to the prosecution and the court are properly exercised, the solution which Parliament has adopted is a reasonable and proportionate response to a substantial public interest, and therefore justifiable.[54]

On this point the House of Lords in *Rezvi* agreed.[55] In *International Transport Roth GmbH and another v Secretary of State for the Home Department*[56] the Court of Appeal did hold by a majority that the scheme under the Immigration and Asylum Act 1999 whereby carriers were held responsible and subject to penalties for the clandestine arrival of illegal entrants into the UK by means of concealment in freight vehicles was inconsistent with Article 6 and Article 1 of the First Protocol to the Convention. In *Lindsay*[57] a distinction was made between the treatment of those who are found to be smuggling for profit and those who are directly or indirectly involved in not-for-profit smuggling. So far as the latter are concerned, the remedy applied by the Commissioners must be proportionate to the activity of which complaint is made. The Court in

---

[51]   R *(Daly) v Secretary of State for the Home Department* [2001] UKHL 26, [2001] 3 All ER 433.
[52]   *De Freitas v Ministry of Agriculture* [1999] 1 AC 69.
[53]   *Ibid*, at 80.
[54]   R v *Benjafield* (CA) [2001] 3 WLR 75; [2001] 2 All ER 609 at 635 (para 88).
[55]   R v *Rezvi* [2002] UKHL 1 para 17 *et seq*.
[56]   *International Transport Roth GmbH and another v Secretary of State for the Home Department* [2002] EWCA Civ 158.
[57]   *Lindsay v HM Customs and Excise Commissioners* [2002] EWCA Civ 267; [2002] 3 All ER 118.

Hoverspeed[58] held that a random search policy for 'booze-cruisers' was unlawful. This is an important and developing area.

Forfeiture Proceedings and Double Jeopardy

The double jeopardy protocol to the Convention prohibits signatory countries from trying or punishing again one who has already been convicted or acquitted.[59] The United Kingdom has not signed (and consequently not ratified) this provision. In the absence of any special provision the courts have tended to read the defence of *autrefois convict* narrowly[60] and to assume that there are no restrictions upon the power of Parliament to impose double penalties.[61] It is still open to the courts in those jurisdictions which do subscribe to the protocol to decide that double jeopardy would be involved in forfeiture following criminal punishment and consequently to provide relief in the case where punishment has been imposed. This will only apply to forfeiture where there is a conviction. The decision of the House of Lords in *R v Smith (David Cadman)*[62] indicates that no such inhibitions afflict the courts of England and Wales. The adoption of the double jeopardy protocol might make a significant difference to the operation of forfeiture law. The fundamental objection to forfeiture on conviction is that, unless treated as a fine, it constitutes double punishment.

Forfeiture Proceedings and the Right to a Fair Trial

The other possible human rights challenge to forfeiture is on the grounds that the imposition of forfeiture, whether or not by a court, constitutes a 'criminal charge' for the purposes of Article 6(2) of the Convention, so as to attract, subject to its

---

[58] *R v HM Customs and Excise Commissioners, ex parte Hoverspeed and others* [2002] EWHC 1630 (Admin).

[59] Protocol 7 Art 4—Right not to be tried or punished twice 1. No one shall be liable to be tried or punished again in criminal proceedings under the jurisdiction of the same State for an offence for which he has already been finally acquitted or convicted in accordance with the law and penal procedure of that State. 2. The provisions of the preceding paragraph shall not prevent the reopening of the case in accordance with the law and penal procedure of the State concerned, if there is evidence of new or newly discovered facts, or if there has been a fundamental defect in the previous proceedings, which could affect the outcome of the case. 3. No derogation from this Article shall be made under Article 15 of the Convention.

[60] *Connelly v DPP* [1964] AC 1254. There is a rule against double *exposure* to punishment, but, if that can be circumvented (for example by the fiction that the thing is at fault) there is no independent rule in English Law against double punishment.

[61] In *R v W* [1998] STC 550 (CA (Crim Div)) the Court of Appeal, asked whether the CPS was wrong to bring a prosecution for theft and false accounting after the Revenue had reached a settlement with the taxpayer and decided not to prosecute, held that the CPS and the Revenue had differing objectives and that the Revenue could not estop the CPS.

[62] [2001] UKHL 68: see Alldridge, 'Smuggling, Confiscation and Forfeiture' (2002) 65 *Modern Law Review* 781.

displacement,[63] the presumption of innocence, the criminal standard of proof and the evidential and procedural guarantees of Article 6(3).[64] In *Goldsmith v Customs and Excise Commissioners*[65] the court accepted that the appellant might well feel that an aspersion of criminality had been cast on him by the proceedings but took a number of factors to indicate that forfeiture proceedings were not covered by Article 6.[66] When the forfeiture has the element of imposing a *penalty*, then Article 6(2) applies.[67]

Whether Article 6 applies to forfeiture provisions is obviously critical to two major overlapping features of the new law. First, increased attention is being given to attempts to seize the finances of terrorism. Powers of seizure in respect of terrorist property use are, without more, forfeiture powers, not confiscation powers.[68] Even though confiscation proceedings upon conviction do not themselves involve a criminal charge,[69] it might have been possible to argue that forfeiture proceedings upon conviction did, or at the very least, that forfeiture proceedings *absent* conviction involved a criminal charge so as to attract the rules under Article 6(2). The second relates to the extended law of cash seizures, which requires separate treatment.

Broadening Customs Seizure, Detention and Forfeitures of Cash

One of the powers whose ambit has increased in the Proceeds of Crime Act is that to seize and retain suspected cash.[70] There is now power to search for such cash[71] with the prior approval of a magistrate or, where that is not, practicable a senior police officer. A code of practice to govern such searches and seizures will be published.[72]

The Act confers power either upon a customs officer (who had it already) or a constable (who, without more, did not) to seize cash of a minimum amount[73]

---

[63] Following *Salabiaku v France* (1991) 13 EHRR 379 and *R v Lambert* [2001] UKHL 37.

[64] *Ali v Best* (1997) 161 JP 393; [1996] COD 28; (1997) 161 JPN 676.

[65] *Goldsmith v Customs and Excise Commissioners* [2001] 1 WLR 1673.

[66] Following *R (McCann) v Crown Court at Manchester* [2001] 1 WLR 1084; Drawing on the ECHR jurisprudence from *Engel v Netherlands* (1976) 1 EHRR 647; *AP, MP and TP v Switzerland* (1998) 26 EHRR 541. See the section below ch 11, Article 6—Fair Trial and the Burden of Proof.

[67] *Bendenoun v France* (1994) 18 EHRR 54; *Georgiou (trading as Mario's Chippery) v United Kingdom* [2001] STC 80; *King v Walden* [2001] STC 822; *Customs and Excise Commissioners v Han and another and other appeals* [2001] EWCA Civ 1040, [2001] STC 1188 *Clingham (formerly C (a minor)) v Royal Borough of Kensington and Chelsea* [2002] UKHL 39.

[68] See the section below ch 10, Forfeiting Terrorist Property Upon Conviction.

[69] *HM Advocate v McIntosh (Sentencing)* [2001] UKPC D1; [2001] 3 WLR 107; *Phillips v United Kingdom* (2001) 11 BHRC 280; *R v Rezvi* [2002] UKHL 1; *R v Benjafield* [2002] UKHL 2.

[70] Cash is defined widely to include notes and coins in any currency, postal orders , cheques, bankers' drafts and bearer bonds. PCA 2002 s 289(6) & (7).

[71] PCA 2002 s 289.

[72] PCA 2002 s 292. The exercise of such powers by members of the executive without such a code would not satisfy the Convention: *Camezind v Switzerland* (1999) 28 EHRR 458.

[73] The minimum amount is to be fixed from time to time by order of the Home Secretary: PCA 2002 s 303.

or more if he has reasonable grounds for suspecting that it is recoverable property[74] or intended by any person for use in unlawful conduct.[75] It may be detained for up to 48 hours in the first instance, and there is provision for the extension of the detention for longer periods.[76] A magistrates' court may then order the forfeiture of the cash or any part of it.[77] The standard of proof is that the court must be 'satisfied' as to its provenance, but the proceedings are civil and the standard of proof is the civil one.[78] There is provision in forfeiture proceedings for the true owner to apply for the release of the cash[79] and for compensation to be paid where no forfeiture order is made to the person from whom cash was seized or to whom it belongs.[80] The initial minimum amount for this scheme is £10,000.[81] The previous legislation was interpreted to deal with 'smurfing' (use of multiple transactions each individually smaller than a limit, but collectively larger).[82] The two limbs of the procedure make this an interesting hybrid: it is a forfeiture procedure so far as it relates to property intended for use in crime, and it is a confiscation procedure so far as it relates to recoverable property. It was argued above that different considerations applied to customs than to other forfeitures—that powers which are justifiable in the customs hall may not be elsewhere.[83] Consequently it is to be regretted that the extension of the cash forfeiture régime did not attract more Parliamentary attention. Legislative creep is manifest again.

The relationship between forfeiture proceedings for cash and civil recovery proceedings requires clarification. The view of the minister was that wherever the assets of a person were cash then the appropriate mechanism was forfeiture, not civil recovery.[84] The availability of magistrates' courts' proceedings is clearly an incentive. Express provision was made in the Act to prevent recovery proceedings being taken in respect of cash *only*.[85]

So far as concerns the forfeiture aspect of the provision, the question of principle that remains is whether the mere fact that property can be shown on the balance of probabilities to be intended for use in crime is itself sufficient to justify a forfeiture. Even if it could be shown beyond reasonable doubt that a person intended to commit a crime, that would not without more be sufficient to justify conviction and punishment. Much of the discussion of the limits of the

---

[74] The definition in PCA 2002 s 304 applies. See the section below ch 11, The 'Civil Recovery' Power.

[75] PCA 2002 s 294.

[76] PCA 2002 s 295.

[77] PCA 2002 s 298.

[78] PCA 2002 s 298(2).

[79] PCA 2002 s 301.

[80] PCA 2002 s 302.

[81] PCA 2002 s 303.

[82] *Commissioners of Customs and Excise v Duffy* [2002] EWHC 425 holds that the court is entitled to aggregate to cover smurfing.

[83] See the section below ch 3, Customs Forfeitures.

[84] HL Debates 14 May 2002 Cols 54–56 (Lord Goldsmith A-G).

[85] PCA 2002 s 282(2).

law of attempts holds that the respects in which the law of attempts differs from a system of 'thought-crimes' is in the conduct requirement.[86] Why should a mere intention be regarded as a sufficient reason for the State to acquire the cash at all and why should the civil burden suffice?

HUMAN RIGHTS' CHALLENGES TO CASH FORFEITURE

The available challenges depend upon the limb of the provisions under which the State seeks the property. So far as the cash forfeiture proceedings are directed against property that is intended for criminal use, they are forfeiture proceedings, and the objections that may be made are identical to those against any other forfeiture without conviction.[87] So far as the proceedings are directed against recoverable property, however, the proceedings are most closely analogous to the civil recovery procedure, and the objections to civil recovery apply equally here.[88]

The principal issues relate to Article 6(2) and the burden and standard of proof, and the First Protocol. Under the previous legislation, in *Butt*, where the civil standard applied, Hallett J dismissed the Article 6 argument:

> It would, in my view, defeat Parliament's clearly expressed and enacted intention if the courts were to find that every case of forfeiture under s 43 [of the Drug Trafficking Act 1994] involves a finding of criminal activity and, therefore, the standard to be applied is the criminal standard of proof.[89]

The First Protocol argument was held to fall the same way. As to the arguments about the 'variable civil' standard of proof, *B v Chief Constable of Avon and Somerset Constabulary*[90] and the speech of Lord Nicholls in *Re H*[91] were discussed and the judge concluded that they did not compel the adoption of the criminal standard or something very close to it.[92] However, *Butt* must now be read in the light of *Clingham v Royal Borough of Kensington and Chelsea*[93] in which the House of Lords held that application of the 'variable civil' standard to anti-social behaviour orders was so riddled with difficulty that the safest course was to adopt the criminal standard. Hallett J's approach to the ASBO cases may no longer be legitimate.

---

[86] Under Criminal Attempts Act 1981 s 1, 'an act more than merely preparatory' to the commission of an offence.

[87] See the section in this ch above, First Protocol—the Right to Recovery.

[88] See the section below ch 11, Assets Recovery and Human Rights.

[89] *Butt v HM Customs and Excise* [2001] EWHC Admin 1066 Para 25.

[90] *B v Chief Constable of Avon and Somerset Constabulary* [2001] 1 WLR 340.

[91] *H (Minors) (Sexual Abuse: Standard of Proof), Re* [1996] AC 563; [1996] 1 All ER 1.

[92] And see the section below ch 7, The Standard and Burden of Proof in Confiscation Proceedings—No Criminal Lifestyle.

[93] *Clingham (formerly C (a minor)) v Royal Borough of Kensington and Chelsea* [2002] UKHL 39.

A COMPARATOR—UNITED STATES' JURISPRUDENCE

The apparent indifference of the courts to the various rights asserted by defendants in forfeiture proceedings is not solely an European phenomenon. By way of a comparator, consider the constitutional law of the United States. In the United States a number of attacks have been made upon the constitutionality of forfeiture.[94] There are three major ways of making the claim that forfeiture is unconstitutional under the federal United States constitution. First, there is the claim that forfeiture involves an excessive fine (which is an eighth amendment claim); secondly, that forfeiture upon conviction, involves double jeopardy contrary to the fifth amendment;[95] thirdly, and most fundamentally, there is a claim about the nature of property and the relationship between the State and private proprietary rights (which is also a Fifth Amendment claim).[96] As to punishment, the US Supreme Court has treated forfeiture as a punishment. In *United States v Bajakajian*[97] it held that the excessive fines clause of the Eighth Amendment applied to the forfeiture of a sum of money when exported unlawfully, but this would only interfere with a few forfeitures.

In *Bennis v Michigan*,[98] Justice Ginsburg—a Clinton nominee—disagreed with the liberal wing of the United States Supreme Court and joined the majority in allowing forfeiture. The State of Michigan seized a car, owned jointly by husband and wife, because the husband had used the vehicle while having sex with a prostitute. The car was therefore a nuisance and subject to abatement pursuant to Michigan Law.[99] The Supreme Court rejected the wife's constitutional claim that her interest in the car was so far removed from anything to do with the crime that it could not be forfeit.[100] The decision has been greeted by (almost[101]) universal disapproval among the critics.[102]

In *United States v Ursery*[103] the double jeopardy argument was made and rejected. The Supreme Court, reaffirming a 'traditional understanding', held

---

[94] Most notably in Leonard Levy, *A License to Steal: The Forfeiture of Property* (Chapel Hill, University of North Carolina Press, 1996).

[95] USCA 5: '. . . nor shall any person be subject for the same offence to be twice put in jeopardy of life or limb . . .'.

[96] USCA 5: '. . . nor shall private property be taken for public use, without just compensation.'

[97] *United States v Bajakajian* (1998) 524 US 321, 118 S Ct 2028. Fletcher N Baldwin '*States v Bajakajian*. The United States Supreme Court tries again' (1998) 1 *Journal of Money Laundering Control* 319–25.

[98] *Bennis v Michigan* (1996) 517 US 1163, 116 S Ct 984.

[99] Compiled Laws s 600.3825.

[100] There were dissents by Stevens, Souter and Breyer JJ.

[101] See Paul Schiff Berman, 'An Anthropological Approach to Modern Forfeiture Law: The Symbolic Function of Legal Actions Against Objects' (1999) 11 *Yale Journal Law and Humanities* 1.

[102] Erik Grant Luna, 'Fiction Trumps Innocence: The *Bennis* Court's Constitutional House of Cards' (1997) 49 *Stanford Law Review* 409.

[103] *United States v Ursery* (1996) 518 US 267; 116 S Ct 2135: and see *State v One 1990 Chevrolet Corvette* (1997) 695 A 2d 502 (RI).

that civil *in rem* forfeitures were not 'punishment' for purposes of the double jeopardy clause in the Fifth Amendment, and that the house of a defendant, in the garden of which he grew marijuana, could be forfeit notwithstanding that he was also subject to a prison sentence.[104] The court held that the fact that drug forfeitures[105] are subject to review for excessiveness under the Eighth Amendment does not mean that those forfeitures are so punitive as to be 'punishment' for double jeopardy purposes. There is to be a two-part test used to determine whether forfeiture is 'punishment' for double jeopardy purposes. This asks, first, whether Congress intended particular forfeiture to be remedial civil sanction or criminal penalty, and, second, whether forfeiture proceedings are so punitive in fact as to establish that they may not legitimately be viewed as civil in nature, despite any congressional intent to establish civil remedial mechanism. The court's reliance upon precedent[106] rather than principle is disappointing, and appears to have given rise to what has been called a 'Constitutional Kleptocracy'.[107] In particular, in *Ursery*, the distinction between 'civil' and 'criminal' forfeiture is never really investigated.[108] It is not clear what the significance of the distinction is. The defendant in a forfeiture case confronts the power of the State to investigate, obtain evidence and pursue issues through the courts.[109]

CONCLUSIONS

Forfeiture remains objectionable in ways that a limited, principled set of confiscation provisions are not. Unless the forfeiture is a fine *in specie* (in which case it could just be levied as a fine, or one of the specific justifications applies), the rationale is quite unclear. The argument should be confronted that forfeiture upon conviction otherwise than as a fine *in specie*, and without a specific justification (such as prevention of crime) is not legitimate. If it follows a conviction then it is double punishment. If there is no conviction then it is an attempt to impose penalties without the procedural rigour of Article 6 and 7. These points are simply made, but strike at the root of the strategy of the Proceeds of Crime Act 2002.

---

[104] See also *Hudson v United States* (1997) 118 S Ct 488.

[105] 18 USCA § 981(a)(1)(A), Comprehensive Drug Abuse Prevention and Control Act of 1970, § 511(a)(6), as amended, 21 USCA § 881(a)(6).

[106] Particularly the prohibition era case of *Various Items of Personal Property v United States* (1931) 282 US 577; 51 S Ct 282.

[107] Stefan B Herpel, 'Toward A Constitutional Kleptocracy' (1998) 96 *Michigan Law Review* 1910, reviewing Levy, *A License to Steal: The Forfeiture of Property* (Chapel Hill, NC, University of North Carolina Press, 1996).

[108] 'The contradictions in the Court's treatment of civil forfeiture, which began in the Nineteenth Century, have only been exacerbated by the decision in *Ursery*.' Herpel, *idem* at 1931.

[109] 'Civil Forfeiture surely has nothing to do with private rights and remedies.' Leonard Levy, *A License to Steal: The Forfeiture of Property* (Chapel Hill, NC, University of North Carolina Press, 1996) 22. See also the section below ch 11, 'The 'Civil Recovery' Power.

7

Statutory Confiscation Provisions

THIS CHAPTER WILL consider the extent of the statutory provisions for confiscation under English Law. Since their initial enactment in the mid-1980s they have become an integral part of the criminal justice process. They provide the most significant means by which the State seizes the proceeds of crime. Their enlargement since 1980 has been one of the principal legislative contributions to the changes in the sentencing system.

If the purpose of confiscation is to prevent a criminal profiting from crime, then confiscation should be a mechanism by which to place the defendant in the *status quo ante*. This is the uncomplicated position associated with the Hodgson Report.[1] The modern application of the rules of English law goes beyond that. In particular, they make no attempt to distinguish between the proceeds of crime, widely understood, and the net profits. A system whose objective was simply to recreate the *status quo ante* would only confiscate the net profits.[2] A clear statement of the purpose of the confiscation provisions is to be found in the following comments.

> The provisions are and were intended to be Draconian. They apply only to convicted criminals. They are designed to ensure that criminals do not profit from crimes which they have committed, but which cannot be specifically identified let alone proved against them. There is no injustice in the procedure. [I]t is not his property and it makes perfectly good sense that he should not be permitted to retain property which does not belong to him and which he came by dishonestly.[3]

CONFISCATION ORDERS

Before the 2002 Act, there were two main parallel confiscation schemes. The original forfeiture provisions, applying only to drugs offences, were in the Drug Trafficking Offences Act 1986 and then the Drug Trafficking Act 1994, as amended. The Criminal Justice Act Part 1988 Part VI, as amended and inserted by subsequent legislation, contained the provisions for the confiscation of

---

[1] D Hodgson, *Profits of Crime and their Recovery* (London, Heinemann, 1984) (hereinafter 'Hodgson Report').

[2] And see Guy Stessens, *Money Laundering: A New International Law Enforcement Model* (Cambridge, Cambridge University Press, 2000) 53–5.

[3] *R v Delaney; R v Hanrahan*, unreported, Court of Appeal, 14 May 1999, *per* Butterfield J.

proceeds of other criminal conduct. There were occasional differences[4] between the rules governing confiscation under the two régimes, but their basic structure was the same, case law under the one statute applied to the interpretation of equivalent provisions in the other,[5] and the arguments for assimilation at least of all the provisions that do not deal with terrorist property were strong.[6] There were separate provisions dealing with terrorist property.[7]

The Predicate Offence(s)—Criminal Conduct

The definition of predicate offences for confiscation orders under the 2002 Act obviates some of the difficulties that arose under the parallel régimes. The definition is wide. What is required is 'criminal conduct',

> 'Criminal conduct' means conduct which constitutes an offence in England and Wales *or* would constitute such an offence if it had occurred in England and Wales.[8]

In order to comply with Article 7 of the European Convention these offences must have been committed after the Act came into force.[9] Following conviction for any offence, indictable or summary, in the magistrates' court, a person must be committed to the Crown Court for confiscation proceedings and *may* be committed for such proceedings in respect of other offences.[10] Where the prosecutor asks the magistrates' court so to do, the court *must* commit the defendant to the Crown Court. Where a person is committed to the Crown Court for confiscation proceedings, the Crown Court will assume responsibility for the sentencing process.[11]

---

[4] Principally, and subject always to human rights provisions affecting the validity of the legislation, (i) the court was required to assume that the assets held by the offender on conviction and his or her previous six years of income relate to the proceeds of drug trafficking, and that the expenditure in the previous six years was met from these proceeds, even following a single conviction; non-drug offences require convictions for two or more 'qualifying offences' before similar assumptions apply; (ii) the court had wider powers to reassess the amount of criminal proceeds and assets held by a drug trafficking offender; (iii) where drug trafficking was in point the court could detain cash above £10,000 found at borders and shown on the balance of probabilities to relate to drug trafficking; (iv) the court could deal with the assets of absconders charged with drug trafficking offences but not yet convicted, and also with the assets of those who die after conviction before a confiscation order is made.

[5] Though compare *R v Miranda* [2000] *Criminal Law Review* 393 and *R v Ingham* [2000] *Criminal Law Review* 698.

[6] Cabinet Office Performance and Innovation Unit, *Recovering the Proceeds of Crime* (London, Cabinet Office, 2000) (hereinafter '*PIU Report*') para 8.7.

[7] See the section below ch 10, Involvement with Terrorist Money.

[8] PCA 2002 s 76(1).

[9] *Welch v United Kingdom* (1995) 20 EHRR 247.

[10] PCA 2002 s 70.

[11] PCA 2002 s 71.

Matters of Jurisdiction—Predicate Offence Overseas

Does is make any difference that the predicate offence is committed overseas? If money is brought to the United Kingdom that has its provenance in illegal behaviour overseas, will the confiscation provisions apply to it? There must be a conviction for a crime justiciable in England and Wales before there can be a confiscation order. So the offence for which there is a conviction must be committed inside the jurisdiction of the courts. But, so far as concerns other offences in respect of which a confiscation order is to be made, there is no such limitation. These were inserted in compliance with the UN Convention.[12]

The critical phrase in the definition of the offences capable of amounting to 'criminal conduct' is '*would constitute such an offence if it had occurred in England and Wales*'.[13] There is no dual criminality requirement. The English Courts are to transpose conduct committed abroad to an English context and determine its lawfulness. It is only necessary to know the nature of the conduct in question and whether that conduct, in England, once translated into English terms, would constitute an offence. Where the offence alleged is a *specific* offence under the foreign tax legislation the question will arise whether the overseas offence is sufficiently close to the analogous offence for the section to be satisfied. Usually, however, these considerations can be made largely (in the pejorative sense) academic by treating the offences as constituting broader, more general offences, such as conspiracy to defraud or cheating the Revenue.

The Special Case of the Proceeds of Overseas Tax Evasion

The Common Law

Allen[14] and *Smith*[15] hold that tax evasion can constitute a predicate offence for the purposes of the making of a confiscation order when it takes place within England and Wales. Does it make any difference whether the evasion or the gain occurred elsewhere?[16] The common law attitude towards the collection of foreign tax was summarised by *Dicey & Morris* in the following terms: 'English courts have no jurisdiction to entertain an action: (1) for the enforcement, either

---

[12] See the section above ch 5, The Vienna Convention.

[13] PCA 2002 s 76(1).

[14] *R v Allen* (CA) [2000] QB 744; [2000] 2 All ER 142; (HL) [2001] UKHL 45; [2002] 1 AC 509: see the section in this ch, Pecuniary Advantage—the Benefit.

[15] *R v Smith (David Cadman)* [2001] UKHL 68: see the section in this ch, Proceeds Not Just Profits.

[16] It is central to the FATF strategy that it should not. See the section below ch 9, Tax Evasion as the Predicate Offence to Criminal Laundering.

directly or indirectly of a penal, revenue or other public law of a foreign State'.[17] So far as tax laws are concerned, the rationale usually advanced is that:

> ... enforcement of a claim for taxes is but an extension of the sovereign power which imposed the taxes, and that an assertion of sovereign authority by one State within the territory of another, as distinct from a patrimonial claim by a foreign sovereign, is (treaty or convention apart) contrary to all concepts of independent sovereignties.[18]

This principle was upheld in *QRS 1 APS v Flemming Frandsen*[19] where the Court of Appeal said that the prohibition on the enforcement *in English civil law* of foreign revenue and penal laws was absolute. On the face of it, this principle would prevent English courts putting in place confiscation orders or enforcing liability for criminal laundering where the predicate offence is overseas tax evasion. The old rule is, of course, only a common law principle (including a principle of statutory interpretation), which is subject to modification by statute. It follows from a notion of sovereignty that developed long before the 'international community' acquired the importance in international lawmaking now granted it. The assumption is of the other country as an economic competitor, rather than a collaborator, and consequently not entitled to the use of the courts and enforcement machinery of another country. The development of the money laundering régime has been at the forefront of the move from insular views of sovereignty, so it is not surprising that money laundering has become an early test.

There can be little doubt that the reversal of the principle in *Government of India v Taylor*, and its commitment to a view of sovereignty which appears outdated, is now at the centre of Government policy in this area.[20] The Home Office review of jurisdiction[21] recommended that the instantiation of extra-territorial jurisdiction be considered where one of the following factors was present;

(i)   the offence is serious;
(ii)   where, by virtue of the nature of the offence, the witnesses and evidence necessary for the prosecution are likely to be available in the United Kingdom;

---

[17] (Ed Collins) *Dicey & Morris. The Conflict of Laws* (London Sweet & Maxwell, 12th edn, 1993) 100–101. The authority most frequently cited is the speech of Lord Somervell of Harrow in *Government of India v Taylor* [1955] AC 491, 514. See also *In re State of Norway's Application* [1990] 1 AC 723, distinguishing *Government of India v Taylor* in a case where evidence, not direct or indirect enforcement, was required.

[18] Lord Keith of Avonholm in *Government of India v Taylor* at [1955] AC 491 at 511. But see Philip Baker, 'Mutual assistance in the recovery of tax claims: no Government of India in the European Union?' [1999] *British Tax Review* 14–15.

[19] *QRS 1 APS v Flemming Frandsen* [1999] STC 616.

[20] And see Guy Stessens, *Money Laundering: A New International Law Enforcement Model* (Cambridge, Cambridge University Press, 2000) 299: 'The exception of fiscal offences encapsulated the refusal of states to cooperate . . . the interest of international criminal justice was placed second to the economic interests of states.'

[21] Home Office Review of Jurisdiction (1996) cited at Home Office, *Raising Standards and Upholding Integrity The Prevention of Corruption* (London, Stationery Office, 2000) para 2.21.

(iii)   where there is international consensus that certain conduct is reprehensi-
        ble and that concerted action is needed, involving the taking of extra-
        territorial jurisdiction;
(iv)   where the vulnerability of the victim makes it particularly important to
        tackle instances of the offence;
(v)   where it appears to be in the interests of the standing and reputation of the
        United Kingdom in the international community.
(vi)   where there is a danger that the offences would not otherwise be justiciable.

Of these, a case can be made that (i) (ii) (iii) (v) and (vi) may be satisfied in the
case of overseas tax evasion. In particular, money laundering is central to the
internationalisation of criminal law to which (iii) and (v) conduce. Pressure for
change will necessarily be found in this area. The extension of the criminal law
by reversing the principle in *Government of India v Taylor* is something that
could be achieved by clear legislation, but it is not an effect that the courts
should strain to achieve without such clear words. The question is whether the
words of the legislation now in force are adequate to alter the position. It seems
that they are. If tax evasion generates a qualifying benefit then the fact that the
evasion is overseas evasion will not matter.

THE CONFISCATION ORDER

One of the indisputable benefits of the Proceeds of Crime Act 2002 is that it provides assimilation of the previous parallel régimes.[22] The basic power to make a
confiscation order is granted by section 6. The prerequisite is a conviction in the
Crown Court or committal to the Crown Court for sentencing[23] or for consideration for a confiscation order.[24] The triggers which cause the court to consider
the making of an order are notice either from the prosecutor or the Director of
the Assets Recovery Agency[25] or a holding by the court that it considers, even
though it has not been given such notice,[26] that it would be appropriate for it so
to proceed.[27] The legislation directs the court to act as follows before sentencing or otherwise dealing with the offender in respect of that offence or any other
relevant criminal conduct. The court must decide whether or not the defendant
has a 'criminal lifestyle'. The expression 'criminal lifestyle' is not used as in ordinary language, but is defined in the statute.[28] The Joint Parliamentary
Committee on Human Rights was critical of the 'lifestyle' provisions:

---

[22] See the section above ch 4, The Hodgson Committee.
[23] Powers of Criminal Courts (Sentencing) Act 2000 s 6.
[24] PCA 2002 s 6(2).
[25] See the section below ch 11, The Director and the Agency.
[26] There is no analogous power in the court to halt proceedings in which, in the view of the court,
it would not be appropriate to proceed.
[27] PCA 2002 s 6(3).
[28] PCA 2002 s 75.

It should not be forgotten that all these criteria go beyond identifying hallmarks of a criminal lifestyle, leaving courts to assess their significance on the facts of each case. Instead, they amount to statutory presumptions that cannot be rebutted. There may be some empirical evidence for the sociological assumptions which the criteria reflect. However the Government has not provided any such evidence. Even if there is such evidence, it cannot prove a satisfactory basis for preventing the defendant from rebutting the presumption of a criminal lifestyle.[29]

There are three tests, satisfaction of one of which triggers the lifestyle provisions. They are, first, that the offence concerned is one of a group specified in Schedule 2.[30] That list contains offences of drug trafficking, money laundering,[31] directing terrorism,[32] trafficking in people or arms, counterfeiting or intellectual property offences, pimping and blackmail, together with attempting, conspiring and inciting those offences or being party to them. Second, that the offence constitutes 'conduct forming part of a course of criminal activity'.[33] This is defined to mean that there must be three or more other offences from which the defendant gained a benefit in the same proceedings, or at least two previous convictions within the previous six years for such offences.[34] Third, where the offence in question is a continuing offence committed over at least six months.[35] Where the offence is not included by reason of Schedule 2 it will only count where the defendant obtains relevant benefit of £5,000 or more.[36]

The making of the order is then mandatory.[37] If the court finds that the defendant does not have a criminal lifestyle, it must decide whether he benefited from the particular criminal conduct. This is defined to include conduct of which the defendant was convicted in the same proceedings and offences taken into consideration in sentencing.[38] If the court finds that the defendant does have a criminal lifestyle, it must decide whether he benefited from his general criminal

[29] Joint Committee on Human Rights, *Eleventh Report: Proceeds of Crime Bill* (February 2002) para 7. Or, more pointedly, 'I could take up residence in one of the outer suburbs of London in a large property with substantial electric gates, which are especially seen in parts of the Essex fringe. I could acquire two rottweilers called Ronnie and Reggie and buy a 4x4 for my wife—I think that the Vitara is the one that they go for—and a Range Rover for myself. I could wear shades throughout the year and have rings on my fingers that include large sovereigns. I could have small tattoos on my knuckles that are indicative of my general outlook. If I did that, it might be said that I had adopted a criminal lifestyle. However, that does not mean that I would be a criminal.' Dominic Grieve MP, House of Commons Standing Committee B (pt 6) 15 Nov 2001.

[30] PCA 2002 s 75(2)(a) and Schedule 2. The list may be amended without further primary legislation: PCA 2002 s 75(7).

[31] Only the offences under ss 327 and 328: see the section below ch 9, The Specific Money Laundering Offences. Failure to disclose is not covered.

[32] Terrorism Act 2000 s 56 (but not otherwise taking part in terrorism).

[33] PCA 2002 s 75(2).

[34] PCA 2002 s 75(3).

[35] PCA 2002 s 75(2)(c).

[36] PCA 2002 s 75(4)

[37] The Government was defeated in the House of Lords on an opposition amendment to insert a discretion, in exceptional circumstances, not to make the order. HL Debates 25 June 2002 Col 1217. It reversed the defeat in the Commons.

[38] PCA 2002 s 6(4)(c), s 76(3).

conduct. This is defined to include all of the criminal conduct of the defendant, whether before or after the Proceeds of Crime Act.[39] The significance of this is the operation of statutory assumptions that everything by which the defendant has come in the previous six years is the proceeds of criminal conduct.[40]

If the court determines that the offender has benefited, it must determine the amount to be recovered in his case, and make a confiscation order. There is one case where the court does not have a duty to impose a confiscation order, but only a power. If the court is satisfied that a victim of any relevant criminal conduct has instituted, or intends to institute, civil proceedings against the defendant in respect of loss, injury or damage sustained in connection with that conduct the sum required to be paid under that order shall be of such amount, as the court thinks fit.[41]

Change of Circumstances—Variation

Whether or not an order was originally made, when the defendant's circumstances change after the making of a confiscation order it may be varied. A defendant whose realisable property does not suffice to pay the benefits of criminal conduct is thus treated as an undischarged bankrupt in respect of any after-acquired property, however lawful its acquisition. Conversely, however, where the amount of realisable property increases after the making of the order, the order can be revised upwards.[42] In *R v Tivnan*[43] new realisable property had been acquired by the defendant after the initial confiscation order was made and could not be shown to have been acquired through drug dealing. The defendant appealed against the variation of the confiscation order, arguing that assets that had been acquired by honest means after a confiscation order had been made could not be taken into account when determining an application for an increase in the amount to be recovered under a confiscation order.[44] The Court of Appeal held that the intention of Parliament in enacting the relevant legislation was to deprive offenders of *any* benefit gained through dealing in drugs by confiscating their realisable assets up to the level of any profit made, regardless of whether those particular assets arose from drug trafficking. A continuing process was envisaged by the legislation, bearing in mind that it contained no limitation as to time, was expressed in the present tense, that the marginal note

---

[39] PCA 2002 s 76(2).

[40] PCA 2002 s 10.

[41] PCA 2002 s 6(6), replacing CJA 1988 s 71(1C). 'The purpose of this provision is to enable the court to make a confiscation order that is net of any award to the victim, since it is likely that the amount of compensation awarded to any one victim would be less than the net assets. The 'fund' of the criminal's assets is preserved so that victims get compensated before the courts get access.' HC Standing Committee C (Proceeds of Crime Bill) 15th March 1995 Col 15 (Bob Ainsworth).

[42] PCA 2002 s 19–26.

[43] *R v Tivnan (Michael)* [1999] 1 CAR(S) 92; [1998] *Criminal Law Review* 591.

[44] A jurisdiction now exercised under PCA 2002 s 22, replacing CJA 1988 s 74B(3) and DTA 1994 s 16(4).

referred to an increase in realisable property, and there was no indication that the reason for the increase in realisable property was in any way relevant.

Postponed and Reconsidered Determinations

Under the Drug Trafficking Offences Act 1986 as originally enacted, the court was obliged to deal with all matters to do with confiscation *before* sentencing the offender. The waiting period was regarded as unacceptable. The Criminal Justice Act 1993 preserved the original obligation upon the court to deal with confiscation then sentence, but inserted a new section[45] creating an exceptional category to allow the court to sentence immediately and postpone decisions relating to confiscation.[46] Where a court considers that it requires further information before determining whether the defendant has benefited from drug trafficking or any relevant criminal conduct, or in determining the amount to be recovered in his case it may, for the purpose of enabling that information to be obtained, postpone making that determination for such period as it may specify, but unless there are exceptional circumstances the period must not now exceed two years beginning with the date of conviction.[47]

The Court of Appeal policed the limit quite rigorously.[48] The Cabinet Office complained[49] that administrative delay may mean that confiscation orders are simply not obtained. It recommended its extension to two years when there are good reasons to do so,[50] and the Proceeds of Crime Act 2002, which regards postponement of confiscation proceedings is to be the norm, so provides.[51] The Act also provides that a confiscation order is not to be quashed merely because of a courts procedural error in its application of the postponement provisions.[52] This is a curious provision. Historically the courts have been astute in striking down orders and warrants where procedures have not been satisfied. To preclude such scrutiny must invite, at best sloppiness, and at worst inattention to the rights of the defendant.

---

[45] Drug Trafficking Offences Act 1986 s 1A.

[46] And see CJA 1988 s 72A; DTA 1994 s 3.

[47] PCA 2002 s 14. The previous limit had been six months: CJA 1988 s 72A(3); DTA 1994 s 3(3). As to what may amount to exceptional circumstances see *R v Gadsby* [2001] EWCA Crim 1824, [2002] 1 CAR(S) 97; *R v Chuni* [2002] *Criminal Law Review* 420 (illness of trial judge or particular complexity sufficient). In *R v Dhillon; R v Jagdev* [2002] EWCA Crim 1326 the Court of Appeal held that where important legal decisions were expected from higher courts about the validity of the procedures and presumptions for confiscation proceedings, a judge was entitled to have regarded the content of the expected decisions as 'further information' required and to postpone a confiscation hearing beyond the time limit from the date of conviction.

[48] *R v Kelly* [2000] *Criminal Law Review* 393; *Miranda* [2000] *Criminal Law Review* 393; *R v Lingham* [2000] *Criminal Law Review* 696; *R v Matthew Dean Gordon* 2000; *R v Pisciotto* [2002] EWCA Crim 1592 (length of postponement must be specified).

[49] *PIU Report* para 8.24 and Box 8.3.

[50] *Ibid* para 8.24 and conclusion 22.

[51] PCA 2002 s 14(5), with power to postpone for longer in exceptional cases: s 14(4).

[52] PCA 2002 s 14(11), with exceptions, s 14(12).

There is power for the issue of whether to make a confiscation order to be reconsidered when, within six years of the conviction, evidence comes into the hands of the prosecutor that was not available on the relevant date.[53] The amount confiscated must not be more than would have been the recoverable amount had the assessment taken place immediately upon conviction but is subject also to a 'justice' test[54] in which fines are to be taken into account.[55]

Death of the Criminal

There was provision in the earlier legislation for confiscation where the defendant is dead.[56] It is very doubtful, however, whether confiscation of the property of a deceased person is consistent with the European Convention on Human Rights.[57] There is no such provision in the 2002 Act. However, so long as it does not offend Article 6, the civil recovery procedure, which does not require a conviction, might be invoked against the estate.[58]

Making the Order—Assessing the Benefit

The basic rule is the wide one that, 'A person benefits from conduct if he obtains property as a result of or in connection with the conduct'.[59] When the lifestyle provisions do not come into play, the courts must determine the proceeds of the specific criminal conduct , which includes the offence in question together with any offences taken into consideration in sentencing.[60]

> (4) For the purposes of this Part of this Act a person benefits from an offence if he obtains property[61] as a result of or in connection with its commission and his benefit is the value of the property so obtained.

The value of assets is the market value net of the costs of sale.[62] If the proceeds have been invested so as to appreciate then the greater sum is confiscated.[63] In computing the amount of the confiscation order the formula is to determine the defendant's benefit from the conduct concerned, which is the 'recoverable

---

[53] PCA 2002 s 19–22.
[54] PCA 2002 s 19(6)(a) and analogous provisions of ss 20–22.
[55] PCA 2002 s 21(7)(b).
[56] DTA 1994 s 19.
[57] 'It is a fundamental rule of criminal law that criminal liability does not survive the person who has committed the criminal act. Inheritance of the guilt of the dead is not compatible with the standards of criminal justice in a society governed by the rule of law.' *AP, MP and TP v Switzerland* (1998) 26 EHRR 541, para 48.
[58] See the section below ch 11, The Civil Recovery Power.
[59] PCA 2002 s 76(4).
[60] PCA 2002 s 6(5).
[61] 'Property' includes 'money': PCA 2002 s 85(1).
[62] PCA 2002 s 79(2); *R v Cramer (John Charles)* (1992) 13 CAR(S) 390.
[63] PCA 2002 s 80.

amount'.[64] Unless the available amount is less,[65] the recoverable amount is the total of the values of the free property[66] *minus* the amount payable in respect of prior obligations,[67] plus the total in values of all tainted gifts.[68] The benefit obtained may be reconsidered whether or not[69] there was an order made in the first instance,[70] so long as fresh evidence is available.

As with any other set of rules dealing with the collection of monies by the State, there is provision for interest to be payable on sums unpaid under confiscation orders, and for those sums to be subject to the same collection mechanisms as are available for the original sums. The amount of the interest, for the purposes of enforcement, is be treated as part of the amount to be recovered from him under the confiscation order,[71] and the rate of interest is that for the time being applying to a civil judgment debt.[72]

Tainted Gifts

As with the disposal of property in contemplation of or in order to avoid its loss upon a bankruptcy, there are provisions allowing property that is the subject matter of 'tainted' gifts of other disposals to be included in the realisable property.[73] Gifts otherwise than to a *bona fide* purchaser for value made within the period of six years prior to the institution of proceedings[74] may be added to the sum of realisable property, and a confiscation order may extend to them or their proceeds.[75] Where the property has appreciated in value in the hands of a third party who is not a *bona fide* purchaser s/he may be liable for the higher sum.[76] In the event that the property has diminished in value in the hands of a third party who is not a *bona fide* purchaser, s/he will only be liable to the extent of its depreciated value.[77]

In determining the amount of realisable property, and in determining applications for certificates of inadequacy,[78] one claim that occurs frequently is that the defendant is no longer able to lay his/her hands upon the property. This is no defence. Even when confiscation was discretionary, the ability or otherwise

---

[64] PCA 2002 s. 7(1).

[65] PCA 2002 s.7.

[66] Defined in PCA 2002 s 82 as not being subject to forfeiture under specified statutory provisions.

[67] PCA 2002 s 9(2).

[68] PCA 2002 s 9(1)(b) and s 77 and s 78. See next section.

[69] PCA 2002 s 22.

[70] PCA 2002 s 21.

[71] PCA 2002 s 12.

[72] Ie under Judgments Act 1838 s 17—PCA 2002 s 12((2).

[73] PCA 2002 s 77.

[74] The definition of the commencement of proceedings is in PCA 2002 s 85(1). A charge or a court order is required.

[75] PCA 2002 s 78: this is now mandatory (following DTA 1994 s 8), not discretionary as under CJA 1988 s 74(10).

[76] PCA 2002 s 81.

[77] PCA 2002 s 81(1)(a).

[78] PCA 2002 s 23–4.

of the defendant to recover the property was not relevant to the exercise of the discretion. In *Re S (Confiscation Order)*[79] it was held, at the stage when a court was charged with assessing whether the realisable property of a defendant was adequate to pay the amount remaining to be recovered under a confiscation order,[80] the court was not concerned with making inquiries about assets dissipated since the confiscation order was made. Such inquiries came at a later stage when the applicant, having been granted his certificate, sought to make an application for variation of the confiscation order.[81]

Proceeds Not Just Profits

Where the 'criminal lifestyle' assumptions do not come into play, the proceeds are quantified on the basis of the offence for which there is a conviction, together with any other relevant offences.[82] So far as concerns the drug trafficking legislation, it was held repeatedly[83] that the power to make confiscation orders extended beyond the net profit that the defendant made. Thus it is clear that the assessment of proceeds is such that the forfeiture rules operate *punitively*, not simply as a means of restoring the *status quo ante*.[84] Under the drug legislation the definition of 'proceeds' was very wide.[85] A drug dealer was not entitled to a deduction for purchase of stock, distribution expenses or anything of that nature. The supposed justification is that it is inappropriate to allow a deduction for expenditure on activity that is, *ex hypothesi*, illegal.[86] The underlying aim is clearly one that rejects the 'reparative' philosophy of Hodgson and shows an unequivocal commitment to the use of confiscation as a punitive device going beyond the restoration of the *status quo ante*.[87] The rule is punitive to the extent that it confiscates money unrelated to the profit made. There is a principle at stake here. If the target of confiscation is the profits that are made in the conduct of criminal conduct, then confiscation provisions should deal only

[79] *In Re S (Confiscation Order), Re* The Times, 1 November 1994.
[80] Under the legislation preceding PCA 2002 s 7.
[81] Under CJA 1988 s 83(3), now PCA 2002 s 23.
[82] PCA 2002 s 6(2), s 6(4)(c).
[83] *R v Osei* (1988) 10 CAR(S) 289, *R v Smith (Ian)* [1989] 1 WLR 765; [1989] 2 All ER 948, *R v Comiskey* (1990) 12 CAR(S) 562, *R v Simons* (1994) 15 CAR(S) 126, *R v Banks* [1997] 2 CAR(S) 110, *R v Simpson (David)* [1998] 2 CAR(S) 111, [1998] *Criminal Law Review* 292. This line of cases was approved in *R v Smith (David Cadman)* [2001] UKHL 68 at para 25 *per* Lord Rodger.
[84] And compare the *Hodgson Report*, see the section above ch 4, The Hodgson Committee, and *SEC v Bilzerian* (1994) 29 F 3d 689; 308 US App DC 43 for forfeiture in the US, which only targets profits.
[85] DTA 1994 s 4 (a) any payments or other rewards received by a person at any time (. . .) in connection with drug trafficking carried on by him or another person are his proceeds of drug trafficking; and (b) the value of his proceeds of drug trafficking is the aggregate of the values of the payments or other rewards.
[86] Guy Stessens, *Money Laundering; A New International Law Enforcement Model* (Cambridge, Cambridge University Press, 2000) 53.
[87] See the section above ch 4, The Hodgson Committee.

with profits. If the argument is that it is impossible or impracticable to make the deductions it should be noted that the deductions are allowed for the purposes of the assessment to tax of unlawful trading.[88]

Under the Criminal Justice Act 1988, the quantification of the benefit operated the same extensive principle, which is retained in the 2002 Act:

> 76(4) A person benefits from conduct if he obtains property as a result of or in connection with the conduct . . .
> . . . (7) If a person benefits from conduct his benefit is the value of the property obtained.

That is, no set-off is allowed in respect of the expenses involved in committing the crime. To the extent that the expropriation exceeds the profit, the legislation does not only seize the profits of crime. The benefit may be direct or indirect. Drugs bought with money not raised from drug trafficking and not later sold cannot be the subject of a confiscation order but may be of a forfeiture order.[89]

What is objectionable about the 'proceeds not just profits' doctrine is that it creates an unjustifiable further punishment and that the amount is calculated by reference to the overheads on the crime. The full impact of the 'proceeds not just profits' doctrine is seen in corruption offences. Corruption is the subject of concerted international action, the law of the United Kingdom has been under review, and the United Kingdom Government has (finally) discharged its obligation under the Paris Convention of the OECD[90] to penalise the bribery of public officials overseas.[91] Bribes need only represent a small percentage of an overall transaction involving exchange of value. In the case of an employment acquired corruptly (for example, by a bribe), the benefit, for the purposes of a confiscation order, is the gross salary paid. This is a very harsh rule indeed. Until 1968 it was not, without more, a crime to gain employment by deception,[92] as, for example, to one's qualifications. Civil liability would be reduced to take into account the expenses incurred (including the work done) and the employer's duty to mitigate his/her loss. Where the court makes a confiscation order, however, apparently no deduction can be made in respect of work done, or of deductions at source for tax and national insurance. This has the effect that the Exchequer would benefit twice—once from the tax paid on the salary and once from the confiscation order, to the exclusion of other creditors, which would be an absurdity equalling *Smith (David Cadman)*.[93] At the least, in circumstances

---

[88] Subject to the rule that unlawful payments may not be deducted: Income and Corporation Taxes Act 1988 s 577A. Thus, for the purposes of taxation, a drug dealer may deduct the payment for a car, but not for drugs. See the section below ch 11, The Taxation Jurisdiction of the ARA.

[89] *R v Butler* (1993) 14 CAR(S) 537.

[90] *Convention on Combating Bribery of Foreign Public Officials in International Business Transactions*, Paris, 17 December 1997 (Cm 3994).

[91] Anti-Terrorism, Crime and Security Act 2001 s 106–108.

[92] *Lewis* (1922) Somerset Assizes, cited in JC Smith, *The Law of Theft* (London, Butterworths, 1st edn, 1968).

[93] *R v Smith (David Cadman)* [2001] UKHL 68, see the section in this ch, Pecuniary Advantage—The Benefit.

of this sort, the part of the confiscation order that is attributable to the tax that has been deducted cannot be regarded as being a deduction justified by a principle against allowing persons to profit from crime, but must itself be part of the punishment, raising questions of double punishment.

In the case of a commercial contract gained by bribery, the sums involved may be very large indeed. If A, working for and with the connivance of company B, enters into a collusive agreement with C, working for and with the connivance of company D to confer, for example a construction contract, then the bribe which A gave C may be insignificant compared to the gross value of the contract, yet it is that which will form the basis of the confiscation order.[94] The 'proceeds not just profits' doctrine faces a series of challenges on human rights' grounds, which are best considered after the more general challenges to confiscation.[95]

Pecuniary Advantage—The Benefit

A special case of benefit from crime is where the defendant does not obtain property but still obtains an advantage. These are the cases where, for example, the defendant defers a liability to pay a debt. The issue has become most acute in the case of tax evasion, assessing the benefit of which has raised issues for the courts. If a person has evaded a direct tax (such as income tax or corporation tax) or an indirect tax (VAT or excise duty) s/he will have more money or other property than s/he would otherwise. Tax evasion usually constitutes more general fraud offences such as obtaining the remission of liability debt by deception,[96] conspiracy to defraud the Inland Revenue or cheating the Revenue.[97] Nonetheless there remains doubt as to whether or not tax evasion can constitute a predicate offence for the purposes of the criminal laundering offences[98] and consequently the reporting requirements.[99] There never was any serious doubt as to whether tax evasion can constitute a predicate offence for the purposes of making a confiscation order. Tax evasion is such conduct.

---

[94] There is no corollary to the doctrine that the confiscation order should target proceeds not just profits. In *Attorney-General's Reference (No 25 of 2001), Re* [2001] EWCA1770; [2001] STC 1309 an attempt to extend the range of the confiscated property beyond the unpaid tax to the whole of the undeclared profits was rejected.

[95] See the section in this ch, Proceeds Not Just Profits—The Human Rights Challenges.

[96] Theft Act 1978 s 2.

[97] There is now a summary offence (Finance Act 2000 s 144, as to which see David C Ormerod, 'Summary evasion of income tax' [2002] *Criminal Law Review* 3).

[98] Those under PCA 2002 s 327–29, replacing CJA 1988 ss 93A–93C and DTA 1994 s 49–51. See the section below ch 9, The Specific Money Laundering Offences.

[99] Money Laundering Regulations 1993 para 2(3) uses suspicion of one of the laundering offences as the trigger for the obligation to report. See the section below ch 12, Sector Guidance Notes and the Identification of Suspicion.

The specific provision for quantifying the benefit from tax evasion for the purposes of making an order has no substantial changes from the Criminal Justice Act 1988.[100] Section 76(5) of the Proceeds of Crime Act 2002 provides:

> If a person derives a pecuniary advantage as a result of or in connection with the conduct, he is to be taken to obtain as a result of or in connection with the conduct a sum of money equal to the value of the pecuniary advantage.

The use of the expression 'pecuniary advantage' was not an especially felicitous one, given the disastrous history of section 16(2)(a) of the Theft Act 1968.[101] The reason for the repeal of section 16(2)(a) of the Theft Act 1968 was the difficulties that arose when the debt was not extinguished by the crime.[102] The same problem arises under the confiscation provisions. A person who evades tax is still liable to pay it. But in the context of the law of proceeds of crime there are two further difficulties that did not obtain in the case of the offence of obtaining a pecuniary advantage. First, under section 16(2)(a) it was not necessary to *quantify* the advantage. It was sufficient that there was (deemed to be) one. A confiscation order requires a quantity. Secondly, if the advantage is to be used as a basis for criminal liability or for the invocation of the reporting régime, it will be necessary to *identify* the property which represents the advantage.[103]

There is no definition of 'pecuniary advantage' in the 1988 or the 2002 Act. There was some earlier case law that tax evasion was covered[104] and the Court of Appeal in *R v Allen*[105] clearly held that 'pecuniary advantage' is to be given its natural meaning, and that will include the cases which were deemed to be pecuniary advantages under section 16(2)(a) of the Theft Act 1968,[106] including the deferral of a liability to taxation. Allen was convicted of failure to pay or to declare liabilities for income and corporation tax due in respect of certain offshore companies he managed. A confiscation order was made. He appealed, contending that the confiscation order was unlawful because the failure to meet his tax liabilities did not result in the gain of any pecuniary advantage. He main-

---

[100]   CJA 1988 s 71(5).

[101]   A 'judicial nightmare': *R v Royle* [1971] 1 WLR 1764; [1971] 3 All ER 1359. See *DPP v Turner* [1974] AC 357; *DPP v Ray* [1974] AC 370; *MPC v Charles* [1977] AC 177; Criminal Law Revision Committee, *Thirteenth Report, Section 16 of the Theft Act 1968* (Cmnd 6733, 1977); Theft Act 1978; *R v Lambie* [1981] 1 WLR 78; [1981] 1 All ER 332; Theft Act 1978; *R v Preddy* [1996] AC 815; [1996] 3 All ER 481; Theft (Amendment) Act 1996.

[102]   See especially *DPP v Turner* [1974] AC 357; *DPP v Ray* [1974] AC 370; *MPC v Charles* [1977] AC 177; JC Smith, *The Law of Theft*, 2nd edn (London, Butterworth, 1972) para 256 *et seq*. Criminal Law Revision Committee Thirteenth Report, *Section 16 of the Theft Act 1968* (Cmnd 6733).

[103]   See the section below ch 9, Identifying the Property.

[104]   *R v Tighe* [1996] 1 CAR(S) 314, *R v Travers* [1998] *Criminal Law Review* 655, *R v Martin*, *R v White* [1998] 2 CAR 385.

[105]   *R v Allen* [2000] QB 744; [2000] 2 All ER 142, on appeal from *R v Dimsey; R v Allen* [1999] STC 846, [1999] 8 CL 555.

[106]   *R v Dimsey & Allen* [2000] 1 CAR(S) 497 at 500–501 *per* Laws LJ. In *United States v Montgomery* (CA) [1999] 1 All ER 84 at 96D to E, Stuart-Smith LJ. indicated that there was no reason to accord a restricted meaning to the expression 'pecuniary advantage' in s 71(5).

tained that no advantage had accrued because he was still subject to the same liability to pay the Revenue even if the sum due under the confiscation order was paid in full.[107] The Court of Appeal held, dismissing his appeal, that it was clear that Parliament intended that a confiscation order could be made in respect of an unforgiven or outstanding debt. Laws LJ said:

> In short, the fact that the tax remains due does not mean that its evasion did not confer a pecuniary advantage, nor indeed that that pecuniary advantage consisted of the whole of the tax withheld, the value of the liability that was evaded. By his crime the appellant evaded payment of £4 million tax. That sum constituted the proceeds of the offence. . . . The fact that he remained in law liable to pay the tax, the fact even, were it so, that the Revenue might later recover it, does not, in our judgment, yield the proposition that the proceeds of his crime were one penny less than the whole of the tax evaded.[108]

Although, having granted leave on another issue, the House of Lords could have re-opened any question in the case, the matter was not considered further in *Allen*. Had Allen's contention been upheld either in the Court of Appeal or the House of Lords, it would not only have succeeded so far as concerned tax evasion but also so far as concerned any deferment of any debt. The Court of Appeal in *Allen* held that a person who 'benefits' from tax evasion benefits to the extent of the tax evaded.[109] The court held, although apparently without full argument, that the quantity of the unpaid tax is the quantity of the benefit. The obvious objection is that if the advantage is the deferral, then the value of the advantage is the value of the deferral, not the total liability. This follows clearly from the language of the statute, and also from principle: the idea of the statute is to deprive the defendant of what he acquired by crime. Since he still owed the tax, the only additional gain was the deferral.

The Court of Appeal then departed from *Allen* in *Smith (David Cadman)*.[110] The facts are commonplace. The defendant had smuggled 1.25 million cigarettes on board a boat into the UK—enough 'baccy to keep many chapters of clerks in serious pulmonary complaints. The excise duty payable on that quantity of cigarettes would have been £130,666.40. The excise duty point was the time when the cigarettes were charged with duty at importation and the duty became payable at that point.[111] Smith was convicted and the cigarettes were forfeit.[112] The question arose whether, notwithstanding their forfeiture, there could be a confiscation order in respect of the excise duty on the cigarettes. The

---

[107] He further contended that liability for the tax due rested with the offshore companies rather than with him as an individual. See *R v Allen* [2001] UKHL 45; [2002] 1 AC 509, *R v Dimsey* [2001] UKHL 46; [2002] 1 AC 509.

[108] [2000] 1 CAR(S) 497 at 500–501.

[109] So as to satisfy CJA 1988 s 71(5), now PCA 2002 s.76(5).

[110] *R v Smith (David Cadman)* (CA) [2001] 1 CAR(S) 61.

[111] Importation took place at a point at the mouth of the Humber. Excise Goods (Holding Movement, Warehousing and REDS) Regulations 1992, paras 4–6.

[112] The forfeiture power is conferred by Customs and Excise Management Act 1979 s 49.

Court of Appeal held that it could not, and *Allen* was distinguished on the basis that:

> It is true to say that the liability for duty on the cigarettes was incurred . . . and was evaded, and indeed is still due because, although the cigarettes themselves were forfeited, the appellant remains liable to duty on those forfeited cigarettes. But there was, in the view of this court, no benefit to the defendant as a result of that deferment. He never had or sold on the cigarettes; he has not retained any sum from which he could be said to have benefited and indeed he now remains liable for the duty.[113]

The difficulty is that in cases of tax evasion the liability *will* always remain, and that if this is the determinative issue it should also have decided *Allen*. The two cases could not stand one with another. After some procedural problems,[114] a further appeal was heard and allowed by the House of Lords.[115] The question of law certified as being of general public importance was:

> Whether an importer of uncustomed goods, who intends not to enter them for customs purposes and not pay any duty on them, derives a benefit under section 74 of the Criminal Justice Act 1988 through not paying the required duty at the point of importation, where the goods are forfeited by HM Customs following importation, before their value can be realised by the importer.

The answer of the House of Lords was in the affirmative. Lord Rodger of Earlsferry delivered the only speech. It is noteworthy for its commitment to a harsh approach to the confiscation legislation. He held, following *Allen*, but again apparently without argument, that the value of the pecuniary advantage was the value of the entire liability to duty, and that the subsequent fate of the cigarettes was irrelevant to the confiscation order. If they had been lost, liability to pay duty would have remained.[116] That they were seized is likewise irrelevant. If Lord Rodger is correct about the operation of section 71(5) (now Proceeds of Crime Act 2002 s 75(5)) a defendant is treated as having received an advantage far greater than s/he actually has, and then has an amount confiscated equivalent to the larger amount, the confiscation still doing nothing to clear his liability to tax or to forfeiture of the cigarettes, and a defendant who secures the extinguishment of a debt fares better than one who only defers the liability.

In *Smith* the case for the defendant seems to have been argued on the lines that there was no 'pecuniary advantage', and the certified question asks whether there was a benefit at all, not, if there were one, its quantity. Lord Rodger dismissed, on the basis of ordinary language, the argument that there was no benefit.[117] To that there can be no objection. There is no question that evading or deferring a debt falls within the natural meaning of 'pecuniary advantage', but that does not resolve the issue as to its *extent*. Under section 16(2)(a) of the Theft

---

[113] Para 31 *per* Burton J.

[114] *Sub nom: R v Cadman-Smith* [2001] *Criminal Law Review* 644; see [2001] UKHL 68 para 6.

[115] *R v Smith* [2001] UKHL 68.

[116] Paras 17–18.

[117] Paras 18–20, following Laws LJ in *Dimsey & Allen* [2000] 1 CAR(S) 497 at 500.

Act 1968 a determination of *quantum* was unnecessary, but it is critical here, and the defendant would have been on far firmer ground disputing it.

Lord Rodger said:

> [T]he offender who has derived a pecuniary advantage from his offence is treated as a person who has obtained 'property' as a result of or in connection with the commission of the offence, the 'property' in question being a sum of money equal to the value of the pecuniary advantage. Under section 74(5) for the purposes of making a confiscation order the value of the property is its value to the offender when he obtained it. In this case the respondent derived a pecuniary advantage by evading the duty at the moment when he imported the cigarettes. The sum equalling that pecuniary advantage is treated as property obtained by the respondent at that moment.[118]

The final two sentences are open to serious question. Lord Rodger's conclusions do not follow from the statute. The alternative approach to the statute, and one which accords better with the natural meaning of the expression 'pecuniary advantage', is to recognise that the liability to pay the tax remains, but that the extent of the 'pecuniary advantage' to the defendant is the value of the *deferral* of the liability, not of the *debt* itself. This would usually be only a fraction of the liability itself. The question would be: what is it worth (to the defendant) that s/he did not pay the duty on the spot, but paid later? In a case such as *Smith* the value will be negligible, but since he remained liable to pay the duty, there was no further profit of crime with which the law need have concerned itself.

Lord Rodger's view, following *Allen*, is that 'the pecuniary advantage' is equal in value to the property from whose custody it derives. This is like saying that the value of the advantage accruing from having £100 on deposit at five per cent for a year is £100, when it is actually £5. But the statute is clear:

> . . . he is to be treated for the purposes of this Part of this Act as if he had obtained as a result of or in connection with the commission of the offence a sum of money equal to the value of the pecuniary advantage.

Deferral of a liability to tax will generally have some value, but the value is not the same as the total liability. The Theft Act 1968 did not extend to making the section 16 offence a predicate offence either for the offence of handling stolen goods[119] or for the making of an order for the restitution of property to or for the compensation of a victim of theft.[120] It would be curious if, for the purposes of confiscation provisions, the analogous provision were not only to apply, but to apply so as to generate a confiscation order based on an artificially inflated valuation of the advantage gained. It is respectfully suggested that, so far as relates to the value of the pecuniary advantage, Lord Rodger misread an unhappily drafted statute. In a case such as this the value of the deferral of the duty is negligible and the powers of the Customs and Excise to recover the debt so

---

[118] Para 26.

[119] Theft Act 1968 s 24(4).

[120] Theft Act 1968 s 28(6), (incorporating the definition for the purposes of handling stolen goods, in s 24(1) and (4)). See now Powers of Criminal Courts (Sentencing) Act 2000 s 130.

great that the appropriate course to adopt would have been not to issue the confiscation order but for the Customs and Excise to assess the defendant to duty, and, if appropriate, penalties.

The upshot of *Smith* was that a case note[121] was used as the basis for a proposed amendment to the Proceeds of Crime Bill, moved at the Commons Report stage, the effect of which would have been to reduce the benefit attributed to a smuggler by the amount of any forfeitures.[122] The amendment was withdrawn when the Government agreed to reconsider the issue.[123] A similar amendment was then introduced at the House of Lords Committee stage.[124] The Government was happy with *Smith* and the amendment was defeated.[125] Lord Rooker said:

> For example, if an offender steals a television and subsequently drops and breaks it while carrying it to his home, he would still be liable to have the value of the television confiscated from him even though he could not sell the television in order to make any money. There is no reason why a pecuniary advantage that has been lost should be treated any differently.[126]

Lord Rooker reads 'pecuniary advantage' to mean 'debt' and not 'deferral'. From the point of view of clarity it would have been better for the amendment to deal directly with the definition of 'pecuniary advantage', but the area is probably past saving. What remains is a statute which says clearly, consistently with principle, that when a person obtains a pecuniary advantage by obtaining the deferral of a debt, the value of the advantage is the value of the deferral, but two House of Lords' decisions which hold that the value of the advantage is the value of the debt (without the alternative apparently having been suggested) and a statement by a minister during the Committee stage of a Bill re-enacting the statute, endorsing the decisions of the House of Lords,[127] again without adverting to the possibility that the value of the advantage is the value of the deferral. This may be an area where *communis error facit ius*. Unless a later House of Lords is prepared to overrule *Smith* and to treat Lord Rooker as not having adverted to the right question, later defendants who fall foul of the ruling will have to fall back upon Convention rights. In the case where a confiscation order is made in the value of unpaid tax and then the tax is demanded, it might be pos-

---

[121] Alldridge, 'Smuggling, Confiscation and Forfeiture' (2002) 65 *Modern Law Review* 781.

[122] House of Commons Reports 26 February 2002 vol 380 cols, 634–639, Amendment 41 (Dominic Grieve MP).

[123] *Ibid* col 639 (George Foulkes).

[124] HL Debates 22 April 2002 col 57 (Lord Kingsland).

[125] HL Debates 22 April 2002 cols 57–59 (Lord Rooker).

[126] HL Debates 22 April 2002 col 58.

[127] Technically, it is possible that the statement of the minister may not be taken into account by a later court interpreting s 75(5): *Pepper v Hart* [1993] AC 593; [1993] 1 All ER 42 limits the availability of reference to Hansard to cases where the Parliamentary speaker is dealing with the words under consideration by the subsequent court. Lord Rooker was speaking against an amendment dealing with the relationship between confiscation and forfeiture, not the meaning of the expression 'pecuniary advantage'.

sible to assert a First Protocol right. However, the Convention right that most clearly embodies the moral claim on Smith's behalf is a right not to be made subject to double jeopardy. That will become available if and when the United Kingdom adopts the double jeopardy protocol.[128] But the fundamental irrationality is that the criminal whose crime extinguishes a debt is treated better than one whose crime defers its payment.

Benefit and Knowledge?

A confiscation order may be made against a person convicted of drug trafficking offences in respect of any payment or other reward received by him 'in connection with drug trafficking'[129] only if it is shown that the recipient knew that the payment was made in connection with drug trafficking. The Court of Appeal so held in *Richards*.[130] This was an unexpected decision. If the objective of the law is simply to deprive the defendant of the proceeds of crime, then it ought to make little difference whether the defendant knew or did not know of their provenance (subject, perhaps, to some kind of defence based upon change of position by *bona fide* purchasers). The effect of the general application of the Criminal Justice Act 1988 definition in the new legislation[131] is that knowledge is no longer required.

Joint Ownership of Property

In any system based upon the appropriation of property from criminals by the State, there will be problems over any property of which the defendant is not the sole owner. The difficulty of third party interests in property arises most clearly when it is a substantial asset whose seizure would occasion significant inconvenience, typically a matrimonial home. In the case of forfeiture, based upon the fiction of the thing as criminal, the 'consistent' approach seems to be that forfeiture overrides third party interests (subject to some exception where the object was stolen).[132] This is not the position taken by English law.[133] Only the defendant's interest is subject to confiscation, and in the case of confiscation orders there is no such fiction and in a series of decisions the courts have leaned against holding that a confiscation order should be enforced to the point of compelling the sale of a matrimonial home.[134]

---

[128] See the section above ch 6, Forfeiture Proceedings and Double Jeopardy.
[129] DTA 1994 s 2(3).
[130] *R v Richards* [1992] 2 All ER 572; 95 CAR 230.
[131] PCA 2002 s 76(4).
[132] See discussion of *Bennis v Michigan*, Above, ch 6 A Comparator—United States' Jurisprudence.
[133] Powers of Criminal Courts (Sentencing) Act 2000 s 144(1)(b): Above, ch 6 A Comparator—United States' Jurisprudence.
[134] *R v Hackett (Kevin Peter)* (1988) 10 CAR(S) 388; [1990] CLY 1242, *R v Holah (Steven Richard)* (1989) 11 CAR(S) 282 and *R v Lee (Raymond)* [1996] 1 CAR(S) 135.

The courts hold a preference against selling the matrimonial home. In *Customs and Excise v A*[135] the Court of Appeal held that nothing in the Drug Trafficking Act 1994 precluded the court from making a property adjustment order under the Matrimonial Causes Act 1973, and exceptionally, for the order to put the entirety of the property in the hands of the wife. The preference against selling the matrimonial home is by no means an absolute one.[136] Where it is necessary to compel the sale of the matrimonial home, so far as the division of the equitable interest in the matrimonial home was concerned, it is necessary to hold an enquiry.[137] Where orders are made against both partners, the court must determine the respective shares arising from any joint benefit of drug trafficking and make separate confiscation orders accordingly.[138]

In *Re Norris*[139] an attempt by a wife to reopen the question of the extent of her interest on the basis that she was not a party to the case against her husband, was rejected by the Court of Appeal, but the House of Lords allowed her appeal.[140] The House held it was not an abuse of process for W to attempt to reopen the issue of ownership of the matrimonial home in the High Court. The Crown Court exercised a criminal function, but if there was a dispute as to civil law rights the Crown Court had to leave the interested third party to pursue a civil remedy in the civil courts. The court also operated as a public authority within the meaning of the Human Rights Act 1998, and consequently fell under the duty to act compatibly with Convention rights generally, not just those of defendant. Lord Hobhouse explicitly stated that had the legislation not itself given rise to this conclusion, it would have been necessary to explore the question whether the interests of the wife in the property were protected under the Human Rights Act 1998.[141] Third party interests are explicitly recognised in Scotland[142] but no such explicit provision was thought necessary in England and Wales.

Defendant Absconds

Where the defendant absconds after the trial has reached a verdict, a confiscation order may still be made.[143] More questionably, there is provision for the

---

[135] *HM Customs & Excise (2) Richard Long v (1) MCA (2) JMA* [2002] EWCA Civ 1039, reversing in part *Re A, A v A* [2002] All ER (D) 128 (Munby J).

[136] *R v Taigel (Peter John)* [1998] 1 CAR(S) 328.

[137] *R v Robson* (1991) 92 CAR 1.

[138] *R v Porter* [1990] 3 All ER 784.

[139] *Re Norris* (CA) [2000] 1 WLR 1094.

[140] *Re Norris* (HL) [2001] UKHL 34, [2001] 3 All ER 961.

[141] The rights in question were presumably under the First Protocol, but possibly also under the right to private *and family* life. The Article 8 argument was mentioned by the Joint Committee on Human Rights, *Eleventh Report: Proceeds of Crime Bill* (February 2002) para 29.

[142] PCA 2002 s 98.

[143] PCA 2002 s 27.

making of an order when the defendant's trial is not completed, and a period of two years has elapsed.[144] At the time of the enactment of the Proceeds of Crime Act 2002 the power, which had been in existence since 1993 for drugs offenders, had never been used.[145]

The Standard and Burden of Proof in Confiscation Proceedings—No Criminal Lifestyle

The Hodgson Committee had divided on the allocation of the burden of proof in respect of confiscation orders.[146] The majority favoured the imposition of a burden upon someone convicted of drug trafficking, but in respect of no other offences.

> The reasons advanced are that the trafficking in hard drugs inflicts such terrible social harm and is, by its nature, so difficult to detect that when a wholesaler is caught and convicted condign measures are justified to ensure that he enters prison stripped of his ill-gotten gains. We are not here speaking of mere couriers or retailers but their employers, and we believe that any new investigative techniques should be limited to those convicted of supplying hard drugs in substantial amounts.[147]

The more liberal wing of the committee took the contrary view:

> . . . [O]ur principles of criminal procedure are tested most strongly where defendants are unpopular or have been accused of the most offensive behaviour but they ought to withstand that test. One of the most basic principles is that a person is presumed innocent until proved guilty. This presumption now forms part of the European Convention on Human Rights (Article 6(2)). That presumption must mean that a defendant is entitled to stay silent, to be uncooperative, to insist that the Crown prove its case with or without his help.[148]

This debate resounds through the history of the legislation on laundering. The Vienna Convention endorsed shifting the burden of proving that items were acquired lawfully onto the defendant.[149] When the power was put in place to make confiscation orders, the burden of proving that the property in question had unlawful provenance was placed on the prosecution.

Following an early reverse, it is now clear that *where* the burden is on the prosecution in respect of a confiscation order, the standard of proof is the balance of probabilities. In *R v Dickens*[150] the Court of Appeal laid down, under the Drug Trafficking Offences Act 1986, that it was for the prosecution to prove

---

[144] PCA 2002 s 28.

[145] HL Debates 22 April 2002 col 99 (Lord Rooker).

[146] *Hodgson Report*, 82–3.

[147] *Hodgson Report*, 82–3: they suggested (in 1984) that the drugs be class A and the sum perhaps £100,000.

[148] *Hodgson Report*, 83.

[149] Art 5(7).

[150] *R v Dickens* [1990] 2 QB 102; [1990] 2 All ER 626; see also *R v Enwezor* (1991) 93 CAR 233.

to a criminal standard (that is, beyond reasonable doubt) that D had benefited from drug trafficking and the amount of the benefit, but that if there was prima facie evidence that property was held by D since his convictions or transferred to him since the beginning of a period of six years ending when proceedings were instituted, a judge could assume that it was a payment or reward related to the drug trafficking. This was a liberal stand, clearly contrary to the intention that had been expressed during the passage of the legislation.[151] It was in response to this case that Parliament introduced section 71(7A) Criminal Justice Act 1988, which makes the standard of proof that applicable in civil proceedings.[152] This rule is maintained in the 2002 Act, which adopts 'the balance of probabilities'.[153]

In the debates on the relevant provisions the minister responsible referred to a judgment in a care case:

> The balance of probability standard means that the court is satisfied that an event occurred if the court considers that, on the evidence, the occurrence of the event was more likely than not. When assessing the probabilities the court will have in mind as a factor, to whatever extent is appropriate in the particular case, that the more serious the allegation the less likely it is that the event occurred and, hence, the stronger should be the evidence before the court concludes that the allegation is established on the balance of probability. Fraud is usually less likely than negligence. Deliberate physical injury is usually less likely than accidental physical injury . . . built into the preponderance of probability standard is a generous degree of flexibility in respect of the seriousness of the allegation.
>
> Although the result is much the same, this does not mean that where a serious allegation is in issue the standard of proof required is higher. It means only that the inherent probability or improbability of an event is itself a matter to be taken into account when weighing the probabilities and deciding whether, on balance, the event occurred. The more improbable the event, the stronger must be the evidence that it did occur before, on the balance of probability, its occurrence will be established.[154]

This raises the possibility of a 'variable civil standard'.[155] The same issue arises as to the burden under the civil recovery[156] procedure and as to cash forfeitures.[157] If, in spite of a commitment in the statute to 'the balance of probabilities' and to that as meaning something quite different from the criminal

---

[151] HL Debates vol 472 col 92, 4 March 1986 (Lord Glenarthur). Note that the above cases were before *Pepper v Hart* [1993] AC 593; [1993] 1 All ER 42 rendered admissible such aids to construction.

[152] DTA 1994 s 2(8) was in identical terms.

[153] PCA 2002 s 6(7).

[154] HC Debs Standing Committee B Tuesday 20 November 2001 (Bob Ainsworth), quoting Lord Nichols in *Re H (Minors) (Sexual Abuse: Standard of Proof), Re* [1996] AC 563; [1996] 1 All ER 1.

[155] And see IH Dennis, *The Law of Evidence* (London, Sweet & Maxwell, 2nd edn, 2002) 395 *et seq.*

[156] See the section below ch 11, Evidence.

[157] *Butt v HM Customs and Excise* [2001] EWHC Admin 1066. See the section above ch 6, Human Rights Challenges to Cash Forfeiture. *Butler v United Kingdom* (2002).

standard, it might be that law is now not far from the position in *R v Dickens*.[158]
If so, satisfaction of the standard by the prosecutor or the ARA so as to secure
orders for confiscation, forfeiture and civil recovery will all be quite difficult. If,
on the other hand, the variable standard does not commit the courts to anything
resembling the criminal standard,[159] then the problems of proof which have
been said to beset the State will be eased.

The Standard and Burden of Proof in Confiscation Proceedings—Applying the Lifestyle Provisions

From the Proceeds of Crime Act 1995 forward, when the provisions which are
now the 'lifestyle' provisions are triggered, the legislation has placed the burden
upon the defendant of proving on the balance of probabilities that the property
in question[160] was *not* the proceeds of crime. The practical justification for this
is that without shifting the burden of proof there is little chance that the confiscation procedures will ever yield sufficient money to make them worthwhile.
The legal justification that is offered seems to be that the defendant is best
placed to know the provenance of his/her assets.[161] This argument is commonly
used to support the making of exceptions to the general rule in the law of evidence that 's/he who asserts must prove'. It is used, for instance, to support the
rule that the burden of disproving the facts underlying an assessment to taxation
is on the taxpayer.[162] The most obvious case where somebody might be assumed

[158] Discussing what is now PCA 2002 s 241(3), Vera Baird MP quoted from Lord Bingham in *B v Chief Constable of Avon and Somerset Constabulary*, [2001] 1 WLR 340. He said:

It should, however, be clearly recognised . . . that the civil standard of proof does not invariably mean a bare balance of probability . . . The civil standard is a flexible standard to be applied with greater or lesser strictness according to the seriousness of what has to be proved and the implica- tions of proving those matters.
I have no doubt that, in deciding whether the—
question in respect of truth of criminality—
is fulfilled, a magistrates' court should apply a civil standard of proof which will for all practical purposes be indistinguishable from the criminal standard.
She went on: 'Granted, the Bill sets out, and the background documentation sets out as a pol- icy, a hierarchy of proceedings so that the choice will be to prosecute on the criminal burden of proof when prosecution is possible and to resort to civil recovery only when it is not. It is not prac- tical for the burden of proof in civil recovery ever to be as high as that in criminal proceedings, or one would not be able to succeed where one had already failed. Consequently, there are real conundrums in respect of the standard of proof.' (HC Debates 26 Feb 2002: Column 657–8).

[159] *Per* Hallett J in *Butt v HM Customs and Excise* [2001] EWHC Admin 1066. Note especially that the decision of the HL in *Clingham v Royal Borough of Kensington & Chelsea* [2002] UKHL 39 seems to render such a reading illegitimate.

[160] Meaning property acquired by 'general criminal conduct'—'all his criminal conduct'—PCA 2002 s 76(2), extending to cover property acquired in the 6 years prior to the proceedings: PCA 2002 s 10(2).

[161] HL Debates 22 April 2002 cols 66–67 (Lord Goldsmith, A-G).

[162] John Tiley, *Revenue Law*, 4th edn (Oxford, Hart, 2000) 69. See also the pre-Human Rights Act rules on implied shifting of the burden of proof onto the defendant in a criminal case. Under *R v Hunt* [1987] AC 352 the courts had greater license to place the burden on the defendant when s/he was best placed to know.

to know all the facts but does not have to prove them is in respect of *mens rea* in criminal cases. The defendant might be the only one who knows whether or not an act was intentional, but the prosecution must still prove that it was.[163]

The issue of principle is clearer cut.[164] So far as concerns the decision in particular cases, the fundamental risk is of error.[165] Any rules that place the burden upon the defendant to show something not to have been will generate more incorrect findings of guilt or confiscation orders than where the burden is on the prosecution. In the criminal justice climate of the early twenty-first century this sort of risk is one legislators are eager to bear.

Corporate Defendants

There is increasing emphasis in various areas of criminal law upon corporate criminal liability. In recent years this has become an article of faith in the internationalisation of criminal law. The creation of corporate criminal liability is thought to resolve issues that would otherwise be problematic. It is thought that complex managerial structures can impede the ascription to one human being of the responsibility, and that a sanction imposed upon an institution can act as a catalyst for the reorganisation of the management and supervisory structures.[166] The Vienna Convention made no mention of corporate liability, but many subsequent international instruments do require it. The Council of Europe is heading a drive for the imposition of corporate criminal liability among member and candidate States.[167] The seventh of the 40 recommendations of the FATF holds that corporate liability should be imposed 'where possible'. The obvious advantage from the point of view of law enforcement is that it may be easier to proceed successfully in respect of assets held by a corporation than by an individual. At the very least, the individual should not be able to secure immunity for the property by using a 'corporate veil'. The response in England and Wales to corporate criminality has been lukewarm, but the shift of focus towards approaching the financial aspects of crime, and placing less emphasis upon criminal trial, will inevitably direct more attention towards more widespread use of corporate criminal liability.[168] During the debates on the Proceeds of Crime Act 2002 the

---

[163] *Woolmington v DPP* [1935] AC 462.

[164] Paul Roberts, 'Taking the Burden of Proof Seriously' [1995] *Criminal Law Review* 783; 'The Presumption of Innocence brought home? *Kebilene* deconstructed' (2002) 118 *Law Quarterly Review* 41.

[165] For the expression of the law of evidence in terms of allocation of the risk of incorrect decisions, see A Stein, 'The Refoundation of Evidence Law' (1996) IX *Canadian Journal of Law and Jurisprudence* 279.

[166] United Nations, *Commentary on the United Nations Convention against Illicit Traffic in Narcotic Drugs and Psychotropic Substances 1988*, (New York City, New York, United Nations, 1998) paras 3.54–3.55.

[167] This was one of the objectives of the Octopus II programme, which operated from 1997–1999.

[168] And see generally Celia Wells, *Corporations and Criminal Responsibility*, 2nd edn (Oxford, Oxford University Press, 2001).

Attorney-General made clear his view that there was no reason not to apply the 'lifestyle' provisions to corporate defendants,[169] but amendments which would have had the effect of making this explicit were rejected.[170]

Confiscation—Human Rights Objections

There is a range of human rights' claims that can be made against Confiscation Orders. It has been central to the continuation of the crusade against money laundering that they should be able to be sidestepped or ignored by the courts. The Convention has hitherto given defendants little purchase.

Legitimacy of the Shifted Burden

The lifestyle provisions create a series of assumptions which the court is to make.[171] It is assumed that any property the defendant obtained or held in the six years before the relevant day[172] was obtained by general criminal conduct, that expenditure incurred by him was met from property obtained as a result of general criminal conduct, and that he obtained any property free of any other interests. The force of the lifestyle provisions is that that they allow an assessment to be made that a defendant had wealth that, in fact, s/he did not.[173] The objection to the assumptions is exactly the same. Harmful consequences are to be imposed upon a defendant in consequence of a legal fiction. Human rights challenges have been abundant but unsuccessful.

Under the Convention there are two major questions. They are whether Article 6 applies at all to confiscation proceedings, and if it does, whether it falls within the cases where the presumption of innocence may be displaced. If it were once granted that the confiscation procedure falls within Article 6 of the Convention, the lifestyle provisions might seem to be inconsistent with Article 6(2) (the presumption of innocence) and postponements in confiscation proceedings (which are the norm) with Article 6(3) (to be 'informed promptly of the nature and cause of the accusation against him').[174] This was noticed by the Appeal Court of the High Court of Justiciary in *McIntosh v HM Advocate*,[175] holding the assumptions under the Proceeds of Crime (Scotland) Act 1995 (the equivalent provisions in Scotland to the Proceeds of Crime Act 1995) to be inconsistent with Article 6(2), and invalid.[176] In *R v Benjafield*[177] the Court of

---

[169] HL Debates 25 June 2002 col 1216 (Lord Goldsmith A-G).
[170] HL Debates 11 July 2002 col 840 (Lord Goodhart).
[171] PCA 2002 s 10.
[172] Usually the day proceedings started—PCA 2002 s 10(8).
[173] And see the observations on the standard of proof, above pp 145 *et seq*.
[174] *Rezvi*, at para 12 *per* Lord Steyn.
[175] *McIntosh v HMA* 2000 SCCR 1017; [2000] UKHRR 751.
[176] Under the constitutional arrangement in Scotland embodied in Scotland Act 1998 s 57(2).
[177] *R v Benjafield* [2001] 3 WLR 75; [2001] 2 All ER 609.

Appeal in England held, following the decision of the High Court of Justiciary, that the presumption of innocence *prima facie* applied to confiscation proceedings. The Judicial Committee of the Privy Council, in a critical decision for the relationship between the confiscation provisions and the Human Rights legislation, then allowed the appeal in *McIntosh* and held that since the defendant had already been convicted, there was no question of the presumption of innocence being available.[178] Delivering the leading judgment, Lord Bingham's view was that:

> [the respondent] cannot overcome the problem of showing either that he is 'charged' or that he is accused of any 'criminal offence'. He faces a financial penalty (with a custodial penalty in default of payment) but it is a penalty imposed for the offence of which he has been convicted and involves no accusation of any other offence.[179]

A decision to like effect was taken by the European Court of Human Rights in *Phillips v United Kingdom*.[180] The dissent relied upon a series of decisions to the effect that Article 6 should apply at every stage in the criminal process.[181] There is much to be said for Ashworth's suggestion that neither decision is convincing because the adoption of the assumptions going back six years does involve an aspersion as to past wrongdoing going beyond the offence in respect of which there is a conviction,[182] but the chapter was apparently closed by the decisions of the House of Lords in *Rezvi*[183] and *Benjafield*,[184] both following *McIntosh*. These decisions end any argument that Article 6 applies to confiscation proceedings, and, since the Proceeds of Crime Act lifestyle provisions are equivalent in principle, must validate them also.[185] There is little reason to suppose that the decisions under the 'statutory assumptions' in the Criminal Justice Act 1988 and Drug Trafficking Act 1994 will not apply equally to the lifestyle provisions under the Proceeds of Crime Act 2002. Nonetheless 'with the possible exception of the Irish Republic . . . post conviction reversal of the burden of proof typically yields modest results and crime proceeds income is not redirected towards the police or to development agencies'.[186]

---

[178] *HM Advocate v McIntosh (Sentencing)* [2001] UKPC D1; [2001] 3 WLR 107.

[179] Para 25.

[180] *Phillips v United Kingdom* (2001) 11 BHRC 280.

[181] *Minelli v Switzerland* (1983) 5 EHRR 554, a decision to award costs against the defendant in criminal defamation proceedings that were stopped before judgment was reached.

[182] See note by AJA at [2001] *Criminal Law Review* 818.

[183] [2002] UKHL 1.

[184] *R v Benjafield* [2002] UKHL 2.

[185] Note that the same line of reasoning does not apply to actions to confiscate the assets of a defendant against whom no criminal charge has been brought. *McIntosh* and *Phillips, Rezvi* and *Benjafield* do not guarantee the consistency of the civil recovery procedure with the Convention. See the section below ch 11, The Director and the Agency.

[186] Michael Levi, 'Following the Criminal and Terrorist Money Trails' in Petrus van Duyne and Klaus von Lampe (eds), *Criminal finances and organizing crime in Europe* (forthcoming); Michael Levi, *Best Practice Report No 3: Reversal of the Burden of Proof in Confiscation of the Proceeds of Crime* (Strasbourg, Council of Europe, 2001).

Article 7 and Retroactivity

Confiscation orders may only be made consistently with the Convention in respect of offences committed after the relevant confiscation legislation came into force.[187]

Confiscation and the First Protocol

The other general human rights' objection that can be made to the confiscation provisions is that they interfere with the right of property under the First protocol. This argument was ventilated and dismissed in the cases of *Rezvi*[188] (dealing with the Criminal Justice Act 1988) and *Benjafield*[189] (dealing with the Drug Trafficking Act 1994). In order to satisfy the protocol the provisions had to be proportional to the objective sought. The test was laid down in *De Freitas v Ministry of Agriculture*.[190] In *Rezvi*[191] Lord Steyn, applying this test, held that the 1988 Act was passed in furtherance of a legitimate aim, and that the measures were rationally connected to that aim.[192] So long as the proportionality requirement is satisfied,[193] the First Protocol will present no further obstacle. The particular question of the 'proceeds not just profits' doctrine was not raised.

Proceeds Not Just Profits—the Human Rights Challenges

Even if confiscation orders in general, whether or not under the lifestyle provisions, prove Convention-proof, particular questions arise as to the 'proceeds not just profits' doctrine. The principle against permitting a person to benefit from crime is a legitimate and defensible but also a limited principle.[194] It does not support the 'proceeds not just profits' doctrine.[195] The element of a confiscation order that goes beyond profits is open to challenges that have been ruled out elsewhere.[196] The human rights challenge to seizures which (i) extend beyond profits; and (ii) are not part of the punishment for the crime will have very much the same bases as the human rights challenge to forfeiture which (i) does not prevent crime and (ii) is not of an item whose possession is itself illegal, and the

---

[187] *Welch v United Kingdom* (1995) 20 EHRR 247.
[188] [2002] UKHL 1.
[189] [2002] UKHL 2.
[190] [1999] 1 AC 69.
[191] [2002] UKHL 1 para 14–15.
[192] See also *Benjafield* [2002] UKHL 2 para 8 for the drug legislation.
[193] See the section above ch 6, First Protocol—The Right to Property.
[194] See the section above ch 3, Qualifying and Limiting the Principle Against Allowing Criminals to Keep the Profits of Crime.
[195] See the section above ch 3, The Nature of the Claim of the State to the Profits of the proceeds of Crime.
[196] See the section above in this ch, The Standard and Burden of Proof in Confiscation Proceedings—Applying the Lifestyle Provisions.

underlying philosophical issue about the nature of the personal right of property against the State again arises.[197] In addition to the other challenges to confiscation, there could be a challenge specifically directed against the confiscation of 'proceeds not just profits' under Article 6, Article 7 (where there is an attempt to apply the rules retroactively), the First Protocol (quiet enjoyment of property) or (should the United Kingdom accept it) the double jeopardy protocol.

Article 6

The penalty element of the 'proceeds not just profits' doctrine may also bring cases within Article 6 that might otherwise not have been. The Article 6 argument in respect of that part of a confiscation order that extends beyond the profits of crime is as follows. The rationale for saying that Article 6 does not apply to the order is that the person against whom the confiscation proceedings are brought is not 'charged with a criminal offence' for the purposes of Article 6, but simply undergoing proceedings which do not themselves involve a fresh charge or finding of liability.[198] In the case where the defendant is exposed to the operation of the 'proceeds not just profits' doctrine s/he faces a fresh penalty. The existence of this penalty might change the characterisation of the proceedings. If it does, then a number of consequences follow.

Burden and Standard of Proof: the basis of the decisions in the line of cases holding that Article 6 does not apply to confiscation proceedings[199] is that the defendant is merely being treated in respect of the offence for which there has been a conviction(s). If Article 6(2) applies, this would put in question the statutory expression of the standard of proof as the 'balance of probabilities'.[200] If the 'proceeds not just profits' does trigger Article 6(2), then, subject to its being displaced, the burden would fall on the prosecution and the standard will be the criminal one.

Informing the defendant of the charge: in *Rezvi*,[201] Lord Steyn made the point that if Article 6 were to apply to confiscation proceedings, then a difficulty would immediately be presented.

---

[197] Compare the section above ch 6, First Profotol—The Right to Property.

[198] This is the basis of the holdings in *HM Advocate v McIntosh (Sentencing)* [2001] UKPC D1; [2001] 3 WLR 107, *Phillips v United Kingdom* (2001) 11 BHRC 280, *R v Rezvi* [2002] UKHL 1 and *R v Benjafield* [2002] UKHL 2: above, 148 *et seq*.

[199] And compare the position as to forfeiture in the section above ch 3, Forfeiture.

[200] This assumes that in proceedings of this sort 'balance of probabilities' has a meaning distinct from 'beyond reasonable doubt'. See the discussion of *H (Minors) (Sexual Abuse: Standard of Proof), Re* [1996] AC 563; [1996] 1 All ER 1 and *B v Chief Constable of Avon and Somerset Constabulary* [2001] 1 WLR 340, in the section in this ch, The Standard and Burden of Proof in Confiscation Proceedings—No Criminal Lifestyle and now see also *Clingham v Royal Borough of Kensington & Chelsea* [2002] UKHL 39.

[201] [2002] UKHL 1.

After all, a 'criminal charge' gives rise to a 'minimum right' under Article 6(3)(a) 'to be informed promptly . . . of the nature and cause of the accusation against him.' This provision fits in uneasily with confiscation proceedings with its elaborate step-by-step machinery designed to obtain information to enable the court eventually to decide whether a confiscation order should be made and, if so, in what sum.[202]

That is, irrespective of the burden of proof, the procedure is too much an inquisitorial one to satisfy the Convention. This is an interesting point of view, because what it implies is that whenever it is possible to find a 'criminal charge' in confiscation proceedings, then the entire procedure, rather than just the period to which it applies (as under Article 7) or the rules of procedure or evidence or as to lawyers (as under more usual Article 6 challenges) is vulnerable to challenge, and that whatever is done to meet the more specific Article 6 and 7 challenges will fail.

First Protocol Property Rights

Unlike forfeiture, which might be able to be defended against a First Protocol claim on the grounds that it regulates the *use* of property, confiscation extending beyond profits could not, because there is no property whose use is necessarily controlled by the use of confiscation orders.[203] If confiscation is to be justified by relation to the 'general interest ' requirement in the first sentence, then that justification needs to be made out, and an explanation must be offered as to why confiscation extending only to profits is not sufficient. In this context it is important to notice that for the purposes of the liability to tax of someone trading illegally, deductions may be made for business expenses, so long as those expenditures are not themselves illegal.[204]

Double Jeopardy

The double jeopardy Protocol (Protocol 7 Article 4) to the European Convention on Human Rights states:

> **Right not to be tried or punished twice** 1. No one shall be liable to be tried or punished again in criminal proceedings under the jurisdiction of the same State for an offence for which he has already been finally acquitted or convicted in accordance with the law and penal procedure of that State. . . .

It is the expressed intention of the Government to accede.[205] So far as concerns the 'proceeds not just profits' doctrine, the relevant words are, 'No one shall be liable to be tried or punished again in criminal proceedings under the jurisdiction of the same State for an offence for which he has already been finally . . .

---

[202] Para 12.
[203] And compare the section above ch 6, First Protocol—The Right to Property.
[204] Income and Corporation Taxes Act 1988 s 577A.
[205] *Rights Brought Home* (Cmnd 3782, 1997) para 4.15.

convicted.' There seems no reason why confiscation proceedings should not be held to be 'criminal proceedings' for the purpose of the protocol notwithstanding that there is no 'criminal charge' for the purposes of Article 6.[206] Consequently, if the United Kingdom does adopt the protocol then there is at least a strong argument that the operation of the 'proceeds not just profits' doctrine contravenes it. The element of the confiscation order that is not profit must be penalty, and, since the 'normal' penalty will already have been fixed, this is a second and consequently unwarranted one. It is difficult to ses how the United Kingdom Government can accede to the double jeopardy principle while the 'proceeds not just profits' doctrine remains in force.

RELATIONSHIP OF CONFISCATION TO OTHER ADVERSE CONSEQUENCES[207]

As with the provisions as to forfeiture,[208] the relationship between confiscation orders and other liabilities of the defendant is critical to the evaluation of the purpose of the legislation, and to questions of double jeopardy. Should there still be a set-off between the punishment that is imposed, and the sum that can be confiscated? That is, is the confiscation order independent of any fine, any other penalty or forfeiture order that the court imposes, or is it part of an overall sentencing package? The court must take account[209] of the confiscation order in imposing a fines, compensation orders,[210] forfeiture orders[211] and deprivation orders.[212]

As to the question of priority between confiscation order and compensation orders, if it appears to the court that the individual will not have sufficient means to satisfy both the orders in full, it shall direct that so much of the compensation as will not in its opinion be recoverable because of the insufficiency of his or her means shall be paid out of any sums recovered under the confiscation order.[213]

Does the fact that a confiscation order is made stand in the way of forfeiture in respect of what is substantially the same property? The answer given by the House of Lords in *Smith (David Cadman)*[214] is in the negative. In that case Lord Rodger said:

---

[206] The '*Engel* criteria' are satisfied. Ben Emmerson and Andrew Ashworth, *Human Rights and Criminal Justice* (London, Sweet and Maxwell, 2001) see the section in this ch above, Proceeds Not Just Profits.

[207] And see the discussion of double counting in the section above ch 6, Confiscation, Forfeiture and Double Counting.

[208] And see above, p 117.

[209] PCA 2002 s 13.

[210] Powers of Criminal Courts (Sentencing) Act 2000 s 130, replacing Powers of Criminal Courts Act 1973 s 35.

[211] Misuse of Drugs Act 1971 s 27.

[212] Ie under Powers of Criminal Courts (Sentencing) Act 2000 s 143, as to which see the section above ch 6, Forfeiture Upon Conviction.

[213] PCA 2002 s 13(5) and (6).

[214] [2001] UKHL 68: see the section in this ch, Proceeds Not Just Profits.

I am accordingly satisfied that the decision of the Court of Appeal on this point was wrong. It is worth adding that, if adopted, their interpretation would go a long way to making the confiscation provisions ineffective against smugglers. After all, there will be few, if any, cases where customs officers will fail to seize contraband goods which they find in the hands of smugglers. The decision of the Court of Appeal would mean that in any such case, for the purposes of section 71(5), the smugglers would derive no pecuniary benefit from evading the excise duty and so no confiscation order could be made against them. Fortunately, the terms of the legislation do not lead to that result.[215]

By implication Lord Rodger's view that the availability of other means of proceeding against the defendant (in this case, the forfeiture of the cigarettes[216]) does not argue against the availability of confiscation. The obvious answer is that it might not be so bad if confiscation provisions were ineffective (meaning, apparently, inapplicable) against smugglers against whom forfeiture provisions were instituted. On the contrary, this might have been precisely what was intended, or what would have been intended had it been considered, precisely *because forfeiture was already available in those cases.* To allow both forfeiture *and* confiscation is unnecessary and unfair. Nonetheless, both Houses of Parliament rejected amendments directed towards altering this position.[217]

Whether or not satisfactory justifications can be advanced for forfeiture more generally, forfeiture in customs proceedings has always been used as a rough and ready mixture of criminal and civil sanctions.[218] The customs authorities have, for many years, had the power to forfeit contraband that is being smuggled.[219] Confiscation was introduced to deal with perceived deficiencies in the forfeiture régime.[220] Those deficiencies do not, however, obtain in the customs field. Lord Rodger need not have been unhappy, therefore, had the confiscation provisions not applied to customs forfeitures. The State has enough power already.

PROCEDURE—THE INTERVIEW AND THE PROSECUTOR'S STATEMENT

When the prosecutor or the Director requires a confiscation hearing, the prosecutor or the Director (as the case may be) is required to give the court a statement detailing the defendant's benefit from criminal conduct. The basis from

---

[215] Para 29.

[216] No mention is made of the other enforcement mechanisms available to the Customs and Excise (in particular, the power to impose penalties), but they might be thought a further reason against confiscation in *Smith*.

[217] See the section in this ch, Proceeds Not Just Profits.

[218] Sufficiently civil not to attract the protections of Article 6(2) of the European Convention to those against whom it is deployed: *Goldsmith v Customs and Excise* [2001] 1 WLR 1673.

[219] Above, ch 4 Statutory forfeiture p 73.

[220] *R v Cuthbertson* [1981] AC 470, [1980] 2 All ER 401, see the section above ch 4, The Origins of Confiscation Law.

which confiscation proceedings follow is the prosecutor's statement of matters relevant to determining that the defendant has benefited, and the extent to which s/he has benefited.[221] The defendant can be ordered to provide information.[222] The police conduct the interview and engage in other enquiries to determine the extent of the defendant's wealth for the purposes of assessing the amount of the defendant's 'realisable property' that can form part of a confiscation order. The purpose of the interview is the production of the prosecutor's statement that informs the deliberations as to the amount of the order. Failure to attend for interview without reasonable excuse or to answer questions is something from which adverse inferences can be drawn.[223] Failure to answer may also be the subject of contempt proceedings.[225]

The information that is gathered for the statement is acquired by interviews with the defendant and the use of production orders and orders to provide information. Acceptance of the statement by the defendant creates an agreed set of facts. In *R v Emmett*[225] the defendants argued that in accepting prosecution statements as to their proceeds of drug trafficking they had acted under a mistaken view of the law in that they had assumed that drugs that had been seized by customs and excise officers could by themselves amount to a benefit from drug trafficking under the 1986 Act. The House of Lords held that the section of the 1986 Act[226] providing that the court might treat the defendant's acceptance of a statement tendered to the court by the prosecutor under section 3(1)(a) as conclusive of the matters to which it related did not, on its true construction, exclude the general right to appeal against a confiscation order. Consequently a defendant was entitled to argue on appeal that his acceptance of a section 3(1) statement had been based on a mistake of law or fact, the question not being what mistake his counsel had made but what mistake he had made; but that here, however, the defendants had not established that their agreement to the confiscation orders had been as a result of the mistaken view of the law alleged by them.

In responding to the prosecutor's statement the defendant is granted the privilege against self-incrimination, but not, apparently, the right that admissions be not used in respect of subsequent confiscation or other proceedings otherwise than for 'an offence'.[227] Unless the prosecutor's statement is controverted, it is taken as fact.[228] It is possible to update the statement, either at the instance of the prosecutor or the court.[229] It is open to the defendant to accept the prosecutor's statements completely or to a limited extent.[230] As long as a copy of the

[221] PCA 2002 s 16.
[222] PCA 2002 s 18(2).
[223] PCA 2002 s 18(4).
[224] PCA 2002 s 18(5).
[225] *R v Emmett* [1998] AC 773; [1997] 4 All ER 737.
[226] Drug Trafficking Offences Act 1986 s 3(1): see now PCA 2002 s 17(2).
[227] PCA 2002 s 17(6), s 18(9).
[228] PCA 2002 s 17(2).
[229] PCA 2002 s 16(6).
[230] PCA 2002 s 17(2).

statement has been served upon the defendant prior to the hearing the court may require the defendant to indicate to what extent he accepts each allegation in the statement and, so far as he does not accept any such allegation, to indicate any matters he proposes to rely on.[231]

ENFORCEMENT OF CONFISCATION ORDERS

Under the previous régime the expense of the use of the High Court was thought a substantial impediment to success. The principal weapons in the armoury of the Crown Prosecution Service were charging orders and restraint orders. A charging order was a mechanism for putting in place a legally enforceable charge upon property. Section 78 of the Criminal Justice Act 1988[232] gave the High Court power to make a charging order on realisable property for securing the payment to the Crown. Charging orders were abolished by the Proceeds of Crime Act 2002.[233] They were replaced by the cheaper and more pro-active enforcement tool of receivership. A restraint order prevents dealing in the property. The principal shifts in the enforcement machinery under the Proceeds of Crime Act are the moving of the proceedings to the Crown Court, the abolition of charging orders and the more widespread use of receivership—to be paid for, ultimately, out of the assets seized. Various minor faults in the pre-existing scheme are also removed. There was, in particular, no provision for a judge to order the transfer to the State of the ownership of restrained assets. Where assets were restrained or detained they had, under the previous régimes to be released to the defendant before they could be subject to a confiscation order. This made the enforcement procedure significantly less efficient.[234]

Restraint Orders

It is not enough to have powers to confiscate assets. It is necessary to have the means to prevent the defendant from concealing or moving or alienating the assets so as to place them beyond the reach of the English courts during the time in which a decision is being made as to whether or not to prosecute and, if successful, confiscate. Restraint orders are intended to prevent dealing in a bank account or other assets of a person under investigation. They have the effect of prohibiting any person from 'dealing' with any realisable property.[235] Where

---

[231] PCA 2002 s 17(1).
[232] The equivalent provision is DTA 1994 s 27.
[233] PCA 2002 Schedule 12.
[234] *PIU Report* para 8.38 recommended the alteration of this rule: PCA 2002 s 49(2)(a) achieved it.
[235] Dealing includes removing of the property from the jurisdiction (PCA 2002 s 41(9)), but the further definition which appeared as CJA 1988 s 77(9) and DTA 1994 s 26(8) ('For the purposes of this section, dealing with property held by any person includes (without prejudice to the generality

there is an application for a restraint order affecting land, an inhibition may be entered at the Land Registry.[236] The application may be by the prosecutor, the Director or an accredited financial investigator.[237] An order may be made both against the defendant (or person under investigation) and any other person holding realisable property. An exception is made for the reasonable living and legal expenses of the person against whom the order is made, and for the expenses of carrying on a trade, profession or vocation.[238] However the property subject to the restraint order may not be used to pay for legal challenges to it.[239] Public funding for legal expenses will be available. Restraint orders may be made only on an application by the prosecutor, the director or an accredited financial investigator;[240] and may be made on an *ex parte* application to a judge in chambers.[241]

Whatever the theoretical benefits, before the Proceeds of Crime Act 2002 restraint orders did not prove successful in practice. The Crown Prosecution Service has limited resources and the cost of the High Court hearings was thought a deterrent to seeking the orders. The numbers of restraint orders per year declined in the late 1990s,[242] prompting the proposal from the Cabinet Office that they should be able to be granted by the Crown Court (not the High Court).[243] The powers[244] now conferred on the Crown Court[245] are exercisable where an investigation has been started[246] with regard to an offence and there is reasonable cause to suspect that the alleged offender has benefited from his criminal conduct.[247] The court may then make a restraint order, which prohibits any specified person from dealing[248] with any realisable property held by him. It had power to vary or discharge the order.[249]

The court must discharge the order if proceedings in respect of the offence are not instituted (whether by the laying of an information or otherwise), or (as the

---

of the expression)—(a) where a debt is owed to that person, making a payment to any person in reduction of the amount of the debt.) is no longer included.

Where property subject to a restraint order is the subject of another legal action the leave of the Crown Court is required, and any court has power to stay the action if it learns that a restraint order has been applied for or made. PCA 2002 s 58(5).

[236] PCA 2002 s 47.
[237] PCA 2002 s 42(2).
[238] PCA 2002 s 41(3).
[239] PCA 2002 s 41(4).
[240] PCA 2002 s 42(2).
[241] PCA 2002 s 42(1)(b).
[242] *PIU Report* table 8.1.
[243] *PIU Report* para 8.30.
[244] Which may not be exercised where there has been undue delay in continuing the proceedings or application in question: PCA 2002 s 40(7).
[245] Under the preceding legislation the High Court exercised this jurisdiction. The move is the outcome of dissatisfaction noted in the *PIU Report* that only 252 orders were made in 1997 and 247 in 1998. HL Debates 22 April 2002 col 105 (Lord Bassam of Brighton).
[246] Under the preceding legislation the court had to be satisfied that a person was to be charged.
[247] PCA 2002 s 40(2): for other analogous conditions see s 40(3)–(8).
[248] PCA 2002 s 41(9).
[249] PCA 2002 s 42.

case may be) no application is made, within such time as the court considers reasonable.[250] There is no appeal against the decision of the Crown Court to grant a restraint order. An appeal does lie against the Crown Court's decision to vary or discharge an order. A person dissatisfied with an order is consequently forced to apply first to the Crown Court for its variation or discharge[251] and only then to the Court of Appeal Civil Division.[252] However the appeal can then address the issues *de novo* rather than consider, as a narrow point of law, whether the decision to refuse to discharge or vary the order was correct.[253] Once property is subject to a restraint order, appeal against the decisions of the Crown Court is to the Court of Appeal and thence the House of Lords.[254]

There is a general right of appeal against any order of the High Court,[255] but this does not apply to the Crown Court. Consequently a prosecutor denied an order is specifically granted the right to appeal.[256] Restraint orders may be made against third parties.[257] There is a power to seize property subject to a restraint order in order to prevent its being removed from the jurisdiction.[258] Although the hearing is in the Crown Court, the rules of evidence in applications for restraint orders are the rules of evidence in civil cases, and hearsay is admitted.[259]

Enforcement of Restraint Orders

As with any other order of the court the ultimate sanction for failure to comply is to be treated as being in contempt of court.[260] In making restraint orders the jurisdiction of the courts is closely analogous to that in respect of *Mareva* orders.[261] The objective in both cases being to strike a balance at an interlocutory stage between keeping assets available to satisfy a final order, and meeting the reasonable requirements of the owner in the meantime.[262] The civil analogy only proceeds so far: the court has no jurisdiction to imply a cross-undertaking

---

[250] PCA 2002 s 41(7) and s 42(3).

[251] PCA 2002 s 42(3).

[252] PCA 2002 s 43, preserving the effect of *Re Owen (disclosure order)* [1991] 2 QB 520; [1991] 1 All ER 330, approved in *AT&T Istel v Tully* [1993] AC 45. Leave is required: s 89(1).

[253] Standing Committee B 29th November 2001 (Bob Ainsworth MP).

[254] PCA 2002 s 43, 44.

[255] Supreme Court Act 1981 s 18.

[256] PCA 2002 s 43(1), 44(2).

[257] *Re D (Restraint Order: Non-party)*, *The Times* 25 Jan 1995. This now follows from the words of PCA 2002 s 41(1): '. . . prohibiting any specified person from dealing with any realisable property held by him'.

[258] PCA 2002 s 45(1).

[259] PCA 2002 s 46, which was added at the House of Lords Committee stage.

[260] And for utterly wilful, deliberate and contumacious delays, see *Re T* [1996] COD 103.

[261] As to which see Mark SW Hoyle, *The Mareva injunction and related orders*, 3rd edn (London, LLP, 1997). They are now called freezing orders and governed by Civil Procedure Rules 1998 Part 25 r. 25.1(1)(b).

[262] *Re Peters* [1988] QB 871; [1988] 3 All ER 46.

in damages on the part of the prosecution when applying for a restraint order as a means of indemnifying innocent third parties affected by the order against any abuse or misuse of proceedings.[263]

As to the making of subsidiary orders, the *Mareva* analogy looms large:

> Counsel for the commissioners points out that a court faced with the making or variation of a restraint order or a charging order is not concerned with the making of a confiscation order or a process of execution in satisfaction of such an order. It is concerned solely with the preservation of assets at a time when it cannot know whether the accused will or will not be convicted. Such a jurisdiction is closely analogous to that exercised by the courts in relation to *Mareva* injunctions and might, not inaccurately, be referred to as a 'Drugs Act *Mareva*'. Under the *Mareva* jurisdiction the interest of the potential judgment creditor has to be balanced against those of actual creditors, whether secured or unsecured, and of the defendant himself who may succeed in the action and should be fettered in his dealing with his own property to the least possible extent necessary to ensure that the processes of justice are not frustrated. [The power to make restraint orders] is consistent with such a purpose, subject to what counsel for the commissioners described as a 'legislative steer', namely that, so far as is reasonable taking account of the fact that the accused may be acquitted and that, unlike the position under the *Mareva* jurisdiction, there is no counter-undertaking in damages although there is a discretionary power to award compensation,[264] the value of the realisable property shall be maintained in order that it may be available to satisfy any confiscation order.[265]

In *Re Owen*[266] the Court of Appeal held that the power to make a restraint order included an inherent power to make ancillary orders to ensure that the exercise of its jurisdiction was effective to achieve its purpose. Apparently to extend the residual High Court jurisdiction to the Crown Court, this is now made explicit in the statute.[267] Where the overseas asset was land or securities obtaining whose value depended on completion of formalities abroad, it may still not be possible for the court to make an appropriate order.[268]

Management Receivers

Receivers always performed two distinct functions in the confiscation scheme. 'Management' receivers manage property pending conviction or acquittal and 'enforcement receivers' dispose of it so as to satisfy a confiscation order. This division of functions is now explicit in the Proceeds of Crime Act 2002. Where a restraint order has been made, a management receiver may be appointed by

---

[263] *Re R (restraint order)* [1990] 2 QB 307; [1990] 2 All ER 569.

[264] DTA 1994 s 19: now PCA 2002 s 72.

[265] *In Re Peters* [1988] 3 All ER 46 at 51, [1988] QB 871 at 879 *per* Lord Donaldson of Lymington MR. See also *Re Piper* [2000] 1 WLR 473, [1999] 4 All ER 473.

[266] *In Re Owen* [1991] 2 QB 520; [1991] 1 All ER 330: followed in *DPP v Scarlett* [2000] 1 WLR 515 and approved in *US v Montgomery* [2001] UKHL 3; [2001] 1 WLR 196.

[267] PCA 2002 s 41(7) .

[268] *DPP v Scarlett* [2000] 1 WLR 515. The court cannot order the performance of acts outside its jurisdiction.

the Crown Court on the application of the person who applied for the restraint order.[269] The powers of a management receiver are set out so as to make clear that they are exercised with a view to maintaining the value of the amount available for confiscation.[270] Receivers may dispose of depreciating assets.[271] Costs of receivership are normally met out of the assets under the receiver's control.[272] In *Re Andrews*[273] the Court of Appeal held that the costs were still payable from the assets, but in that case the effect of the First Protocol was not argued. The argument was then made and rejected in *Hughes v Customs & Excise*.[274] The shift to the imposition of the costs upon the assets is a central part of the strategy of the 2002 Act.

When an enforcement receiver is appointed, property in the hands of a management receiver (except property realised for the management receiver's remuneration and expenses) is handed over to the enforcement receiver.[275] Further provisions deal with the legal liability of Proceeds of Crime Act receivers,[276] who are not placed under the same obligation as other receivers (for example, in insolvency) in respect of the payment of the taxes of the person whose property is under receivership.[277] Receivers' actions may be challenged by persons concerned in the Crown Court.[278]

Enforcement Receivers

Where a confiscation order has been made and the magistrates' court will be responsible for its enforcement, the Crown Court may appoint an enforcement receiver to help enforce the order. The powers of an enforcement receiver are similar to those of a management receiver but the enforcement receiver has power to realise the property. After satisfying the confiscation order, the receiver is obliged to pay any remaining sums in his/her hands to those with an interest in the property.[279] Where the Director is enforcing a confiscation order, the main enforcement tool is the appointment of a receiver. The powers of the Director's receiver are similar to those of an enforcement receiver.[280]

---

[269] PCA 2002 s 48.

[270] PCA 2002 s 49.

[271] PCA 2002 s 49(2)(b) and s 49(10)(a). Challenges are possible on the grounds, for example, of irreplacability: s 49(8).

[272] PCA 2002 s 49(2)(d).

[273] *Re Andrews* [1999] 1 WLR 1236; [1999] 2 All ER 751.

[274] *Hughes v Customs and Excise Commissioners* [2002] EWCA Civ 734.

[275] PCA 2002 s 51(5).

[276] Who are protected from liability for anything done by them to property that is not realisable property unless they are negligent: PCA 2002 s 61.

[277] PCA 2002 s 448 and Schedule 10 part 1.

[278] PCA 2002 s 62(3).

[279] PCA 2002 s 56. The Crown Court must give those with interests in the property concerned a reasonable opportunity to make representations. PCA 2002 s 54(4). Analogous provisions deal with Director's Receivers: PCA 2002 s 56.

[280] PCA 2002 s 56.

Restraint Orders, Receivers and Human Rights

Under the preceding legislation, the question arose whether or not it was consistent with the First Protocol to engage in restraint at all, and to pay the receiver (if one was appointed) out of the assets under restraint, and whether a defendant who was not convicted should still have to pay the costs of restraint proceedings.

(i) *Restraint and the First Protocol*: in *Hughes v Commissioners of Customs & Excise*[281] Simon Brown LJ held that the régime of restraint and receivership orders is not contrary to the First Protocol. He asserted that there is a significant public interest in ensuring that criminals do not profit from their crimes and that the proceeds of crime are confiscated in the event of conviction. This public interest extends to preventing the dissipation of assets prior to trial to ensure that any confiscation order made will not be thwarted.[282]

(ii) *Paying the receiver*: as to the payment of the receiver out of the assets of an unconvicted or acquitted defendant, the judge at first instance had held there to be a violation of the protocol but the Court of Appeal held that the question was whether the measures taken are (i) in the public interest, (ii) appropriate for achieving its aim, (iii) proportionate, and (iv) achieve a fair balance between the demands of the general interest of the community and the requirements of the protection of the individual's right.[283] Following the analogy of the defendant who is acquitted after having been detained pending trial, the Court of Appeal held that no legally remediable wrong is necessarily done to one who is made to defend him/herself through legal procedures but who is found not to be liable.[284]

(iii) *Paying for legal challenges:* the property subject to the restraint order may not be used to pay for legal challenges to it.[285] So long as confiscation proceedings are outside the scope of Article 6 of the European Convention, there is no prospect of a successful challenge to this rule as to restraint orders under Article 6(3)(c), which gives a person the right to 'defend himself . . . through legal assistance of his own choosing'.

(iv) *Article 6(2) and the privilege against self-incrimination:* the Crown Court has jurisdiction, when making a restraint order, to order the defendant to disclose the full value, nature and whereabouts of all his/her assets so as to render the restraint order effective, provided that the disclosure require-

---

[281] *Hughes v Commissioners of Customs & Excise* [2002] EWCA Civ 734.

[282] Para 52, citing *Raimondo v Italy* (1994) 18 EHRR 237: see the section above ch 6, First Protocol—The Right to Property.

[283] Citing *Sporrong & Lonroth v Sweden* (1983) 5 EHRR 35 and *Lithgow v United Kingdom* (1986) 8 EHRR 329.

[284] Compensation is only available on serious default: PCA 2002 s 72.

[285] PCA 2002 s 41(4).

ment is made subject to a condition that no disclosure made in compliance with the order is to be used as evidence in the prosecution of an offence alleged to have been committed by the person required to make the disclosure.[286] In *Re Thomas (Disclosure order)*[287] the Court of Appeal, by a majority, rejected the suggestion[288] that there was *no* danger of self-incrimination where the supplying of information was ordered. The way in which the danger has hitherto been averted is by a condition in the order that information gleaned may only be used for the purposes of determination as to the proceeds of crime, and that it is not admissible in any subsequent criminal proceedings. The problem cases, as in the case of any 'fruit of the forbidden tree' cases, will be those where the availability of the incriminatory evidence to the authorities gives the opportunity to find other incriminating evidence for production at the trial.

In *Re C*[289] it was held that a restraint order requiring the defendant to identify persons with whom he had done business, should expressly stipulate that evidence obtained as a direct result of disclosure under the order must not be used in any prosecution against the defendant. To rely on the general discretion to exclude evidence on grounds of unfairness[290] was not sufficient protection for the accused. The defendant was entitled to an absolute guarantee against self-incrimination. These decisions require reappraisal in the light of the developments that have taken place since, both as to Article 6 and to the privilege against self-incrimination. The privilege against self-incrimination forms part of the right to a fair trial,[291] but its limits and rationale remain unclear.[292] In *McIntosh, Phillips, Rezvi* and *Benjafield*[293] the highest courts held that the fair trial guarantees of Article 6(2) and (3) of the Convention do not apply to confiscation proceedings. The fact that the defendant had already been convicted placed him/her in a less advantageous position, in which s/he was unable to rely upon the presumption of innocence. So far as concerns other offences than those the subject of the proceedings, however, Article 6 and the privilege against self-incrimination will be available.

---

[286] *Re Owen (Disclosure order)* [1991] 2 QB 520; [1991] 1 All ER 330, *Re Thomas (Disclosure order)* [1992] 4 All ER 814.

[287] *Re Thomas (Disclosure order)* [1992] 4 All ER 814.

[288] *Re Thomas (Disclosure order)* [1992] 4 All ER 814 *per* Leggatt LJ (dissenting) at 819, holding that confiscation, being *reparative*, is not a punishment, and consequently not something against which the privilege against self-incrimination *need* operate as a shield. This suggestion seems unlikely to survive the more recent concessions (*eg per* Lord Bingham in *HM Advocate v McIntosh (Sentencing)* [2001] UKPC D1; [2001] 3 WLR 107, Para 25) that a confiscation order is a penalty.

[289] *Re C (Restraint Orders: Identification)* [1995] COD 263.

[290] Police and Criminal Evidence Act 1984 s 78.

[291] *Saunders v United Kingdom* (1997) 23 EHRR 313.

[292] Peter Alldridge and Bert Swart, 'The Privilege against Self-Incrimination in Proactive Policing' in SA Field and C Pelser (eds) *Invading the Private* (Aldershot, Dartmouth, 1998) 253; *Brown (Margaret) v Stott* [2001] 2 WLR 817; [2001] 2 All ER 97; *R v Allen* [2001] UKHL 45; [2002] 1 AC 509.

[293] See the section above in this ch, Legitimacy of the Shifted Burden.

Could evidence gained by these questions be used in subsequent criminal proceedings against the defendant? At the time of *Saunders v United Kingdom*,[294] it was thought that the privilege against self-incrimination might extend quite widely.[295] It is now clear that the privilege may be displaced by public interest considerations[296] and that it does not apply to requests for information made by the tax authorities.[297] It is unlikely that the orders will any longer necessarily incorporate an undertaking not to use information gained in subsequent prosecutions. The question is whether it could be used in that subsequent trial consistently with Article 6. The grounds upon which *Saunders* was distinguished in *Brown v Stott* were unsatisfactory,[298] but it is suggested that the decision is correct, and that *Saunders* itself is the source of the difficulty.

The problem with any régime that permits the use, for any other limited purpose, of self-incriminatory evidence is that it is impossible to put the toothpaste back in the tube. With financial information, which is frequently well documented, once the authorities have some idea (as a result of the evidence which is only admissible for specific purposes, for example, the determination of liability to taxation) of the facts it is relatively easy to secure further evidence that would be admissible in criminal proceedings to prove them.[299]

(v) *Costs of restraint proceedings*: as to the costs in the legal proceedings, the court in *Hughes* held that Schiemann J's judgment in *Re W*[300] had been correct and that the costs of restraint proceedings, upon an acquittal, should indeed be borne by the public rather than by the acquitted defendant.[301]

Prison as Alternative

The mechanism for the enforcement of unpaid confiscation orders is to treat the order as if it were a fine.[302] When a confiscation order is made it carries with it

[294] *Saunders v United Kingdom* (1998) 23 EHRR 313, [1998] 1 BCLC 362.

[295] It was upon this basis that the amendments in the Youth Justice and Criminal Evidence Act 1999 Schedule 3 were brought forward.

[296] *Brown (Margaret) v Stott* [2001] 2 WLR 817; [2001] 2 All ER 97.

[297] *R v Allen* [2001] UKHL 45; [2002] 1 AC 509.

[298] Andrew Ashworth, 'Criminal Proceedings After the Human Rights Act: the First Year' [2001] *Criminal Law Review* 855.

[299] A *witness* is entitled to claim privilege in relation to any piece of information or evidence on which the prosecution might wish to rely not only in establishing guilt but also in making their decision to prosecute: *Sociedade Nacional de Combustiveis de Angola UEE v Lundqvist* [1991] 2 QB 310.

[300] *In re W*, *The Times*, 13 October 1994.

[301] The power to award 'such compensation as the court considers just' (PCA 2002 s 73) upon discharge of the order under would extend to such payments.

[302] PCA 2002 s 35(2).

the sanction of a specified period of imprisonment in default of payment.[303] This term is to be served consecutively to any term for the principal offence.[304] Failure to pay a confiscation order prevents a person from being rehabilitated under the Rehabilitation of Offenders Act 1974.[305] Magistrates have discretion whether or not to commit to prison but must exercise the discretion keeping in mind that the defendant cannot *choose* to serve the default term instead of paying.[306] The magistrates are primarily obliged to consider other methods of enforcement short of committal (which is an acknowledgement of defeat). The existence of a confiscation order is regarded as evidence that on the date it was made there were assets to meet it. The defendant may seek a certificate of inadequacy[307] in the case where the assets have diminished in value since the making of the order. The principle upon which prison sentences are set is that the object is not to provide additional punishment, but rather to encourage compliance.[308]

Is there any kind of defence that can be mounted to a committal order, or is committal entirely a mechanical consequence of non-payment? The table of terms of imprisonment in default of payment of fines and other orders in section 139(4) of the Powers of Criminal Courts (Sentencing) Act 2000 specifies maximum terms, and the task of the sentencer is to fix an appropriate default term within the relevant band in the exercise of his discretion. Where the amount of the judge's order was near to the bottom of the bracket, it is inappropriate for the maximum default term to be ordered.[309] The legislation directs that the confiscation order be enforced as a fine. The problem is that committal to prison on default of payment of a fine is only imposed in the case where the non-payment amounts to wilful and culpable neglect.[310] In this respect a more punitive practice upon non-payment seems to obtain for confiscation orders than for other fines.[311]

Priority of Confiscation Orders Relative to Other Debts

The victim of the crime(s) in respect of which the order is to be made has priority over confiscation orders.[312] The satisfaction of confiscation orders takes precedence over any other obligations of the defendant or the recipient from him/her of a tainted gift. Any property subject to a restraint order, and any proceeds of property realised by and in the hands of the receiver, is excluded from

---

[303] Powers of Criminal Courts (Sentencing) Act 2000 s 139(2).
[304] PCA 2002 s 38(2)
[305] PCA 2002 Schedule 11 para 7.
[306] PCA 2002 s 38(5).
[307] PCA 2002 s 23–4 DTA 1994 s 17(1); Civil Procedure Rules 1998 (SI 3132), Order 115, r 9.
[308] And see s 31 DTA 1994: s 82(4); CJA 1988.
[309] *R v Szrajber* (1994) 15 CAR(S) 821.
[310] Magistrates Courts Act 1980 s 82(4)(b)(i).
[311] *R v Harrow Justices, ex parte DPP* [1991] 1 WLR 395; [1991] 3 All ER 873, *R v Liverpool Magistrates' Court, ex parte Ansen* [1998] 1 All ER 692.
[312] PCA 2002 s 6(6).

the distribution of assets upon a bankruptcy.[313] The idea is to prevent defendants using bankruptcy to defeat the purpose of the confiscation legislation. When both are possible, the procedure that starts first is the one that takes precedence. If confiscation proceedings have commenced, they take precedence over bankruptcy proceedings. If bankruptcy proceedings have started before any confiscation proceedings have begun, the bankruptcy proceedings take precedence.[314] Discharge of a bankrupt does not release the bankrupt from liability to pay a confiscation order.[315] Analogous provisions deal with the insolvency of a company rather than of an individual.[316]

The approach to the question of priorities is contentious. The rule in insolvency law that the Revenue is preferred over other unsecured creditors was long criticised, and it has now been altered.[317] During the passage of the Proceeds of Crime Act the arguments advanced by the Government for a system which, on the face if it, takes money from innocent traders and places it into the Consolidated Fund were: first, there is a risk of criminals attempting to fabricate debts to manipulate their proceeds into the hands of their criminal associates;[318] second that 'without a precedence system, criminals could run up large amounts of genuine debts so as to leave a little as possible available for confiscation';[319] third, it would be wrong to allow creditors to be paid out of the proceeds of crime.[320] The first two reasons are pragmatic, consequentialist arguments. It is difficult to know whether the fears are well founded or not. The third propounds a moral precept, apparently absolute, as to how the profits of crime should be regarded. It involves a move away from the more flexible, defeasible way in which the principle against allowing people to profit from crime operates at common law,[321] towards an absolutist view.[322] So long as the civil recovery action is constituted as a proprietary action, and consequently that the ARA can secure priority over creditors by bringing a recovery action, it would be strange if confiscation orders were not themselves prioritised.[323]

---

[313] PCA 2002 s 417(2).

[314] PCA 2002 s 418.

[315] PCA 2002 Schedule 11 inserting sections after Insolvency Act 1986 s 306.

[316] PCA 2002 s 430 (dealing with floating charges), s 431 (limited liability partnerships).

[317] Enterprise Act 2002 s 251.

[318] HL Debates 27 May 2002 col 1100 (Lord Rooker).

[319] *Ibid*. Rather unrealistically, Lord Falconer suggested that if the payment was so important to the creditor, then the creditor should seek security for the debt. HL Debates 25 June 2002 col 1234. See also HC Debates 18 July 2002 cols 518 *et seq*.

[320] HL Debates 27 May 2002 col 1101 (Lord Rooker).

[321] See the section above ch 3, Qualifying and Limiting the Principle Against Allowing Criminals to Keep the Profits of Crime.

[322] And see the section above ch 3, The Nature of the Claim of the State to the profits or the Proceeds of Crime.

[323] The Government suffered a defeat in the House of Lords (HL Debates 25 June 2002) on an opposition amendment: it had to use its Commons majority to restore this position.

External Confiscation Orders

There are arrangements under which orders of overseas' courts may be enforced in the United Kingdom. Prior to the 2002 Act, under enabling legislation[324] the courts could be directed to enforce 'external confiscation orders' from designated territories. These were orders made by the courts in the designated country for the purpose of recovering, or recovering the value of, the proceeds of crime. When governed by the external confiscation order procedure all the enforcement mechanisms that would be available were the order a confiscation order from a court in England and Wales are available. The full rules were set out in subordinate legislation.[325] In one important respect the statutory instruments have been held to be significantly wider than the corresponding statute. There is no requirement that criminal proceedings be in train in order for the overseas forfeiture order procedure to apply.[326] Although the *Acts* (Criminal Justice Act 1988, Drug Trafficking Act 1994) gave jurisdiction to make restraint orders *pending criminal proceedings* only, the *Orders* give jurisdiction to make restraint orders pending any proceedings, including civil actions directed at assets rather than offenders, where the purpose was to recover the proceeds of drug trafficking. In *United States v Montgomery*[327] it was held that the 1991 Order could apply, despite the fact that the proceedings were instituted before the Order came into force, as the ban on retrospective penal legislation,[328] which applied to domestic proceedings under the Act, was deliberately omitted from the 1991 Order[328a].

Part 11 of the Proceeds of Crime Act 2002 changes the position. The designation procedure, which had not worked very successfully, is abolished. Reciprocity of enforcement within the United Kingdom is guaranteed.[329] With other jurisdictions rules are to be put in place by Order in Council to provide the equivalent powers for the enforcement of external as internal orders,[330] and the same goes for external the investigations.[331] Property may be frozen in the United Kingdom which may be needed to satisfy overseas orders in respect of the recovery of criminal proceeds, and for the enforcement of the orders by the realisation of property in any part of the United Kingdom.[332] Since restraint orders may be granted from the start of a criminal investigation, the Home

---

[324] DTA 1994 s 39; CJA 1988 s 96.
[325] CJA 1988 (Designated Countries and Territories) Order 1996 SI 278; DTA 1994 (Designated Countries and Territories) Order 1996 SI 2880 (1996).
[326] *Re JL, Sub nom: Re Drug Trafficking Offences Act 1986 (Designated Countries and Territories) Order 1990, The Times,* 4 May 1994.
[327] *United States v Montgomery* [2001] UKHL 3, [2001] 1 WLR 196.
[328] CJA 1988 s 102(4)
[328a] Criminal Justice Act 1988 (Designated Countries and Territories) Order (SI 1991/2873), the precursor of the 1996 Order cited above fn 325.
[329] PCA 2002 s 443.
[330] PCA 2002 s 444.
[331] PCA 2002 s 445.
[332] PCA 2002 s 444.

Secretary may, by Order in Council, provide for the courts of England and Wales to restrain assets at the request of a foreign jurisdiction at an earlier stage in proceedings than is possible at present.[333]

Investigative powers are to be made available in respect of overseas investigations.[334] These will be provided by Orders in Council, which will be subject to annulment in pursuance of a resolution of either House.[335] The powers in respect of domestic investigation orders and warrants are made available for external investigations[336] and there will be equivalent offences in relation to external investigations.[337] Such offences would include the offence of prejudicing an investigation and the offence of failing to comply with a customer information or disclosure order in respect of an overseas investigation. External investigations are defined as the overseas equivalents to domestic confiscation, money laundering and civil recovery investigations.[338] Disclosure orders, however, will not be available for external money laundering investigations.[339] An external order is enforceable in the United Kingdom regardless of the form it takes.[340] It does not matter whether the order was made in criminal proceedings or not.[341] There is another scheme[342] for the enforcement by Order in Council of forfeiture orders made overseas. These are limited to the 'instrumentalities' of crime.

Levels of Confiscation

In England and Wales there is no question that the profits of the sale of drugs, or other serious crimes, have generated significant and increasing sums. It is also clear that the sums have not approached those originally mooted. By the end of 1992 £35m had been ordered to be confiscated under the 1986 Act and £15m had actually been realised.[343] More recent data are set out in Tables 1 and 2.[344]

The years to April 1998 and 1999 yielded 3.5 and 6.0 million.[345] Confiscation orders were made in about 18 per cent of drug trafficking cases and far fewer (0.3 per cent in 1998)[346] Criminal Justice Act cases. The collection rate is about 40 per cent.[347] These are very small amounts compared to the amount posited by the law enforcement authorities.

---

[333] PCA 2002 s 444.
[334] PCA 2002 s 444.
[335] PCA 2002 s 444, 445.
[336] *Ibid.*
[337] PCA 2002 s 445(1)(b).
[338] PCA 2002 s 447(3).
[339] PCA 2002 s 445(3).
[340] Ie whether *in rem* or *in personam*: PCA 2002 447(2)(b).
[341] PCA 2002 s 447(2)(a), giving statutory effect to *Re S-L* [1996] QB 272; [1995] 4 All ER 159.
[342] Under Criminal Justice (International Co-operation) Act 1990.
[343] HL Debates 3 Nov 1992 vol 539 col 1383 (Lord Glenarthur).
[344] These tables are taken from a written answer by Alun Michael, HC Debates 2 Dec 1998, cols: 197–199. Notes in text.
[345] *PIU Report* table 4.2.
[346] *PIU Report* table 4.4.
[347] *PIU Report* para 8.35.

Table 1: Drug trafficking confiscation orders (England and Wales) 1992–1996

Year	Amount ordered to be confiscated	Downward variation on appeal	Default sentences (DTOA 1986)[348]	Amount available for confiscation	Amount remitted to consolidated fund
	£				
1992	9,129,863	500,000[349]	1,271,000	7,358,863	5,180,900
1993	9,678,118	594,000	579,000	8,505,118	5,380,000
1994	25,373,426	489,000	2,537,000	22,347,426	5,135,000
1995	18,337,490	1,201,000	848,000	16,288,490	5,343,000
1996	10,471,336	1,643,000	1,342,000	7,486,336	7,415,000
Total	72,990,233	4,427,000	6,577,000	61,986,233	28,453,900

Table 2: Proceeds of criminal conduct—confiscation orders made under the Criminal Justice Act 1988 and the 1988 Act as amended by the Proceeds of Crime Act 1995 (England and Wales) 1992–1996

Year	Amount ordered to be confiscated	Downward variation on appeal	Default sentences (unamended CJA)[350] (20)	Amount available for confiscation	Amount remitted to consolidated fund
	£				
1992	1,354,000	[351]	1,000	1,353,000	481,600
1993	412,000	44,000	156,000	212,000	266,000
1994	3,042,000	17,000	471,000	2,554,000	1,318,559
1995	3,653,000	355,000	513,000	2,785,000	1,024,000
1996	6,070,000	217,000	82,000	5,771,000	1,343,000
1997					
Total	14,531,000	633,000	1,223,000	12,675,000	4,433,159

[348] Default sentences served under the Drug Trafficking Offences Act 1986 served to expunge the debt owned by the defendant.

[349] Estimate—no figures available for 1992.

[350] Default sentences served under the unamended CJA 1988 served to expunge the debt owed by the defendant.

[351] No figures available.

8

Investigatory Powers

IT IS IMPOSSIBLE to make sense of the law of money laundering without reference to the enforcement powers that are necessary implications of the legal
framework, and the burdens that framework imposes. They are significant in
their own right, but also as the thin end of a number of wedges. The enlistment
of the financial services' industry to assist the police in the apprehension of
offenders and the confiscation of their property has not proved enough for the
authorities. There are other powers, going some way beyond those powers
available under the régime for the investigation and prosecution of 'normal'
crime.[1] The major investigatory powers under the Proceeds of Crime Act 2002
are set out in Part 8 and apply to:

1. Investigation to determine whether a person has benefited from his/her criminal conduct and the extent and whereabouts of his benefit (a confiscation
   investigation);
2. Investigation to determine whether property is recoverable or associated
   property, who holds it and its extent and whereabouts (a civil recovery investigation);[2]
3. Investigation to determine whether a person has committed a money laundering offence.[3]

The Secretary of State is obliged to issue a statutory code of practice in relation
to the investigation powers.[4] A breach of the code will not necessarily render a
person liable to criminal or civil proceedings but the code will be admissible as
evidence in criminal or civil proceedings.[5] Little distinction seems to have been
made between those powers for the investigation of crimes and those that do
not.[6] For the purposes of the investigatory powers simply benefiting from

---

[1] By virtue of the amendment to Police and Criminal Evidence Act 1984 s 116 a drug trafficking
offence as defined in paragraph 1 of Schedule 2 to the PCA 2002 is always a 'serious arrestable
offence', as are the new principal 'all crime' money laundering offences under PCA 2002 ss 327–329:
PCA 2002 Schedule 11 para 14.

[2] These powers are not available if civil recovery proceedings have been started (PCA 2002 s
341(3)(a)), or an interim receiving order has been made (PCA 2002 s 341(3)(b)) or cash has been
seized and detained.

[3] PCA 2002 s 341.

[4] PCA 2002 s 377.

[5] PCA 2002 s 377(6) and (7).

[6] Applications in respect of confiscation and money laundering investigations must be made to a
judge entitled to exercise the jurisdiction of the Crown Court. Applications in respect of civil recovery investigations must be made to a High Court judge. PCA 2002 s 343, 344.

criminal conduct is regarded as the equivalent of the commission of a serious criminal offence.[7] The investigation is protected by an offence of prejudicing an investigation either by tipping-off or by tampering with evidence.[8]

PRODUCTION ORDERS

A circuit judge has power, on application by an appropriate officer,[9] to make an order to produce particular material or material of a particular description to a constable for him to take away, or give a constable access to it, within such period as the order may specify.[10] The Human Rights Act 1998 requires judges not to act incompatibly with Convention rights. A Government attempt to remove the 'public interest' test and rely wholly upon Convention rights was finally abandoned.[11] The conditions which must be satisfied before the order is made are: that there are reasonable grounds for suspecting that a specified person has benefited from any criminal conduct, and that there are reasonable grounds for suspecting that the material to which the application relates—(i) is likely to be of substantial value (whether by itself or together with other material) to the investigation for the purposes of which the application is made; and (ii) does not consist of or include items subject to legal privilege or excluded material.[12] There is provision for access to premises[13] and for information stored in electronic form.[14]

The House of Lords considered the scope of the analogous power under the preceding legislation[15] in *ex parte Bowles*.[16] In this case the question was whether a particular application for a warrant to gain access to material held by an accountant should have been brought under the 'normal' procedure for obtaining a warrant,[17] or in an application for a production order, or whether it made no difference. The major point was whether a production order should be made if the purpose of the police in applying for the order is not to carry out an investigation into whether someone has benefited from criminal conduct or into the extent or whereabouts of the proceeds of criminal conduct, but to carry out an investigation into whether someone has committed an offence and to obtain evidence to bring a prosecution.

---

[7] This is a further instance of the amplification of concern connected with the 'moral panic'.

[8] PCA 2002 s 342(2).

[9] PCA 2002 s 345(1). The application is usually heard *ex parte* in chambers: PCA 2002 s 352(1).

[10] The presumption is that the period shall be 7 days: PCA 2002 s 345(5).

[11] HC Debates 24 July 2002 col 1050 *et seq* (Bob Ainsworth).

[12] PCA 2002 s 348.

[13] PCA 2002 s 347.

[14] PCA 2002 s 349.

[15] CJA 1988 s 93H.

[16] *R v Southwark Crown Court, ex Parte Bowles* [1998] AC 641; [1998] 2 All ER 193.

[17] The normal procedure was under Police and Criminal Evidence Act 1984 s 9 and Schedule 1. The application in *Bowles* was in respect of material in the hands of an accountant, which is 'special procedure material' for the purposes of the Police and Criminal Evidence Act 1984 since it is held in confidence. Police and Criminal Evidence Act 1984 s 14(1).

On appeal Lord Hutton agreed and spelt out the legal position in the case where there were two possible grounds for the application:

> I consider that in the great majority of cases the circuit judge will not be faced with a situation where it appears that the police are actuated both by the purpose of investigating the proceeds of criminal conduct and by the purpose of investigating the commission of an offence, and that the judge will only have to consider whether he is satisfied (in addition to the matter specified in [what is now Proceeds of Crime Act 2002 section 346(2), formerly section 93H(4)]) that the purpose of the application is to investigate the proceeds of criminal conduct. Secondly, in my opinion the nature of the dominant purpose test is well stated in Wade and Forsyth on *Administrative Law* 7th edn. p 436:
>
> > Sometimes an act may serve two or more purposes, some authorised and some not, and it may be a question whether the public authority may kill two birds with one stone. The general rule is that its action will be lawful provided that the permitted purpose is the true and dominant purpose behind the act, even though some secondary or incidental advantage may be gained for some purpose which is outside the authority's powers. There is a clear distinction between this situation and its opposite, where the permitted purpose is a mere pretext and a dominant purpose is *ultra vires.*
>
> Accordingly I consider that if the true and dominant purpose of an application under [Proceeds of Crime Act 2002] section 93H is to enable an investigation to be made into the proceeds of criminal conduct, the application should be granted even if an incidental consequence may be that the police will obtain evidence relating to the commission of an offence. But if the true and dominant purpose of the application is to carry out an investigation whether a criminal offence has been committed and to obtain evidence to bring a prosecution, the application should be refused.'
>
> I further consider that if the police discover evidence of the commission of an offence in the course of an investigation consequent upon an order properly made under [Proceeds of Crime Act 2002 s 345, formerly section 93H], the fact that the evidence was discovered in this way would not be a reason for the exclusion of the evidence under section 78 of PACE on the ground of unfairness at a trial where the prosecution sought to adduce such evidence.

There is specific provision for the obtaining of information that is in the hands of Government departments.[18] Where a production order or an order to grant entry is not complied with, proceedings may follow for contempt of the Crown Court[19] or (where dealing with a High Court Order) the automatic High Court contempt jurisdiction.

SEARCH AND SEIZURE POWERS

The 'normal' powers under which magistrates issue search warrants are conferred by section 9 of the Police and Criminal Evidence Act 1984 and deal with

[18] PCA 2002 s 350.
[19] PCA 2002 s 351(7).

suspected crime. They would not necessarily extend to the enquiry into whether any person has *benefited* from any criminal conduct or from drug trafficking offences. There may be cases where there is such a benefit but that there is no crime which could provide the basis for a search warrant under PACE. The Proceeds of Crime Act 2002 provides additional powers, modelled upon and analogous to the PACE powers. The effect is that benefiting from criminal conduct is treated, for most purposes, *as if it were* a serious arrestable offence for the purposes of the powers under the Police and Criminal Evidence Act 1984. The search and seizure power is an invasive power that is subjected to a Code of Practice.[20]

There is power to order the search of premises.[21] The general provisions of part II of the Police and Criminal Evidence Act 1984 apply to warrants issued under these powers, save that the seizure of special procedure material[22] is permitted and that applications may be made without notice to the person whose premises are to be searched.[23] Where the warrant relates to a confiscation investigation or a money laundering investigation, the warrant is to be executed by a constable.[24] Where it is a civil recovery investigation it must be a named[25] member of the ARA.[26] A warrant may be issued where a production order has been made and not complied with or where the person involved is abroad or otherwise *incommunicado*, or where it is impossible to describe the material involved.[27]

As with many areas of law which depend upon scrutiny by the courts of orders which are sought, the test is whether or not adequate scrutiny will indeed be provided before warrants are granted. There are some reported instances in which courts have quashed orders that are drafted in terms too wide. Hence in *R v Thames Magistrates' Court, ex parte Hormoz*[28] an order to banks to disclose *all* of the applicant's financial affairs about which they had information was quashed because it was drafted too widely and the evidence was insufficient to found the magistrate's required reasonable grounds for belief that money had been laundered. Counsel was invited to re-draft the order, but by that time the benefit of surprise would have been lost. In *R v Southwark Crown Court, ex parte Sorsky Defries*[29] a firm of accountants, applied for judicial review following the issue of a search warrant and the subsequent seizure of documents from their premises. It was held that the judge should have satisfied himself that the material was of substantial value, considering the warrant's serious effect on

[20] Under PCA 2002 s 377.
[21] PCA 2002 s 352.
[22] Police and Criminal Evidence Act 1984 s 14.
[23] PCA 2002 s 353.
[24] PCA 2002 s 353(10)(a).
[25] Subject to the power to use pseudonyms: PCA 2002 s 449.
[26] PCA 2002 s 353(10)(b).
[27] PCA 2002 s 353.
[28] *R v (1) Thames Magistrates' court (2) Her Majesty's Customs & Excise, ex parte Farrokh Hormoz* [1998] *Criminal Law Review* 732.
[29] *R v Southwark Crown Court, ex parte Sorsky Defries* [1996] COD 117.

personal liberty, rather than relying on the information given to him by an officer of the Investigation Division of the Customs and Excise. He should have given reasons for his decision in this case, to show that everything appropriate had been considered in such a short space of time.[30] In the case in point, the search was outside the warrant, which made the search and the seizure of the documents covered by the warrant unlawful.

DISCLOSURE ORDERS

In a confiscation or civil recovery investigation (but not a money laundering investigation) the Director may apply to a judge for a disclosure order.[31] If such an order is made, the Director may use the extensive powers[32] throughout the investigation to require the answering of questions, delivery up of documents and disclosure of information. The Director is made the sole judge of the relevance of any of these matters.[33] The judge exercises his/her functions in accordance with the Human Rights Act, and so must consider the application of the proportionality test[34] as to whether a continuing order (rather than a one-off production order) is necessary for the purposes of the investigation. Sanctions for failure to comply with the orders are provided.[35] Statements made in response to this coercion are not able to be used subsequently to incriminate the person concerned.[36] Legal professional privilege operates, save that a lawyer may be required to produce the name and address of a client.[37]

CUSTOMER INFORMATION ORDERS

The Proceeds of Crime Act 2002 introduced customer information orders.[38] A customer information order requires all (or a targeted sample of) banks and other financial institutions to provide details of any accounts held by the person who is the subject of a confiscation or a money laundering investigation.[39] The order can also apply to persons who appear to hold property that is subject to a

[30] In any event, the warrant was invalid because the 1990 Act enabled Part II of the 1984 Act to include offences abroad, which meant that s 19 of the 1984 Act remained apposite to domestic offences only.

[31] PCA 2002 s 357.

[32] Set out in PCA 2002 s 357(4).

[33] PCA 2002 s 357(5).

[34] Above, .

[35] PCA 2002 s 359.

[36] PCA 2002 s 360(1). This stems from the reading given to *Saunders v United Kingdom* (1998) 23 EHRR 313 in the production of Schedule 3 to the Youth Justice and Criminal Evidence Act 1999. That this reading was over-extensive has been shown in *Brown (Margaret) v Stott* [2001] 2 WLR 817; [2001] 2 All ER 97 and *R v Allen* [2001] UKHL 45; [2002] 1 AC 509.

[37] PCA 2002 s 361(1).

[38] Defined in PCA 2002 s 363.

[39] PCA 2002 s 363.

civil recovery investigation.[40] There are offences of non-compliance and knowingly or recklessly making a misleading statement.[41] Since the statements are compelled from the institution, they may not be used subsequently to incriminate the institution.[42]

ACCOUNT MONITORING ORDERS

The other significant procedural innovation contained in the 2002 Act is the account monitoring order, modelled upon the terrorist provisions.[43] This is an order requiring a financial institution to supply specified information in relation to an account during a specified period of up to 90 days.[44] The information will usually be in the form of a bank statement. An account monitoring order may be obtained in respect of all three types of investigation and may be applied for by an appropriate officer.[45] Again, since the statements are compelled from the institution, they may not be used subsequently to incriminate it.[46] The account monitoring order is designed to meet concern at the expense in multiple applications for production orders.[47] The judge exercises his functions in accordance with the Human Rights Act, and so must consider the application of the proportionality test as to whether a continuing order (rather than a one-off production order) is necessary for the purposes of the investigation.

RIGHTS OF DETAINED PERSONS

The criminal provisions include the duty to report, and the Money Laundering Regulations 1993 and the consent rules[48] contemplate the existence of a person receiving notice (usually from NCIS) that an investigation is in train, will create a greater need than usual to secure continuing secrecy. This is one of the inevitable outcomes of the predominantly proactive method of policing money laundering. In consequence, the rules relating to the rights of detained persons to have someone informed and to legal advice are attenuated in the case of an enquiry into whether or not somebody has benefited from criminal conduct equally as if a serious arrestable offence were under investigation, so that the exercise of those rights can be deferred where a police officer of the rank at least

[40] PCA 2002 s 363(2)(b).
[41] PCA 2002 s 366.
[42] PCA 2002 s 367(1). Above, n 36.
[43] Terrorism Act 2000 Schedule 6A, substituted by Anti-Terrorism, Crime and Security Act 2001 Schedule 2.
[44] PCA 2002 s 370.
[45] PCA 2002 s 370(1).
[46] See n 36 above.
[47] The Regulatory Impact Statement to the Proceeds of Crime Bill set the saving at about £1m *per annum*.
[48] PCA 2002 s 335. See the section below ch 9, 'Tipping Off'.

of superintendent has reasonable cause to believe that the detained person has benefited from the offence and that the recovery of the value of the property obtained by that person from or in connection with the offence or of the pecuniary advantage derived by him from or in connection with it will be hindered by telling the named person of the arrest.[49] This is a further means by which benefiting from criminal conduct or drug dealing, even before its criminalisation, has been assimilated in its enforcement consequences to being a serious arrestable offence.

EVIDENCE-GATHERING AND ENFORCEMENT POWERS OVERSEAS

If it were possible to escape the enforcement régime simply by expatriating profits, then any attempt to regulate money laundering would be useless. Consequently, the powers of the court extend to property of the defendant overseas. The legislation prior to the Proceeds of Crime Act 2002 was largely silent on the conditions under which requests for assistance in the freezing and realisation of property in jurisdictions outside the United Kingdom might be made.

Under Article 7 of the Vienna Convention, parties signatory are obliged to afford each other the 'widest measure of mutual legal assistance in [narcotics] investigations, prosecutions and judicial proceedings'. Under Article 5(4)(b), when a request is received by another party having jurisdiction over an offence established in accordance with the Convention, the 'requested party shall take measures to identify, trace and freeze or seize proceeds, instrumentalities [and] property . . . for the purpose of eventual confiscation'. If forfeitable property is in the territory of a party, it may either enforce the other party's order, or its own, against the property. The Criminal Justice (International Co-Operation) Act 1990 allowed the United Kingdom Government to ratify the 1975 European Convention on Mutual Legal Assistance. It replaced the previous system, under the Extradition Act 1870, of '*Commissions Intérrogatoires*' by Mutual Legal Assistance Treaties (MLATs). MLATs allow the parties to obtain documentary evidence and other forms of assistance to assist law enforcement authorities in investigating and prosecuting criminal matters. They provide for a broad range of co-operation in criminal matters, including: (1) obtaining witness statements on oath and authenticated documentary evidence, including banking evidence ; (2) providing documents, records and evidence; (3) serving legal documents; (4) locating or identifying persons; (5) executing requests for searches and seizures; and (6) providing assistance in proceedings relating to the forfeiture of the proceeds and instrumentalities of crime (7) temporary transfer of prisoners, with their consent, to assist with criminal investigations and proceedings and service

---

[49] Police and Criminal Evidence Act 1984 s 56(5A) and (5B) , s 58(8A) and (8B). PCA 2002 Schedule 11 para 14.

of summonses, judgments and other procedural documents; restraint and confiscation of proceeds of crime.

The 'central authority' charged with the administration of the service of process in the UK and the obtaining of evidence in the UK from within the UK, is NCIS. It may use the investigation powers of the Serious Fraud Office in London and the Crown Office in Edinburgh in cases of serious or complex fraud;[50] this central authority also enforces confiscation orders made by overseas courts. Action by the central authority is initiated by receipt of a request from a court, tribunal or other central body overseas.[51] The Criminal Justice (International Co-operation) Act 1990 first provided for reciprocal arrangements for the service of summonses and other judicial documents.[52] The provision for mutual provision of evidence[53] is subject to a 'dual criminality' provision that applies only to fiscal offences.[54] The legislation was drafted so as to confer upon the Secretary of State absolute discretion in screening out requests from jurisdictions that he would not wish to be seen to help.[55] The search powers of the Police and Criminal Evidence Act 1984[56] apply when material relevant to an overseas investigation which is conducted on behalf of a signatory nation is in point and where the offence would amount to a serious arrestable offence for the purposes of that Act.[57]

During the 1990s, the MLAT procedure was not very successful. The number of requests to the UK Central Authority did not rise commensurately with other enforcement activity, such that by 2000 it was said that 'problems with international confiscation action are becoming so acute that assets overseas are being ignored for confiscation purposes'.[58] A new EU Convention on Mutual Legal Assistance[59] was signed in May 2000, supplementing the 1959 Council of Europe Convention.[60] Crucially, under the new Convention, assistance is to be given in the manner indicated by the requesting State, unless that is unlawful in the requested State. Requests can be transmitted directly between judicial authorities without the involvement of central authorities. All outgoing requests must pass through the UK Central Authority for mutual assistance in criminal matters in the Home Office. Requests may be made for prohibitions upon deal-

---

[50] And see Home Office Judicial Co-operation Unit Organised and International Crime Directorate, *Seeking Assistance in Criminal Matters from the United Kingdom: Guidelines for judicial and prosecuting authorities*, 2nd edn (London, Home Office, 1999).

[51] HL Debates, vol 513 col 1230 (12 Dec 1989) (Earl Ferrers).

[52] Ss 1 and 2.

[53] Ss 3 and 4.

[54] S 4(3): No definition is given of the word 'fiscal' but the Explanatory Report to the additional Protocol to the 1957 European Convention suggest that 'fiscal offences' are offences in connection with taxes, duties, customs and exchange.

[55] S 4(3)(1).

[56] Especially Police and Criminal Evidence Act 1984 ss 9–13 and Schedule 1.

[57] Police and Criminal Evidence Act 1984 s 116.

[58] Cabinet Office Performance and Innovation Unit, *Recovering the Proceeds of Crime* (London, Cabinet Office, 2000) (hereinafter '*PIU Report*') para 11.10, box 11.2.

[59] EU Convention on Mutual Legal Assistance OJ C 197 12.07.2000, 24.

[60] European Convention on Mutual Assistance in Criminal Matters (1959) ETS 30.

ing with property or, where a confiscation order has been made, its realisation. Under the Proceeds of Crime Act 2002, there is provision for enforcement abroad by means of a request for assistance[61] to the receiving country to prevent dealing in the realisable property in question.[62] Where a confiscation order has been made the request for assistance can ask that the property is realised.[63]

A PARTICULAR QUESTION IN EVIDENCE

One of the mechanisms by which the prosecution can operate in circumstances where witnesses are unwilling or unable to give evidence in person is by using the rules relating to the admissibility of this evidence under sections 23–26 of the Criminal Justice Act 1988. The problem for the defence is obvious. If the basis for the admissibility of the evidence is that the witness was afraid, then this will give an impression that is highly unfavourable to the defendant. If the evidence is not admitted, then a charter is put in place for the 'knobbling' of witnesses. The challenge that can be made against the use of section 23 is that it removes from the defendant the right to confront his/her accuser.[64]

These kinds of questions arise frequently in the area of money laundering because of the international nature of the crime. In *R v Belmarsh Magistrates Court, ex parte Gilligan*[65] the prosecution put before the court two written statements by C, the first speaking to C's guilt and a second statement, made to the Garda, in which C said he was unwilling to give evidence as he was in fear for his life and that of his girlfriend and child. The magistrate admitted the first statement in evidence under section 23 of the Criminal Justice Act 1988, relying on the second statement to be satisfied that C had not attended to give evidence because of fear. G applied for judicial review contending: that the magistrate had been wrong to admit C's written statement, and that as a result of the answers given by D in cross examination there was insufficient evidence to establish a *prima facie* case that the money found on the applicant was the proceeds of drug trafficking. The Divisional Court held that the magistrate had been wrong to rely upon the second statement, describing the witness's fear, to justify admitting his first statement. Fear causing the absence of a witness had to be proved by admissible evidence and the second statement could not be relied upon as admissible evidence. In order to satisfy the requirements of section 23 of the 1988 Act, it was necessary for the court to hear oral evidence as to fear. That could be given, for example, by a police officer. In the instant case there

---

[61] Proceeds of Crime Act 2002 s 74.
[62] Proceeds of Crime Act 2002 s 74(2).
[63] Proceeds of Crime Act 2002 s 74(3).
[64] Andrew L-T Choo, *Hearsay and Confrontation in Criminal Trials* (Oxford, Clarendon Press, 1996); Richard D Friedman, 'Thoughts from across the water on hearsay and confrontation' [1998] *Criminal Law Review* 697.
[65] *R v Belmarsh Magistrates Court, ex parte Gilligan* [1998] 1 CAR 14; [1997] COD 342.

had been no oral evidence and the statement could not prove itself.[66] In *R v Radak and others*[67] the defendant and others were charged with various money laundering offences arising out of allegations that a substantial sum of money had been transferred out of S's New York bank account by deception and without S's authority. The prosecution case rested on S's evidence, but S refused to attend the UK trial, allegedly through fear. Accordingly, the prosecution applied to read out two statements made by S.[68] The trial judge did not exercise his discretion to exclude the statements to be read under section 26 of the Act, concluding that the risk of unfairness to D was minimal. The Court of Appeal held that the judge had erred in approaching the issue of the risk of unfairness to D by making a speculative comparison between the outcome if S gave oral evidence and was cross examined and the result if S's statements were admitted but the jury were given evidence as to S's refusal to attend. Where the proceedings are civil, hearsay evidence will be admissible.

ENFORCEMENT POWERS AND HUMAN RIGHTS

The question of the consistency of these provisions with the Convention is resolved, so far as concerns the privilege against self-incrimination, by the express provisions dealing with the privilege against self-incrimination,[69] and so far as the various other aspects in which they might run up against the Convention, by the requirement that the judicial powers be exercised in accordance with it, including the 'proportionality' rule.

In the case of the intrusive powers the major countervailing human rights argument is from the right to private life. The right to private life extends to the financial transactions of the person concerned. Privacy of financial information is central to the forms of autonomy that are protected directly and indirectly by privacy rights. Does the privacy claim provide any purchase beyond the contractual privacy enshrined in *Tournier*?[70] There are obvious reasons for the requirement of privacy. People with substantial wealth are targets for criminal of many sorts. Many people have reasons not to wish the disposition of their money (for example, to unpopular causes). Nonetheless Blum *et al* argue that 'When the issue of legal accountability is at stake, the right of privacy must give way.'[71] This is to go too far. It is axiomatic that privacy is not a strong right, and that it must give way when confronted by any plausible countervailing law

---

[66] And see *R v Denton (Clive)* [2001] 1 CAR 16.

[67] *R v Radak, Adjei, Butler-Rees & Meghjee* [1999] 1 CAR 187; [1999] *Criminal Law Review* 223.

[68] Pursuant to the CJA 1988 s 23: and see IH Dennis, *The Law of Evidence*, 2nd edn (London, Sweet & Maxwell, 2002) 597 *et seq*.

[69] PCA 2002 s 360(1), 367(1), 372(1).

[70] *Tournier v National Provincial and Union Bank of England* [1924] 1 KB 461.

[71] Jack Blum *et al*, *Financial Havens, Banking Secrecy and Money-Laundering*, UNDCP technical series issue 8 (NYC, NY, UN, 1998) 68.

enforcement claim.[72] Nonetheless, the relationship between the claim of privacy and the claims of law enforcement must be a proportional one, not one in which the claims of law enforcement have a 'trump' value.

The question has arisen[73] whether the right to private life could be invoked as a response to a question in a confiscation investigation. A requirement under tax legislation to produce a list of private expenditure was held to amount to an interference with private life.[74] In order to be defensible under the Convention the interference must be 'necessary in a democratic society' for one of a series of objectives. In determining 'necessity' the court has left a wide margin of appreciation to the States in question.[75]

In the case where the questioning is of persons convicted of crimes with victims (especially frauds) the invasion may be justified as being for 'the protection of the rights and freedoms of others'. In the case where the crime in respect of which there is a conviction is part of a continuing criminal enterprise, and the money which the invasion would trace is further to be deployed in crime, then the invasion of the right to private life can be justified as being 'for the prevention of crime'. However, where there is no justification on either of these grounds, it should be noted that no separate justification is contemplated under Article 8(2) of the Convention that the invasion of privacy was justified to recoup the proceeds of crime, and, so far as the questioning represents an interference with private life, questioning could indeed be resisted upon this ground.

Section 6 of the Human Rights Act 1998 states that where a public authority has acted in a manner which incompatible with a complainant's Convention rights, a court may grant any remedy within its powers which it considers 'just and appropriate'. In the context of a criminal trial or of confiscation proceedings, this extends to cover the making of an order to exclude the evidence obtained in breach of Article 8. The outstanding question is whether the admission of evidence obtained in breach of Article 8 is *ipso facto* a breach of Article 6. The authorities suggest that it is not.[76]

---

[72] Peter Alldridge and Chrisje Brants, 'Introduction' in Alldridge and Brants (eds), *Privacy, Autonomy and Criminal Law* (Oxford, Hart, 2000) 1, 19.

[73] Ewan Bell, 'The ECHR and the Proceeds of Crime Legislation' [2000] *Criminal Law Review* 783, 793.

[74] *Friedl v Austria* (1996) 21 EHRR 83.

[75] Ben Emmerson and Andrew Ashworth, *Human Rights and Criminal Justice* (London, Sweet and Maxwell, 2001) 199 *et seq*.

[76] *R v P* [2002] 1 AC 146; [2001] 2 All ER 58; *Khan v United Kingdom* (2001) 31 EHRR 45; [2000] 8 BHRC 310; *R v McLeod* [2002] EWCA Crim 989. Ben Emmerson and Andrew Ashworth, *Human Rights and Criminal Justice* (London, Sweet & Maxwell, 2001) 426.

9

Beyond Confiscation—Criminalisation

IT IS ONE thing to provide for the *confiscation* of the profits of crime. It is another, and a significant further step, to make criminal the process of disposing or otherwise dealing in the proceeds of crime.[1] Someone who disposes of the assets will frequently be able to be dealt with under existing legislation, for example, for handling stolen goods or as a party to other offences. The criminalisation of money laundering has gone far beyond that. As with the confiscation legislation, there are two distinct threads in the history of the English legislation. The first, dealing with the proceeds of drugs offences, was in the Drug Trafficking Act 1994. The second, dealing with the proceeds of other criminal conduct, was in Part VI of the Criminal Justice Act 1988, in both cases, as amended. The criminalisation of money laundering involves a radical restructuring of the law of complicity. It might not go so far as to create a 'crime of being a criminal',[2] but shifts the emphasis in the enforcement process onto what is done with the profits, rather than what is done to acquire them. The offences are now assimilated in the global money laundering offences in the Proceeds of Crime Act 2002.

The following offences are created:[3]

Concealing, disguising, converting, transferring the proceeds of criminal property or removing them from the jurisdiction;[4]
Entering into or becoming concerned in an arrangement which s/he knows or suspects facilitates the acquisition retention use or control of criminal property by or on behalf of another;[5]
Acquisition, possession or use of the proceeds of criminal property.[6]

There is also a 'tipping off' offence,[7] and, extending beyond the earlier law, which only covered the case of laundering the proceeds of drug dealing,[8] an

---

[1] For a critique of the underlying assumptions, see the section above ch 3, Justifying Criminalisation.

[2] Gerard E Lynch, 'RICO: The Crime of Being a Criminal' (1987) 87 *Columbia Law Review* 661.

[3] These are all originally derived from Article 3 of the Vienna Convention, which was adopted both in the European Directive (Article 2) and the Strasbourg Convention (Article 6).

[4] PCA 2002 s 327, replacing DTA 1994 s 49 and CJA 1988 s 93C.

[5] PCA 2002 s 328, replacing DTA 1994 s 50 and CJA 1988 s 93A.

[6] PCA 2002 s 329, replacing DTA 1994 s 51 and CJA 1988 s 93B.

[7] PCA 2002 s 333, replacing DTA 1994 s 53 and CJA 1988 s 93D.

[8] DTA 1994 s 52.

offence *in the regulated sector*[9] of failure to inform the authorities of suspected transactions,[10] both of which merit separate treatment.

THE PREDICATE OFFENCE AND THE CRIMINAL PROPERTY

As with the provisions dealing with confiscation, the preliminary requirement is that there be a predicate offence. The definition of predicate offence for the purposes of the *crimes* of laundering money is, on the face of the legislation, identical to the definition for the purposes of the confiscation orders. 'Criminal conduct' means conduct which constitutes an offence in England and Wales *or* would constitute such an offence if it had occurred in England and Wales.[11]

The other important pre-requisite for the laundering offences is 'criminal property'. Property is criminal property if

(a) It constitutes a person's benefit from criminal conduct or it represents such a benefit (in whole or in part and whether directly or indirectly); and
(b) The alleged offender knows or suspects that it constitutes or represents such a benefit.[12]

It is the second part that inserts (part of) the *mens rea* requirement for the offences in the Act. The word 'knowledge' has been used in many statutes, and its interpretation in this context is unlikely to give rise to many difficulties.[13] It will include actual knowledge, shutting one's mind to the obvious, and (probably) knowledge of circumstances that would indicate the facts to an honest and reasonable person. More problematic is the notion of suspicion. Usually the word 'suspicion', with or without a requirement of reasonable grounds, is used to generate a liberty to act or not act. 'If X has reasonable grounds to suspect' is a well known formula. Under the money laundering provisions, however, suspicion generates the duty, not the liberty, to act. Two justifications are advanced for the use of suspicion as the base line for conviction under the offence. First, it is said that disclosure based upon any higher standard (such as belief) would

---

[9] PCA 2002 Schedule 9 part 1 defines the regulated sector. The definition stems from Money Laundering Regulations 1993 Article 4, as amended by Financial Services and Markets (Consequential Amendments and Repeals) Order 2001 (SI 3649) Article 439. The Schedule can be amended without full Parliamentary scrutiny.

[10] PCA 2002 s 330.

[11] PCA 2002 s 340(2) (criminal laundering): PCA 2002 s 76(1) (confiscation): see the section above ch 7, The Predicate Offence(s)—Criminal Conduct.

[12] PCA 2002 s 340(3).

[13] Stephen Shute, 'Knowledge and Belief in the Criminal Law', in Stephen Shute and AP Simester (eds), *Criminal Law Theory—Doctrines of the General Part* (Oxford, Oxford University Press, 2002) 171; AP Simester and GR Sullivan, *Criminal Law: Theory and Doctrine* (Oxford, Hart, 2000) 136–8.

involve a dilemma as to whether or not to disclose based upon what might be a finely balanced assessment of the facts. The obligation to disclose suspicion removes that problem. Secondly, it is said that law enforcement agencies act upon suspicion and that a great deal of 'intelligence' could be lost if all that could be disclosed were beliefs.[14] Neither of these justifications is at all powerful. As to the first, it is true that the law would be easier to administer (in terms of proof) and easier for the citizen to know when to disclose if the obligation to disclose were based upon suspicion. But that is not itself a reason for imposing a potentially onerous duty upon the citizen more widely than otherwise it would have been. As to the second, the justification advanced (the generation of 'intelligence' by the police) is an extremely dubious one. It is by no means self-evidently a good thing for the police to collect and store large quantities of information based upon nothing but subjectively held suspicions. The positive side is that they might be able to use this information to direct investigations and to obtain convictions that would not otherwise be gained. The negative is that the police will acquire a large amount of unreliable information that might form the basis for intrusive investigations and ill-advised prosecutions.[15]

In these offences, both knowledge and suspicion are to be judged subjectively. It does not matter that there were reasonable grounds to suspect if, in fact, that defendant did not suspect. This has led to complaints by prosecutors about the difficulties of proof imposed by this subjective requirement. The Cabinet Office claimed that the professional who 'turns a blind eye' avoids liability, and use this as the justification for the introduction of an objective test of 'reasonable rounds to suspect.[16] This, however, is contentious for two reasons. First, 'knowledge' in criminal statutes has been held to comprehend 'wilful blindness'.[17] Second, it would be inconsistent with the general understanding that negligence is not sufficient for a conviction for a serious crime.[18]

TAX EVASION AS THE PREDICATE OFFENCE TO CRIMINAL LAUNDERING

For the purposes of a confiscation order, all that is necessary is that the amount of the order be quantified. For the purposes of the criminal laundering provisions it is necessary to *identify* the specific property involved. The previous definitions of 'predicate offences' so as to exclude *some* criminal offences implies,

---

[14] Earl Ferrers, HL Debates vol 540 col 753 (22 Nov 1992).

[15] The third justification, mentioned during the debates on the Criminal Justice Act 1993, that this is the mental state required by the Convention, simply moves the enquiry elsewhere.

[16] Cabinet Office Performance and Innovation Unit, *Recovering the Proceeds of Crime* (London, Cabinet Office, 2000) (hereinafter '*PIU Report*') para 9.59 et seq.

[17] AP Simester and GR Sullivan, *Criminal Law: Theory and Doctrine* (Oxford, Hart, 2000) 135 et seq.

[18] AP Simester and GR Sullivan, *Criminal Law: Theory and Doctrine* (Oxford, Hart, 2000) 138 et seq. Andrew Ashworth, *Principles of Criminal Law*, 2nd edn (Oxford, Oxford University Press, 1999) 197.

that there is money made by *some* crimes which may still be disposed of lawfully, and for which the laundering apparatus may lawfully be used. This in turn impacted upon levels of reporting, because the people charged with reporting may profess a belief that funds whose origins they suspect derive from criminal offences which are not covered by the reporting requirements, and it provides difficulties in securing both confiscation orders and realising assets. A firm conducting relevant financial business may have been able to say that its suspicions were that the client was laundering unlawfully acquired money, but that their suspicion was that it was the product of an offence not specified in the definition. The 2002 Act takes a more expansive view, attempting to eliminate this problem by including all offences.

The difficult cases, however, are where the alleged 'criminal property' is the outcome of evasion or deferment of a debt.[19] The provision dealing with pecuniary advantages for the purposes of the criminal laundering provisions[20] is in identical terms to that for the making of confiscation orders.[21]

> Where a person derives a pecuniary advantage as a result of or in connection with the commission of an offence, he is to be treated for the purposes of this Part of this Act as if he had obtained as a result of or in connection with the commission of the offence a sum of money equal to the value of the pecuniary advantage.

This will apply where the property in question is the subject matter of a debt, usually of tax evasion. As in the case of confiscation, and because of its great significance to the relationship between criminal justice and taxation, it requires especial attention.

When laundering of money gained otherwise than from drugs was introduced to the statute book, in Part VI of the Criminal Justice Act 1988, it was only as a basis for the making of confiscation orders. Provisions to make laundering a series of independent substantive crimes were introduced later. *Allen*[22] decides that tax offences *are* predicate offences for the purposes of the making of a confiscation order. In the face of the international movement for including tax evasion within the category of predicate offences to laundering,[23] and for not distinguishing between predicate offences for the purposes of confiscation and criminal provisions, there are obvious attractions to applying the same definition to criminal laundering. However, extensive readings of criminal statutes should not be adopted merely on the grounds of simplicity and it is worthwhile at least to consider the case against the extension of predicate offences to criminalise laundering the proceeds of tax evasion.

---

[19] And as to confiscation of the proceeds of tax evasion, see the section above ch 7, Pecuniary Advantage—The Benefit.

[20] PCA 2002 s 340(5).

[21] PCA 2002 s 76(5), see the section above ch 7, Pecuniary Advantage—The Benefit.

[22] *R v Allen (Brian Roger)* [2001] UKHL 45; [2002] 1 AC 509, see the section above ch 7, Pecuniary Advantage—The Benefit.

[23] See the section above ch 7, Pecuniary Advantage—The Benefit.

It was in the mid-1990s that the Financial Action Task Force and a number of other international bodies began to broaden the category of offences capable of amounting to predicate offences. The G7 Finance ministers, at a meeting in London in May 1998, called for international action to enhance the capacity of anti-money laundering systems to deal effectively with tax-related crimes. The plan was that the following objectives would be furthered: the extension of suspicious transaction reporting to money laundering related to tax offences; giving permission to money laundering authorities to the greatest extent possible to pass information to their tax authorities to support the investigation of tax-related crimes; and the communication of such information to other jurisdictions in ways which would allow its use by tax authorities.[24]

A Financial Action Task Force directive, issued on 2 July 1999 in the form of an 'interpretative note' to its Forty Recommendations on money laundering,[25] proclaimed that 'suspicious transactions should be reported by financial institutions regardless of whether they are also thought to involve tax matters.' It warned Governments that 'to deter financial institutions from reporting a suspicious transaction, money launderers may seek to state, *inter alia*, that their transactions relate to tax matters.' Late in 1999, the Tampere European Council meeting[26] placed enormous emphasis upon money laundering, calling, in particular, for an increase in consistency in the definition of predicate offences, the adoption of the Amending Directive and the greater availability of all relevant information for the purposes of exchange, irrespective of arguments from banking secrecy. At the IMF meeting in Washington DC in April 2000 the Chancellor of the Exchequer, Gordon Brown, told world economic leaders that he wants Britain to spearhead a major international crackdown on offshore tax havens, money laundering and financial crime.[27]

Of course, almost everything involving money laundering has an international dimension, and the fear which is never far from the surface in discussions of laundering the proceeds of tax evasion relates to the large sums of money that—it is suspected—are laundered through the City of London, bringing valuable business.[28] The Money Laundering Regulations supply the regulatory framework for the conduct of 'relevant financial business'—the requirements of knowing the customer, reporting suspicious transactions and the responsibilities of the Money Laundering Reporting Officer.[29] The claim by regulated financial institutions that might provoke most concern in the context of the 1993 Regulations is this:

---

[24] <http://utl1.library.utoronto.ca/www/g7/finance/fm980509.htm> Point 16
[25] See the section above ch 5, Financial Action Task Force.
[26] Julian Schutte, 'Tampere European Council Presidency Decisions' (1999) 70 *Revue Internationale de Droit Pénal* 1023 at 1034–5.
[27] *Daily Telegraph*, 17 April 2000.
[28] And see Lord Rooker HL Debates 27 May 2002 col 1067.
[29] See the section below ch 12, The Money Laundering Reporting Officer.

we [the firm conducting relevant financial business] did not think that the money that we were handling was the proceeds of drug dealing: we only thought that it was the proceeds of tax evasion.

If this is a good defence, then the regulatory framework will be substantially less effective, but if it is not, the costs to the professions of the additional monitoring and reporting of suspected tax evasion will be very substantial.[30]
There is a further consideration relating to the substantive law of taxation. Schemes to avoid tax frequently depend upon complex routings of deals without apparent commercial rationale. Money movements under a tax avoidance scheme make money movements that *are* laundering the profits of crime less easy to detect. If the law of taxation could be altered in such a way as to discourage 'artificial' avoidance schemes then the laundering disposals would no longer sit midst their camouflage. This can be used as an argument for general anti-avoidance rules.

It may not be essential for tax evasion to be a predicate offence for money laundering charges[31] . . . but if financial and other institutions are permitted not to pass on information about conduct that otherwise would be suspicious on the grounds that they think (or say they think) that the funds are 'only' tax money. . . . Given that few institutions have satisfactory methods of satisfying themselves and others that particular funds are not the proceeds of crime and are tax evasion/avoidance the tax exemption both facilitates the cognitive judgment that they can do the business without informing the authorities and denies the authorities information that might be used for identifying the laundering of drug and fraud proceeds.[32]

In 2000, in a supplementary note to evidence given to the Treasury select committee, the then Paymaster General (Melanie Johnson) set out the UK Government's position:

In the UK there is no specific offence of 'tax evasion'. The offences with which tax evaders are commonly charged include offences under the Theft Act 1968 and the common-law offence of cheating the public revenue. These are included within the definition of criminal activity for the purposes of the Criminal Justice Act [1988], which extends to all indictable offences. This means that laundering the proceeds of tax evasion is considered a serious offence in the UK, and that financial institutions and others have a statutory obligation to report suspicions of tax evasion to the National Criminal Intelligence Service. This obligation extends to the proceeds of offences committed overseas, where the relevant conduct would have been criminal if it had occurred in the UK. In this way, the UK clearly sets out that we do not wish to provide a haven for dirty money.[33]

---

[30] And for further consideration of the application of the legal framework to tax offences, see this section above.

[31] And see this section above.

[32] Jack Blum *et al*, *Financial Havens, Banking Secrecy and Money-Laundering*, UNDCP technical series issue 8 (New York City, NY UN, 1998) 51.

[33] Dated 28 February 2000, supplementary to evidence given on 8 February 2000.

Guidance Notes[34] given under the Money Laundering Regulations 1993 to the professions were altered to accommodate the harder line against laundering the proceeds of tax evasion. In 1994 the guidance notes published, for example, by the Institute of Chartered Accountants stated that the NCIS had 'indicated'[35] that they only wished to receive reports of suspicious financial transaction derived from the profits of serious crimes including drug trafficking, terrorist activity, major thefts and fraud, robbery, forgery and counterfeiting, blackmail and extortion.'[36] The current (1999) Guidance Notes reflect a far more proactive view on the part of the NCIS than informed the previous set. They assert that: 'Suspected tax evasion should be treated no differently to any other crime that is covered by the money laundering legislation.'[37] That is true, if indeed it is covered, but we are entitled to ask whether the NCIS is correct and that tax evasion is indeed covered.

There is also a political agenda here. The NCIS has its own empire to build. One of the ways in which the Economic Crimes Unit of the NCIS can establish its claim upon our attention is to show the type of crime against which it is directed to be serious and to be on the increase. If the NCIS contention is correct, then the amount of money which can be claimed to be laundered is the total 'black and 'grey' economies of the world multiplied by the mean number of transactions *per* unit of currency *per* unit of time. Greater obligations to report will boost this figure.

When the criminal laundering provisions were put in place, the assumption was made, without any real consideration, that the same definition could serve to define predicate offences for the purposes both of confiscation and of defining criminal laundering. It might have been argued that since the consequences of something falling within the definitions of 'criminal conduct' and 'criminal property' for the purposes of a confiscation order were less grave than when imposing criminal liability, a more restrictive approach should be taken in the latter case. Moreover, the definition for the purposes of a confiscation order assumes that a criminal conviction has been achieved in respect of an offence over which the courts in England and Wales *do* have jurisdiction. The definition

---

[34] The Guidance Notes do not, of course, have the direct force of law, but rather—as with the Highway Code—are matters to which the court is entitled to have regard. (Money Laundering Regulations 1993 para 5 (3). In determining whether a person has complied with any of the requirements of paragraph (1) above, a court may take account of—(a) any relevant supervisory or regulatory guidance which applies to that person.)

[35] Whether or not it was lawful to do so: *R v Metropolitan Police Commissioner, ex parte Blackburn* [1968] 2 QB 118, [1968] 1 All ER 763 holds that while the police may put in place priorities, it is not open to the police to decide not to enforce particular criminal laws. Indicating that it did not wish to receive reports of other cases of laundering not only manifests intention not to enforce the law in those cases but also purports to grant permission to professional—not to discharge their legal duty by making reports. (Author's note).

[36] ICAEW Technical release 11/94.

[37] ICAEW Technical release 15/99. The British Bankers Association also presented new guidelines to its members in June 1999, stating that the financial proceeds of tax evasion can be viewed by British authorities as laundered money.

of 'criminal conduct' in respect of the money laundering offences and the reporting obligation has no such connection to the jurisdiction as a predicate. It might have been thought that these considerations could argue for differential treatment, on the one hand, of confiscation orders, and, on the other, the imposition of reporting requirements and criminal liability.

Should dealings by the tax evader[38] or others with his/her own property be regarded as dealings in the proceeds of crime, or 'money laundering'? Much turns upon the answer to this question. If tax evasion is a predicate offence to money laundering, any firm dealing with the proceeds of tax evasion and engaging in 'relevant financial business' for the purposes of the Money Laundering Regulations 1993 will come under the regulatory framework which governs money laundering, and so will have an obligation to operate reporting procedures to deal with cases of clients suspected of tax evasion. Bankers or accountants who do not operate such procedures, or who fail to report knowledge or suspicion that clients are committing the laundering offences, will themselves be liable to criminal penalties.[39] The thrust of Government policy has clearly been towards the view that tax evasion should provide a predicate offence.[40]

There are, however, three major avenues left along which to argue that tax evasion does not provide a predicate to criminal laundering. The first turns on the difficulty of identifying the property. The second turns on the application of Article 8 of the European Convention on Human Rights, by means of the Human Rights Act 1998.[41] The third depends on the availability of other mechanisms for the gathering of information on tax evasion and the undesirability of mixing the systems of tax gathering and criminal justice. It can be encapsulated in an Article 6 claim. Each argument proceeds from the assumption, that criminal statutes should be construed narrowly.[42]

Identifiying the Property

As to the identification of the property, it should be noted that when the court makes a confiscation order, what it needs to know is *how much* property represents the proceeds of crime. For the purpose of a confiscation order it is unnecessary to identify the specific property. For the purpose of a confiscation order the question to which the definition of the predicate offence provides an answer is '*how much* property?' It is enough to set a global value. When convicting someone for a laundering offence, on the other hand, it is necessary that the particular property in respect of which laundering is alleged was (directly or indi-

---

[38] Or, of course, any other person who unlawfully obtains a pecuniary advantage.
[39] Money Laundering Regulations 1993 para 5(2). See the section below, The Money Laundering Regulations 1993.
[40] See the section above ch 7, Pecuniary Advantage—The Benefit.
[41] In force since 2 October 2000.
[42] And see the section in ch 4, A Note on the Interpretation of Laundering Legislation.

rectly) the proceeds of crime, and the appropriate mental state[43] must be held in respect of an item of property. The definition needs to answer the more specific question '*which* property'? The difficulty is that the liability to pay tax is a debt that is not, without more,[44] attached to any specific part of the taxpayer's property.[45] The only case where it might be said with certainty that a particular item of property 'in whole or in part represents' a sum by which a defendant has benefited by not paying tax is when the liability to tax is so great that the property in question must necessarily account for some of the property in question.[46] Thus when the laundering transaction involves shares worth £30,000 out of total property owned by the defendant of £300,000 the shares might be said to represent unpaid tax where the liability to tax exceeds £270,000.[47] So far as concerns triggering the regulatory régime, this argument would only work where the regulated institution knows the total wealth of the client. In practice this will seldom be the case. Where the property cannot be identified as representing the evaded tax, there is no offence. This is briefly stated but a major stumbling block for attempts to operate the reporting procedures against the proceeds of tax evasion, or of any offence involving non-payment of a debt. Even if the property can be identified as a matter of law, the mental state implied in 'criminal property' (that the alleged offender knows or suspects that it constitutes or represents such a benefit) provides further possible defences to one charged: one is that s/he did not know or suspect the property represented the benefit of criminal conduct because it did not. The other is that s/he did not know or suspect the property represented the benefit of criminal conduct because s/he did not understand the relevant law. If this negatives the relevant *mens rea* it can provide a defence.[48]

Privacy

As to privacy, if the argument is correct that the property which A has because s/he criminally did not pay a debt (as in the case of tax evasion, but also of making off without payment and similar offences) *is* the proceeds of crime for the purposes of the criminal laundering provisions, then there would be no part of

[43] Ie 'Knowledge or suspicion' that the money had dubious provenance for the purpose of the definition of 'criminal property' in PCA 2002 s.340(2).

[44] It is unlikely that there would ever be anything in the nature of a 'Quistclose trust' (*Barclays Bank Ltd v Quistclose Investments Ltd* [1970] AC 567, [1968] 3 All ER 651).

[45] This makes the assumption that, where the pecuniary advantage is the deferral of a debt, the value of the advantage (for the purposes of PCA 2002 s 340(5)) is the value of the debt, not the value of the deferral. A *fortiori*, if the position espoused above (in section above ch 7, Pecuniary Advantage—The Benefit) that the value in question should be that of the deferral, is correct, the task becomes yet more difficult.

[46] Even this would involve giving a meaning to the word 'represents' wider than for the purposes of the law of restitution.

[47] And note that under the tracing rules in civil recovery, PCA 2002 s 305–306, a debt may not be followed into other property absent a *Quistclose* trust.

[48] *R v Smith (DR)* [1974] QB 354; [1974] 1 All ER 632.

the property of the client to which the reporting requirements and their atten-
dant liabilities would not attach, because there is no severable part of the property that is identifiable as the benefit. Any part of his/her property *might* be the
benefit, granted the appropriate *mens rea* in its regard. Consequently, dealings
with property which might be assisting the other to retain (etc) the property will
be criminal if that other is a tax evader, whatever part of their property is in
point, whereas if the property in question is, for example, the product of fraud
or drug dealing, only activities assisting the other to retain the specific proceeds,
direct or indirect, of that offence will be covered.

The significance of this is that if the category of predicate offences to criminal
laundering includes tax evasion offences, then its consequences, in terms both of
reporting requirements and of the demands of the criminal law, are *more* onerous than for those other offences where the proceeds of crime *are* able to be
identified and differentiated from the other property of the person holding it.
Article 8 of the European Convention on Human Rights protects the right to
private life, and only permits invasions of the right to private life so far as 'is necessary in a democratic society'.[49] A person's financial affairs, including the relationship between client and accountant, are clearly covered by the article. To
compel disclosure in breach of the obligation of confidentiality which exists
between professional adviser and client is *(prima facie)* a breach of the right to
private life.[50] If it is only 'necessary' (for the purposes of the Convention) for
reporting restrictions to apply in respect of *some* transactions of suspected drug
dealers or terrorists (that is, where suspicion exists that the transactions under
consideration deal with the proceeds of drugs offences or are terrorist property),
it is difficult to say that *every* transaction of a person suspected of tax evasion
should be reported. The Human Rights Act 1998 states that where possible
statutes should be construed so as to comply with the Convention.[51] If the only
way of achieving consistency with the right of privacy is to say that predicate
offences are defined differently for the purposes of the confiscation than the
criminalisation provisions, this may be what the Act requires.

Fair Trial

As to the question of fair trials, there are dangers in assimilating, on the one
hand, interactions between the individual and the police, and, on the other,
those between the individual and the authorities concerned with tax, social
security and immigration, to one undifferentiated interface between the individual and a monolithic State.[52] Tax authorities have very significant powers,

---

[49] Article 8(2).
[50] *Friedl v Austria* (1996) 21 EHRR 83.
[51] Human Rights Act 1998 s 3(1): above, p 83.
[52] Hence the Security Administration (Fraud) Act 1996. This is not to accept without question
that the information given to one branch of Government for its own purposes was never disclosed
to another.

against which fewer safeguards are available than in the case of the police. It appears, for example, that the privilege against self-incrimination is not available in the case of requests by tax authorities for information.[53] The Revenue may require the production of records and has power to levy fines without recourse to the courts.[54] The Revenue has not, hitherto, had frequent recourse to the criminal law as a means of dealing with tax evasion. Rates of prosecution are extremely low. A move towards greater interdependence between the systems of tax collection and criminal justice would be a very significant change.[55] If it is to be adopted, this should be as a result of full and open discussion, not by means of the change in enforcement policy as to existing legislation, upon which the NCIS alighted during 1999.[56]

If tax evasion *is* a predicate offence to criminal laundering, then, since almost all income from unlawful sources is taxable, there is a danger that the chosen enforcement mechanism—against, for example, drug dealers—will be to treat the money as the proceeds of tax evasion. If the prosecution need establish nothing other than that the money was undeclared income[57] then, unless the sentences for laundering vary according to those which would have been available for the predicate offence,[58] they will not put themselves to the trouble of proving any other, more serious 'criminal conduct' as a predicate. Moves towards taxation rather than confiscation as a means of recouping the profits of crime, or moves to charging laundering the proceeds of tax evasion rather than those of any substantive offence as a means of punishing people involved in acquisitive crime, are radical ones, which endanger the traditionally accepted distinctions between the systems of taxation and criminal justice. Similarly, the use of the investigative powers of the Revenue to generate evidence of crime, and the deployment of its power to raise assessments against alleged offenders is not a step to be undertaken lightly, because of the dangers of discriminatory treatment arising from enhanced State powers.

If the issue of identification could be resolved, neither the argument from privacy nor that from the right to a fair trial provides an entirely compelling ground for distinguishing the definition of 'criminal conduct' for the purposes of confiscation orders from that for criminal liability and for reporting, but the sorts of moves which are contemplated by the extension of the money laundering jurisdiction into the field of tax evasion are, potentially at least, very significant, and their implications need to be considered fully, and these challenges require answers.

---

[53] *R v Allen* [2001] UKHL 45; [2002] 1 AC 509: Taxes Management Act 1970 s 19A–20A.

[54] Taxes Management Act 1970 Part X, Finance Act 1994 s 8.

[55] See the section below ch 11, Taxation, Money Laundering and Criminal Justice.

[56] See the section in this ch, Tax Evasion and the Predicate Offence to Criminal Laundering. And see further on the taxation jurisdiction of the ARA, the section below ch 11, The Taxation Jurisdiction of the ARA.

[57] *PIU Report* paras 10.21 *et seq.*

[58] The basis upon which sentencing for criminal laundering is to proceed is as yet unclear. See below, section at 207.

THE SPECIFIC MONEY LAUNDERING OFFENCES

Once there is a predicate offence, and criminal property that can be attributed to it, three major money laundering offences come into play, each of which derives from the Vienna Convention. They have been slightly simplified by the 2002 Act. The substantive alterations which have been made are that laundering offences can now be committed in respect of the property of the defendant, not just that of another.

Concealing or Transferring Criminal Property[59]

Actus Reus

'Concealing or disguising' carries a wide meaning. It can include references to concealing or disguising the nature, source, location disposition, movement or ownership of the property or any rights with respect to it.[60] The crime also extends to cases where the defendant converts[61] or transfers that property or removes it from the jurisdiction.[62] In *R v Macmaster*[63] it was construed to cover the conversion into a foreign currency of the proceeds in sterling of drug trafficking. Although the intention to hide is not explicitly made part of the offence the use of the strong words 'conceal' or 'disguise' may well be taken to comprehend intention to hide if those are the elements charged. There has been a certain amount of case law in the United States that might restrict the notion of 'concealment' on this ground.[64] Because the offence is so widely drawn, there is a substantial degree of overlap between this offence and that of handling stolen goods.[65]

Mens Rea

The *mens rea* is imported by the definition of 'criminal property': the defendant must be shown to have had knowledge or suspicion that the proceeds are, in whole or in part,[66] the proceeds of a predicate offence. The omission of any further *mens rea* term in the definition is deliberate. During the passage of the 2002

[59] PCA 2002 s 327.

[60] PCA 2002 s 327(3).

[61] The context requires that the expression does not have the technical meaning it carries in the law of torts (which is negated by consent), but bears its 'normal' meaning of 'change'.

[62] PCA 2002 s 327(1)(e).

[63] *R v Macmaster* [1999] 1 CAR 402.

[64] *US v Saunders* (1991) 928 F 2d 946 (buying car in daughter's name did not satisfy 'intention to conceal or disguise'); *US v Patino-Rojas* (1992) 974 F 2d 94 (intent to structure transaction to avoid reporting requirement meets intent element); *US v Posters 'n' Things* (1992) 969 F 2d 652 (mixing proceeds with legitimate assets in a single account indicates intent to disguise or conceal).

[65] Theft Act 1968 s 22.

[66] PCA 2002 s 340(7).

Act there was discussion of the possibility of insisting upon a *mens rea* element of 'knowingly concealing'. This amendment was defeated.[67] It might still be able to be argued, however, that the use of words like 'conceal' (rather than, say, 'retain') itself implies a mental state. Under the preceding legislation there could only be a conviction for concealing or transferring where the behaviour takes place *for the purpose* of avoiding prosecution for a predicate offence or the making or enforcement in his case of a confiscation order. This requirement has now gone.

Defences

Defences are provided in the cases of authorised disclosures, intended disclosures and lawful justification.[68]

Assisting Another Person to Retain the Benefit[69]

Actus Reus

The offence is committed by someone who enters into or becomes concerned in an arrangement which s/he knows or suspects facilitates the acquisition, retention use or control of criminal property by or on behalf of another. 'Entering into or becoming concerned in an arrangement whereby' is not unlike becoming a party to a criminal conspiracy, but is wider. The offence will consequently attract the condemnation of those who do not like that offence.[70] The 'entering or becoming concerned' can happen explicitly or implicitly. To 'facilitate' is not difficult to define in this context. The best guess is that the courts will attach to it a meaning like that of 'aid' when dealing with the liability of accomplices.[71] This will leave open questions (in the pejorative sense, perhaps, academic), as to whether or not there can be assisting by omission.[72] The use of the expression 'enters into an arrangement' is thought to be sufficiently positive that it is doubtful whether that offence can be committed by omission, but 'becomes concerned' probably can.

Mens Rea

In addition to the 'knowledge or suspicion' requirement to generate 'criminal property' there is a 'knowledge or suspicion' requirement as to whether the

---

[67] Standing Committee B 17 January 2002 cols 971 *et seq.*
[68] PCA 2002 s 327(2).
[69] PCA 2002 s 328.
[70] Phillip E Johnson, 'The Unnecessary Crime of Conspiracy' (1973) 61 *California Law Review* 1137; Paul Marcus, 'Criminal Conspiracy Law: Time to Turn Back from an Ever Expanding, Ever More Troubling Area' (1992) 1 *William and Mary Bill of Rights Journal* 1.
[71] AP Simester and GR Sullivan, *Criminal Law: Theory and Doctrine* (Oxford, Hart, 2000) 190.
[72] AP Simester and GR Sullivan, *Criminal Law: Theory and Doctrine* (Oxford, Hart, 2000) 194 *et seq.*, *R v Clarkson* [1971] 1 WLR 1402; [1971] 3 All ER 344.

arrangement facilitates the acquisition, control, retention or use of the property. Once again this is a respect in which the offence extends beyond criminal conspiracy, which would require intention that the arrangement have that consequence.[73]

Defences

Defences are provided in the cases of authorised disclosures, intended disclosures and lawful justification.[74]

Acquisition, Possession or Use of Criminal Property[75]

Actus Reus

'Acquisition' in a similar context has been held to be able to be performed passively.[76] In order to possess property it is necessary that there be knowledge that there is something.[77] Possession only applies to tangible property, but 'acquire' also encompasses intangible property.[78]

Mens Rea

No further mental state is required than that to generate 'criminal property'.

Defences

Defences are provided in the cases of authorised disclosures, intended disclosures and lawful justification. There is also a defence of 'good consideration'[79] that protects, for example, lawyers acting for alleged traffickers.[80]

---

[73] Criminal Law Act 1977 s 1.

[74] PCA 2002 s 328(2).

[75] PCA 2002 s 329.

[76] *Attorney General's Reference (No 1 of 1988)* [1989] 1 AC 971; [1989] 2 All ER 1 dealing with the acquisition of knowledge for the purposes of insider dealing, under legislation now repealed.

[77] *Warner v Metropolitan Police Commissioner* [1969] 2 AC 256 (1968) 52 CAR 373.

[78] Such as that which is contemplated under PCA 2002 s 340(6).

[79] PCA 2002 s 329(2)(c).

[80] And see *Barham (Edward John Frederick), Re* (unreported) *Sub nom: In the Matter of the Drug Trafficking Offences Act 1986, Re* (1995), distinguishing *Customs and Excise Commissioners v Norris* [1991] 2 QB 293.

Defences and the Burden of Proof

Money Laundering Offences—Expressly Placing the Burden on the Defendant

For many years it was clearly open to Parliament to place the burden of proof explicitly or implicitly[81] upon the criminal defendant.[82] This followed from the consideration that Parliament was sovereign. Under the previous law, and before the decision of the House of Lords in *Lambert*, there were provisions in the definitions of money laundering offences expressly placing the burden of proof on the defendant,[83] and some which were held impliedly to achieve that end.[84] Then came the Human Rights Act 1998. Article 6(2) guarantees the presumption of innocence, but it was established early that a defendant could bear an onus, but not the whole burden of proof, and that certain reasonable presumptions are permissible.[85] In *Salabiaku v France*[86] the court held:

> Article 6(2) does not therefore regard presumptions of fact or law provided for in criminal law with indifference. It requires states to confine them within reasonable limits which take into account the importance of what is at stake and maintain the rights of the defence.[87]

The sorts of things which militate against the shifting of the burden are the seriousness of what is at stake and any question of the adverse assumption being an automatic one. In *Hoang v France*,[88] the phrase 'importance of what is at stake' was taken to indicate that the more serious the offence, the less likely it was that shifts in the burden would be tolerated, and the absence of automatic reliance by the judges upon the presumptions in the French customs code.

In *R v Director of Public Prosecutions ex parte Kebilene and Others*,[89] there were suggestions in the speech of Lord Cooke that only an evidential burden could be placed upon the defendant,[90] and Lord Steyn[91] referred to a body of decisions in other common law jurisdictions[92] that might argue against the possibility of shifting the burden onto the defendant. Lord Hope held that the test was one of proportionality, to be answered by reference to the following questions:

> (1) What does the prosecution have to prove in order to transfer the onus to the defence?

---

[81] *R v Hunt (Richard)* [1987] AC 352.
[82] *Woolmington v DPP* [1935] AC 462.
[83] *R v Colle* (1992) 95 CAR 67, *R v Butt* [1999] *Criminal Law Review* 414.
[84] *R v Gibson* [2000] *Criminal Law Review* 479.
[85] *Lingens v Austria* (No.1) (1982) 4 EHRR 373.
[86] *Salabiaku v France* (1988) 13 EHRR 379.
[87] Para 28.
[88] *Hoang v France* (1993) 16 EHRR 53.
[89] *R v Director of Public Prosecutions ex Parte Kebilene and Others* [2000] 2 AC 326.
[90] At 372: and see the note of Sir John Smith [2000] *Criminal Law Review* 479, 480.
[91] *R v Director of Public Prosecutions, ex Parte Kebilene and Others* [2000] 2 AC 326 at 369.
[92] *Attorney-General of Hong Kong v Lee Kwong-kut* [1993] AC 951 (PC); *Reg. v Whyte* (1988) 51 DLR (4th) 481; *R v Oakes* (1986) 26 DLR (4th) 200; *State v Mbatha* [1996] 2 LRC 208.

(2) What is the burden on the accused—does it relate to something which is likely to be difficult for him to prove or does it relate to something which is likely to be within his knowledge or to which he readily has access?

(3) What is the nature of the threat faced by society which the provision is designed to combat?[93]

The House, however, expressed no decided view. It further considered the question of the application of the Convention in *R v Lambert*[94] holding that the status of the affirmative defences to drugs offences in sections 4, 5 and 28 of the Misuse of Drugs Act 1971 *was* affected by the Human Rights Act. The House held that the natural meaning of the words placing upon the defendant an affirmative duty was *prima facie* inconsistent with Article 6(2). The next question was whether there were reasons that could be advanced, under *Salabiaku* and later cases, for the displacement of the presumption. The House held that while there were such reasons, they did not satisfy the test of proportionality. Section 3 of the Human Rights Act 1998 required the House to interpret statutes consistently with the Convention. The House held therefore, that whilst it was not the natural meaning of the words, the statute would bear the secondary meaning that an *evidential* and not a *legal* burden was imposed upon the defendant.[95] If the 'secondary interpretation' is available which is consistent with Article 6(2), then section 3 of the Human Rights Act and *Lambert* require that it be adopted. Where there is no such interpretation available a declaration of incompatibility can be made.

It was held in *Hunt*[96] that it is possible for Parliament to place the burden of proving something on the defendant by implication, but that this inference should not lightly be drawn. The criteria to be applied were that the court should have regard to three things—the wording of the statute, the seriousness of the offence and the ease for the respective parties of proving the matter in question.[97] In *Gibson*[98] the court applied *Hunt* and held the burden to have shifted. The case has been the subject of strong criticism.[99] One of the *indicia* to which reference had been made in *Hunt* was whether the defendant had particular access to proof or disproof of the fact asserted: where it was a matter specifically within the defendant's knowledge, it was thought to provide an indicator that it might be legitimate to place the burden upon the defence.[100] This idea does indeed argue for moving the burden, but the argument proves too much, as it might apply, for example, equally to *alibi*. Another criterion derived

---

[93] [2000] 2 AC 326 at 386.

[94] *R v Lambert* [2001] UKHL 37; [2001] 3 All ER 577.

[95] For comments, see Paul Roberts, 'Drug dealing and the presumption of innocence: The Human Rights Act (almost) bites' (2002) 6 *International Journal of Evidence and Proof* 2002 17.

[96] *R v Hunt* [1987] AC 352.

[97] See *per* Lord Griffiths at 374–5. And see Glanville Williams, 'The Logic of Exceptions' [1988] *Cambridge Law Journal* 261.

[98] *R v Gibson* [2000] *Criminal Law Review* 479.

[99] By Sir John Smith, note to *R v Gibson* [2000] *Criminal Law Review* 479.

[100] [1987] AC 352 at 360–363, *per* Lord Griffiths.

from *Hunt* is the seriousness of the offence:[101] the more serious the offence, the less the court should be inclined towards the imposition of any burden of proof upon the defendant. The case law under Article 6(2) of the Convention,[102] on the other hand, suggests that the burden may shift only where the offence is a serious one.

In *Lambert* the House held that the burden could only be shifted onto the defence, consistently with the Convention, in the case where three criteria were satisfied:[103]

> (1) What does the prosecution have to prove in order to transfer the onus to the defence? (2) What is the burden on the accused—does it relate to something which is likely to be difficult for him to prove or does it relate to something which is likely to be within his knowledge or to which he readily has access? (3) What is the nature of the threat faced by society which the provision is designed to combat?[104]

The final criterion in *Salabiaku* and *Kebilene* indicates that the more serious the offence alleged, the stronger the argument for shifting the burden to the defence (when that is done explicitly). The final criterion in *Hunt* holds that the more serious the offence alleged, the weaker the argument for holding that a statute has implicitly shifted the burden to the defence. It is difficult to see, therefore, how *Hunt* can have survived *Lambert*.

In redefining the offences in the 2002 Act notice was taken of these matters.[105] The form in which the offences are cast is for there to be a provision stating 'but a person does not commit an offence if' followed by the conditions of the 'defence'. Unless there is a backlash against *Lambert*, the legal and evidential burdens under these defences will fall upon the prosecution.

The Discretion to Disclose

In respect of compelled (that is, within the regulated sector) or voluntary disclosures (disclosures by any person carrying out a trade profession business or employment outside the regulated sector)[106] there is no civil liability, for example for breach of confidence.[107] In addition to these protected disclosures, there is also a category of 'authorised disclosure' which permits people to complete

---

[101] [1987] AC 352 at 362 *per* Lord Griffiths.

[102] *Hoang v France* (1993) 16 EHRR 53; *Salabiaku v France* (1988) 13 EHRR 379; *R v Lambert* [2001] UKHL 37 and Lord Hope's criteria in *R v Director of Public Prosecutions ex Parte Kebilene and Others* [2000] 2 AC 326, 386.

[103] Following *Salabiaku v France* (1988) 13 EHRR 379 and *Kebilene* [2000] 2 AC 326.

[104] *Kebilene* at 386 *per* Lord Hope.

[105] And see Joint Parliamentary Committee on Human Rights, *Third* and *Eleventh Reports* (2001 and 2002 respectively).

[106] PCA 2002 s 337(2).

[107] PCA 2002 s 337(1).

transactions they know or suspect to constitute one of the principal offences, but which has been authorised (usually by the NCIS).[108]

The Obligation to Inform—Failure to Disclose Suspicion

There is no general duty upon citizens to report criminal offences to the police. The offence of misprision of felony[109] was abolished in 1967.[110] The offence of misprision of treason still exists, but is obsolescent. There is an offence under section 4 of the Criminal Law Act 1967 of doing without lawful authority or reasonable excuse any act with intent to impede the apprehension or prosecution of a person. There is also an offence of failure to notify the authorities of acts of terrorism, which, after a brief hiatus, reappeared on the statute book as part of the emergency legislation package in 2001.[111] The money laundering legislation, however, relies for what efficacy it has upon compelled disclosure. Before the 2002 Act there was an obligation upon everyone to inform the authorities of knowledge or suspicion in respect of drug[112] or terrorist[113] money laundering. The Home Office Working Group on Confiscation recommended the extension of the offence of failure to disclose proceeds to which Part VI of the 1988 Act applies.[114] The Cabinet Office accepted this proposal.[115] This is another case where the demands of consistency have been taken to be that the scope of the criminal law should expand. Rational development of the law might equally be achieved by abolishing the offence altogether.[116] By 2000 there had only ever been one conviction.[117] The 2002 Act contains an offence of failure to disclose suspicion that extends to money laundering. While there was no specific offence of failure to report money laundering other than that relating to drug trafficking or terrorist activity, there is an offence under the Money Laundering Regulations where a firm[118] conducting relevant financial business failed to maintain procedures to ensure that all known and suspected cases are properly reported.[119]

---

[108] PCA 2002 s 338.

[109] See *Sykes v Director of Public Prosecutions* [1962] AC 528; (1961) 45 CAR 230.

[110] Criminal Law Act 1967 s 12.

[111] Terrorism Act 2000 s 38B, inserted by Anti-Terrorism, Crime And Security Act 2001 s 117. The new offence is similar to that which was found in the Prevention of Terrorism (Temporary Provisions) Act 1989 s 18, which had been repealed by the Terrorism Act 2000. S 18 was related only to acts of terrorism in Northern Ireland. The new offence has no such geographical limitation.

[112] DTA 1994 s 52.

[113] Terrorism Act 2000 s 19.

[114] Home Office Working Group on Confiscation, 3rd Report: *Criminal Assets* (London, Home Office, 1998) 20.

[115] *PIU Report* para 1.32.

[116] And see the section above ch 1, The General and the Particular in Criminal Lawmaking.

[117] *PIU Report* box 9.4.

[118] Liability extends to individuals as well as to the body corporate: Money Laundering Regulations 1993 para 6.

[119] Money Laundering Regulations 1993 para 14.

Actus Reus

The Proceeds of Crime Act extended the scope of the 'failure to report' laundering offences to cases of the laundering of the proceeds of any criminal conduct, but restricted its application to the regulated sector.[120] It is an offence if:

(a) a person knows or suspects, or has reasonable grounds upon which to know or suspect, that another person is engaging in money laundering;[121]
(b) the information, or other matter, on which that knowledge or suspicion, or upon which the reasonable grounds arise, is based came to his attention in the course of the business in the regulated sector,[122] and
(c) he does not disclose the information or other matter to a constable, or when subject to the reporting regulations, the relevant reporting officer.[123]

The offence is subject to defences of 'reasonable excuse',[124] legal professional privilege[125] and failure of the employer properly to train.[126]

Mens Rea

Under the previous law it was necessary that a person knew or suspected that another person is engaged in drug money laundering.[127] Now negligent failure to disclose can constitute a serious offence. This generated much discussion in the Parliamentary debates.[128] Liability for negligence is unusual anyway, and this offence involves a negligent omission. Five years is very severe penalty for a negligent failure. There is a general understanding that negligence is not sufficient for a conviction for a serious crime. The understanding is due only in part to a lasting commitment amongst many criminal law theorists to the 'subjective' principle of criminalisation, but even putting that aside there are reasons why liability for negligence should be restricted. Ashworth argues to a position where:

... negligence may be used as an appropriate standard for criminal liability where: (i) the harm is great; (ii) the risk is obvious; and (iii) the defendant has the capacity to take the required precautions.[129]

---

[120] PCA 2002 s 330(3)(b).
[121] Ie the commission of one of the offences under PCA 2002 s 327–329.
[122] The sector is defined in PCA 2002 Schedule 9 Part 1.
[123] PCA 2002 s 330(2)–(4). There are similar offences for nominated officers (ie Money Laundering Reporting Officers) and other nominated officers. PCA 2002 s 331, 332.
[124] PCA 2002 s 330(6)(a).
[125] PCA 2002 s 330(6)(b).
[126] As before, the burden will fall on the prosecution throughout.
[127] DTA 1994 s 52.
[128] HL Debates 27 May 2002 cols 1067–1070.
[129] Andrew Ashworth, *Principles of Criminal Law*, 3rd edn (Oxford, Oxford University Press, 1999) 199.

The issues are unlikely to arise whether attributes personal to a particular person should be ascribed to the reasonable person for the purposes of the test.[130] The questions both of the size of the harm and the obviousness of the risk (but particularly the first) directs us back to consideration of the harm in the laundering offences.[131] The offence which is usually cited as an example of a case where the seriousness of the harm might justify criminal liability for negligence (or gross negligence) is manslaughter. The harm is clear and serious: someone is dead. This is not the case in money laundering. The harm is distant and unclear.[132] The major comparator offences[133] (handling, smuggling, counterfeiting, drug dealing) cannot be committed negligently. Theft cannot be committed negligently. If there is some exceptional justification for the imposition of liability for negligence, it is in need of clear articulation. This is not to be found in the debates on the Proceeds of Crime Act 2002. The willingness of the Government to extend liability without a specific explanation or clear foundation is a clear example of the operation of the 'moral panic' about laundering.[134]

One offence or two? There are strong arguments for the negligence offence to be separated from the offences requiring consciousness. The driving analogy is, in this context, powerful. Nonetheless the Government took the view that one wide offence was better.

> The key argument against splitting the offence is that the prosecution would then have to decide whether to risk basing an indictment on knowledge, or suspicion. That is the problem with the current *régime*—it is very difficult to prove subjective knowledge. It is highly likely that prosecutors would go for the lesser offence if the proposed single offence were split, as the offence containing the subjective tests would be used only rarely, if at all.[136]

The minister's justification seems to assume that in the drafting of an indictment the prosecutor is not entitled to charge alternative counts, one more serious than another. S/he is. The indictment would, in any event, have to allege some fault, and if the minister were correct, the same argument would apply to the new offence, in which, on his reasoning, the prosecutor would charge a fault element other than negligence 'rarely, if at all'.[137]

'Tipping-off'

One of the peculiarities in the statutory scheme for the criminalisation of money laundering is the 'tipping-off' offence, which, together with the duty to inform,

---

[130] This issue is much debated in the literature on criminal liability for negligence. AP Simester and GR Sullivan, *Criminal Law: Theory and Doctrine* (Oxford, Hart, 2000) 138 *et seq.*

[131] See the section above ch 3, Justifying Criminalisation.

[132] See the section above ch 1, The Harm in Laundering.

[133] See the section below in this ch, Sentencing Money Launderers.

[134] See the section above ch 1, Moral Panics.

[136] Bob Ainsworth, HC Debates 27 Feb 2002 col 739.

[137] And see, on the question of grading and dividing offences, Andrew Ashworth, *Principles of Criminal Law*, 3rd edn (Oxford, Oxford University Press, 1999) 199–200.

places the citizen who knows what is or might be going on in an entirely different position from that which s/he has in respect of almost any other crime.[138] On several occasions the courts have had to consider the extent to which the giving of warnings to somebody who is or might be committing a criminal offence itself constitutes a criminal offence. The twentieth century marked a move from holding that there was no duty not to warn someone off who might otherwise be apprehended[139] to holding that the offence of obstructing a police officer would be committed.[140]

The offence of tipping-off a launderer is committed when a person knows or suspects that a disclosure has been made by a nominated officer, and s/he discloses to any other person information or any other matter which is likely to prejudice that investigation, or proposed investigation.[141] There is protection for a professional legal adviser when the disclosure is to, or to a representative of, a client, in connection with the giving by the adviser of legal advice to the client; or to any person in contemplation of, or in connection with, legal proceedings; and for the purpose of those proceedings.[142] The protection does not apply in relation to any information or other matter that is disclosed with a view to furthering any criminal purpose.[143] It is a defence for the defendant that s/he held legal professional privilege, that s/he did not know or suspect that the disclosure was likely to be prejudicial in the way mentioned in that subsection.[144] The maximum penalty for this offence on conviction on indictment is imprisonment for a term not exceeding five years or a fine or to both.[145]

Reconciling Professional Duty With Not Tipping-off

The obvious problem for professional advisers is that they may wish to terminate their relationship with any client whom they know to be suspected of laundering offences, or in respect of whom they themselves have made a report to

---

[138] '[T]o tip off a burglar's accomplice that he is being investigated for money laundering is an offence, but to tip him off that he is being investigated for the perpetration of the burglary is [without more—PA] not.' Simon Gleeson, 'The Involuntary Launderer: the Banker's Liability for Deposits of the Proceeds of Crime', in Peter Birks (ed) *Laundering and Tracing* (Oxford, Oxford University Press, 1995) 115 at 116.

[139] 'Suppose a party of men are engaged in the offence of night poaching, and a person passing near warns them that the police are coming, I think it is clear that that could not be held to be an offence within this section. We must not allow ourselves to be warped by any prejudice against motor cars, and so to strain the law against them.' *Bastable v Little* [1907] 1 KB 59 at 62 *per* Lord Alverstone CJ, (surprisingly) followed in *Bennett v Bale* [1986] *Criminal Law Review* 404.

[140] *Green v Moore* [1982] 1 QB 1044; [1982] 1 All ER 428: and see also Regulation of Investigatory Powers Act 2000 s 54, creating a further 'tipping-off' offence.

[141] PCA 2002 s 333(1).

[142] PCA 2002 s 333(2)(c).

[143] And see, for the interpretation of this sort of provision, the discussion in *R v Central Criminal Court, ex parte Francis & Francis* [1989] 1 AC 346; [1988] 3 All ER 775, below, ch 12 section lawyer/client confidentiality.

[144] PCA 2002 s 333(2)(a): the burden now on the prosecution (unlike CJA 1988 s 93D(6); DTA 1994 s 54(6)).

[145] PCA 2002 s 334.

the police, and yet they do not want, by so doing to lay themselves open to the accusation of having tipped-off the person under investigation. In *Barclay's Bank v Taylor*[146] the Court of Appeal held that a bank disclosing confidential documents in compliance with an access order is under no implied obligation either to oppose the orders or notify its clients. The position in which the adviser is placed is clearly a difficult one, which called for further guidance from the courts. This was forthcoming in *C v S*.[147] C, a company wishing to trace allegedly misappropriated funds, appealed against the court's refusal to make orders against B, a bank, for discovery of documents to help C obtain relief against other defendants. B, however, had made a series of money laundering reports to the NCIS. The NCIS informed B that disclosing information to C could contravene the 'tipping-off' provisions in the 1988 Act. The NCIS letter to B read: 'Please continue to operate the account in accordance with normal business practice'. Whilst it had been accepted by the parties that the disclosure sought would not interfere with any investigation, the Court of Appeal took the opportunity to offer general guidance on the action to be taken in situations where there was a conflict between the fight against crime and a private body's right to redress in the case of misappropriation of funds.

The Court of Appeal gave the following guidance:

> On becoming aware that a party was seeking or had obtained an order which might involve the disclosure of information which could prejudice an investigation, a financial institution should inform the NCIS or other investigating authority, which could then identify the material which it did not want disclosed; where the NCIS approved of partial disclosure, but that was unacceptable to the applicant, the matter would have to be referred to the court, ensuring that the judge was aware of all the difficulties. The extent to which the matter could be resolved in open court and the applicant could participate in the proceedings would depend on the circumstances of each case; it was for the court to decide what evidence it would need in deciding what order to make, bearing in mind that it had to have material on which to act if an applicant was to be deprived of his normal rights. It was for the NCIS to show that there was a real prospect of prejudice to its investigation, and the court should consider whether a partial order might be preferable to no order, and whether an adjournment of the whole or part of the issue might be effective to remove the risk of prejudice.[148]

The way in which the case was fought generated denunciation and comparison to Kafka.[149]

> But subject to such safeguards, the Court of Appeal accepted the legitimacy of the secret procedure and of the possibility that parties to a civil action may be denied the facility of disclosure or other similar remedies without being allowed to utter a word in their own defence. There is no doubt that if the police could, by secret means, prevent litigants from taking measures to protect their legitimate interests without any

---

[146] *Barclay's Bank v Taylor* [1989] 1 WLR 1066; [1989] 3 All ER 563.
[147] *C v S and others* [1999] 2 All ER 343; [1999] 1 WLR 1551.
[148] Lord Woolf MR [1999] 2 All ER 343 at 349.
[149] Adrian Zuckerman, 'A case of secretive and opaque justice?' *The Times*, 8 February 2000.

court supervision, an unacceptable scope for unwarranted interference with private rights would be created. [. . .]

More disturbing still is the fact that the possibility of a secretive judicial process remains. The timely disclosure of the whereabouts of stolen assets may be the only way of retrieving them. The denial of this facility to an innocent person without the due process of the law, the linchpin of which is the right to be heard, is difficult to justify, no matter how strong the countervailing interest in the prosecution of drug offences.[150]

It is clear that in the event of conflict between civil and criminal law duties the criminal law takes precedence. The court would not make an order that it would otherwise make if it would result in a person being required to commit a criminal offence.[151] The court gave the NCIS substantial powers at a point where a party to legal proceedings intended to apply or had applied for disclosure of information by the financial institution concerned. At that point, the NCIS should be informed and given the opportunity to identify the material it did not wish to be disclosed and to indicate its preference as to how the matter should be handled.

The issues were reconsidered in *Bank v A Ltd*.[152] A bank was informed that one of its customers was under investigation, and applied *ex parte* to the court for direction as to how to proceed. The judge made an order freezing the accounts and ordered that the information leading to its making should remain confidential, and made no provision for the communication of the order to A. The order came to A's attention, presumably when he tried to use the account. He brought an action to challenge it. It was discharged on the ground that the judge had exceeded his powers. The court made it clear that the mere suspicion on the part of the bank would not deprive the customer of liberty to use the account. The police were to be invited to provide the information to the court on the basis of which the order should be made.

The Court of Appeal held that the bank should have approached the Serious Fraud Office with a view to reaching an agreement as to the information that it could disclose and if agreement had not proved possible, it ought to have sought directions from the court, making the Serious Fraud Office the defendant. The court would then have had the power to make an interim declaration under the Civil Procedure Rules 1998[153] setting out the information upon which it would be appropriate for the bank to rely. This approach is acceptable if (but only if) a further condition is satisfied. Some kind of provision is made better than those currently existing in English Law for exempting from criminal liability people acting upon official advice.[154] The courts cannot say, on the one hand, that the

---

[150] Zuckerman, *ibid*.
[151] The court cited *Rowell v Pratt* [1938] AC 101, 106.
[152] *Bank of Scotland v A Ltd* [2001] EWCA Civ 52; [2001] 1 WLR 751.
[153] Civil Procedure Rules 1998 Part 25 r 25 1(1)(b).
[154] Andrew Ashworth, 'Testing fidelity to legal values: official involvement and criminal justice' (2000) 63 *Modern Law Review* 633.

bank should take the advice of the SFO, but that acting upon their advice will not provide any legal shield. Second, there needs to be some other mechanism for oversight of the advice given by the SFO (or whichever enforcement agency is in point).

After consultation, provisions were inserted in the Proceeds of Crime Act 2002 to give clearer guidance for the assistance of the financial sector in the case where a report is made to the NCIS as to a suspected transaction. The new legal mechanism is granting power to police officers, customs officers or nominated officers[155] to consent to the performance of what would otherwise be unlawful transactions.[156]

One of the difficulties had been that the NCIS had not been responding with sufficient speed to requests for permission to carry out a transaction. The 2002 Act puts in place a notice period of seven working days: if consent to a transaction being made is not refused before the end of the notice period, the transaction may proceed.[157] This is a long time for banks to put off customers who are active account users without tipping them off. The moratorium period is the period of 31 days starting with the day on which the nominated officer is given notice that consent to the doing of the act is refused.[158]

NUMBERS OF CONVICTIONS

Information taken from the Home Office court proceedings database showing the number of persons convicted for money laundering offences during the period 1991 to 2000 in England and Wales is given in Table 3. Data for other European Union (EU) States are not collected regularly. The data in Table 4 have been produced from a paper produced by the Financial Action Task Force (FATF) and were collected from the mutual evaluations of FATF members of which two rounds have occurred since 1991.[159]

---

[155] Who require their own consent PCA 2002 s 336.
[156] PCA 2002 s 335.
[157] PCA 2002 s 335(2)
[158] PCA 2002 s 335(6).
[159] HC Debates 9 Nov 2001 Column: 495W (Bob Ainsworth).

Table 3: Number of offenders convicted at all courts for money laundering offences, by type of offence, England and Wales, 1991–2000[12]

Code	Offence	1991	1992	1993	1994	1995	1996	1997	1998	1999	2000
	Drug money laundering offences										
93/49	S49 Drug Trafficking 194 (previously S14 Criminal Justice (Inter-national Co-operation) Act 1990	15	15	15	1	15	15	4	15	12	5
93/50	S50 Drug Trafficking Act 1994 (previously S24 Drug Trafficking Offences Act 1986)[13] Assisting another person to retain the benefit of drug trafficking	17	17	4	4	3	2	11	9	9	16
93/51	S51 Drug Trafficking Act 1994 (previously S23A Drug Trafficking Offences Act 1986 as inserted by S16 Criminal Justice Act 1993) Acquisition, possession or use of other proceeds of drug trafficking	16	16	16	15	15	3	13	7	9	5
93/52	S52 Drug Trafficking Act 1994. Failure to disclose knowledge or suspicion of money laundering	16	16	16	15	15	15	15	15	15	15
93/53	S53 Drug Trafficking Act 1994 Disclosure of information likely to prejudice an investigation ('tipping-off')	16	16	16	15	15	15	15	15	15	15
	Total drug money laundering offences	15	15	4	5	3	5	28	16	30	26
	Offence of laundering proceeds of other crime										
53/26	S93A Criminal Justice Act 1988[14] as inserted by S29 Criminal Justice Act 1993 Assisting another to retain the benefit of criminal conduct	16	16	16	15	15	2	10	4	4	9

Table 3: *cont.*

Code	Offence	1991	1992	1993	1994	1995	1996	1997	1998	1999	2000
Offence of laundering proceeds of other crime											
53/27	S93B Criminal Justice Act 1988[14] as inserted by S30 Criminal Justice Act 1993 Acquisition, possession or use of proceeds of criminal conduct	16	16	16	15	15	6	4	2	5	6
53/28	S93C Criminal Justice Act 1988[14] as inserted by S31 Criminal Justice Act 1993 Concealing or transferring proceeds of criminal conduct	16	16	16	15	15	15	1	4	15	9
53/29	S93D Criminal Justice Act 1988[14] as inserted by S32 Criminal Justice Act 1993 Disclosure of information likely to prejudice an investigation ('tipping-off')	16	16	16	15	15	15	15	15	15	15
	Total for offences of laundering proceeds of other crime	15	15	15	15	15	8	15	10	9	24
	Total for all offences	15	15	4	5	3	13	43	26	39	50

[12] Excludes any convictions in Staffordshire

[13] Court Proceedings data prior to 1993 cannot separately identify offences under S24 Drug Trafficking Offences Act 1986 (since consolidated and replaced by S50 Drug Trafficking Act 1994) from other drug offences. For the years 1993, 1994 and 1995, a special exercise was undertaken to identify this specific offence. However as a 100 per cent. response from courts was not achieved 'estimates' for these three years were made.

[14] Sections 93A to 93D Criminal Justice Act 1988 came into force in February 1994.

[15] Nil return

[16] Not applicable

[17] Not available

Note:

All data are given on a principal offence basis[160]

---

[160] HC Debates 19 Feb 1998 column: 784W Written Answer 29789 (Alun Michael).

Table 4: Number of convictions for money laundering offences, in certain EU countries[161]

Country	Year	Convictions
Belgium	1994–99	182
Denmark	1994–99	88
Germany	1994	16
	1995	15
	1996	30
Italy	1994	
	1995	125
	1996	
Ireland	1995–99	11

The numbers are low. The responses to the exigencies of the Vienna Convention both in the United Kingdom and elsewhere suggest that the use of the criminal sanction against launderers has not been the first resource of prosecutors, and reduces the strength of the claim that it is imperative that such crimes should be on the statute book.[162]

SENTENCING MONEY LAUNDERERS

It would have been peculiar had the objectives of the law, and the harms which they seek to prevent, so elusive at the point where the crime is defined, suddenly become pellucid at the point of sentence. They did not. If there is to be sensible sentencing then it must rest upon a developed account of what actually is wrong with money laundering. In an area where there is so little guidance, the starting point is the sentencing *maxima*. Under the current legislation they are severe, and are set out in Table 5.

There is not yet sufficient case law for a sentencing standard to have developed.[163] If the only legislative clues to a proper account of the seriousness of the offence are not reliable indicators, then regard must be had to the behaviour of the courts and to considerations of principle.[164] The language of the courts suggests that in sentencing three people, one for possession of x grams of drug y having a 'street value' of £z, one for selling x grams for £ z, and the last for laundering £ z, the approach of the court should be that the sentence of the dealer is greater than that of the launderer is greater than the possessor.

[161] Source: Financial Action Task Force: HC Debates 9 Nov 2001 Column: 497W (Bob Ainsworth).

[162] See the section above ch 3, Justifying Criminalisation. The argument that the criminal offences exist largely to provide triggers for the reporting requirements is strengthened.

[163] In *R v O'Neill* [2001] EWCA Crim 1660 the court reserved its position (at para 96) on the appropriate sentence for laundering.

[164] And compare Jonathan H Hecht, 'Airing the Dirty Laundry: The Application of the United States Sentencing Guidelines to White Collar Money Laundering Offense' (1999) 49 *American University Law Review* 289.

Table 5: Laundering—sentencing *maxima*

	Criminal Justice Act 1988	Drug Trafficking Act 1994	Terrorism Act 2000	Proceeds of Crime Act 2002
Assisting another person to retain the benefit of criminal conduct or of drug trafficking	14 years[165]	14 years[166]	14 years[167]	14 years[168]
Acquisition, possession or use of the proceeds of criminal conduct or of drug trafficking	14 years[169]	14 years[170]	14 years[171]	14 years[172]
Concealing or transferring the proceeds of criminal conduct or of drug trafficking	14 years[173]	14 years[174]	14 years[175]	14 years[176]
Failure to disclose knowledge or suspicion of laundering	5 years[177]			5 years[178]
Tipping-off	5 years[179]	5 years[180]	5 years[181]	
Failing to comply with the requirement to operate a proper reporting system	2 years[182]	2 years[183]		

In some early decisions on money laundering the courts took the view that this was not an area of sentencing in which any guidelines could be laid down.[184] In 1999, for the first time, a sentencing case came before the courts in which the launderer had no other allegation against him/her. The court took a very harsh

[165] CJA 1988 s 93A(6).
[166] DTA 1994 s 54(1).
[167] Terrorism Act 2000 s 19(8).
[168] PCA 2002 s 334.
[169] CJA 1988 s 93B(9).
[170] DTA 1994 s 54(1).
[171] Terrorism Act 2000 s 19(8).
[172] PCA 2002 s 334.
[173] CJA 1988 s 93C(4).
[174] DTA 1994 s 54(1).
[175] Terrorism Act 2000 s 19(8).
[176] PCA 2002 s 334.
[177] CJA 1988 s 93D(9).
[178] PCA 2002 s 334.
[179] CJA 1988 s 93D(9).
[180] DTA 1994 s 52.
[181] PCA 2002 s 334.
[182] Money Laundering Regulations 1993 para 5(2).
[183] Money Laundering Regulations 1993 para 5(2).
[184] *R v Morgan*, *The Times*, 5 April 1994, nonetheless holding that the sentence under consideration was correct. See also *R v O'Meally* (1994) 15 CAR(S) 831.

line indeed.[185] Nonetheless, there are so few cases decided on the sentencing of offenders under the money laundering legislation that there is little guidance as to the underlying rationale of the offence to be found in the sentences that have been imposed.[186] In seeking to place sentencing on a rational footing, there are two major approaches. One is to have regard to possible comparators— offences that might be thought to provide analogies.[187] The other is to seek the basis for sentencing by reference to aggravating and mitigating factors. Both test the possible justifications for the crime. As to the first, there are four serious offences to which there are some similarities.

Drug Dealing?

There are some indications in the earlier cases and legislation on laundering that the launderer is regarded more agreeably than the trafficker. There is Court of Appeal authority for the proposition that 'those who launder money are nearly as bad as those who deal the drugs'[188] but neither were reasons given nor the full consequences of that statement have been worked through. This statement again assumes that the seriousness of the act of laundering is directly related to that of the predicate, yet unless laundering is a form of complicity there is no reason why the vice in laundering should be in any way related to the means by which the money was acquired.

It was easier to see a direct connection between the gravity of drug dealing and that of laundering at the time when the *only* laundering offences were offences of laundering the proceeds of drug dealing. At that time the governing rationale might well have been that laundering was a form of complicity in dealing, and, following a relatively unsophisticated theory of complicity, the liability of the accomplice was a function of, and generally was guilty of a less serious offence than the perpetrator. This view is far more difficult to sustain now the range of predicate offences has grown so much wider.

[185] *R v Ussama-el-Kurd* (*The Guardian*, 26 February 1999): defendant fined £1m, and jailed for 14 years. On appeal, conviction and sentence stood. [2001] *Criminal Law Review* 234 (CA). And see *R v Izzigil* [2002] EWCA Crim 925.
[186] Guidance is arriving: *R v Sabharwal* (*Tarsemwal Lal*) [2001] EWCA Crim 392 (*bureau de change* conspiring to launder £52m from—12 years; *R v Metcalfe* (*Jason Peter*) [2001] EWCA Crim 1343; *R v Cuenca-Ruiz* [2001] EWCA Crim 2418 attempt to launder about £1m—5 years, reduced to 3.
[187] And see Eric C Tew, 'Note: Establishing Uniformity: the Need for a *per se* Rule Against the Grouping of Money Laundering and Fraud Counts under The Federal Sentencing Guidelines' (2001) 42 *William and Mary Law Review* 1077.
[188] *R v Greenwood* (1995) 16 CAR(S) 614.

Counterfeiting?

If the contentions of some economists[189] are accepted, and money laundering does indeed threaten the economies of countries, then the best way to categorise money laundering may well be as a means of undermining the unit of exchange. In that sense the offence might be characterised as resembling offences of counterfeiting money, with commensurate sentences. Counterfeiting money is more than a means of obtaining by deception.[190] If the counterfeit is successful, there will be no identifiable loser, but the introduction of counterfeit currency into circulation will generate an increase—albeit very small, even when the sums of counterfeit currency are quite large—in the rate of inflation. But that is not the real risk either in counterfeiting or laundering. The sources of anxiety are that there will be an alternative source to the 'legitimately' powerful issuer of money, and that the existence of such a source will be subversive of respect for that established authority. In the same way, money laundering—converting worthless 'dirty' money into valuable 'clean' money can be regarded as a mechanism for 'printing one's own money' and in that sense comparable to laundering.

Handling Stolen Goods?

Offences of handling have the obvious similarity to offences of laundering in that they are offences of disposal of unlawfully acquired property. There is a substantial overlap between handling and laundering offences and there have been suggestions that the laundering offences are little but an updated version of handling.[191] In many ways the panic surrounding laundering now has echoes of that surrounding Wild and the other thief-takers in the eighteenth century. Handling offences were amongst the first in which the liability of the instigator of crimes came to be regarded as more serious than that of the individual thieves. In *Metcalfe* the Court cited *R v Rance*[192] as an appropriate comparator. In that case handling of computers worth £0.25m generated a penalty of two and a half years.

Smuggling

Dealing, handling and counterfeiting operate as comparators to laundering without sharing its most significant distinguishing feature—its international character. Reform efforts continually target the changes in enforcement proce-

---

[189] See the section above ch 7, The Economic Consequences of Laundering in Individual Jurisdictions.

[190] And see generally Law Commission, *Criminal Law: Report on Forgery and Counterfeit Currency* (London, HMSO, 1973).

[191] By Professor Sir John Smith, note to Gibson [2000] *Criminal Law Review* 479: Lord Bassam of Brighton, HL Debates 27 May 2002 cols 1064–1065.

[192] *R v Rance: Attorney General's Reference Number 70 of 1999* [2000] 2 CAR(S) 28.

dure that would be necessary to prevent money being spirited away through other jurisdictions. The economic accounts of the gravity of laundering rely for their force upon the effect of laundering upon *two or more* national economies.[193] If the only serious economic damage from laundering depends for its effect upon the international movement of money and goods,[194] then there is clearly a case to be made for restricting the application of the criminal sanction, if it is to be imposed at all, to the cases where the proceeds of crime are moved between jurisdictions. In this account the closest comparator crimes to laundering are smuggling and (in jurisdictions where exchange controls exist) exchange control violations. The peculiarity of smuggling[195] is that it takes its significance from the boundaries. In this sense the closest analogy might be the illegal importation of drugs. Sentencing practice is unclear on the question whether illegal importation 'counts' for the purpose of sentencing as simple possession (in the case where the importation was for personal use) or as possession with intent to supply (in the case where there is intention to sell (the drugs on).[196] If the harm in the activity of launderers is identified as stemming from their moving the proceeds of crime between jurisdictions, then the smuggling analogy might be most appropriate. If it is, then it should be noted that penalties for smuggling have traditionally been very high.

Aggravating and Mitigating Factors

The second approach to the classification of laundering offences is to consider some of the possible variables. Does it, and should it matter, to the sentence imposed upon someone convicted of a laundering offence:

1. that the money laundered was a large or a small amount?
2. that the money laundered was the product of a more serious or a less serious crime?
3. that the laundering was done knowingly rather than suspecting that the money was of unlawful provenance?
4. that it can be shown that the availability of the laundering route made the difference between the crime being committed and not?
5. that the money was acquired inside or outside the jurisdiction, or was to be invested inside or outside the jurisdiction?
6. how the money, when laundered, was to be deployed?

[193] See the section above ch 2, The International and Global Economic Consequences of Laundering.
[194] See the section above ch 2, The Economic Consequences of Laundering in Individual Jurisdictions.
[195] That is, for these purposes, offences under the Customs and Excise Management Act 1979 s 50.
[196] And see Alldridge, 'Dealing with Drug Dealing' in AP Simester and ATH Smith (eds), *Harm and Culpability* (Oxford, Oxford University Press, 1996) 239, 245.

In each of these cases an argument can be made that the distinction should be regarded as having significance. Taking them in turn: As to (1), in all property crime, *ceteris paribus*, *quantum* is significant. As to (2), if the wrong in money laundering is seen as relating so closely to the harm of the predicate offence as for it to amount to a form of complicity, then the nature of the predicate offence should inform the degree of seriousness attached to the laundering transaction. On the other hand, if the punishment is *not* being directed against a form of complicity but against the causing of economic harms, then sentencing will ignore the nature of the predicate offence. If the offence is directed against both, then subject to considerations about *mens rea* , both will be taken into account. Thus far there has been no suggestion that there should be differential sentencing according as to whether the offence was charged under the Drug Trafficking Act 1994 or the Criminal Justice Act 1988 (that is, whether the predicate offence was .a drug trafficking offence or not),[197] but that would be a consistent consequence of the 'complicity' position.

In *R v Basra (Ajaib Singh)*[198] the defendant appealed against a sentence of five years imprisonment imposed following conviction for an offence of assisting another person to obtain the benefit of criminal conduct, the evasion of VAT, Excise Duty and other taxes.[199] He contended that he ought to have been sentenced on the basis of the guidelines for this kind of evasion.[200] The Court of Appeal held that there was no necessarily direct relationship between the sentence for the laundering offence and the original antecedent offence. Nevertheless the sentence for laundering the proceeds of crime should not be wholly disproportionate to the sentence imposed for the original antecedent offence in circumstances where the retention of the proceeds of criminal conduct, was facilitated by the defendant.

As to (3), how significant is it that the laundering was done knowingly rather than suspecting that the money was of unlawful provenance? It is standard treatment of questions of *mens rea* that the 'higher' mental state will give rise either to a separate offence or at the least a greater punishment for the same offence. The issue in money laundering is, however, rather different, because the defendant *can* be expected to have regard to his/her *own* mental state. It is the existence of the mental state (knowledge, suspicion, belief) that gives rise to the obligation to report, or not to take part in the process.

A person generally will not know when she is reckless as to some consequence (like damage to property), because the nature of the enquiry is such that it generally can only be conducted *ex ante*. A person can know whether or not they

---

[197] Sentencing for the terrorist money offences may differ, because the nature of the offences is of preparation for crime rather than disposal of its profits. See the section in this ch, Involvement With Terrorist Money.

[198] *R v Basra (Ajaib Singh)* [2002] EWCA Crim 541; *The Times*, 1 April 2002.

[199] It goes without saying that the point made about *Smith (David Cadman)*, see the section above ch 7, Pecuniary Advantage, was not argued.

[200] In *R v Dosanjh (Barjinder)* [1998] 3 All ER 618.

suspect the provenance of funds with which they deal. If they suspect, then they know they suspect, and the obligation arises just as much as if they know they know. If the knowledge or suspicion is taken to be merely the thing which imposes the obligation to act,[201] or not to act[202] then it will not affect sentence. If the knowledge or suspicion is not merely a precondition to that obligation but also a *mens rea* descriptor of the way in which the obligation is discharged, then it will be taken into account.

A causal issue is raised by (4), which will arise rarely in practice but which focuses attention again upon the rationale for the offence, and calls for comparisons with the developing area of law which deals with *agents provocateurs*. One of the principal reasons which is asserted[203] for the existence of the offences is that people who commit crimes will be less likely to do so if it is less easy to have access to the profits in useable form. If it could be established that the predicate offence would not have happened without the availability of the launderer, then there is a case for suggesting that the launderer's participation was as *instigator*—as in the case of the participation of a handler in a theft to order of a unique artefact. In this case the solution most consistent with the internal logic of the system is for the commissioning launderer to be treated as a handler of stolen goods.

As to (5), if the source jurisdiction of the money or other aspects of the 'money trail' take on international elements, then similar questions arise with a charge of possession with intent to supply: does it make a difference that drugs possessed in jurisdiction A are intended for supply in jurisdiction B, having been made in jurisdiction C? Which jurisdiction is most legitimately aggrieved? Suppose someone is arrested in an airport in jurisdiction A through which they are in transit. They are in the course of carrying banknotes, generated by the sale of drugs, from jurisdiction B to jurisdiction C, where the proceeds are going to be banked, with a view to their eventual investment in jurisdiction Z. How this contributes to the evaluation of the moral wrong in or the sentence for laundering depends upon the obligation which the country B has to country C. The rhetoric of the 'international community' and the operation of multi-national enforcement groups and mechanisms seek to suggest that whichever is the sentencing jurisdiction ought to sentence on the basis that all the offences took place in a cumulative international jurisdiction to which all the harm ascribed to the laundering could be imputed. If this position were not adopted, then sentencers would have to filter out harms ascribable elsewhere. That, however, would be inconsistent with the imposition of liability in the first place.

---

[201] In the case of the offence of failing to disclose or failing to operate a proper system under the regulations.

[202] In the case of the offences of assisting another person to retain the benefit of criminal conduct or drug dealing or acquisition, possession or use of the proceeds of criminal conduct or drug dealing.

[203] See the section above ch 3, Punishing Laundering Removes the Incentive to Commit Predicate Offences.

As originally conceived, the major comparators in sentencing were drugs offences, and the distinction between the drug dealer and the launderer of money is crucial to the assessment of the gravity of laundering. There are enormous differences in scale between the degrees of participation either might have in the whole enterprise. The dealer might be operating on a wholesale or retail basis: the launderer might be putting a few hundred pounds in a building society or transferring millions into a tax haven.

In the case of (6), would it be a defence to give the money to charity, or another good cause, or to the Exchequer? The issue here is whether the use to which the money is to be put has any effect upon the degree of turpitude that is ascribed to the launderer. If the harm against which the offences stand is to do with the empowerment of the 'wrong' people, then it ought to be taken into account.

The latest cases are still equivocal. In *R v Metcalfe (Jason Peter)*[204] the defendant received, and the Court of Appeal approved a sentence of five years' imprisonment for laundering the proceeds of a series of armed robberies by placing a number of large bets, usually at short odds. The court appears to have treated his offence as a serious one because it was seen as a form of complicity in other serious offences. In *R v Everson*[205] a sentence of seven years for conspiring to launder was held to be adequate but not excessive. Clearly if the criminal laundering provisions are to be used more frequently, then a more refined account of the harm (for the purposes of sentence) is required.

---

[204] *R v Metcalfe (Jason Peter)* [2001] EWCA Crim 1343.
[205] *R v Everson* [2001] EWCA Crim 2262, [2002] 1 CAR(S.) 132.

10

Acquisition and Deployment of Money for Terrorism

T ERRORISM NEEDS MONEY just as much as it needs the personal commitment of its active members. Much of the resources available to terrorism are the proceeds of crime—from kidnapping for ransom, armed robbery, extortion ('revolutionary taxes') and drug trading. Where the terrorist organisation has acquired the property by criminal means, then it is liable to confiscation under the 'regular' legislation, and no special provision is required in order to allow the State access to it. Beyond that, terrorism in its 'purest' form presents something of a challenge to confiscation legislation, or any legislation whose predicate is that the criminal acts for profit, because terrorism is not necessarily done for profit. Funding of terrorism has attracted the attention of supranational organisations.[1] If the only applicable provisions were confiscation provisions, they would have no purchase against money intended for use in terrorism that had not itself been acquired in terrorist crime. In the case of money for use in terrorism it is the use to which the money is to be put, not its provenance, which attracts the attention of the law. In order to target money before it comes to be used for the purchase of the *impedimenta* of terror, *forfeiture* and criminalisation *are* therefore the only available mechanisms.

The 'harm' threatened by one who intends to deploy money for terrorist ends is not the extremely remote one of the reduction of confidence in a market, or damage to the economy, or bringing the law into disrepute, but the rather more immediate fear that the money will be used for the purchase of weapons and explosives or otherwise to fund acts of terror. Although it is not clear that the attack required very large sums of money, the financial aspects of terrorism were thrust to the top of the global political agenda by the attacks on the East Coast of the United States on 11 September 2001.[2] Legislative reactions to these events risk being 'knee-jerk' responses from legislators keen to avoid inaction, and so require close scrutiny.

---

[1] UN Convention for the Suppression of the Financing of Terrorism, 9 December 1999.
[2] Tony Blair, HC Debates 14 September 2001 cols 606 and 609. And see Michael Levi, 'Following the Criminal and Terrorist Money trails' in Petrus van Duyne and Klaus von Lampe (eds), *Criminal finances and organizing crime in Europe* (forthcoming).

The enactment of the Terrorism Act 2000 created a new framework for terrorism law. There are criminal laundering provisions and also a set of forfeiture provisions that contain strong analogies to the confiscation provisions under the Proceeds of Crime Act.

The critical definition is the very wide one of 'terrorist property', which means—(a) money or other property which is likely to be used for the purposes of terrorism (including any resources of a proscribed organisation), (b) proceeds of the commission of acts of terrorism, and (c) proceeds of acts carried out for the purposes of terrorism.[3] This definition serves in the place of a requirement, in the confiscation régime, of a predicate offence. The most noteworthy distinction between the criminal laundering provisions and the terrorist money provisions is that, whilst under subsections (b) and (c) there must have been prior criminal activity, under section 14(1)(a) there need be no prior or contemplated offence to trigger the laundering jurisdiction, and no mental state is necessary. Likelihood is sufficient to give rise to terrorist property. Once there is, or is believed or suspected to be 'terrorist property' in contemplation a series of offences come into play.

Terrorist Fund-Raising

It is an offence to invite another to provide money or other property,[4] to receive money or other property[5] and to provide money or other property,[6] intending or knowing that it should be used, or having reasonable cause to suspect that it may be used, for the purposes of terrorism. It is an offence to use money or other property for the purposes of terrorism, or to possess money or other property, intending that it should be used, or having reasonable cause to suspect that it may be used, for the purposes of terrorism.[7] It is also an offence to enter into or become concerned in an arrangement as a result of which money or other prop-

---

[3] Terrorism Act 2000 s 14(1): Reference to proceeds of an act includes a reference to any property which wholly or partly, and directly or indirectly, represents the proceeds of the act (including payments or other rewards in connection with its commission), and the reference to an organisation's resources includes a reference to any money or other property which is applied or made available, or is to be applied or made available, for use by the organisation. (Terrorism Act 2000 s 14(2).)

[4] Terrorism Act 2000 s 15(1).

[5] Terrorism Act 2000 s 15(2).

[6] Terrorism Act 2000 s 15(3).

[7] Terrorism Act 2000 s 16.

erty is made available or is to be made available to another,[8] for terrorist purposes. This last is a very broad offence indeed. There is no requirement that the property involved be terrorist property. All the offences are open to the objection that liability for a serious criminal offence should not be generated by a negligently made mistake.[9]

Criminal Laundering Provisions

The law on the laundering of terrorist property developed piecemeal. There was a provision, similar in effect to the legislation preceding the Proceeds of Crime Act 2002, making it a crime to enter into or otherwise to be concerned in an arrangement whereby the retention or control by or on behalf of another person is facilitated.[10] There was also a crime of failing to disclose knowledge or suspicion of dealing with terrorist property, gained in the course of a trade, profession, business or employment,[11] and offences of raising terrorist funds and some forfeiture provisions.[12]

Now a person commits an offence if he enters into or becomes concerned in an arrangement which facilitates the retention or control by or on behalf of another person of terrorist property—(a) by concealment, (b) by removal from the jurisdiction, (c) by transfer to nominees, or (d) in any other way.[13] It is a defence for a person charged to prove that he did not know and had no reasonable cause to suspect that the arrangement related to terrorist property.[14]

---

[8] Terrorism Act 2000 s 17.

[9] See the section above ch 9, section headed The obligation to inform—failure to disclose suspicion.

[10] Prevention of Terrorism (Temporary Provisions) Act 1989 s 11.

[11] Prevention of Terrorism (Temporary Provisions) Act 1989 s 18, creating a wider offence which for these purposes is analogous to the 'failure to disclose' crime under DTA 1994 s 52, as to which see the section above ch 9, Mens Rea.

[12] Prevention of Terrorism (Temporary Provisions) Act 1989 ss 9, 10, 13.

[13] Terrorism Act 2000 s 18: this offence is clearly analogous to those under DTA 1994 s 50; CJA 1988 s 93A and now PCA 2002 s 327 considered in the section above ch 9, Concealing or Transferring the Proceeds of Crime.

[14] Terrorism Act 2000 s 18(2). As for the significance of the decision in *R v Lambert* [2001] UKHL 37; [2001] 3 WLR 206 for this sort of provisions purporting to shift the burden of proof see above, p 195. *Kebilene* itself dealt with Terrorism Act 2000 s 16. See Paul Roberts, 'The presumption of innocence brought home? *Kebilene* deconstructed.' (2002) 118 *Law Quarterly Review* 41. *Lambert* suggests that the evidential burden only will be on the defence. Judicial responses to *Lambert* have not been such as to embrace it whole-heartedly. Paul Roberts, 'Drug dealing and the presumption of innocence: The Human Rights Act (almost) bites' (2002) 6 *International Journal of Evidence and Proof* 2002 17. See now *R v Daniel* [2002] EWCA Crim 959 (shifted burden acceptable in the offence under Insolvency Act 1986 s 352). *Re SL v DPP* [2001] EWHC Admin 882; [2002] 2 All ER 854 (and in possession of an offensive weapon).

Coupled with the definition of terrorist property in terms of its 'likely use', this goes a long way towards criminalising stupidity. All these offences command sentences of 14 years.[15]

The Offence of Failure to Inform[16]

Where a person believes or suspects that another person has committed an offence of dealing with terrorist cash[17] and bases this belief or suspicion on information that comes to his/her attention in the course of a trade, profession, business or employment,[18] the person commits an offence if he does not disclose to a constable[19] as soon as is reasonably practicable (a) the belief or suspicion, and (b) the information on which it is based.[20] It is a defence to prove[21] that the defendant had a reasonable excuse for not making the disclosure. There is a saving for information covered by legal professional privilege.[22] The maximum penalty is five years.[23] Instead of 'knowledge or suspicion', as under the 1989 Act and the Proceeds of Crime Act 2002[24] the *mens rea* requirement is of 'belief or suspicion'.[25] Disclosures in the prescribed manner are protected from legal action.[26] As an early response to the difficulties to which the conflict between the tipping-off provisions and the duty to the client has given rise, actions with the express approval of a constable are exempt under the terrorism legislation.[27]

Forfeiting Terrorist Property Upon Conviction

Since there are not necessarily any profits in view from offences of terrorism, expropriation by the state of property involved or suspected of being involved in terrorism is by means of forfeiture, not confiscation.[28] The basic forfeiture

---

[15] Terrorism Act 2000 s 22.

[16] And compare the section above ch 9, The Obligation to Inform—Failure to Disclose Suspicion.

[17] Those under Terrorism Act 2000 ss 15 to 18. Terrorist cash is defined in Anti-Terrorism, Crime and Security Act 2001 Schedule 1 para 1.

[18] This formulation is based on that in the DTA 1994 s 52.

[19] Or to the authorised officer: s 19(4).

[20] Terrorism Act 2000 s 19(1)–(3).

[21] Terrorism Act 2000 s 19(3). Again, *Kebilene* and *Lambert* suggest that an evidential burden only will fall on the defence, but subsequent cases are more equivocal. See the section above ch 9, Money Laundering Offences—Expressly Placing the Burden on the Defendant.

[22] Terrorism Act 2000 s 19(5).

[23] Terrorism Act 2000 s 19(8).

[24] PCA 2002 s 331(2).

[25] And see the section above ch 9, Criminal Property.

[26] Terrorism Act 2000 s 20.

[27] Terrorism Act 2000 s 21.

[28] If it is acquired by criminal means then the confiscation procedures under the PCA 2002 may be used.

provision is section 23. According to the offence of which there has been a conviction, the property must be in the possession or under the control of the defendant at the time of the offence,[29] and at that time, he must have intended it should be used, or had reasonable cause to suspect it might be used, for the purposes of terrorism,[30] or the property must be property to which the arrangement[31] in question related, and property which, at the time of the offence, he knew or had reasonable cause to suspect would or might be used for the purposes of terrorism.[32] There is further provision for the forfeiture of any money or other property that, wholly or partly, and directly or indirectly, is received by any person as a payment or other reward in connection with the commission of an offence under sections 15 to 18.[33] This is in essence a confiscation provision directed against the case where the terrorist offence yields profits. The only sop to the rights of third parties is the rule that where a person other than the convicted person claims to be the owner of or otherwise interested in anything which can be forfeited by an order under this section, the court shall give him an opportunity to be heard before making an order.[34]

The obvious comparator to forfeiture under section 23 of the Terrorism Act 2000 is forfeiture under section 143 of the Powers of Criminal Courts (Sentencing) Act 2000.[35] The powers of forfeiture in respect of terrorist property are wider in the following respects. First, under section 143 it is necessary that the property 'was used or intended to be used for committing or facilitating the commission of *any* offence' whereas under section 23 it is necessary that the defendant, 'intended [that the property] should be used, or had *reasonable cause to suspect [it] might be used,* for the purposes of terrorism.' Secondly, as to third party rights, under section 143, only the *defendant's* interest in the property is forfeit. Under section 23, third parties only have the right to be heard[36] before the forfeiture is ordered, but once ordered, it applies equally against third parties. That is, this is a forfeiture provision in the mould of *Bennis v Michigan,*[37] with less regard for third party rights. Thirdly, under section 143 there are issues as to what constitutes an 'item' for the purposes of forfeiture.[38] Section 23, on the other hand is drafted in very expansive terms. The court may order the forfeiture of any money or other property that, wholly or partly, and directly or indirectly, is received by any person as a payment or other reward in connection with the commission of the offence.[39]

---

[29] Terrorism Act 2000 s 23(2)(a).
[30] Terrorism Act 2000 s 23(2)(a)(b).
[31] For the purposes of the crime under Terrorism Act 2000 s 18: s 23(5).
[32] Terrorism Act 2000 s 23(2).
[33] Terrorism Act 2000 s 23(6).
[34] Terrorism Act 2000 s 32(7).
[35] See the section above ch 6, Forfeiture upon Conviction.
[36] Terrorism Act 2000 s 23(7).
[37] Above ch 6 A Comparator—United States' Jurisprudence (p 121).
[38] *R v Attarde* [1975] *Criminal Law Review* 729, interpreting the section expansively.
[39] Terrorism Act 2000 s 23(6), borrowing from CJA 1988 s 93C(2) and DTA 1994 s 49(2).

Seizure and Detention

There is provision, analogous to that in the Proceeds of Crime Act,[40] for the seizure and detention of cash where an authorised officer has reasonable grounds for suspecting that it is intended to be used for the purposes of terrorism, that it forms the whole or part of the resources of a proscribed organisation, or that it is terrorist property.[41] Further provisions deal with extensions of the seizure.[42] A magistrates' court or the sheriff has power to forfeit the cash if satisfied on the balance of probabilities that the cash is cash of the appropriate kind.[43]

Financial Information Orders (Bank Circulars)

One of the innovations in the Terrorism Act 2000 is the introduction[44] of general bank circulars to be issued by constables when investigating terrorist offences. These orders, which are issued by circuit judges, direct banks, on pain of criminal liability, to supply designated information. The information is to be provided in such manner and within such time as the order may specify, and notwithstanding any restriction on the disclosure of information imposed by statute or otherwise.[45] This is the model for customer information orders.[46]

At the Labour Party conference in September 2000 the Secretary of State for Northern Ireland announced the creation of a Commission in Northern Ireland that is to have power to forfeit without conviction.[47] The model would be that of the Irish Criminal Asset Bureau. As with many of these powers, the disruptive force they bring to bear upon targeted organisations is probably more significant than any actual successes they will have. Whether, this can be done consistently with the European Convention will depend upon three contentious matters being dealt with: forfeiture itself, shifted burdens of proof and confiscation and forfeiture without conviction.

---

[40] PCA 2002 Ch 3: see the section above ch 6, Broadening Customs Seizure, detention and Forfeitures of Cash.

[41] Anti-Terrorism, Crime and Security Act 2001 Schedule 1.

[42] Anti-Terrorism, Crime and Security Act 2001 Schedule 1, replacing Terrorism Act 2000 s 26–27.

[43] And compare cash forfeiture in non-terrorist cases: see the section above ch 6, Broadening Customs Seizure, Detention and Forfeiture of Cash.

[44] By Schedule 6: Terrorism Act 2000 s 38. Such orders have previously been available in Northern Ireland.

[45] Terrorism Act 2000, Schedule 6.

[46] PCA 2002 s 363.

[47] 'We will seize terrorist assets, says Mandelson', *The Guardian* (London) 26 September 2000. The full legislation was not introduced, perhaps because the decision of the High Court of Justiciary in *HM Advocate v McIntosh (Sentencing)* 2001 JC 78; 2000 SLT 1280; 2000 SCCR 1017; [2000] UKHRR 751 had placed much of the confiscation legislation in question, and there was little point in legislating while the matter was unresolved. The Financial Investigations (Northern Ireland) Order 2001 was far more limited.

Terrorist Money Laundering Law—Human Rights Challenges

The extensions of the law relating to terrorist money laundering beyond the régime which applies more generally is something which, as with other aspects of the special treatment of persons suspected or convicted of offences involving terrorism, together with the fact that the provisions for seizure upon conviction are forfeiture provisions rather than confiscation provisions, gives rise to a slightly different set of human rights arguments.

Forfeiture upon Conviction and Article 6

McIntosh, Phillips, Rezvi and *Benjafield*[48] dealt with the argument that the shift in the burden of proof involved in the procedure for making the statutory assumptions is a violation of Article 6(2) by holding that a person who is the subject of confiscation proceedings is not 'charged with a criminal offence' for the purposes of Article 6 of the Convention, and consequently the presumption of innocence does not apply to someone who has already been held by a court to be guilty. There is little reason to suppose that this same argument would not operate to prevent any attempt to argue that an Article 6 right was infringed when someone was subject to forfeiture proceedings under section 23.

Forfeiture without Conviction and Article 6(2)

The case of forfeiture without conviction is less clear. In *Goldsmith v Customs and Excise Commissioners*[49] the court accepted that the appellant might well feel that an aspersion of criminality had been cast on him by the proceedings but[50] took a number of factors to indicate that forfeiture proceedings are not covered by Article 6(2).[51] The consequence of a successful claim under Article 6 would be that the burden of proof would fall on the prosecution, and the standard would be the criminal standard.[52] This now appears to have been ruled out by the case law on cash forfeiture.[53]

---

[48] See the section above ch 7, Legitimacy of the Shifted Burden.

[49] *Goldsmith v Customs and Excise Commissioners* [2001] 1 WLR 1673: see the section above ch 6, Forfeiture Proceedings and the Right to a Fair Trial.

[50] Following *R (McCann) v Crown Court at Manchester* [2001] 1 WLR 1084.

[51] Drawing on the ECHR jurisprudence from *Engel v Netherlands* (1976) 1 EHRR 647 to *AP, MP and TP v Switzerland* (1998) 26 EHRR 541.

[52] Ben Emmerson and Andrew Ashworth, *Human Rights and Criminal Justice* (London, Sweet and Maxwell, 2001) 279 *et seq.*

[53] *Butt v HM Customs and Excise* [2001] EWHC Admin 1066.

Forfeiture Provisions and Property Rights

Here the arguments are very similar to those considered above.[54] So long as the court is prepared to hold that the measures taken by the State are proportional[55] to the ends sought by the legislation, the argument from the First Protocol is unlikely to succeed.[56]

Double Jeopardy

It was argued above that the fundamental objection to forfeiture provisions operating upon conviction is that they involve double jeopardy, and that this is something which has hitherto been ignored by English Law. Should the United Kingdom accede to the double jeopardy protocol, account will need to be taken of its effect upon forfeiture in this area.[57]

---

[54] See the section above ch 6, First Protocol—The Right to Property.
[55] *Ibid.*
[56] And compare above, *ibid.*
[57] See the section above ch 6, Forfeiture Proceedings and Double Jeopardy.

11

Confiscation without Conviction— 'Civil Recovery'

THERE ARE MANY reasons why a person suspected of profiting from criminal activity might not be subject to criminal conviction, and it might be thought that they should not all stand in the way of the State having access to the profits. Under the United States' system,[1] once the Government showed probable cause the burden did shift to the defence.[2] The existence of lessened procedural safeguards inevitably led to heightened incidence of error, and in 2000 the burden was placed back onto the State.[3] Under the Comprehensive Drug Abuse Prevention and Control Act 1970[4] the law enforcement agency keeps the proceeds it seizes.[5] The standard of proof was 'probable cause'.[6] Whilst it is true, in comparison to the United Kingdom, that the sums of money seized are very significant,[7] the experience in the United States is some way from providing the unqualified success claimed for it by the advocates of such a system. Boudreaux and Pritchard provide a corrective:

> Legislators benefit from civil forfeiture in two ways; (1) civil forfeitures free up funds that would otherwise have gone to law enforcement agencies; and (2) civil forfeiture increases the cost of prohibited substances, thus fostering more violence in the prohibited industry. Politicians exploit this violence to expand government power, notwithstanding their role in fostering the very criminal activity that they rail against.[8]

The proceeds of civil forfeiture partially relieve taxpayers of the burden of paying taxes for law enforcement. The result is more law enforcement than otherwise people would be prepared to pay for.[9]

---

[1] Scott A Hauert, 'Comment: An Examination of the Nature, Scope, and Extent of Statutory Civil Forfeiture' (1994) 20 *Dayton Law Review* 159.

[2] *United States v 900 Rio Vista Blvd* (1986) 803 F 2d 625, 629.

[3] Civil Asset Forfeiture Reform Act 2000 Pub L 106–185, 114 Stat 202.

[4] Amended to include monies used in and proceeds of trafficking and real property, and codified at 21 USC s 881(a)(4).

[5] 28 USC s 524(c).

[6] 19 USC s 1615.

[7] The Federal Government received the following amounts from asset forfeiture in criminal cases: 1986: $93.7m; 1987: $177.6m; 1988: $205.9m; 1989: $580.8m; 1990: 459.6m; 1991: $643.6m; 1992: 531.0m; 1993: $555.7; 1994: $549.9m. Eric Blumenson and Eva Nilsen, 'Policing for Profit: The Drug War's Hidden Economic Agenda' (1998) 65 *University of Chicago Law Review* 35 at 63.

[8] Donald J Boudreaux and AC Pritchard, 'Civil Forfeiture and the War on Drugs: Lessons from Economics and History' (1996) 33 *San Diego Law Review* 79, 84.

[9] And see Marc B Stahl, 'Criminal Law: Asset Forfeiture, Burdens Of Proof and The War On Drugs' (1992) 83 *Journal of Criminal Law & Criminology* 274.

The major driving force behind the way in which the power of confiscation without conviction works in the United States is that the enforcement authorities are given the incentive that they, rather than central funds, receive some of the property seized. Is this a legitimate way for payments to the police to be set up? This is a question at the heart of the relationship between the market forces and policing. There is a range of arguments as to why this should not be. First, Blumenson and Nilson[10] argue that an important conflict of interest is created for the police, on the ground that there will be financial incentives in place to adopt policing practices which, absent these incentives, would not be optimal. There are some areas of government in which there cannot be a market without risk of corruption. Policing, they argue, is not an area into which the market can be introduced without harmful effects. Secondly, it is argued because the police activity will be directed toward the money rather than the drugs (which have no lawful market) the policing strategy will be such that the drugs remain in circulation. The incentives will incline rational police to target the least culpable participants. Reverse stings—where police pretend to sell drugs to seize the money of the buyer—are now common in the United States.[11] Thirdly, a system of incentivised forfeiture gives the police financial incentives to neglect other pressing crime problems. Business judgements supplant or get in the way of broad law enforcement goals.[12] Fourthly, economic rewards are so high as to generate incentives for the police to behave unlawfully in their pursuit. Lastly there is the strong argument of principle from the separation of powers that the police should not be self-financing. The response in the Cabinet Office proposals for UK legislation is that the problems in the United States' experience have been a function of direct hypothecation, and that a system of pooling funds to be made available on a bid basis, rather than allocating them to the force involved would operate better.[13] The first bids for the Recovered Assets Fund were invited in 2002.[14]

THE IRISH LEGISLATION

In Ireland, the Money Laundering Directive was implemented by the enactment of the Criminal Justice Act 1994. That Act also made provision for the making of an order, by the trial court, for the confiscation of goods on the conviction of an offender, which was adequate to deal with what were described to us as 'second tier criminals'. The legislation was similar to the confiscation provisions in

---

[10] Eric Blumenson and Eva Nilsen, 'Policing for Profit: The Drug War's Hidden Economic Agenda' (1998) 65 *University of Chicago Law Review* 35, 56.

[11] And see also J Mitchell Miller and Lance H Selva, 'Drug Enforcement's Double-edged Sword' (1994) 11 *Justice Quarterly* 313.

[12] Eric Blumenson and Eva Nilsen, n 10 above, at 78.

[13] Cabinet Office Performance and Innovation Unit, *Recovering the Proceeds of Crime* (London, Cabinet Office, 2000) (hereinafter '*PIU Report*') para 12.9.

[14] <http://www.homeoffice.gov.uk/oicd/fct.htm>

England and Wales. The political and social impetus to do something about criminal property came in the aftermath of the murder in 1996 of Veronica Guerin, a specialist organised crime newspaper reporter.[15] The Proceeds of Crime Act 1996 and the Criminal Assets Bureau Act 1996[16] were a comprehensive package of measures on the seizure of criminal assets and, have been said to provide a model for adoption in other European jurisdictions.[17] Those measures are supplemented by the Disclosure of Certain Information for Taxation and Other Purposes Act 1996 which authorises the exchange of information between the Revenue Commissioners and the Garda (the Irish police). Until the 1996 Act, the Revenue were unable lawfully to pass any information about such income onto the police. In summary, the legislation provides for the making of applications to the High Court to seize assets that are suspected to be derived from criminal activity. Seizure can be and is ordered without a prior conviction or proof of criminal activity on the part of the respondent, who, to defeat the claim, is required to establish, on the balance of probabilities, the innocent origins of his/her wealth.

The policy of the CAB is that all the targets for action must meet the *prima facie* standard of criminality. Actions may not be brought on the basis of police beliefs alone.[18] The CAB informs the judge of substantial funds coming into the possession or control of persons who have no occupation, or no occupation that would prima facie merit such income and wealth. Once the case passes this threshold of reasonable suspicion, the burden shifts to the defendant to demonstrate that the funds or the property are the proceeds of legitimate activity. If the case involves fraud, then the victims receive restitution from the seizures.

The Act is a confiscation and not a forfeiture provision and does not apply to the instrumentalities of crime. The Criminal Assets Bureau Act 1996 has as its objectives:[19] the identification of the assets, wherever situated, of persons which derive or are suspected to derive, directly or indirectly, from criminal activity; the taking of appropriate action under the law to deprive or deny those persons of the assets or the benefit of such assets, in whole or in part, as may be appropriate, and the pursuit of any investigation or the doing of any preparatory work in relation to any proceedings arising from these objectives mentioned.

The Criminal Assets Bureau (CAB) is characterised by its multi-agency nature, being staffed by officers from the Irish Police, the Revenue Commissioners and the Department of Social Welfare. The Act provides for:

[15] And see *R v Belmarsh Magistrates Court, ex parte Gilligan* [1998] 1 CAR 14; [1997] COD 342.

[16] See Fachtna Murphy and Barry Galvin, 'Targeting the financial wealth of criminals in Ireland: the law and practice' (1999) 9 *Irish Criminal Law Journal* 133; Eamonn J Walsh 'The enforcement of money laundering legislation' (1999) 9 *Irish Criminal Law Journal* 204; J Paul McCutcheon, 'Select bibliography on confiscation of criminal assets and money laundering' (1999) 9 *Irish Criminal Law Journal* 221

[17] It is this upon which reliance is placed in Home Office Working Group on Confiscation, 3rd Report: *Criminal Assets* (London, Home Office, 1998) 26 *et seq.*

[18] Criminal Assets Bureau Act (Ire) 1996 s 3.

[19] Criminal Assets Bureau Act (Ire) 1996 s 4.

interlocutory freezing orders for proceeds greater than IR£10,000; civil procedures in the High Court; the operation of the civil standard of proof of criminal activity; the belief of a chief superintendent of police or authorised officer of the Revenue to be admissible evidence;[20] and for property not held to be innocent to be frozen for seven years before disposal for the benefit of the Central Fund.

The proceedings are, in effect, a civil trial by *affidavit*, including the *affidavit* of the senior police officer whose asserted belief may be taken by the court to be evidence of fact,[21] with evidence being sworn about the possession of substantial wealth without any visible lawful means of generating it, and about previous convictions and associates of the target. As in a civil case, if the defendant chooses not to contest the allegations, s/he forfeits the case: it is the defendant who has to satisfy the court on the balance of probabilities that his/her possession of the property is innocent.

In the five years to 2002 the Bureau has recovered £IR21m and collected £IR28m out of a total of £IR56m demanded on criminal assets.[22] A number of elements of the Irish legislation give cause for concern: confiscation of property in the absence of a prior conviction; the reversal of the onus of proof;[23] the extent of the powers of search; and the anonymity of Criminal Assets Bureau officers. The Irish courts have consistently rejected constitutional challenges to the legislation.[24] At the time of writing, none of the challenges has reached the European Court of Human Rights.

FORFEITURE AND CONFISCATION BY OTHER MEANS

One use to which the powers to seize and freeze have been put is simply to seize the property and then not restore it to its owner, placing the onus upon the owner to do something to recover it. In *Webb v Chief Constable of Merseyside*[25] the police simply refused to return seized money, and when sued for it, made a claim of *ex turpi causa*. They were able to prove, on the balance of probabilities, that the money concerned was the proceeds of drug trafficking, but no prosecution was brought. Even though the standard of proof was the balance of probabilities, the judge required 'strong and cogent evidence' because of the nature of the crime that was alleged.[26] It was clear that title to the money would

---

[20] This kind of provision is mirrored in the Criminal Justice (Terrorism and Conspiracy) Act 1998. It is very doubtful whether it would survive a challenge under Art 6 of the European Convention.

[21] Proceeds of Crime Act 1996 (Ire) s 8.

[22] HL Debs 22 April 2002 col 35 (Lord Brooke of Sutton Mandeville).

[23] John Meade, 'The disguise of civility: civil forfeiture of the proceeds of crime and the presumption of innocence in Irish law' (2000) 1 *Hibernian Law Journal* 1.

[24] *Murphy v M (G)* [2001] IESC 63.

[25] *Webb v Chief Constable of Merseyside* [2000] 1 QB 427; [2000] 1 All ER 209. And see also *Slater v Commissioner of Police of the Metropolis*, *The Times*, 23 January 1996.

[26] And see IH Dennis, *The Law of Evidence*, 2nd edn (London, Sweet & Maxwell, 2002) 395, and the varying interpretations of the civil standard in confiscation legislation, above, .

pass under a contract for the sale of drugs, even though the contract is illegal. The police had no claim to title but had seized some of it under section 23(2) of the Misuse of Drugs Act 1971[27] and some under section 19 of the Police and Criminal Evidence Act 1984.[28] Powers of detention in both cases are identified by section 22 of the 1984 Act.[29] The police made a half-hearted claim that they were entitled to retain the money in order to find the real owner. The Court of Appeal held that the statutory power of the police to hold on to the property had been exhausted and that the plaintiff *was* the real owner. The real issue was whether the illegality by which the money had been obtained by the dealer stood in the way of recovery being made. The argument for the police had three facets. First, that the plaintiff could not establish title without relying on his own illegality; secondly, that his possession of the money would itself amount to an offence, so that for the court to order that he be granted possession would implicate it in that; and thirdly, that it would be absurd for the court to lend its assistance to the completion of a criminal enterprise.

As to the first, the court held that it was not necessary that the plaintiff assert illegality in order for the claim to succeed. As to the second, an exception had been made in the *Bowmakers* case[30] to the general rule that to deal with cases where the actual possession of the matter under dispute would be criminal (pornography, drugs themselves, firearms and so on). The court held that the case in point did not fall within the exception. This turns on consideration of the text of sections 49–51 of the Drug Trafficking Act 1994. The court accepted the argument that no crime is *necessarily* committed by a person holding on to the proceeds of their own drug dealing—for example simply storing them in a deposit box. This was correct, but provides a very technical basis for the decision. As to the third, the court was able to rely upon the fact that the simple possession of the proceeds of drug dealing is not itself a crime, and that the order or the court would not necessarily achieve anything more than that. It is true that the money laundering crimes did not cover the case of a defendant who simply retains the money, puts it in a bank deposit box, or spends it in a 'normal' transaction. The court was apparently influenced by the consideration that the claims made by the police did not sit easily with their decision not to prosecute. May LJ did contemplate the possibility that the court might decline to grant relief to plaintiffs where to grant it might be to assist (directly or indirectly) the plaintiff in his criminal act, but he concluded:

> In my judgment, the court should not extend the law in the way suggested. Although from the Chief Constable's perspective the money is the proceeds of crime, from

[27] 'If a constable has reasonable grounds to suspect that any person is in possession of a controlled drug in contravention of this Act, . . . the constable may—[. . .] (c) seize and detain, for the purposes of proceedings under this Act, anything found in the course of the search which appears to the constable to be evidence of an offence under this Act.'

[28] Which is the general power to seize during a lawful search.

[29] s 22(1) . . . anything which has been seized . . . may be retained so long as is necessary in all the circumstances.

[30] *Bowmakers v Barnett Instruments Ltd* [1945] KB 65.

another perspective the court should not, in my view, countenance expropriation by a public authority of money or property belonging to an individual for which there is no statutory authority. There is statutory machinery for the prosecution of those who deal in drugs and for the confiscation upon conviction of the proceeds of their drug dealing. There is statutory machinery for the confiscation upon conviction of the proceeds of other serious crime. There is statutory machinery for the forfeiture of the cash proceeds of drug trafficking which are being imported into or exported from the United Kingdom.[31] There is no statutory power to confiscate the proceeds of drug dealing within the United Kingdom where the person entitled to possession of the money is not convicted of a drug trafficking offence.[32] [. . .] It is one thing to prosecute to conviction and to take positive steps authorised by statute to confiscate the proceeds of crime from the convicted defendant. It is quite another to resist the claim of an innocent person by asserting some or all of the ingredients of what might have been a prosecution; or to effect confiscation in this way from a convicted person against whom statutory confiscation machinery has not been used. Innocent claimants would, I am sure, be deterred from pursuing entirely proper claims for the return of money or property to which they were entitled. I can foresee quite unacceptable possible consequences of the development of the law for which the Chief Constable contends in these cases.[33] If statutory provision for civil confiscation is inadequate, it is for Parliament to strengthen them after proper consideration of all the implications.[34]

Viewed against the background of the Cabinet Office review, the provocation and then the defence of the action by the police was a 'win–win' strategy. Either they would win the case (in which case the only legislation on civil forfeiture that would be necessary would be to clarify issues as to the destination of seized goods), or they would lose, generating further pressure for legislation.[35]

THE ASSETS RECOVERY AGENCY

The Hodgson Committee had considered forfeiture without a criminal conviction and found 'this concept of quasi-criminal forfeiture troubling. It can too easily be used as a way of penalising criminal conduct without the safeguards of the ordinary criminal process.'[36] With the passing years, acceptance of 'civil

---

[31] The reference is to Drug Trafficking Act 1994 s 42, now PCA 2002, ch 3: see the section above ch 6, Broadening Customs Seizure, Detection and Forfeitures of Cash.

[32] And see now the section below in this ch, The Director and the Agency.

[33] The correctness of the cases (cited without demur in *Webb*) in which interlocutory injunctions were granted to Chief Constables (*Chief Constable of Kent v V* [1983] QB 34; *West Mercia Constabulary v Wagener* [1982] 1 WLR 127; *Chief Constable of Hampshire v A. Ltd.* [1985] QB 132; *Chief Constable of Leicestershire v M* [1989] 1 WLR 20) was left open *by Lord Nicholls* in *Blake v Attorney-General* [2001] 1 AC 268 at 289; [2000] 4 All ER 385 at 402.

[34] This view was affirmed in *Attorney-General v Blake* [2001] 1 AC 268 at 293; [2000] 4 All ER 385 at 404 *per* Lord Steyn.

[35] *Webb* was followed in *Costello v Chief Constable of Derbyshire* [2001] EWCA Civ 381; [2001] 3 All ER 150. The police behaviour was probably in contravention of the First Protocol to the ECHR. See Graham Battersby, 'Acquiring title by theft,' (2002) 65 *Modern Law Review* 603.

[36] D Hodgson, *Profits of Crime and their Recovery* (London, Heinemann, 1984) (hereinafter 'Hodgson Report') 97.

recovery' has become far closer to the orthodox. It is the proposal to follow suit—particularly following the Irish model, that formed the basis for the Third Report of the Home Office Working Part on Confiscation[37] and which was endorsed during 2000 by the Cabinet Office.[38] It has now led to the establishment by the Proceeds of Crime Act 2002 of the Assets Recovery Agency. The Agency is to exercise three major powers. First, although it has no direct prosecution role, the Director may intervene at the point of conviction to set in train confiscation proceedings. In this regard the relationship in this regard between the CPS and the ARA is the subject of a memorandum of understanding.[39] Secondly, the Agency has the power to bring 'civil recovery' proceedings against people who have not been convicted.

The areas identified by the Government as giving rise especially to the need for a confiscation power independent of the criminal courts are where:

rules of criminal procedure or evidence, having no bearing on the issue of the attribution of assets to criminal conduct, protect a respondent from conviction, with the result that no prosecution ensues or that the case results in an acquittal;[40]

there may be convincing evidence that particular property was obtained through criminal conduct, but insufficient evidence to establish which of a group of identified individuals were involved in the crime, with the result that no prosecution has proved possible;

the respondent is wholly beyond the reach of prosecution, perhaps because he is abroad in circumstances in which he cannot be extradited, or because he has died;

the crime in question was committed abroad in circumstances where there is no extra-territorial jurisdiction to prosecute.[41]

Thirdly, the Agency exercises a taxation jurisdiction. It may exercise the powers of a tax inspector to raise assessments to taxation upon persons suspected of having benefited from unlawful income. Consideration must be given by the Agency to the exercise of the three powers in that order. That is, if prosecution and conviction is a reasonable prospect, then that is the avenue that should be followed. Failing that, a recovery order, and only failing that should the taxation jurisdiction be considered.

The Director and the Agency

The pivotal figure in the new arrangements is the Director of the Assets Recovery Agency, acting to implement a strategy of raising the priority given to

---

[37] Home Office Working Group on Confiscation, *3rd Report: Criminal Assets* (London, Home Office, 1998).

[38] *PIU Report.*

[39] HL Debates 22 April 2002 col 32 (Lord Rooker).

[40] The characterisation of the rules of criminal procedure or evidence as a nuisance is unfortunate.

[41] *Proceeds of Crime Bill: Publication of Draft Clauses* (London, The Stationery Office, CM 5066) para 5.5.

asset confiscation, align incentives and promoting co-operation between law enforcement bodies. The ARA is to house a centre of excellence in respect of financial crime. In this way the responses that previously were insufficiently co-ordinated are focused. 'Joined-up' government implies increased links between government bodies and greater investment of personnel in financial investigation and specialist investigation powers for complex cases. Revenue officials are seconded to the Agency.[42] Following the Irish model, the staff of the Agency other than the Director may have pseudonyms.[43] The Director must produce an annual plan setting out objectives, performance targets,[44] priorities and resource allocations,[45] and produce an annual report.[46] The Secretary of State is obliged to produce a Code of Practice dealing with the discharge by the Agency of its obligations.[47]

The Act separates civil recovery from the prosecution function. The Director will not be a prosecution authority. S/he will, on the other hand, have a duty of co-operation with the prosecution and law enforcement authorities, and a statutory basis to obtain information from those authorities. The duty of the law enforcement authorities to enforce the criminal law will remain unchanged and where they initiate criminal proceedings, confiscation rather than civil recovery will be the expected method of recovery. The Director does have power, independently of the prosecution authorities, to request evidence from overseas.[48] The Director is a public authority and consequently must act in all respects consistently with the Human Rights Act 1998. If he does not, persons affected have a cause of action.[49]

Use of Information by and Disclosure of Information to and by the Director

The Director has many means of acquiring information. Various Government services are empowered to disclose information to the Director. It is a general principle that where a power is given for a particular purpose it is not permissi-

---

[42] *PIU Report* para 10.12.
[43] More strictly, pseudonyms: PCA 2002 s 449.
[44] 'They are likely to include the number of confiscation orders obtained by the agency and the value of those orders; the number of successful civil recovery actions and the amounts recovered through that route; the number of successful taxation cases and the amounts recovered; and the proceeds recovered as a percentage of the number of confiscation orders made, in respect of those cases for which the agency is responsible for enforcement. Some measure will need to be applied to international co-operation on confiscation matters, the performance of the centre of excellence and the agency's financial performance. We will also seek to include a measure of the agency's involvement with the Secretary of State's priorities and other Government priorities.' (Bob Ainsworth MP HC Debates 26 Feb 2002: Column 586–7).
[45] PCA 2002 Schedule 1 para 6(3)(b).
[46] PCA 2002 Schedule 1 para 6(3)(c) and (e).
[47] PCA 2002 s 377.
[48] PCA 2002 s 376.
[49] Human Rights Act 1998 s 6.

ble to use that power for a collateral purpose.[50] Consequently some flexibility is granted.

> Information obtained by or on behalf of the Director in connection with the exercise of any of his functions may be used by him in connection with his exercise of any of his other functions.[51]

The Director has extensive powers under the Proceeds of Crime Act 2002 to acquire information. However in some respects the powers s/he holds *qua* tax inspector are greater.[52] Tax authorities have power to elicit information that would be privileged as against a prosecuting authority. Different controls exist for the exercise of the powers of a tax inspector to require information and documents[53] than in his/her other capacities. On the face of it the section seems to imply that information elicited by deploying the powers of a tax inspector would be able to be used either for the bringing of a confiscation or civil recovery proceedings. Information acquired, for example, by the use of a disclosure order would not be able to be used in those proceedings.[54] If the Agency keeps to the plan of considering the exercise of its taxation powers last, (confiscation or recovery proceedings having been ruled out) then can those decisions be reconsidered and the incriminating evidence acquired by the use of the powers of the tax inspector used? If it can, then the use of those powers might frequently be preferred to the use of the Proceeds of Crime Act powers. The Director may disclose information to any person or body for a range of purposes.[55] S/he may not disclose information obtained by the exercise of his/her revenue functions.[56]

Accredited Financial Investigators

The Act introduces a novel category—the accredited financial investigator. A system for the accreditation of financial investigators is provided.[57] The Secretary of State has power to issue a code of practice for the regulation of the

---

[50] *R v Special Commissioner and another ex parte Morgan Grenfell* [2002] UKHL *per* Lord Hobhouse at para 48.

[51] PCA 2002 s 435.

[52] In particular, the privilege against self-incrimination was never available in response to a tax return before the Human Rights Act 1998, and the Act has made no difference: *Funke v France* (1993) 16 EHRR 297, *Brown v Stott* [2001] 2 WLR 817, [2001] 2 All E.R. 97, *R v Allen* [2001] UKHL 45; [2002] 1 AC 509. On legal professional privilege see now *R v Special Commissioner and another, ex parte Morgan Grenfell* [2002] UKHL 21: see the section below in this ch, Lawyer/Client Confidentiality.

[53] The principal powers are those set out in Taxes Management Act 1970, s 20, s 20A, s 20B, s 20C and s 20D.

[54] See the section above ch 8, Disclosure Orders.

[55] PCA 2002 s 436. The disclosure of information to the Director is governed by PCA 2002 s 438. Disclosures of information that contravene the Data Protection Act 1998 or are prohibited by Part 1 of the Regulation of Investigatory Powers Act 2000 are not permitted: s 438(8).

[56] PCA 2002 s 438(2).

[57] PCA 2002 s 3.

conduct of accredited financial investigators.[58] The Director may provide different classes of accreditation for different purposes.[59]

THE 'CIVIL RECOVERY' POWER

The major innovation in the Proceeds of Crime Act is the advent of the 'civil recovery' power. As in the United States and Ireland, the use of the word 'civil' in this context carries some danger of terminological inexactitude. The process is only civil in the sense that the civil standard of proof (maybe) applies. It still involves an exercise of the full powers of the State against the citizen, something that is in danger of being camouflaged by the expression 'civil' or the naming of a claimant other than the State. Nor is it in any real sense 'recovery' by the State of something it once had. An agency operating under the Irish model would only be 'civil' in the senses that the standard of proof that would apply is the civil one, civil courts are used and that there would be no requirement of a criminal conviction before an order could be made. In every other respect this would be an exercise of the power of the State against designated individuals in a way that has nothing in common with the resolution of disputes by means of the civil law.

The enforcement authority[60] may take proceedings against any person he thinks holds recoverable property. 'Recoverable property' is property that has been obtained through unlawful conduct or property that represents such property.[61] The nature of the recovery power is that the Director is granted a right over the property in question, of the character of a traceable proprietary interest, with safeguards for certain protected prior rights. It is to be exercisable through the High Court by means of a procedure, governed by the existing Civil Procedure Rules,[62] during which the disputed property may be placed under the control of an interim receiver.[63] The Director will not have a claim against a person who acquires criminal property for full value, in good faith and without notice of its alleged criminal origins.[64] This exception is consistent with a standard principle of the civil law on property. Because the property is critical, an order may be made in respect of a person whether or not domiciled, present or resident in the United Kingdom. There is a financial threshold for proceedings.[65]

The basic premise of the recovery procedure is that it confers a proprietary right that enables the enforcement authority to follow the property into the hands of others than the person who first unlawfully acquired it[66] and to trace

---

[58] PCA 2002 s 377.
[59] PCA 2002 s 3(4).
[60] Under PCA 2002 s 34. That is, for these purposes, (in England and Wales) the Director: PCA 2002 s 316(1).
[61] PCA 2002 s 304.
[62] Civil Procedure Rules 1998 (SI 1998 No 3132).
[63] PCA 2002 s 304 to 310.
[64] PCA 2002 s 308(1). Only executed consideration will do: PCA 2002 s 314(4).
[65] To be specified by order. PCA 2002 s 287.
[66] PCA 2002 s 305.

it into property that 'represents' the unlawfully acquired property.[67] Accrued profits are included.[68] Mixed property is simply divided proportionately according to source, rather than by a 'last in first out rule'.[69]

It is expressly provided that there can be no provision in a recovery order inconsistent with Convention rights,[70] nor can there be a recovery where the defendant has not given value but obtained the recoverable property in good faith and has changed his/her position and it would not be just and equitable to make the order.[71]

'Property Obtained Through Unlawful Conduct'

In order to be subject to the procedure, there must be 'property obtained through unlawful conduct'. This is conduct which is unlawful under the criminal law of the part of the United Kingdom in which it takes place, or which takes place in another country, is unlawful there and would be unlawful in the relevant part of the United Kingdom.[72] Property that was stolen is obtained through unlawful conduct. In this case the true owner is given precedence over the enforcement authority. Various other types of person and property are exempted.[73] At the margins, a similar set of issues arises as to confiscation orders.

Profits or Proceeds?

As for confiscation, the right to recover apparently extends beyond profits to proceeds. It was argued above that in the case of confiscation this extension is not a legitimate one and is not consistent with the European Convention.[74] The argument applies *a fortiori* in the case of the recovery procedure. A power to sue for property that represents the profits of crime is one thing: power to sue for property that does not is another. Nonetheless the Act explicitly excludes the possibility of deductions for expenses.[75]

---

[67] PCA 2002 s 305–6.

[68] PCA 2002 s 306. This does not, of course, depend upon the money having been invested lawfully. The enforcement authority might benefit from such a windfall as in *Foskett v McKeown* [2001] 1 AC 102; [2000] 3 All ER 97.

[69] PCA 2002 s 306.

[70] PCA 2002 s 266(3)(b).

[71] PCA 2002 s 266(3)(b), and on the meaning of 'just and equitable', s 266(6).

[72] PCA 2002 s 241.

[73] PCA 2002 s 281–2.

[74] See the section above ch 7, Confiscation Orders.

[75] PCA 2002 s 242(2)(b).

Tax Evasion and Other Pecuniary Advantages?

Although a confiscation order may be made in respect of evaded tax[76] it need not follow from that that the recovery procedure applies to it (or to other evaded debts). Generally if it is possible to identify the property in the first place as being the proceeds of tax evasion, then there will be no especial difficulty in locating property into which it is traced. If, on the other hand, the property cannot be identified, then, since this is an *in rem* action, there will no *rem*. Indeed, the definitions differ[77] and it might be thought that in the case of suspected tax evasion the usual course will be for the Assets Recovery Agency (or the Revenue) to exercise its taxation jurisdiction.[78] If the profits of overseas crime *are* covered, and tax evasion is covered, there is no reason why the profits of overseas tax evasion should not be covered.

Recoverable and Associated Property

Where only part of a property[79] may be recoverable, or there are several interests in a property, some of which are not recoverable, the non-recoverable part is called 'associated property'.[80] Property is recoverable if it as obtained through unlawful conduct or it represents[81] property so obtained.[82] Property obtained in place of representative property may itself become representative property, but there is provision to prevent double counting.[83] Property obtained through conduct that contravened the criminal law of another country is also to be recoverable, provided that the conduct would also be criminal under domestic law if it occurred here.[84]

Evidence

One of the ideas underpinning the use of the civil recovery power is the use of the laxer rules as to the admissibility of evidence in civil proceedings. Leaving

---

[76] See the section above ch 7, Pecuniary Advantage—The Benefit.

[77] Confiscation orders fasten upon 'the benefit of criminal conduct' PCA 2002 s 76(4)–(5)—which *does* cover the proceeds of tax evasion, whereas it as at least arguable that 'obtained through criminal conduct' (rather than 'obtained or retained') (s 242) does not cover the case of evasion or deferment of liability to tax.

[78] See the section below in this ch, Taxation, Money Laundering and Criminal Justice. Note that by taking on the tax affairs of a subject the ARA does not acquire the Board of Inland Revenue's powers to prosecute: PCA 2002 s 323(3)(b).

[79] Defined for this part PCA 2002 s 316 incorporating by reference the definition in s 242.

[80] PCA 2002 s 245, s 309.

[81] PCA 2002 s 305.

[82] PCA 2002 s 304.

[83] PCA 2002 s 308(9)

[84] PCA 2002 s 241(2)(a).

aside possible obstacles provided by the Human Rights Act 1998,[85] the advantages to the Agency are clear. Hearsay evidence is more readily admissible; the rule against self-incrimination is no bar to the admission in civil recovery proceedings of evidence obtained from a respondent under compulsion; and the Director's right of recovery applies retrospectively to existing criminal proceeds, ie to property which was obtained through criminal conduct that occurred before the Act came into force.[86]

The civil standard of proof rather than the criminal (ie the balance of probabilities rather than proof beyond reasonable doubt) applies.[87] It is necessary for the judge to decide 'on the balance of probabilities' whether it is proved that the matters alleged to have constituted unlawful conduct have occurred'.[88] Again, the question arises as to the meaning of the standard of proof. The minister said:

> The civil test has degrees or scales of weight, and we expect that the recovery of the proceeds of crime will be a matter near the upper end of the civil test.[89]

If, however a respondent fails to provide evidence of the legitimate origins of property, or fails to provide an explanation for such a failure, the court, in considering whether the Director has discharged the burden of proof upon him, is to be able to draw such inferences as it thinks fit.[90] Information obtained from respondents under compulsion, whether by the Director under the disclosure order procedure,[91] or by the High Court during civil recovery proceedings, is subject to the rule against self-incrimination and will not be capable of being used as evidence in any subsequent prosecution of the person providing the information, except a prosecution for giving false information.[92]

Third Party Rights

The confiscation order procedure overrides any provisions that would otherwise prevent, penalise or restrict the vesting of the property in the trustee for civil recovery. Consequently it affects property rights of persons other than s/he against whom the order s made, and it is necessary to make provision so that those rights have effect after a confiscation order. A right of pre-emption is

---

[85] See the section below in this ch, Assets Recovery and Human Rights.
[86] *Proceeds of Crime Bill: Publication of Draft Clauses* (London, The Stationery Office, CM 5066) para 5.8.
[87] Subject to the usual *caveat* as to the variable civil standard: see the section above ch 7, The Standard and Burden of Proof in Confiscation Proceedings—No Criminal Lifestyle.
[88] PCA 2002 s 241(3).
[89] HC Debates 30 October 2001 col 761 (John Denham). See the section above ch 7, The Standard and Burden of Proof in Confiscation Proceedings—No Criminal Lifestyle.
[90] PCA 2002 s 241(3).
[91] See the section above ch 8, Disclosure Orders.
[92] Proceeds of Crime Act s 360(1).

typical in this regard.[93] If a person does suffer loss as a result of the order, s/he may apply for compensation.[94]

Pension Rights

Where the recoverable property consists of rights under a pension scheme, no property is to be treated as associated with that recoverable property. Recoverable property may be recovered from pension funds. Since the property cannot be vested in the trustee for civil recovery, an obligation is placed on the pension trustee or managers to pay to the trustee for civil recovery an amount equal to the pension right held against the fund.[95] There will be regulations and guidance as to calculation and verification.[96]

Third Party Rights

Where the property which was obtained through criminal conduct, or the property which represents property obtained through criminal conduct, is transferred from the criminal's possession to that of another party, the Director will be able to follow it into the hands of the recipient and assert his claim. So, if a drug trafficker places his house in the name of a spouse or associate, the house will remain recoverable by the Director.[97] The Director will not have a complete claim against property of which a third party has been unlawfully deprived, for example through theft, fraud or blackmail.[98]

The Limitation Period

The limitation period for civil recovery proceedings is 12 years from the time the original property was obtained by unlawful conduct.[99]

Vesting the Property—Recovery Orders

If the court finds that property is recoverable it must order its recovery.[100] A recovery order vests the property in the trustee for civil recovery.[101] Property

---

[93] PCA 2002 s 269.
[94] PCA 2002 s 283.
[95] PCA 2002 s 273–275.
[96] PCA 2002 s 275.
[97] PCA 2002 s 305(2).
[98] Proceeds of Crime 2002 s 281.
[99] PCA 2002 s 288, inserting a new s 27A in the Limitation Act 1980.
[100] PCA 2002 s 266.
[101] PCA 2002 s 266(2).

ceases to be recoverable following successful civil recovery or cash forfeiture proceedings or under various other analogous circumstances.[102] The State thus holds a proprietary interest to trump unsecured creditors. The usual distribution upon insolvency is again able to be avoided just as for confiscation orders.[103]

PROCEDURE

Investigation Powers

The procedure is a hybrid. Until the claim form or the Interim Receiverhip Order is issued, the Director has access to civil investigation powers.[104] The procedure is essentially a criminal one. The ARA exercises the powers of search, seizure and interrogation of an investigation into serious crime.[105] The Director may apply for disclosure orders.[106] This is a significant power, whose exercise might yield information not available to the law enforcement authorities in the exercise of their 'normal' powers. The objective, inter alia, is to give the Director the evidence upon which to apply for an interim receiving order. Once the claim form is issued or an interim receivership order is in place, the governing rules are those of civil procedure.[107] Applications for further and better particulars will be available in the case where there is insufficient specificity to the allegations.[108]

The tipping-off provisions[109] apply so that it is an offence to prejudice an investigation with a view to recovery proceedings.[110] This provides a further significant difference from any other civil proceedings. In the case where one party is planning to bring proceedings of which the potential defendant remains blissfully unaware, no criminal offence is necessarily committed by one who tips the defendant off.[111]

Interim Receiving Orders

Where he considers, as may frequently be the case, that there is a risk that property may be dissipated or removed, the Director will be able to apply to the High Court, if necessary without notice and without issuing a claim form, for an

---

[102] PCA 2002 s 308.
[103] And see the section above ch 7, Priority of Confiscation Orders Relative to Other Debts.
[104] PCA 2002 Part 8: see the section above ch 8, Investigatory Powers.
[105] See the section above ch 8, Production Orders.
[106] PCA 2002 s 311.
[107] Civil Procedure Rules 1998 SI 3132.
[108] Schedule to Civil Procedure Rules 1998 Rule 50(3).
[109] See the section above ch 9, 'Tipping-off'.
[110] PCA 2002 s 342.
[111] Though there will usually be a contempt.

'interim receiving order' (IRO).[112] IROs may (but need not always) form the preliminary stage of civil recovery procedure. If granted, an IRO will place the property under the control of an interim receiver, appointed by the court. The order can be for

(i)   the detention, custody or preservation of property, claimed to be recoverable property and associated property and for the prohibition of dealing[114] by the person whose property is covered by the order from dealing with it. The holder of the property and anyone known to own a part of or have an interest in the property will be notified of the order.
(ii) The appointment of a receiver. The role of the receiver will be to prevent dissipation or disposal of the property, to preserve its value, and to make enquiries relating to the property, including in order to identify persons who may have an interest in it.[115]

The Director will have to satisfy the court that there is a 'good arguable case'[116] that the property identified in the application has been obtained through unlawful conduct, and, where the property in relation to which the order is sought includes associated property, the Director will have to satisfy the court that s/he has identified or has taken all reasonable steps to establish the identities of the persons(s) holding that property. The interim receiver may not be on the ARA staff.[117]

Breach of an IRO by someone having notice of it will be a contempt of court.[118] Exclusions from the order may be made to provide for any person's reasonable living expenses or to allow someone to carry on a trade, profession or business.[119] The receiver will always be obliged to take the necessary steps to establish: whether in his view the property is to any extent recoverable or associated property; and whether there is any other property that is recoverable in relation to the same unlawful conduct and if so who holds it.[120] Further powers include the power to seize the property, obtain information about it and require persons to answer questions. Self-incrimination is no answer (though the information gained cannot be used in a prosecution).[121] The receiver's powers

---

[112] PCA 2002 s 246.

[114] PCA 2002 s 252: 'dealing includes disposing of the property, taking possession of it or removing it from the United Kingdom'. PCA 2002 s 316(1).

[115] An inexhaustive list of the powers of the interim receiver, modelled on those under the Insolvency Act 1986, is set out in PCA 2002 Schedule 6. The detailed functions of the interim receiver will be in the court's order.

[116] PCA 2002 s 246(5): the 'good arguable case test' is taken from the law on freezing orders (formerly *Mareva* injunctions): Civil Procedure Rules 1998 (SI 3132) para 25.1(1)(f).

[117] Because s/he becomes an officer of the court and has investigatory duties.

[118] Since it will be a High Court order, no special provision is necessary.

[119] PCA 2002 s 252(3).

[120] PCA 2002 s 247(2).

[121] PCA 2002 Schedule 6 para 2.

are subject to legal professional privilege.[122] The receiver may be given powers of entry, search and seizure and power to require persons to assist in the exercise of those powers. S/he may also be given power to manage property, including selling depreciating assets and carrying on a business.[123] The receiver is subject to a series of reporting duties.[124]

The respondent can be placed under duties to bring the property or documents to a specified place, whether or not they are within the jurisdiction. The court has a duty to supervise the IRO, and that will extend to varying or setting aside the order.[125] The receiver has immunity in respect of dealing with property which turns out not to have been property specified in the order, unless s/he is negligent.[126] Once the claim form is issued the duty of taking whatever further steps are needed to establish the facts about the property is placed on the interim receiver acting under the Court's direction. Once it has been established that property is neither recoverable nor associated property, it should not remain subject to an interim receivership order.[127]

Trustee for Civil Recovery

The person appointed by the court to give effect to a civil recovery order is called the trustee for civil recovery (TCR).[128] The TCR acts on behalf of the enforcement agency[129] and may come from the ARA staff. The TCR is under a duty to secure the property vested in him/her[130] and to maximise the amount realisable from it.[131] The powers of the trustee for civil recovery are set out in Schedule 7 to the Act. There is provision to render tax neutral the vesting of the property in the TCR. Because the civil recovery procedure transfers property to the TCR, a civil recovery claim will be treated in the same way as any other civil proprietary claim in insolvency proceedings. The enforcement authority will have to ask the leave of the insolvency court, but will thus be able to 'jump the queue'.[132]

Relationship to Criminal Proceedings

Formally, the civil recovery procedure is available whether or not the criminal proceedings have been brought and, if they have, whether or not they were

---

[122] PCA 2002 Schedule 6 para 4. HC Standing Committee B col 710–711 (Bob Ainsworth).
[123] PCA 2002 Schedule 6 para 5(2)(b).
[124] PCA 2002 s 255.
[125] PCA 2002 s 251.
[126] And compare enforcement and management receivers: see the section above ch 7, Enforcement of Confiscation Orders.
[127] PCA 2002 s 263.
[128] PCA 2002 s 267.
[129] PCA 2002 s 267(4).
[130] PCA 2002 s 267(5).
[131] PCA 2002 Schedule 10 Part 5.
[132] PCA 2002 s 311.

successful.[133] This is no more a violation of the double jeopardy principle than to allow any other civil proceedings to be decided against someone who has been acquitted in criminal proceedings. During the passage of the Bill an amendment was rejected which would have provided a defence to recovery proceedings that other proceedings had failed. This was rejected but nonetheless undertakings were given during the passage of the Bill that:

> Only when prosecution is ruled out will other routes be pursued; the reasons for ruling it out will be part of the normal decisions taken by the prosecution agencies.[134]

If honoured, this meets the concern expressed by the Hodgson Committee. At a very late stage, a clause was inserted to constrain the guidance to be given to the Director by the Secretary of State such that it 'must indicate that the reduction in crime is in general best secured by means of criminal investigations and criminal proceedings'.[135] This is a deeply doubtful proposition to be enshrined in legislation, and it remains to be seen what effect that has.

Death of the Suspect

The civil recovery action, being brought against property, survives the death of the defendant. The consistency of this provision with the Convention rights of the deceased depends upon a more general holding being made that the civil recovery procedure is not governed by Article 6. If it is, then the law appears to be clear that proceedings cannot be brought against the estate of a dead person the real effect of which is to bring criminal charges against that person.[136]

ASSETS RECOVERY AND HUMAN RIGHTS

The Agency is a public authority and subject to the Human Rights Act 1998.[137] Moreover there is provision that recovery orders may only be made consistently with the Convention.[138] What further kinds of human rights issues might arise which could provide possible defences? The first depends upon the classification of the proceedings for the purposes of Articles 6 and 7. If the proceedings, notwithstanding being called 'civil' are classified as involving criminal charges for the purposes of Article 6 or involving penalties for the purposes of Article 7, then clear consequences follow.

---

[133] PCA 2002 s 240.
[134] HC Debates 30 October 2001 col 846 (Bob Ainsworth MP).
[135] PCA 2002 s 2(6).
[136] *AP, MP and TP v Switzerland* (1998) 26 EHRR 541, para 48.
[137] Human Rights Act 1998 s 6.
[138] PCA 2002 s 266(3)(a).

Retroactivity and Article 7

Article 7 prohibits retrospective criminal legislation. The Act purports to state that the civil recovery power applies whether or not the conduct in question was committed before or after its enactment.[139] If the civil recovery procedure is held to be criminal, then it can only apply to property acquired by crime committed after the enactment of the legislation. This would mean that the plan for between 15 and 20 cases to be brought by the Agency in its first year of operation[140] would fail, and that the full impact of the civil recovery power of the ARA would be postponed for several years. This might not have been thought too bad a thing, because the introduction of the legislation is so huge an undertaking. As to the nature and severity of the penalty, for the purposes of Article 7, the Government's position was that the recovery of the property is reparative and preventative (because it might be used for further criminal purposes) but not punitive. The Joint Parliamentary Committee on Human Rights disagreed and found the Government's confidence to be misplaced, because of the absence of a conviction.[141] At the Lords' Committee Stage, Lord Lloyd of Berwick pointed out that this view flew in the face of the decision in *Welch*.[142] He was quite categorical:

> . . . the first retrospective recovery order made against a respondent whose own unlawful conduct is in issue will be bound to be challenged in the European Court of Human Rights under Article 7 and the challenge is bound to succeed.[143]

The Government stuck to its guns, still attempting to distinguish *Welch* on the ground that in the case of civil recovery there had been no conviction.[144] The Government was defeated on an amendment proposed by Lord Lloyd which would have restored the right to judge and jury when an allegation was made such as would trigger the civil recovery procedure.[145] A guillotine motion prevented the Lords amendment being discussed in the Commons debate on the

---

[139] PCA 2002 s 413(5).

[140] HL Debates 13 May 2002 cols 72–73 (Lord Goldsmith A-G).

[141] *Eleventh Report* para 24. Lord Lloyd of Berwick remarked: 'That is simple nonsense. It is the kind of argument which, as Lord Atkin once said in a famous case, might have found favour with the Court of King's Bench in the time of Charles I, but surely should not find favour today. One might as well say that a prisoner's sentence is reparative in nature because in some way he is paying a debt to society.' HL Debates 25 March 2002 vol 633 col 48.

[142] *Welch v United Kingdom* (1995) 20 EHRR 247. HL Debates 13 May 2002 vol 635 col 67. The Attorney-General's reliance (HL Debates 13 May 2002 vol 635 cols 72) upon the *absence* of a conviction as providing a distinction is wholly unconvincing, and recalls the observation in an analogous context of Lord Prosser in *McIntosh v HM Advocate* 2001 JC 78, [2000] UKHRR 751: '[T]he suggestion that there is less need for a presumption of innocence in the latter situation appears to me to be somewhat Kafkaesque, and to portray a vice as a virtue.' (Para 30).

[143] HL Debates 13 May 2002 col 66.

[144] HL Debates 11 July 2002 col 855 (Lord Goldsmith A-G).

[145] The amendment is set out at HL Debates 11 July 2002 col 857.

Lords Amendments.[146] The Lords were incandescent.[147] The Government nonetheless removed the amendment and headed resolutely for the precipice. The effect of a successful Article 7 claim would be that the civil recovery procedure could only apply to offences committed after the Proceeds of Crime Act 2002 comes into force. It is difficult to see how this can be resisted.

Criminal Charge and Fair Trial

If it is the case that the bringing of civil recovery proceedings constitutes a 'criminal charge' for the purposes of Article 6(2) of the Convention, then the proceedings must comply with the constituent elements of a fair trial for the purposes of the Article. *McIntosh, Phillips, Rezvi* and *Benjafield*[148] dealt with the argument that the shift in the burden of proof involved in the procedure for making the statutory assumptions is a violation of Article 6(2) by holding that a person who is the subject of confiscation proceedings is not 'charged with a criminal offence' for the purposes of Article 6 of the Convention, and consequently the presumption of innocence does not apply to someone who has already been held by a court to be guilty. The case of a defendant against whom civil recovery proceedings are brought is different because there will not have been a criminal conviction. Unlike the Irish position, the burden is not shifted in civil recovery proceedings, but wherever it does apply, Article 6 implies (subject to its being displaced—probably not something that could be done implicitly[149]) that the standard of proof imposed upon the prosecution (which is what the ARA would become) is proof beyond reasonable doubt.[150] The adoption of the 'variable civil standard' of proof[151] might satisfy the Convention, but only if it is another way of expressing the criminal standard.[152] If the Agency has to establish beyond reasonable doubt that the allegations in the statement of claim are true then recovery proceedings are deprived of one of their most significant advantages for the Agency over confiscation proceedings.[153]

---

[146] At the end of the Commons debate on the Lords' amendments, a Reasons Committee was established to give the Lords one-sentence reasons for rejecting those Lords' amendments which were rejected. The reason given in this instance was that 'it was not appropriate' to provide the right Lord Lloyd had (temporarily) won.

[147] HL Debates 22 July 2002 cols 58 *et seq.*

[148] See the section above ch 7, Legitimacy of the Shifted Burden.

[149] See discussion of *Salabiaku* and *Hunt*, in the section above ch 9, Money Laundering Offences—Expressly Placing the Burden on the Defendant.

[150] Ben Emmerson and Andrew Ashworth, *Human Rights and Criminal Justice* (London, Sweet and Maxwell, 2001) 279 *et seq.*

[151] See the section above ch 7, The Standard and Burden of Proof in Confiscation Proceedings—No Criminal Lifestyle. This possibility was mentioned by Vera Baird, HC Debates 26 February 2002, col 657.

[152] Exactly what it was held in an analogous context *not* to do: *Butt v HM Customs and Excise* [2001] EWHC Admin 1066. But see now *Clingham (formerly C (a minor)) v Royal Borough of Kensington and Chelsea* [2002] UKHL 39.

[153] Avoidance of a jury, if it is an advantage, is the other.

The European Court of Human Rights has held that the relevant factors in determining whether or not proceedings are criminal (so as to attract Article 6(2) protection), are the form of the proceedings, the substance of the proceedings and the nature and severity of the 'penalty'. The form is less a factor to which to have regard than a precondition. If the form is criminal, that is the end of the matter. The other two criteria are alternatives.[154] It would be very strange if the Convention can indeed be side-stepped simply by holding the recovery proceedings in a civil court. The Joint Committee on Human Rights strongly canvassed the view that it could not.[155] Lord Lloyd was again more forthright:

> I am reminded of an observation made, I think, by the noble and learned Lord, Lord Templeman, in a different context. He said that if we design an agricultural implement for digging and it has a handle and four or five prongs, we have designed a fork. We can call it a spade, if we like, but it remains, in fact and in law, a fork. Likewise, if we design a piece of legislation with the object of depriving a man of some or all of his possessions, after he has been found guilty of unlawful conduct under Part 5, we can describe that as a recovery order, but the European Court will call our bluff and will call it what it is—a confiscation order by another name.[156]

A holding that Article 6 applies to civil recovery proceedings will have impact beyond merely the standard of proof. The governing assumption of the procedure is that the *civil* rules of evidence are to apply, with, for example, hearsay evidence admitted. If Article 6 applies then the question will be whether a criminal conviction (which is what the Convention would interpret a holding of liability in recovery proceedings to be) can, compatibly with the right under Article 6(3)(d) to 'examine and have examined witnesses against him and to obtain the attendance and examination of witnesses in his behalf under the same conditions as witnesses against him,' be based solely or largely upon hearsay evidence.[157] Furthermore, Article 6(3)(c) of the European Convention states that any defendant charged with a criminal offence has the right to defend him/herself with legal assistance of his own choosing. If Article 6 does apply, provisions in the legislation[158] that prevent or place restrictions upon the use of the money that is the subject matter of the litigation will fall foul of this provision.[159]

Lastly, if Article 6 applies to civil recovery proceedings, it is unlikely that it will allow the Agency to allege criminal conduct in general as having been the

---

[154] Ben Emmerson and Andrew Ashworth, *Human Rights and Criminal Justice* (London, Sweet and Maxwell, 2001) 152.

[155] Joint Committee on Human Rights, *Third Report* (2001) para 33, *Eleventh Report* (2002) para 17 *et seq*. See also the speech of Lord Lloyd of Berwick, HL Debates, 25 March 2002 vol 633 col 48.

[156] HL Debates 13 May 2002 col 67.

[157] For detailed consideration of the relationship between the Convention and hearsay evidence see Ben Emmerson and Andrew Ashworth, *Human Rights and Criminal Justice* (London, Sweet and Maxwell, 2001) 462–71.

[158] Ie PCA 2002 s 252(4).

[159] And compare the position for Restraint Orders, see the section above ch 7, Restraint orders, Receivers and Human Rights.

source of the assets in question, without it being forced to specify the particular crimes which gave them rise.[160] An allegation of criminal conduct in general without identifying particular crimes is sufficiently vague as to transgress Article 6.3.a., which states that, 'Everyone charged with a criminal offence has the [right] . . . to be informed promptly, . . . and in detail of the nature and cause of the accusation against him.'[161]

So whilst the Article 7 argument would only have a postponing effect on the 'civil recovery' procedure, a holding that it is governed by Article 6 would reinstall the three major obstacles (the presumption of innocence, the dissipation of the assets in point upon litigation, and the requirement of specificity) the procedure was designed to avert. Early decisions on these issues will be crucial. If the courts hold that the civil recovery procedure involves a criminal charge for the purposes of Article 6, the entire project involved in the 2002 Act will have suffered a severe body blow.

First Protocol

The other major challenge to the civil recovery procedures is by reference to the First Protocol. The extension of the recovery power to proceeds not just profits is open to the same objections as the same extension in respect of confiscation orders.[162] The Government's response was redolent of the arguments mentioned earlier when dealing with the history of forfeiture.[163]

> It is important to bear in mind the purpose of civil recovery, namely to establish as a matter of civil law that there is no right to enjoy property that derives from criminal conduct. This applies no matter who committed the conduct; the focus is on the property, not the person.[164]

The Joint Committee on Human Rights, starting from the position that the general right to enjoy property is not defeated merely by the fact that it derives directly or indirectly from criminal conduct, disagreed.[165]

If correct, the Article 7 argument spells postponement and the Article 6 standard of proof and the First Protocol arguments disaster for the civil recovery procedure. During the Parliamentary debates the Government had very clear

---

[160] This is the position for which the Government argued HL Debates 11 July 2002 cols 850 *et seq.*

[161] Ben Emmerson and Andrew Ashworth, *Human Rights and Criminal Justice* (London, Sweet & Maxwell, 2001) 185–87.

[162] See the section above ch 7, Confiscation Orders.

[163] See the section above ch 6, Forfeiture as an Additional Penalty.

[164] Home Office Memorandum responding to Joint Committee on Human Rights Third Report, (reproduced as the appendix to Joint Committee on Human Rights, *Eleventh Report* (2002) para 24): HL Debates 13 May 2002 col 72 (Lord Goldsmith A-G).

[165] Joint Committee on Human Rights, *Eleventh Report* (2002) para 19, citing *Attorney General v Blake (Jonathan Cape Ltd, third party)* [2001] 1 AC 268; [2000] 4 All ER 385, see the section above ch 3, The Victim as Claimant—Restitutionary and Other Remedies.

notice of the reasons the scheme might fail, yet it chose to emphasise the 'policy' reasons[166] why the power should be able to be exercised retrospectively and should be available on the balance of probabilities, without need to trouble with Article 6(2). These might be thought to be reasons why the Human Rights Act 1998 should not have been enacted. In any discourse about rights it is always possible to find examples of unappealing people who might benefit from particular rights. In his response to the arguments advanced on the basis of the ECHR *jurisprudence* the Attorney-General said:

> I beg to differ fundamentally and strongly with the view of the noble and learned Lord that there will be a challenge which would be bound to succeed in Strasbourg. . . . when there are proceedings after a conviction but which relate to the proceeds of conduct that has not been the subject of a conviction, that constitutes a civil procedure, not a criminal procedure. I emphasise the fact that that applies not just to the case where the confiscation is in relation to the proceeds of the crime for which there has been a conviction, but conduct for which there has not been a conviction.
>
> Secondly, there is other jurisprudence. For example, there is a decision of the European Court in a case called *Raimondi*, in Italian law—the reference of which I shall, of course, give to the noble and learned Lord—which does not appear to be that dissimilar when dealing with Mafia situations; and which, again, is helpful. I also mention the case of *Welch* to which the noble and learned Lord referred.[167]

As to the first, the absence of a conviction *is* critical, because it is the fact of there having been a conviction which enabled the courts to hold confiscation proceedings to fall outwith the scope of Article 6. As to the second, *Raimondi* is a freezing case, not relevant here.[168] It is difficult to account for the behaviour of the Government in this regard.

Even if none of the objections above is successful, there is a further respect in which the civil recovery procedure will run up against the Convention. As noted earlier in respect of confiscation orders,[169] the 'proceeds and not just profits' doctrine must imply that the element of the order that extends beyond the profit of crime is not justified by any reparative principle and must be regarded as punitive. In the case of confiscation orders there could be no Article 6 challenge because the courts have held that Article 6 does not govern confiscation proceedings.[170] But this argument is not available in respect of recovery proceedings, because there is no prior conviction. So whether or not the courts hold for the Government on the more general Article 6 challenge to the civil recovery procedure, the Article 6 challenge to that part of the recovery proceedings which extends beyond the defendant's profit is very powerful.

---

[166] The sum of £440 million is allegedly at large in the hands of 400 'Mr Bigs' HL Debates 13 May 2002 cols 72–73 (Lord Goldsmith A-G).

[167] HL Debates 13 May 2002 col 73 (Lord Goldsmith A-G).

[168] *Raimondo v Italy* (1994) 18 EHRR 237.

[169] See the section above ch 7, Proceeds Not Just Profits.

[170] *R v Rezvi* [2002] UKHL 1; *R v Benjafield* [2002] UKHL 2.

COMPENSATION

The possibility has been mentioned that the instigation of recovery proceedings may have an adverse effect upon third parties. For example, if it becomes known that one client of a particular accountant is the subject of recovery proceedings, then it may be less easy for him/her to recruit or retain clients.[171] Under such circumstances compensation may be payable to third parties.[172]

TAXATION, MONEY LAUNDERING AND CRIMINAL JUSTICE

Traditionally, agencies for taxation and criminal justice have kept their respective information separate.[173] When tax inspectors have come into possession of information that a taxpayer profits from crime, they not been allowed to inform the police, and they have not been allowed to raise assessments to income tax without specifying a source from which the income comes. This will change with the allocation of the powers of tax inspectors to the ARA.[174] The use of the power to raise an assessment to taxation against a person with visible wealth, but no visible lawful source if income, is a new departure. Its advocates[175] regard it as an exercise in integrating the official response to tax evasion and money laundering—in 'joined-up government'. Its detractors see a sinister attempt to aggregate the already intrusive powers of different branches of Government and place citizens continually under an obligation to justify themselves and their possessions to the State.

   One of the successes claimed for the Irish system is from the powers of the Criminal Assets Bureau to levy taxation.[176] The links between the systems for the enforcement of criminal law and the exaction of taxes is becoming increasingly significant for all financial crime. The designation of tax evasion offences as predicate offences for the purposes of confiscation[177] and to (if it is) to criminal laundering[178] is one important development. The further mechanism to be made available is the deployment of the powers of the tax authorities (Inland Revenue and Customs and Excise) against the launderer, as a third arrow (after confiscation orders and recovery orders) in the quiver of the Director. As a means of depriving criminals of their assets, there is much to be said for the powers of the tax author-

---

[171] HC Debates Standing Committee B 13 December 2001 col 689 (Vera Baird).
[172] PCA 2002 s 283.
[173] And see Ann Mumford and Peter Alldridge, 'Taxation as an Adjunct to the Criminal Justice System: the new Assets Recovery Agency *Régime*' [2002] *British Tax Review* (forthcoming).
[174] *PIU Report* para 10.12.
[175] *PIU Report* para 10.16 *et seq.*
[176] See the section above in this ch, The Irish Legislation.
[177] See the section above ch 7, The Common Law.
[178] See section ch 9 beginning Tax Evasion as the Predicate Offence to Criminal Laundering p 184 *et seq.*

ities. They can impose administrative penalties in addition to raising assessments to taxation. They have powers to gather information by demanding the production of records and information about a person's financial affairs. Financial surveillance is becoming more and more crucial to the criminal justice system, and since the Inland Revenue is the best-established State-owned financial surveillance and sanctioning system extant, it is unsurprising that there should be a move to integrate it into investigation and seizure powers relating to the proceeds of crime.

The suggestion that taxation should be used as a weapon against crime is not new.[179] The Hodgson Committee wrote, 'This way of treating people who have offended against the criminal law has attracted judicial praise for its efficiency and cost effectiveness.'[180] There are good reasons why taxation should be used as the *principal* means by which to recover income derived from crime. First of all, it may be more effective in generating revenue than confiscation. This is the Irish experience. Second, the powers that the Revenue has in some respects exceed those of the police. Under the Taxes Management Act 1970 the Board is given very wide powers to assess to tax and impose penalties without bringing the taxpayer before the courts.[181] Even though legal professional privilege is not attenuated in response to an exercise of the Inspector's power under the Taxes Management Act 1970,[182] the privilege against self-incrimination is not available in response to a request for information from the tax authorities.[183] If the objectives of the Inland Revenue are simply expressed in terms of efficient collection of taxes, however, the tax authorities have every reason to avoid pursuit of alleged criminals, because in terms of revenue per unit spent on enforcement, the criminal is not a rewarding target. The development of the 'joined-up' project may involve the deployment of powers that have the less damaging initial objective of taxation (and which need not be subject to such rigorous procedural constraints) to the more damaging end of generating evidence for criminal prosecutions. In this sense each join requires a separate and sufficient justification.

There are, however, fewer reasons for taxation to be relied upon as a *subsidiary* entry into the criminal law—a fall-back when prosecution and confiscation fail. The policy—particularly against suspected drug dealers—of charging tax evasion and trying to place the onus upon them to account for their belongings is one which has been deployed for some time in the United States, where prosecution is a far more common way in which to proceed against tax

---

[179] And see Russell Baker, 'Taxation: Potential Destroyer of Crime' (1951) 29 *Chicago-Kent Law Review* 197.

[180] *Hodgson Report* pp 72–3, citing *Patel v Spencer* [1976] 1 WLR 1268; *A-G v Johnstone* (1926) 10 TC 758.

[181] Taxes Management Act 1970 Part X.

[182] The decision of the Court of Appeal in *R (on the application of Morgan Grenfell & Co Ltd) v Special Commissioner of Income Tax* [2001] EWCA Civ 329, holding that where legal professional privilege was not expressly retained it was Parliament's intention to remove it, was reversed by the House of Lords in *R v Special Commissioner and another, ex parte Morgan Grenfell* [2002] UKHL 21: see the section below ch 12, Lawyer/Client Confidentiality.

[183] *R v Allen* [2001] UKHL 45; [2002] 1 AC 509.

defaulters.[184] This kind of policy is open to question. Much has been made, for example, of the fact that Al Capone was finally convicted of tax evasion. The underlying claim seems to be that tax evasion liability served as a useful fall-back for authorities who were unable to acquire sufficient evidence to secure a conviction for the 'real' offence. This is not necessarily a good thing. The principle of legality requires that if the authorities want to claim that Capone is a murdering racketeer they should be compelled to make that allegation in court, and produce evidence of those offences. If the traditionally accepted categories are to be abolished this should be done consciously. Greater attention needs to be given to the question of the relationship between tax evasion and other offences for the purposes of money laundering.[185]

The Taxation Jurisdiction of the ARA

The Director may take on general Revenue functions[186] where s/he has reasonable grounds to suspect that income, profits or gains arising or accruing to a person (including a company) in respect of a chargeable period arises from criminal conduct.[187] The Director serves a notice on the Board of the Inland Revenue vesting certain functions[188] of the Revenue in the Director. The revenue functions may only be delegated to staff of the ARA.[189] Information gained in the exercise of these functions is not unlawfully to be disclosed.[190] The Director has equivalent power over Inheritance tax[191] and to the taxation of discretionary trusts.[192] For the purposes of the taxation jurisdiction, 'criminal conduct' does not extend to cover offences under the care and management of the Board of Inland Revenue, for example tax fraud.[193] Appeals from the exercise of the taxation jurisdiction lies only to the Special Commissioners, who exercise this jurisdiction sitting with specially qualified assessors.[194]

In general, despite the absence of clear authority on the point, it seems that unlawfully or illegally obtained income remains subject to taxation.[195] Thus, for example, the export of whisky to the United States during Prohibition was

---

[184] And see Ann Mumford and Peter Alldridge, 'Taxation as an Adjunct to the Criminal Justice System: the new Assets Recovery Agency *Régime*' [2002] *British Tax Review* (forthcoming).
[185] And see further Alldridge, 'Are Tax Evasion Offences Predicate Offences for Money Laundering?' (2001) 4 *Journal of Money Laundering Control* 350.
[186] Defined at PCA 2002 s 323(1).
[187] PCA 2002 s 317. 'Criminal Conduct' is defined (s 326(1) as for civil recovery save that tax frauds are excluded (327(2)).
[188] PCA 2002 s 323.
[189] PCA 2002 s 324.
[190] PCA 2002 s 325.
[191] PCA 2002 s 321.
[192] PCA 2002 s 322.
[193] PCA 2002 s 326(2).
[194] PCA 2002 s 320.
[195] John Tiley, *Revenue Law*, 4th edn (Oxford, Hart, 2000) 110.

held to be taxable,[196] as was the income of a prostitute.[197] Where unlawful activity is taxed under schedule D, deductions may be made for lawful[198] business expenses.[199]

The Cabinet Office review had identified as an obstacle to the taxation of suspicious income the rules, apparently stemming from the early history of the schedular system of assessment, first, that in order for an assessment to be made to income tax (but not those to capital gains tax or corporation tax), there must be an identifiable source of income to which it is to be attributed, such as a particular trade;[200] and, secondly, that the income had to be attributable to a specified year.[201] Under its power to raise an assessment to tax, the Agency may raise a tax demand where neither a source of income nor a year of assessment has been identified.[202] In the case of a person who is in receipt of suspected criminal proceeds and has no tax history there may be no obvious taxable source to which income represented by unexplained assets can be attributed. This may be the case, for example, where there are grounds for suspecting that income has accrued from one or more of a number of possible criminal activities but it is impossible to identify which. The Government's contention is that such a rule does not change substantive tax law, in particular the boundary between taxable and non-taxable activity, but it should help to prevent suspected recipients of criminals' assets from avoiding tax by refusing to identify the source of their

---

[196] *Lindsay v IRC* (1932) 18 TC 43.

[197] See *Inland Revenue Commissioners v Aken* [1990] 1 WLR 1374; [1990] STC 497, reserving the point explicitly by pointing out that prostitution is not *ipso facto* illegal, but doubting the decision of the Supreme Court in Ireland in *Hayes v Duggan* [1929] 1 IR 406. The granting of the taxation jurisdiction to the ARA would be pointless did income tax not apply to illegal profits.

[198] The issue became a live one because bribes of public officials overseas were deducted until the insertion of Income and Corporation Taxes Act 1988 s 577A by the Finance Acts 1992 and 1993. The International move against permitting such bribes, culminating in the Paris Convention of the OECD, Convention on Combating Bribery of Foreign Public Officials in International Business Transactions, Paris, 17 December 1997 (Cm 3994). S 577A states: 'Expenditure involving crime. (1) In computing profits chargeable to tax under Schedule D, no deduction shall be made for any expenditure incurred in making a payment the making of which constitutes the commission of a criminal offence. (1A) In computing profits chargeable to tax under Schedule D, no deduction shall be made for any expenditure incurred in making a payment induced by a demand constituting—(a) the commission in England or Wales of the offence of blackmail under section 21 of the Theft Act 1968, (b) the commission in Northern Ireland of the offence of blackmail under section 20 of the Theft Act (Northern Ireland) 1969, or (c) the commission in Scotland of the offence of extortion. (2) Any expenditure mentioned in subsection (1) or (1A) above shall not be included in computing any expenses of management in respect of which relief may be given under the Tax Acts.'

[199] The taxing section (Income and Corporation Taxes Act 1988 s 18) applies to the 'profits' of a trade, profession or vocation. This is clearly differentiable from proceeds. So the 'proceeds not just profits' doctrine will not extend to the tax jurisdiction. The position differs in the case of VAT. In cases such as *Einberger v Hauptzollamt Freiburg* [1984] ECR 1177, the Court of Justice has held that VAT does not arise on the unlawful importation of drugs: see *R v Goodwin and Unstead* [1997] STC 22; *R v Citrone and another* [1998] STC 29; [1999] *Criminal Law Review* 327. But where lawful services compete with lawful ones the unlawful ones are not given a competitive advantage: *HM Customs and Excise Commissioners v Polok* [2002] EWHC 156; [2002] STC 361 (prostitution).

[200] And see John Tiley, *Revenue Law*, 4th edn (Oxford, Hart, 2000) 132.

[201] *PIU Report* para 10.22.

[202] PCA 2002 s 319.

income, and place the onus on the taxpayer to displace the tax assessment by providing evidence on appeal that assets came from a non-taxable source.[203]

The Taxation Jurisdiction—Human Rights Challenges

Article 6—Fair Trial and the Burden of Proof

Again, the burden and standard of proof provide a potential challenge. *McIntosh, Phillips v United Kingdom, Rezvi* and *Benjafield*[204] dealt with the argument that the shift in the burden of proof is a violation of Article 6(2) by holding that the presumption of innocence does not apply to someone who has been held by a court to be guilty and is consequently unavailable in proceedings for a confiscation order. Persons against whom a tax assessment is made by the Agency will not necessarily (or usually) have been convicted. As for the bringing of recovery proceedings, so too the levying of tax by the Agency must deal with Article 6(2).[205]

In principle,[206] under Article 6(2) the person against whom a 'criminal charge' is made *is* entitled to the presumption of innocence. So the danger to the proponent of ARA is that the use either of 'civil' forfeiture provisions and of taxation as a means of avoiding the exigencies of the European Convention so far as concerns criminal charges will fail, and that by using civil actions or taxation to perform functions which are essentially those of criminal charges will simply subject those areas of law to Article 6 of the Convention. If it does apply then the allocation of the burden of proof onto a taxpayer who is accused, expressly or impliedly, of criminal behaviour, will require early consideration by the courts.

When an assessment to income tax is raised, whether by the Revenue under the present system or under the proposed system by the ARA, the traditional position is that the burden is upon the taxpayer to disprove liability.[207] So far as

---

[203] The new jurisdiction also generates a curious new ground upon which it might become possible to challenge an assessment to tax. In the case where an assessment was made by ARA, its being lawful would depend upon ARA having jurisdiction, which would in turn depend upon the Director having the specified reasonable grounds. The claim, 'the Director did not have reasonable grounds to suspect that my income, gains or profits resulted from the proceeds of crime. Consequently I am not liable to tax.' would be novel.

[204] *HM Advocate v McIntosh (Sentencing)* [2001] UKPC D1; [2001] 3 WLR 107, *Phillips v United Kingdom* (2001) 11 BHRC 280, *R v Rezvi* [2002] UKHL 1, *R v Benjafield* [2002] UKHL 2.

[205] See the section above in this ch, Criminal Charge and Fair Trial.

[206] That is, subject to the possibility of the presumption being displaced on 'proportionality' grounds—*Salabiaku v France* (1991) 13 EHRR 379; *R v Lambert* [2001] UKHL 37: see the section above ch 9, Money Laundering Offences—Expressly Placing the Burden on the Defendant.

[207] This was regarded by Lord Greene MR as beyond argument in *Norman v Golder* [1945] 1 All ER 352, following as it did from the wording of Income Tax Act, 1918 s 137(4), (now Taxes Management Act 1970 s 50(6)) and was restated, eg, in *Gamble v Rowe* [1998] STC 1247, 71 Tax Cas 190. In respect of a number of other taxes the convention appears to be that the burden is placed on the taxpayer *save in respect of allegations of impropriety.* See, eg, Finance Act 2001 Sch 6, Part XI para 122(3) (climate change levy); Finance Act 1996 s 55(4) (landfill tax); VAT Act 1994 s 60(7); Finance Act 1994 s 16(6) (customs fraud); Finance Act 1994 s 60(9) (insurance premium tax).

concerns taxation in the UK, this rule has hitherto drawn little adverse comment. The same rule proved so unpalatable to American taxpayers as to generate a legislative response.[208] Tiley says of the rule that 'it may be rationalised on the basis that [the taxpayer] knows all the facts and therefore should have to prove them'.[209] This position, and its implication that the usual rules relating to the allocation of the burden of proof do not apply in tax cases,[210] might have been sustainable had tax remained disjoined from criminal justice, and, in particular, had it not been for the Human Rights Act 1998.

The question must now be confronted whether the raising of an assessment to income tax constitutes a 'criminal charge' for the purposes of the guarantees in Article 6.[211] Will Article 6(2) only apply in the case of appeals against the imposition of *penalties*, or will it apply also to reverse the assessments to tax upon which the penalties are based? The preponderance of authority is still in favour of the position, that an assessment to taxation does not *without more* constitute a criminal charge. In *King v Walden*,[212] Jacob J, setting out the factors leading to his decision, was careful to distinguish the case of an assessment without penalties (which did not constitute a criminal charge for the purposes of Article 6) from the case where penalties are imposed (which would). However, the abandonment of the disjunctive position will leave in question the traditional position as to the burden of proof in tax appeals. The fact that the assessment is raised by an organ of Government whose principal duty is the reduction of crime, rather than the collection of revenue, is a starting point to an attack upon an assessment from the Director—even one without penalties— on the basis that the proceeding is essentially punitive and in nature part of the criminal justice system.

The position as to assessments without penalties, however, is not so critical, because it is clear that the availability of penalties is one of the factors most attracting the Government to the tax jurisdiction, and if it is rendered unavailable by the presumption of innocence then the plan will have failed. What, then, about an assessment that does include penalties? It seems certain that Article 6 covers an assessment composing of penalties. Administrative tax penalties had been held by the Strasbourg court to constitute 'criminal charges' for these purposes in *Bendenoun v France*.[213] In *Georgiou (trading as Mario's Chippery) v United Kingdom*,[214] the Strasbourg court ruled that a civil penalty imposed for dishonest evasion of VAT pursuant to section 13(1) of the Finance Act 1985

---

[208] Ann Mumford, 'The new American Bill of Rights' [1997] *British Tax Review* 481.

[209] John Tiley, *Revenue Law*, 4th edn (Oxford, Hart, 2000) 69.

[210] The usual rule is 'he who asserts must prove'. The most obvious case where somebody might be assumed to know all the facts but does not have to prove them is in respect of *mens rea* in criminal cases. The defendant might be the only one who knows whether or not an act was intentional, but the prosecution must still prove that it was: *Woolmington v DPP* [1935] AC 462.

[211] Philip Baker, 'Taxation and the ECHR' [2000] *British Tax Review* 211.

[212] *King v Walden* [2001] STC 822: on appeal from [2000] STC (SCD) 179.

[213] *Bendenoun v France* (1994) 18 EHRR 54.

[214] *Georgiou (trading as Marios Chippery) v United Kingdom* [2001] STC 80.

amounted to a 'criminal charge' within the meaning of Article 6(1). In *Customs and Excise Commissioners v Han and another and other appeals*[215] the Court of Appeal divided 2–1 in holding that Article 6 does apply to the imposition of penalties under the VAT legislation.[216] In *King v Walden*[217] Jacob J, applying the *Benendoun* criteria,[218] held that the system for imposition of penalties for fraudulent or negligent delivery of incorrect tax returns or statements is covered by Article 6(2). His reasons were as follows:[219]

(a) Plainly the system is intended to punish the defaulting taxpayer and to operate as a deterrent;

(b) The amount of fine is potentially very substantial;

(c) The amount of fine is not related to any administrative matter. In particular the fine is not limited to the administrative and other extra cost of dealing with the taxpayer concerned;[220]

(d) The amount of fine imposed depends upon the degree of culpability of the taxpayer, the less culpable the more mitigation there is. Mitigation is an essentially criminal rather than civil consideration;

(e) It is accepted that generally it is not for the taxpayer to show that the determination of penalties was wrong. On appeal the burden of proof lies on the Crown. In this regard there is a clear distinction between a penalty determination and an appeal against ordinary assessment where the burden of showing it was wrong lies on the taxpayer.[221]

That Article 6 applies is not itself conclusive, however of the allocation of the burden of proof. Although Article 6(2) is not expressed to have exceptions, the presumption of innocence, which it embodies, can be displaced.[222] In determining whether or not a shift in the burden of proof is warranted on the grounds of its proportionality to the ends sought, the burden is on the State to show that the legislative means adopted were not greater than necessary.[223] It follows from this short discussion that it is very unlikely that the Director can exercise power to impose tax penalties, without the burden of proof falling onto the Director to prove beyond reasonable doubt the facts upon which s/he relies.[224] The position simply as to assessments to taxation is unclear.

---

[215] *Customs and Excise Commissioners v Han and another and other appeals* [2001] EWCA Civ 1040, [2001] STC 1188.

[216] And see *JB v Switzerland* [2001] ECHR 31827/96; (2001) 3 ITLR 663.

[217] See n 212 above. By the time the case went on appeal ([2001] EWCA Civ 1518) the House of Lords had decided (in *Lambert*) that the Human Rights Act 1998 had no application before 2 October 2001.

[218] See n 213 above and accompanying text.

[219] Para 71.

[220] The judge pointed out that the cost to the State of dealing with Mr King, taking into account the Revenue's internal costs as well as the cost of the Commissioners, probably greatly exceeded the fine actually imposed, namely £58,000.

[221] Emphasis added.

[222] See the section above ch 9, Money Laundering Offences—Expressly Placing the Burden on the Defendant: *Salabiaku v France* (1988) 13 EHRR 379.

[223] *R v Lambert* [2001] UKHL 37, [2001] 3 WLR 206 *per* Lord Steyn at para 37.

[224] Joint Parliamentary Committee on Human Rights, *Eleventh Report Proceeds of Crime Bill* (2002) paras 17–24.

Article 6 and Article 7—Specificity

The other area of the taxation jurisdiction that may be open to challenge is the provision that the assessment to taxation need not specify any particular source of income, nor allocate the income to any given year of assessment. Need the director specify the conduct alleged to have generated the income (in which case the same problems will have to be faced as arose with civil recovery) or is the mere fact that the defendant acquired the income (or whatever, had it been acquired lawfully, would have been taxable)?

Assessments may only be made by the ARA when it has jurisdiction. The Agency cannot deny that an allegation of criminality of an undisclosed nature is implied in the assessment. Now in order to proceed towards civil recovery the ARA would at least have to give sufficient particulars of the criminal conduct alleged for the defendant to be able to mount a defence.[225] Can it sidestep this requirement by the exercise of its tax jurisdiction, simply asserting that the defendant received income on which tax was not paid? The intention of the Act was clearly that this should be possible. But this can only be achieved consistently with the Convention if Article 6(2) does not apply. If it does, the tax jurisdiction will add little.

---

[225] See the section above in this ch, Criminal Charge and Fair Trial.

12

Money Laundering and the Professions

To APPROACH MONEY laundering solely from the perspective of the legal mechanisms available directly against launderers and their impact upon human rights is to miss important aspects of the impact of money laundering upon the legal environment. The other side of the coin is to do with financial services' regulation and its relationship to the duties of professionals. The advent of money laundering regulation has altered the nature of the relationships many professionals have with their clients. The argument for regulation and reporting requirements is that only thus can suspicious transactions be located. The argument against regulation is that the regulatory structures are just a further unnecessary intrusion, expense, and disruption of professional relationships, which do little to catch launderers or to affect levels of laundering.[1] This final chapter will deal with the effect upon the legal status of professionals which has been wrought by the developments described elsewhere in the book.

THE MONEY LAUNDERING REGULATIONS 1993

The Money Laundering Regulations 1993 are the principal mechanism by which the EU Money Laundering Directive was implemented.[2] All those dealing with securities and investments in a 'relevant financial business'[3] are subject to the provisions of the Money Laundering Regulations 1993. The regulations require that firms carrying on such business must have internal reporting procedures to ensure that specific standards are met in the reporting of particular transactions and there is disclosure to a constable. This is a positive duty for which failure to comply can lead, on conviction on indictment, to two years' imprisonment and/or a fine.[4] The Money Laundering Regulations 2001[5] extended the money laundering régime to *bureaux de change* and similar institutions, established a register of money service operators and gave power to the Customs and Excise to investigate and prosecute breaches.

---

[1] Duncan E Alford, 'Anti-money laundering regulations: a burden on financial institutions' (1994) 19 *North Carolina Journal of International Law and Commercial Regulation* 437.
[2] No 91/308/EEC: see the section above ch 5, The Money Laundering Directive.
[3] Defined in Money Laundering Regulations 1993 para 4.
[4] Money Laundering Regulations 1993 para 5(2).
[5] SI 3641.

'Relevant Financial Business'

The Money Laundering Regulations apply to banks, building societies and credit institutions, individuals and firms engaged in the investment business, insurance companies and *bureaux de change*.[6] The contrast between the general and specific approach to legislating[7] is seen again in respect of the question of what is to amount to a relevant financial business—that is, which businesses are to have the duty of putting in place reporting requirements and the other internal procedures that are demanded by the Directive. It is probably true that the original location of the majority of most laundering was in the banking sector, and so that was regarded as being the problem. It is also true that there is no transaction involving the transfer of funds that, by its nature, is incapable of being the means by which money is laundered. The same money that could be laundered by being put through bank accounts can also be laundered by way of insurance premiums or fine art or cars or casinos or any other markets.[8]

In the area of laundering, the argument (from consistency) for covering *every* transaction is made stronger because of the assumption that the rational criminal is being addressed, and that the shape of the regulatory framework will affect his/her behaviour because s/he will be able to rely upon the promulgated rules and practices. The rational criminal will aim to avoid their force if possible. If it is known that only transactions over a certain value (as for the $10,000 cash transaction reporting in the United States and the €15000 limit under the Regulations) are targeted, either by exclusions in the written rules or the practice of the officials who enforce them, then 'smurfing' (structuring the transactions into a multiplicity each of which, taken individually, is below whatever threshold is in point) will take place.[9] If it is known that money laundering regulation applies more rigorously to some areas of financial services regulation than to others, then the rational launderer will choose the less regulated area. If it is known that there remains one jurisdiction in the world in which absolute banking secrecy is observed, or trustees can be obliged not to name beneficiaries, or there is no mechanism by which to freeze assets, then a great deal of the capital in the world which is being laundered will be directed to that jurisdiction. In these regards, money laundering has many of the characteristics of a legitimate market.

The range of businesses to which the Directive (and hence, whatever implementing mechanism is deployed in the United Kingdom) applies was radically

---

[6] Defined in Money Laundering Regulations 1993 para 4(2)(a).

[7] See the section above ch 1, The General and the Particular in Criminal Lawmaking.

[8] And see ch 2.

[9] In *US v Anzalone* (1985) 766 F 2d 676 the First Circuit Court of Appeals held that structuring transactions to avoid filing requirements was not covered. The decision was reversed by the Money Laundering Control Act 1985: Sarah Welling, 'Smurfs, Money Laundering, and the Federal Criminal Law: The Crime of Structuring Transactions', (1989) 41 *Florida Law Review* 287; Sarah Welling, 'Structured transactions in money laundering: dealing with tax evaders, smurfs, and other enemies of the people', (1988) 15 *American Journal of Criminal Law* 83.

extended by the Amending Directive,[10] to cover a series of non-financial activities and professions perceived as vulnerable to misuse by money launderers. Accordingly, the requirements of the regulations are extended to external accountants and auditors, real estate agents, notaries, lawyers, dealers in high value goods, transporters of funds and casinos. This has been accomplished by rewriting Article 2a of the Directive, so that it will read as follows:

> Member States shall ensure that the obligations laid down in this Directive are imposed on the following institutions:
> 1. credit institutions as defined in point A of Article 1;
> 2. financial institutions as defined in point B of Article 1; and on the following legal or natural persons acting in the exercise of their professional activities:
> 3. auditors, external accountants and tax advisors;
> 4. real estate agents;
> 5. notaries and other independent legal professionals, when they participate, whether:
>   (a) by assisting in the planning or execution of transactions for their client concerning the
>   (i) buying and selling of real property or business entities;
>   (ii) managing of client money, securities or other assets;
>   (iii) opening or management of bank, savings or securities accounts;
>   (iv) organisation of contributions necessary for the creation, operation or management of companies;
>   (v) creation, operation or management of trusts, companies or similar structures;
>   (b) or by acting on behalf of and for their client in any financial or real estate transaction;
> 6. dealers in high-value goods, such as precious stones or metals, or works of art, auctioneers, whenever payment is made in cash, and in an amount of EUR 15 000 or more;
> 7. casinos.

Implementation must be by 15 June 2003. The United Kingdom has yet to make known the means by which it proposes to comply.[11]

'Know Your Customer'

At the heart of the requirements of the Directive, the Regulations and also the FSA rules is the 'know your customer' requirement. When the identification procedures are triggered, there is an obligation[12] as soon as is reasonably practicable after contact is first made between that person and an applicant for business concerning any particular business relationship or one-off transaction to

---

[10] Directive 2001/97/EC of the European Parliament and of the Council of 4 December 2001 amending Council Directive 91/308/EEC on prevention of the use of the financial system for the purpose of money laundering.

[11] HL Debates 27 May 2002 col 1080 (Lord Rooker).

[12] Money Laundering Regulations 1993 paras 7 & 9.

secure the production by the applicant for business of satisfactory evidence of his/her identity; or the taking of such measures specified in the procedures as will produce satisfactory evidence of his/her identity.[13] The triggering events are where the parties form or resolve to form a business relationship between them; where, in respect of any one-off transaction, any person handling the transaction knows or suspects that the applicant for business is engaged in money laundering, or that the transaction is carried out on behalf of another person engaged in money laundering; where, in respect of any one-off transaction, payment is to be made by or to the applicant for business of the amount of €15,000 or more; or where, in respect of two or more one-off transactions it appears at the outset to a person handling any of the transactions that the transactions are linked, and that the total amount, in respect of all of the transactions, which is payable by or to the applicant for business is €15,000 or more.[14] Failure to comply with the Regulations is an offence punishable on conviction on indictment, by imprisonment not exceeding a term of two years or a fine or both.[15] There is a 'due diligence' defence which explicitly places the burden of proof on the defendant.[16] The Financial Services Authority is conducting an exercise on customer identification that will identify best practice that is appropriate when taking on customers and subsequently.[17]

Records of all identification evidence that has been obtained and of all transactions with applicants for business that have been carried out must be kept for five years.[18] Where the applicant for business is or may be acting on behalf of another person, reasonable measures must be taken to obtain evidence of the identity of that other person.[19] Increased attention is now being given to the operation of the regulations in the case where there is no face-to-face contact with the customer. Payment from a bank or building society may be acceptable evidence of a person's identity where it is reasonable to expect the payment to be made by post.[20] Employees are to be trained in the procedures for forestalling or preventing money laundering and in the reporting procedures and in the recognition of money laundering transactions.

Bureaux de Change and Money Transmission Agents

Money Service Businesses (bureaux de change, Money Transmission Agents and Cheque Cashers) are subject to the Money Laundering Regulations but are

[13] Defined in s 11(1).
[14] This is an 'anti-smurfing' provision.
[15] s 5(2).
[16] s 5(4) As to the validity of such provisions see the section above ch 9, Money Laundering Offences—Expressly Placing the Burden on the Defendant.
[17] Financial Services Authority CRED, <www.fsa.gov.uk/handbook/BL5CREDpp/CRED/Chapter_12.pdf >.
[18] Money Laundering Regulations 1993 paras 12 & 13.
[19] Money Laundering Regulations 1993 para 9.
[20] Money Laundering Regulations 1993 para 8.

not subject to any further requirements as to registration or regulation either by a professional body or the Financial Services Authority. The most serious case of criminal laundering to come before the courts in the 1990s was a bureau de change case, in which the defendant was alleged to have laundered £70 million.[21] There is some evidence that the deposits at money transmission agents are made at a level just below that at which, according to the guidelines issued by the agents, additional identification is required.[22] The Cabinet Office proposed a 'light touch' régime to deal with bureaux de change and Money Transmission Agents and Cheque Cashers.[23] This is to involve registration, spot checks on the operation of the Regulations, and sanctions (fines and closure) in the case of non-compliance. The move is driven by an aspiration to address criminal markets.[24]

After the attacks on the United States on 11 September 2001 one of the *foci* of the political response was the use of bureaux de change as mechanisms by which money was laundered.[25] Although there was no evidence that bureaux de change had been used in the preparation of the attacks (the planning and organisation of which were probably not very costly) the introduction of 'emergency' legislation was immediately announced,[26] followed by a Treasury consultation document.[27] The Money Laundering Regulations 2001 followed.[28] They extend the 1993 Regulations to cover bureaux de change and creates a register of money service operators.[29] The regulations provide powers of entry, search, seizure and prosecution to the Commissioners of Customs and Excise in respect of suspected breaches.

Internal Reporting Procedures

Regulation 14 of The Money Laundering Regulations 1993 requires the establishment of internal reporting procedures for the reporting of 'any information or other financial business which, in the opinion of the person handling the business, gives rise to a knowledge or suspicion that another person is engaged in money laundering'. 'Money laundering' is defined by reference to the money

---

[21] *R v Ussama-el-Kurd* [2001] Crim LR 234 (CA).

[22] Cabinet Office Performance and Innovation Unit, *Recovering the Proceeds of Crime* (London, Cabinet Office, 2000) (hereinafter '*PIU Report*') para 9.43.

[23] *PIU Report* para 9.46.

[24] 'Money launderers will need to find more complex and expensive ways of converting their proceeds.' *PIU Report* para 9.47: that is, they will not be stopped but will be forced into less efficient measures.

[25] Eg *The Observer*, 30 September 2001.

[26] By Gordon Brown, Chancellor of the Exchequer, 1 October 2001. The government estimates were of £2.6 bn per annum laundered in bureaux de change, that constituting 65% of their turnover: 'Crackdown on 'dirty money' trade' *The Times* (London) 1 October 2001.

[27] HM Treasury, *A Consultation Document on a Regulatory Régime for Bureaux de Change, Money Transmission Agents and Cheque Cashers* (2001).

[28] SI 3641.

[29] Paras 3–9.

laundering offences,[30] with provision that acts are included which are performed outside the jurisdiction but which, had they been performed within the jurisdiction, would have been offences. The most important unresolved case remains that of laundering the proceeds of tax evasion. It has been argued above that there will normally be insuperable problems in proving that any particular item of property in the hands of an alleged launderer 'directly or indirectly represents' property obtained by the evasion of tax.[31] If that is correct, then the reporting obligation does not apply to laundering the proceeds of tax evasion, wherever committed. This is a critical chasm between the professed intentions of the Government, and its legislation.

The Money Laundering Reporting Officer

Firms are required to establish a central point of contact to handle the reported suspicions of members of the firm.[32] Within any 'relevant financial business' the official charged with the responsibility for ensuring that the business complies with the regulations is the money laundering reporting officer (MLRO). The MLRO must consider reports made under the internal reporting procedures, and, if s/he forms the view that money laundering may be taking place, is required to make a report to a constable.[33]

The position of the reporting officer is—and is intended to be—a difficult one. On the one hand, the MLRO will have a commitment to discharging his/her liability and preventing the involvement of the firm in the laundering of the proceeds of crime. In addition there is the possibility of the firm being held liable to account or as trustee in the event that the laundered funds were the product of fraud, rather than drugs. On the other hand, s/he would not wish for business to be scared off by monitoring which is any more zealous than necessary.[34]

An annual average of 15,000 such disclosures has led to only a handful of money laundering convictions. There are significant delays in processing suspicious transaction reports.[35] In order for the reports to be acted upon effectively it is important that the turnaround time be fast. The Cabinet Office review set targets of 24 hours in 75 per cent of most urgent cases, as against a 1999 average of seven to eight weeks. In view of the speed with which money can be moved, this sort of delay renders much of the reporting useless. The Economic Crime

---

[30] Money Laundering Regulations 1993 para 2(3).
[31] See the section above ch 9, Identifying the Property.
[32] Money Laundering Regulations 1993 para 14.
[33] *Ibid.*
[34] Rowan Bosworth-Davies, 'Living with the Law: A Survey of Money Laundering Reporting Officers and their attitudes towards the Money Laundering Regulations' (1997) 1 *Journal of Money Laundering Control* 245.
[35] *PIU Report* para 9.1.

Unit of the NCIS is said to have been be understaffed.[36] It is hoped that the introduction of time limits will concentrate minds. But as Levi and Osofsky point
out, the constraint is not only with NCIS but also in the resources available in
the forces receiving the reports from the NCIS.[37]

Sector Guidance Notes and the Identification of Suspicion

The Regulations themselves simply provide an obligation to report knowledge
or suspicion that one or other of the laundering offences is taking place. As to
what is to amount to suspicion, sector guidelines, under the general *aegis* of the
Joint Money Laundering Steering Group, have in the past put flesh upon those
bones. This has not been regarded as a successful regulatory mechanism.

The Mechanics of Reporting

Following publication of the Guidance Notes on Money Laundering for Banks
and Building Societies (1990) the number of suspicious transactions reported
were 12,000.[38] The national reception point for disclosures is the National
Criminal Intelligence Service (NCIS). The reports the NCIS received have been
broken down as shown in Table 6.

Table 6: Suspicious transaction reports by sector

Sector	1995 %	1996 (%)	1997 (%)	1998 (%)
Solicitors	1.5	2.0	1.9	1.9
Banks	62.8	48.3	46.1	44.1
IFAs	1.3	2.5	3.6	3.2
Regulators	0.1	0.2	0.2	0.2
Insurance Companies	4.6	3.0	3.7	4.3
Bureaux de Change	4.5	7.0	17.4	1.81
Credit card issuers	0.5	1.1	0.0	0.04
Building societies	18.9	28.7	22.5	19.5
Accountants	0.3	0.5	0.3	0.7
Others	2.4	4.9	2.7	1.5
Unassigned	3.0	1.7	1.7	3.6
Total number of disclosures	13,710	16,125	14,148	14,129

[36] FATF assessment of the United Kingdom, 1996: 'Representatives of the financial sector, who
have been required by the various anti-money laundering initiatives to invest in resources in this
area, have a legitimate expectation to see their efforts matched by greater law enforcement resources
and priorities for money laundering.'
[37] Michael Levi and Lisa Osofsky, *Investigating, Seizing and Confiscating the Proceeds of Crime*,
Police Research Group Crime Detection and Prevention Series Paper 61 (1995) 29–37.
[38] HL Debates 3 Nov 1992 vol 539 cols 1373 and 1385 (Earl Ferrers).

There has been some criticism of the accounting and legal professions on the basis that the preponderance of the reports continues to come from the banking sector. Out of 58,112 reports received by the NCIS over the period 1995–1998, Britain's 225,000 accountants made only 256 and 991 were made by solicitors. A spokeswoman for the NCIS, warned: 'The professional status and expertise of accountants continues to make the sector attractive to launderers.'[39]

Cash Transaction Reporting

The regulatory structure in England and Wales depends upon the operation of the procedures in respect of customer identification and then the identification and reporting of suspicious transactions. There is an alternative (or additional) approach, which has been deployed in other jurisdictions to attempt to control laundering. This is Cash Transaction Reporting (CTR). Banks and other financial institutions, as well as other trades or businesses, are required to identify transactions in cash or cash equivalents above a threshold (currently $10,000) to a central authority, and the same régime applies to cross-border transactions.

Some writers[40] adopt the expressions 'subjective' to describe reporting requirements based upon suspicion and 'objective' to account for reporting requirements based upon cash. The argument for the objective model is:

> . . . obligatory cash transaction reporting has a potential deterrent effect upon money launderers. The knowledge that engaging in significant cash transactions means that identifying information will be forwarded to law enforcement authorities prompts many erstwhile money launderers to avoid financial institutions when seeking to sanitise their funds. Instead they choose more costly and riskier laundering techniques. . . . Finally, the Objective Model leaves less to the discretion of individual financial institutions, thus promoting uniformity and consistency in enforcement.[41]

As to the consistency argument, this is not strong, begs a number of questions and should not be taken to argue very strongly at all for CTR. There is not all that much value in treating consistently a non-suspicious and a suspicious transaction each of the same amount of cash.

CTR has been in place for some time in the United States. The guiding assumption is that if someone is in possession of a large amount of cash there is generally a dubious explanation. Critics of this scheme point to the economic burden placed upon the institutions involved.[42] United States institutions complain of being placed at a competitive disadvantage as against other institutions

---

[39] *The Times*, 14 October 1999.

[40] Ronald Nobel and Court Golumbic, 'A new anti-crime framework for the world: merging the objective and subjective models for fighting money laundering', 30 *New York University Journal of International Law and Politics* 79.

[41] *Ibid* at 82.

[42] Eg Duncan Alford, 'Anti Money Laundering Regulations: A Burden on Financial Institutions' (1994) 19 *North Carolina Journal of International Law and Commercial Regulation* 437.

whose reporting requirements are more closely circumscribed. There were 12.75 million reports filed in 1996.[43] Consequently a great deal of effort is spent processing information relating to benign transactions. The objective model encourages the institutions concerned to behave perfunctorily in respect of their obligations. A subjective requirement will reduce very significantly the quantity of data through which it will be necessary to sift, and thus reduces the costs of assessing the information. The argument for an objective treatment, from the point of view of deterrence is that launderers recognise that so long as there is nothing suspicious about their behaviour then it will not be reported. Cash has two major advantages for the criminal. It is a readily accepted medium of exchange and it is difficult to trace. If these advantages are removed by the advent of e-cash or other alternatives, then whatever use CTR had will disappear.

THE FINANCIAL SERVICES AUTHORITY AND ITS POWERS

Under the Financial Services and Markets Act 2000 the principal regulatory agency charged with the supervision of the markets in which laundering is suspected to take place is the Financial Services Authority (FSA). The philosophy of the Act is to put in place a unitary authority to replace the previous fragmented regulatory framework that has exited hitherto. The FSA's powers are intended to complement those of the existing criminal intelligence and law enforcement bodies. Its principal focus is to be on systems and controls inside the businesses it regulates.

At least on paper, and subject to such matters as resources, the enlarged FSA is one of the most powerful bodies in respect of its specific statutory objectives covering market confidence, public awareness, consumer protection and the reduction of financial crime, of its kind anywhere in the world. It has disciplinary powers against regulated persons and specified employees, as well as powers to fine,[44] to make restitution or compensation orders, to issue public reprimands and to order individuals to be disqualified from the industry. It has extensive powers of investigation,[45] including powers of compulsory questioning.[46] It also has the power to require regulated persons to commission a report from an external auditor or actuary report on any aspect of their business (this power currently applies only in relation to banks).

One of the statutory objectives of the FSA is the 'reduction of 'financial crime'.[47] This is defined as including any offence involving (a) fraud or

---

[43] Ronald K Noble and Court E Golumbic, 'A new anti-crime framework for the world: merging the objective and subjective models for fighting money laundering', 30 *New York University Journal of International Law and Politics* 79 at 132, fn 246.

[44] Financial Services and Markets Act 2000 s 206.

[45] Financial Services and Markets Act 2000 s 170 *et seq.*

[46] Financial Services and Markets Act 2000 s 170 subject to its not being used in a prosecution s 174.

[47] Financial Services and Markets Act 2000 s 6.

dishonesty; (b) misconduct in, or misuse of information relating to, a financial market; or (c) handling the proceeds of crime.[48] There is no need for the 'financial crime' to have taken place in the UK, so long as it would be classified as an offence had it taken place in the UK.[49] It is not clear whether the 'financial crime' objective will cover not only the existing criminal offences (insider dealing, market manipulation[50] and money laundering) but also the new civil offence of market abuse.[51]

The Act also gives the FSA wide rule-making powers in relation to money laundering,[52] as well as powers at its own instance to bring criminal prosecutions under the existing regulations.[53] This heralds a shift away from the consensual 'guidelines' approach taken under the post-Directive regulatory structure by the Joint Money Laundering Steering Group with the sector guidance notes and a 'soft' regulatory structure towards a more prescriptive régime in respect of the financial sectors involved. The assumption is that the Joint Money Laundering Steering Group did not provide a sufficiently powerful framework for effective action against laundering. The rules are relatively detailed.[54] The rules were published in 2001[55]

The FSA regards the regulation of laundering as being an exercise in risk management. The internal mechanisms it put in place include a Money Laundering Co-ordination Committee, a Financial Crime Policy Unit, enforcement teams and a Risk Review unit.[56] The FSA's relationship with the NCIS, with which it has a partnership agreement, is overseen by its Financial Crime Liaison Unit. The FSA adopted[57] the Money Laundering Regulations 1993 as its prescribed regulations for the purpose of the Financial Services and Markets Act 2000.[58] The effect of this is that the FSA may appoint a competent person to conduct an investigation on its behalf when it appears that a person may be guilty of an offence under the Regulations.

---

[48] Financial Services and Markets Act 2000 s 6(3).

[49] Financial Services and Markets Act 2000 s 6(4).

[50] Financial Services and Markets Act 2000 s 47.

[51] Financial Services and Markets Act 2000 s 118: amongst other penalties, there is a 'name and shame' power in s 123.

[52] Financial Services and Markets Act 2000 s 146. 'The Authority may make rules in relation to the prevention and detection of money laundering in connection with the carrying on of regulated activities by authorised persons.'

[53] Financial Services and Markets Act 2000 s 402.

[54] Following FSA, *Money Laundering: the FSA's New Role* (London, FSA, 2000) para 3.20

[55] www.fsa.gov.uk Financial Services Authority, Money Laundering: The FSA's New Role Policy Statement on Consultation and Decisions on Rules (London, FSA, 2001) Annex A.

[56] Financial Services Authority, *The Money Laundering Theme: tackling our new responsibilities* (London, FSA, 2001) para 6.4 .

[57] Financial Services and Markets Act 2000 (Regulations Relating to Money Laundering) Regulations 2001 (SI 1819).

[58] Financial Services and Markets Act 2000 s 168(5).

THE PROFESSIONS AND MONEY LAUNDERING

Money laundering laws have the peculiarity that they rely for their enforcement upon 'an unpaid, involuntary High Street watch of pressed informants'.[59] Those informants are the same professionals who, in some instances at least, are used in order to secure the success of the laundering operation. In an effective money laundering operation one of the screens that separate the identity of the launderer from the money are banking secrecy laws. Another is the lawyer/client privilege. In order to make the legislation work at all, there must be provisions in place to prevent the relationship providing an absolute barrier to investigative progress.

LAWYER/CLIENT CONFIDENTIALITY

The rule relating to confidentiality of communications between lawyer and client are long established and much revered.[60] Lord Taylor of Gosforth CJ said in *R v Derby Magistrates Court, ex parte B*:

> The principle which runs through all these cases, and the many other cases which were cited, is that a man must be able to consult his lawyer in confidence, since otherwise he might hold back half the truth. The client must be sure that what he tells his lawyer in confidence will never be revealed without his consent. Legal professional privilege is thus much more than an ordinary rule of evidence, limited in its application to the facts of a particular case. It is a fundamental condition on which the administration of justice as a whole rests.[61]

The privilege gives the client the right that the content of privileged communications be not disclosed, an immunity against being compelled to give evidence about it, and a right that the lawyer not disclose (without the client's consent) any of the communications with anyone. From the point of view of the investigator, legal privilege is a most serious obstacle provided by legal rules, because in order to surmount it, it is necessary to produce evidence (independent of the evidence which is sought) that the lawyer was party to the criminality.[62] This is very difficult to find when the most obvious source of such evidence—the lawyer's file itself—is barred. In *R v Central Criminal Court, ex parte Francis & Francis*,[63] Lord Goff held that the following statutory statement of the privilege for the specific purposes of search warrants was of general application.[64]

---

[59] Michael Levi, 'Cleaning up the Bankers' Act: the United Kingdom Experience' in Brent Fisse *et al, The money trail: confiscation of proceeds of crime, money laundering and cash transaction reporting* (Sydney, Law Book Company, 1992).

[60] *Berd v Lovelace* (1577) Cary 62; 21 ER 33.

[61] *R v Derby Magistrates Court, ex parte B* [1996] 1 AC 487 at 507; [1995] 4 All ER 526 at 540–541.

[62] IH Dennis, *The Law of Evidence*, 2nd edn (London, Sweet & Maxwell, 2002) 343 *et seq.*

[63] *R v Central Criminal Court, Ex Parte Francis & Francis* [1989] 1 AC 346.

[64] *R v Central Criminal Court, Ex Parte Francis & Francis* [1989] 1 AC 346 at 392.

Subject to subsection (2) below, in this Act 'items subject to legal privilege' means—

(a) communications between a professional adviser and his client or any person representing his client or any person representing his client made in connection with the giving of legal advice to a client

(b) communications between a professional legal adviser and his client or any person representing his client or between such representative and any other person made in connection with or in contemplation of legal proceedings and for the purposes of such proceedings; and

(c) items enclosed with or referred to in such communications and made—

(i) in connection with the giving of legal advice; or

(ii) in connection with or in contemplation of legal proceedings and for the purposes of such proceedings, when they are in the possession of a person who is entitled to possession of them.

In *ex parte Francis & Francis* the House of Lords considered the meaning of the expression 'items held with the intention of furthering a criminal purpose'. The question was whether the person holding the items was the same person as the one who had the intention. A literal reading would have suggested that it did,[65] but the House of Lords held otherwise. A firm of solicitors had files relating to the purchase of a property. The police suspected, on reasonable grounds, that a third party had laundered the proceeds of drug trafficking by financing the purchase of property by members of the family. Although the family members (the clients) and the lawyers did not know this purpose, the claim of privilege did not succeed. The majority adopted a purposive interpretation of section 10. The decision allows the police access to documents in the hands of innocent people.[66] Correspondence between solicitor and client, even if not privileged, will constitute 'special procedure material' for the purposes of the search and seizure provisions of the Police and Criminal Evidence Act 1984 and the extensions in the money laundering legislation.[67]

In the discussions surrounding the amendment of the EU directive, the possibility was been considered of drawing a distinction between the activities of the legal profession involving legal advice, defence and litigation and other less privileged commercial activities.[68] However, in the final Amending Directive, following the burst of activity after 11 September 2001, the privilege is retained. The Amending Directive recognised these concerns, and Article 6 will now contain a reservation providing that:

> Member States shall not be obliged to apply the obligations laid down in paragraph 1 to notaries, independent legal professionals, auditors, external accountants and tax advisors with regard to information they receive from or obtain on behalf of one of their clients, in the course of ascertaining the legal position for their client or per-

---

[65] See the dissenting speech of Lord Bridge [1989] 1 AC at 379.

[66] ALE Newbold, 'The Crime/Fraud Exception to Legal Professional Privilege' (1990) 53 *Modern Law Review* 472.

[67] *R v Guildhall Magistrates Court, ex parte Primlaks Holdings Co* (1989) 89 CAR 215.

[68] Second Report on the Implementation of the Directive (1998) 11.

forming their task of defending or representing that client in, or concerning judicial proceedings, including advice on instituting or avoiding proceedings, whether such information is received or obtained before, during or after such proceedings.[69]

As a principle established at common law, legal professional privilege could, in principle, be displaced by statute. The Court of Appeal held that it had been so displaced, by a statute giving a tax inspector power to request information, in *R (on the application of Morgan Grenfell & Co Ltd) v Special Commissioner of Income Tax*.[70] The decision was unanimously reversed by the House of Lords.[71] The House reasserted the vigour of Lord Taylor's speech in the *Derby Justices* case.

Borrowing from the powers of the Serious Fraud Office,[72] the privilege of the lawyer does not to extend to the names and addresses of clients.[73] In the case where the lawyer acts in good faith but is mistaken as to whether the document in question attracts privilege, there is no explicit defence to a charge of failure to report, but an indication was made during the passage of the Bill that the courts should infer such a defence.[74]

Might the privilege extend further—to accountants and other financial and tax advisers? The argument was made that failure to protect other professionals providing essentially the same service confers a competitive advantage upon lawyers, and that the absence of a privilege might prevent the sort of frankness which makes meaningful audits possible.[75] The Government did not accept it, but a challenge from EU law is a clear possibility.

How does the privilege operate when a warrant or other order is being executed? The courts have insisted that *in general* the right to search is not described in terms too wide to be 'necessary in a democratic society'.[76] In *Niemietz v Germany*[77] the court rejected the argument that Article 8 was not engaged at all when in respect of the lawyer/client relationship. *Niemietz* was applied in *R v Chesterfield Justices, ex parte Bramley*.[78] Police were executing a warrant on premises where there was material known to be privileged. The

---

[69] Inserted by the Amending Directive, see the section above ch 5, The Amending Directive.

[70] *R (on the application of Morgan Grenfell & Co Ltd) v Special Commissioner of Income Tax* [2001] EWCA Civ 329.

[71] *R v Special Commissioner and another, ex parte Morgan Grenfell* [2002] UKHL 21.

[72] Criminal Justice Act 1987 s 2(9).

[73] PCA 2002 s 361(1).

[74] Lord Rooker said, 'The criminal law is quite clear: where a criminal offence is silent as to its mental element, the courts must read in the appropriate mental element. Therefore, in circumstances where a legal adviser did not know that the information was not legally privileged, the courts would read in a requirement that he could not be convicted if he did know. We believe it is best to rely on that rule of interpretation, which is the current situation, rather than try to put anything on the face of the Bill.' HL Debates 27 May 2002 col 1078.

[75] HL Debates 25 June 2002 cols 1324 (Baroness Noakes). And the preamble to the amending Directive requires that 'directly comparable services need to be treated in the same manner when covered by any of the professionals covered by the Directive'.

[76] *Funke v France* (1993) 16 EHRR 297.

[77] *Niemietz v Germany* (1993) 16 EHRR 97.

[78] *R v Chesterfield Justices Ex p. Bramley* [2000] QB 576; [2000] 1 All ER 411.

court held that the magistrate (or, in the case of orders for which a judge is required, the judge) must ask whether the material sought includes privileged material. If it becomes clear that it might, the warrant must be redrawn to recognise the privilege.

Obligations of Lawyers

The obligation to disclose which is placed upon lawyers is recognised in a series of provisions. There are specific exceptions from the 'tipping-off' offences that provide that it is not an offence for the lawyer to advise the client of a disclosure if the disclosure is in connection with giving the of legal advice to a client or to any person in contemplation of or in connection with legal proceedings and for the purpose of those proceedings.[79] This is subject to the provision that there is no exemption from criminal liability for the adviser when the disclosure is with a view to furthering a criminal purpose.[80] A lawyer acting in privileged circumstances is not liable for the offence of failing to inform.[81]

Can the professional bill the client for time that is spent, not in the pursuit of the client's interest, but in the discharge of the reporting obligations in respect of that client? The answer must generally be in the negative, because the relationship between the client and the lawyer is a contractual one. Nonetheless, depending on market conditions, lawyers will raise their fees to accommodate the costs of the surveillance operations that the regulatory *régime* places upon lawyers and other professionals, or make less money.

Finers v Miro[82] was a case where a solicitor's advice to his client, the defendant, appearing to have been given unwittingly, was used to cover up a fraud. The solicitor applied to the court for directions as to how to deal with the assets held by him on the defendant's behalf. It was held that the legal professional privilege could be torn aside, even though it was the solicitor himself who sought to do so. Fraud, it was held, unravelled all obligations of confidence. Accordingly the court was entitled to give directions to disclose sufficient information to enable the liquidator of a United States company to decide whether or not to make any claim to those assets.

Paying the Lawyer

A further difficulty that has arisen is as to the fees of lawyers.[83] If the only money which the client has, or the overwhelming preponderance of it, is liable to con-

---

[79] PCA 2002 s 333(2)(c).
[80] PCA 2002 s 333(4).
[81] PCA 2002 s 330(10).
[82] *Finers v Miro* [1991] 1 WLR 35, [1991] 1 All ER 182.
[83] And see Leonard Levy, *A License to Steal: The Forfeiture of Property* (Chapel Hill, NC, University of North Carolina Press, 1996) 194 *et seq.*; William C. Gilmore, *Dirty money: the*

fiscation as being the proceeds of crime, then the money with which the lawyer is paid will be those proceeds, and the lawyer will be engaged in its laundering. Conversely, if the money is either going to be confiscated or pay for expensive legal advice, the criminal might just as well go up market when choosing a lawyer. Any defendant charged with a criminal offence does have the right, under Article 6(3)(c) of the European Convention, to defend him/herself with legal assistance of his own choosing.

Under the legislation in England and Wales, there is a specific exception to the offence of acquiring the benefits of drug trafficking or of criminal conduct that the sum paid was in exchange for adequate consideration.[84] In *Re Barham*[85] the defendant was convicted under the Drug Trafficking Offences Act 1986 and was made the subject of a confiscation order and a restraint order. He applied to vary the restraint order to pay for legal fees and in fact give unlimited access to his property. The court held that as a matter of principle an applicant should spend his own monies in litigation proceedings rather than be legally-aided, but that the legal expenses he contemplated must be controlled in respect of the reasonableness of the litigation and costs incurred. The defendant was ordered to produce a plan to show that the projected costs were reasonable, indicating intended steps and chances of success. However, the court held that he should not be artificially limited by the restrictions placed on expenditure under the Legal Aid Scheme.

The Proceeds of Crime Act 2002 puts in place more detailed restrictions upon the power of individuals to use the money that is the subject matter of the proceedings to pay his/her lawyers' fees. So far as concerns defending him/herself on a criminal charge, the rule is that the defendant is entitled to deploy his/her resources to pay for the lawyer.[86] So far as concerns restraint proceedings or proceedings to contest receivership orders the statute expressly excludes the property the subject matter of the proceedings from being available to pay for litigation.[87] As to recovery proceedings, the underlying policy is that, unless the courts intervene and hold that the proceedings are governed by Article 6 the defendant will be unable to deploy the resources that are the subject matter of the proceedings to defend a civil recovery action, but must fall back upon other resources or whatever civil legal aid is available. This might provide a disincentive to the bringing of criminal charges.

---

evolution of money laundering counter-measures, 2nd edn (Strasbourg, Council of Europe Press, 1999) at 140 *et seq.*

[84] PCA 2002 s 328(2)(c).

[85] *Barham (Edward John Frederick), Re* (unreported) *Sub nom: In the Matter of the Drug Trafficking Offences Act 1986, Re* (1995), distinguishing *Customs and Excise Commissioners v Norris* [1991] 2 QB 293.

[86] Article 6.3.c of the Convention grants this right.

[87] PCA 2002 s 41(4)(a).

BANKER/CLIENT CONFIDENTIALITY

Why might it be worthwhile for bankers to do business with people who launder money? The short answer is because it is profitable business. The launderer will be more concerned with the other services the bank offers than with the price it charges. The bank does not have to lend money at high rates of interest in order to pay interest to the launderer. The role of banking secrecy laws in money laundering is frequently referred to, but it may well be that the problems in identifying the beneficial owner of money have more to do with the rules of company secrecy than those to do with banks. Information that might be of use to the authorities in following illegally obtained income might be as to the identity of the beneficial owner of the account and the provenance and destination of money in the account.

The relationship between banker and client, unlike that between lawyer and client, does not give rise to an independent head of privilege.[88] The basis of the relationship between a banker and his/her client is one of contractual confidentiality, but there are exceptions, laid down in *Tournier*[89] as overriding legal obligation and express or implied consent by the client.[90] The money laundering provisions that have been put in place over the last 20 years have radically altered the relationship between banker and client because they do represent such an overriding obligation. The reporting provisions have the effect, under certain conditions, of creating for the banker an entirely different relationship with his/her client, no longer as confidant, but as police informant.

Even when the reporting restrictions are not triggered (by the existence of the appropriate suspicion in the bank), the bank can now be compelled to disclose information about the account either by means of the general powers under the Police and Criminal Evidence Act 1984 or under the laundering legislation when there is reasonable suspicion that a person has benefited from criminal conduct. The provisions[91] creating the obligation to disclose significantly modify the relationship between banker and client by providing that the fact that the relationship is constituted as a confidential one does not affect the duties under the section.

Bank secrecy is only a problem when the money has been traced to a specific institution. For law enforcers the problem is far more frequently identifying the institution. Consequently consideration of banking secrecy laws must conclude with one caveat: 'money laundering can proceed very easily without bank secrecy; in fact it may well be that launderers avoid it precisely because it oper-

---

[88] *Robertson v Canadian Imperial* [1995] 1 All ER 824; [1994] 1 WLR 1493.

[89] *Tournier v National Provincial and Union Bank of England* [1924] 1 KB 461.

[90] And compare Peter W Schroth, 'Bank confidentiality and the war on money laundering in the United States' (1994) 42 *American Journal of Comparative Law* 369–91.

[91] PCA 2002 s 352.

ates as a red flag.'[92] Securities brokerages of various forms can be used to launder money as easily as can banks. In principle, the regulatory framework established under the Financial Services and Markets Act 2000 should make a difference.

Corporate Secrecy and Corporate Service Providers

The Foreign Relations Committee of the United States, reporting on the collapse of BCCI, stated that the bank:

> . . . was from its earliest days made up of multiplying layers of entities, relating to one another through an impenetrable series of holding companies, banks-within-banks, insider dealings and nominee relationships. By fracturing corporate structure, record keeping, regulatory review, and audits, the complex BCCI family of entities . . . was able to evade ordinary legal restrictions on the movement capital and goods as a matter of daily practice and routine.[93]

Corporate secrecy may be more of an obstacle to law enforcers than banking secrecy. There is apparently no legal mechanism by which to identify the 'final client' when lawyers, accountants or corporate service providers have opened an account under the name of a 'brass plate' company name.[94] There is no point in knowing that a given bank account belongs to A Ltd if it is impossible to discover who controls A Ltd. Yet none of the advantages of incorporation— particularly limited liability and access to capital markets—actually require any secrecy. The activities of corporate services providers have generated much criticism, but the issues involved are outside the scope of this book.

CIVIL LIABILITY OF PROFESSIONALS (AND OTHER THIRD PARTIES)

In the case where there is no identifiable, aggrieved 'victim' of crime there will be no one attempting to regain the money from the criminal or from others. So in the case of the laundering of drug money, no issue arises of civil liability either from the criminal or a third party to a victim. Possible liability becomes more important in cases where the predicate offences are fraud or corruption rather than drugs. Difficulties faced in identifying the criminal or his/her money has led to attempts by victims of crime to move against the professionals, banks and others through whose hands the money might have passed *en route* to cleanliness. The idea behind this use of restitutionary remedies is to impose liability to

---

[92] Jack Blum *et al*, *Financial Havens, Banking Secrecy and Money-Laundering*, UNDCP technical series issue 8 (New York City, NY, United Nations, 1998) 17.

[93] Executive Summary of the BCCI Affair, A Report to the Committee on Foreign Relations, United States Senate by Senator John Kerry and Senator Hank Brown (December 1992) 102nd Congress 2nd session Senate Print 102–40.

[94] 'Laundry of choice for Criminals' *The Guardian* 10 October 2001.

the owner of funds upon professional intermediaries who take part in their fraudulent movement, even though they did not steal them and did not benefit otherwise than in professional fees.

Whether the remedy available is an action for account or a constructive trust, this is a mechanism that, if successful, can restore the victims of fraud to the *status quo ante*, or better. Once a restitutionary claim is available then profits on investments may also be recovered, and, in the case of a constructive trust, priority can be won over other creditors by asserting a proprietary claim.[95]

Duty to Account and Constructive Trusts

Where a third party dishonestly assists a trustee to commit a breach of trust, the third party is liable to the beneficiary for the loss occasioned by the breach even if the third party has not received any trust property and the trustee has not actually been dishonest.[96] The relevant heads under which constructive trusts may be imposed are (a) knowing assistance[97] of a trustee and (b) and knowing receipt of and dealing with a trust fund. Knowing assistance does require dishonesty. 'Honesty' in this context is to be judged objectively; equated to conscious impropriety or a reckless disregard of the rights of others rather than mere negligence or oversight.[98] The ingredients of knowing receipt are a disposal of assets in breach of fiduciary duty; the beneficial receipt by the defendant of assets traceable as representing the assets of the plaintiff and knowledge on the part of the defendant that the assets are traceable to breach of fiduciary duty.[99] It is doubtful now whether a fiduciary duty is a 'precondition for equity's intervention'.[100] If a professional adviser or bank does report a transaction as being suspicious, it will probably be fixed with that suspicion for the purposes of civil liability. (This can only operate as a disincentive to reporting.)

What then, is meant by 'knowledge' in these circumstances, and in particular, is there an operative doctrine of constructive knowledge? In *Bank of Credit and Commerce International (Overseas) Ltd (in liquidation) and another v Akindele*[101] the question was as to whether dishonesty was necessary to give rise

---

[95] *Agip (Africa) v Jackson* [1991] 3 WLR 116; [1992] 4 All ER 385.

[96] The honesty of the defendant, not the trustee, is in point: *Royal Brunei Airlines Sdn Bhd v Philip Tan Kok Ming* [1995] 2 AC 378; [1995] 3 All ER 97.

[97] *Royal Brunei Airlines Sdn Bhd v Philip Tan Kok Ming* [1995] 2 AC 378; [1995] 3 All ER 97.

[98] *Twinsectra v Yardley* [2002] UKHL 12, where Lord Hutton, giving the leading judgment in this regard, held that the conduct must be dishonest in accordance with the standards of ordinary people but also that the defendant must realise that fact.

[99] *El Ajou v Dollar Land Holdings* [1994] 2 All ER 685.

[100] In *Agip (Africa) Ltd v Jackson* [1991] Ch 547, 566 the Court of Appeal so held, although the principle had been doubted by Millett J (at first instance in *Agip* [1990] Ch 265, 290). Followed in *El Ajou v Dollar Land Holdings plc* [1993] 3 All ER 717, 734. But So far as the process of tracing is concerned the House of Lords held otherwise in *Foskett v McKeown* [2001] 1 AC 102. See also *Bank of Scotland v A* [2001] EWCA Civ 52; [2001] 1 WLR 751 *per* Lord Woolf CJ at 761 *et seq.*

[101] *Bank of Credit and Commerce International (Overseas) Ltd (in liquidation) and another v Akindele* [2001] Ch 437; [2000] 4 All ER 221.

to a constructive trust, and, if so what did dishonesty mean under those circumstances. Nourse LJ[102] held that knowing receipt did not necessarily imply dishonesty, but that the question was whether or not it would be unconscionable for the recipient to retain the benefit.

CONCLUSION

After the Human Rights claims, the imposition of duties upon professionals is the most hotly contested area of Money Laundering law. From a position of scant compliance to one of resentment the mood has shifted at least to unenthusiastic but fearful compliance. Subject to the argument from competition, client confidentiality appears to have been given up by bankers and accountants, and has been retained in the legal profession only by the making of some concessions. Nothing will concentrate professional minds better than a sentence of six months' imprisonment for a solicitor who had pleaded guilty to failing to disclose knowledge or suspicion of money laundering that was not, in the circumstances, excessive.

The period after 11 September 2001 has been a very significant one for money laundering law. Reporting requirements have been extended, and levels of reporting have increased substantially. Human Rights law is being stretched (in the case of confiscation) or ignored (in the case of forfeiture, and perhaps, civil recovery). The professions are being pulled in at least two opposing directions. Operating in a framework in which the FSA is now the principal body operating against laundering, the Proceeds of Crime Act 2002, with its extended powers, is in many respects the logical culmination of what has gone before. The question remains: is it all worth while?

---

[102] Following a line of cases from *Belmont Finance v Williams Furniture (No 2)* [1980] 1 All ER 393.

Index

Lightning Source UK Ltd.
Milton Keynes UK
173865UK00001B/27/A